The Preston Family
of
Walnut Grove
Virginia

The Descendants of
John and Eleanor Fairman Preston

Dr. Edward F. Foley

HERITAGE BOOKS
2006

HERITAGE BOOKS

AN IMPRINT OF HERITAGE BOOKS, INC.

Books, CDs, and more—Worldwide

For our listing of thousands of titles see our website
at
www.HeritageBooks.com

Published 2006 by
HERITAGE BOOKS, INC.
Publishing Division
65 East Main Street
Westminster, Maryland 21157-5026

International Standard Book Number: 978-0-7884-4013-6

TABLE OF CONTENTS

The Preston Family of Walnut Grove, Virginia

-

FOREWORD

The history of the State of Virginia includes the earliest settlement of our nation. Soon after the settlements on the coast by the English in the 17th century, pioneers began to press the frontier of the state westward. The opening and settling of southwestern Virginia began in earnest in the last quarter of the 18th century. With the endorsement and encouragement of the British Crown, great landowners sought to have their lands explored, surveyed and settled. Among these early families were the Beverleys, Paxtons, Smiths and Prestons.

The Prestons of Virginia have been researched quite extensively, but the exact relationship of these various family groups has not yet been exactly determined. These families are referred to by researchers as the Prestons of Smithfield, the Prestons of Bedford and the Prestons of Walnut Grove. Closely associated, the Smithfield and Walnut Grove Prestons are certainly cousins although their exact connections going back to Co. Donegal and Co. Derry, Ireland are yet to be revealed.

Surveyor Robert Preston came to settle in southwest Virginia in 1780 and was granted the land that constituted his plantation called Walnut Grove. The tract is located at Exit 7 of Interstate 81, outside the current city of Bristol, Virginia, on Lee Highway. Today most of the property had been built over. The plantation fields have been replaced by a shopping center and Super-Wal-Mart department store. In 2005 the Walnut Grove cemetery remained intact at one end of the property and the old Walnut Grove mansion house with its log store behind it, still stood at the other end of the property. In 2000 the land on which the house stood was finally sold out of the family after 200 years. The property had been bought by Tramell Investments LLC and scheduled for development. A group who appreciated the importance of this historic property and the Bristol Historical Association arranged for its preservation by relocation to Sugar Hollow Park.

The history of this area of Virginia has been outlined in written works over the years, with references to Walnut Grove and the pioneers who contributed to the development of Washington County mentioned along the way. This book is meant to recognize not only the contributions that these individuals made to developing the state, but also the great human legacy they have left us.

Great care has been taken to make this work as accurate as possible. However, most certainly facts have been maimed or omitted since much of the research can only be done with secondary or tertiary sources. I encourage the reader to help us update or correct any information about the family so the next addition can be that much more accurate. Please feel free to contact the author.

Ed Foley, 2006, DrEdFoley@aol.com.

-

The Preston Family of Walnut Grove, Virginia

ACKNOWLEDGMENTS

This type of family research can only be accomplished over many years of gathering facts and data from many sources. The search to this point has taken the author over 15 years. It only represents the latest chapter in the Preston family history. More of the family history remains to be told and more history stands to be created in the future. There are hundreds of descendants of Robert Preston living today. They continue to expand the legacy he left us.

Among the contributors to this work have been the many descendents and others interested in the history of this section of Virginia. This book builds on early works about the State including Lewis Preston Summer's *History of Southwest Virginia*. Unpublished contributors are many. Perhaps the most complete research done on the various Preston families has been that of Fred Preston, whose work contributed greatly to his book. What began as a hobby concerning his own ancestry (Fred is a descendant of Robert Preston) has turned into a very extensive web site with outlines of many lines of Prestons.

This book is the result of an enormous effort of Preston descendants over the past two centuries to preserve and account for their part in the opening of the frontier. I hope all who have contributed over the years to make this work possible are proud of the results. A special thanks goes to the following researchers who were important to compiling this work. They include Fred Preston, Pat Hines Hall, Wilma Smith and Dale Carter, Robert 'Dr. Bob' Perry Rhea, Frances Rhea Murphy, and Robert Earhart, Fairman Bockhorst, and to Fairman Cumming for his wonderful stories.

The Preston Family of Walnut Grove, Virginia

First Generation

1. **John PRESTON**, b. 1726 in Co. Derry, Ireland, d. 1 Sep 1796 in Bristol, Sullivan Co., TN, buried in Weaver Cemetery, Weaver Pike, Sullivan Co. TN. Born in Ireland, came with wife and three children to America and settled in Washington Co. VA Died at 70 while on a visit to his daughter Jane Preston Rhea. Buried at Weaver Cemetery. a few miles south of Bristol TN. His wife Eleanor died at family the home, Walnut Grove in VA but was carried to Sullivan Co, TN to be buried in grave with her husband.

The Prestons were closely associated with families located in Co. Donegal Ireland in the later part of the 1700's. The Irish Spinning Wheel lists, which is a comprehensive list of residents of the county, lists many of the families who corresponded with John's son Robert and includes names of Irishmen whose letters are in the special Preston collection at William and Mary College in Williamsburg, VA. It is said that the Prestons were from Co. Derry. This may be since they do not appear in Co. Donegal in the early lists of the 17th and 18th century. Appearing on these Spinning Wheel lists are Alexanders, Deans, Lairds, Fairman (Ferman) and Dennisons, families which intermarried with Prestons in Ireland.

Although researchers have not yet established the relationship between John Preston and Col. William Preston of Smithfield Prestons, Col. William was instrumental in the family of John Preston coming to America and settling in Botetourt Co. VA. William wrote to John and son Robert came to America in 1773.   Children Jane and Walter probably came over later with their parents in 1775.

1790 John made his will at about age 65.

1796 John was put to rest on the hill of Weaver Cemetery in Sullivan Co., TN under an unusual marker. His grave is covered with a coffin shaped iron cover with the inscription 'Here lies the Body of John Preston Dec. Sept 1st 1796 aged 70 and Ellnor his wife Dec. Jan 1820 Aged...'

1797 at a court held for Washington Co the 20th day of April 1797 this last Will and Testament of John Preston dec'd was proved by the oaths of John C. and Elizabeth Campbell, the witnesses hereto and ordered to be recorded. An on the motion of Robert Preston, the Executor therein named, who made oath as the law directs, and together with James Montgomery and John Campbell, his securities, entered into and

1

acknowledged their bond in the sum of $4000, conditioned as the law directs. Certificate is to be granted to him for obtaining probate in due form. Teste: And'w Russell, D.C.
Will of John Preston Sr recorded in Washington Co. VA Will Book 2, pg 119.

I, John Preston of Washington Co in the State of Virginia being of perfect mind and memory and calling to mind the mortality of my body knowing it is appointed for all men once to die, do make and order this my last will and testament as followeth, viz:
I recommend my soul into the hands of Almighty God who gave it, and my body to be buried in a Christian manner at the discretion of my Executor, believing that at the general resurrection I shall receive the same again by the almighty power of God, and as touching such worldly estate as it hath pleased God to bless me with, I give and dispose in the manner following:
First I give and bequeath to my wife Eleanor Preston, all of my moveable estate to live upon and make use of as she may think proper, with the advise and consent of my Executor hereafter named, and at her decease to dispose of amongst my children as she may think proper. And as to my lands, I order and allow them to be sold for the best price that can be got, giving reasonable credit not to exceed three or four years, and that in annual payments as nearly equal as the circumstances of the case will allow, and out of the first payments I give and bequeath to my son in law, Matthew Rhea, forty pounds, or a likely young negro girl not under 12 years of age nor over 20 and to my son, Walter Preston, I give and bequeath 60 pounds, or a likely young negro fellow not to exceed 20 years of age, and the remainder of the price of my land I allow to lye in the hands of my Executor and should my wife stand in need her to be supported out of it, and at her decease my son Robert to have an equal share to Walter and the remainder it and to be equally divided between my two sons, Robert and Walter and my son-in-law Matthew Rhea, first allowing all my just debts to be paid out of my estate and I do hereby appoint my son Robert Preston, Executor of this my last will and testament, hereby revoking all others.
In witness whereof I have hereunto set my hand and seal this 4th day of June 1790.
    his
John x Preston
    mark
Signed, sealed and acknowledged in presence of John Campbell, Elizabeth Campbell. He married **Eleanor FAIRMAN**, married in Ireland, b. 1725 in Co. Derry, Ireland, d. 6 Jan 1820 in Walnut Grove,

2

Washington Co. VA, buried in Weaver Cemetery, Weaver Pike, Sullivan Co. TN. Researcher Charles McDonald notes her parentage in his postings on Rootsweb.com (August 2005 mcdonchr@@myway.com) but documentation has not proven this ancestry - parents John Fairman and Elizabeth Colement of Bexley and Winston England respectively.

Died at home in Walnut Grove in Washington Co., VA but was brought to rest with her husband in Sullivan Co., Tennessee.

Children:

+ 2.   i   **Robert 'Col.' PRESTON, Sr.** b. 1750.

+ 3.   ii   **Walter PRESTON** b. 25 Dec 1756.

+ 4.   iii   **Jannette 'Jane' PRESTON** b. 1758.

Second Generation

2. **Robert 'Col.' PRESTON, Sr.**, (1.John[1]) b. 1750 in Co. Derry, Ireland, d. 16 Dec 1833 in Washington Co., VA, buried in Walnut Grove Cemetery Washington Co. VA. Robert was a young man when he was brought from Ireland by a near relative, Col. William Preston of Smithfield, VA. It has been written that he held a commission as surveyor from Oxford College, England and shortly after his arrival began surveying. Evidence of this Oxford commission has not been found, but he did later receive a commission four years after his arrival in VA in 1777.

1773, when 23 years of age, he was a deputy surveyor of Fincastle County. In a document of service, written by Robert himself in 1799, says he came to America in 1773, and his parents were still in Ireland. They came over in early 1775. This trip was apparently arranged by Col. William Preston of the Smithfield Prestons. (Another account notes Robert came to America along with his parents, along his sister Jane and brother Walter in 1775.) It is further reported Robert came to America on one of James Patton's merchant ships 'Walpole'.

1775 in June Rev. Joseph Rhea, minister of Piney Branch Creek in Maryland, formerly of Co. Donegal, Ireland, informed the Presbytery that he desired to visit some parts of Virginia and that his people had consented to his purpose, and furnished him with the unusual traveling credentials. Rev. Rhea was introduced to the Holston Territory by Col. William Preston at the request of Preston's brother-in-law, Rev. John

Brown. The following letter, from the 'Preston and Virginia Papers' by Lyman Draper, was written by Rev. Brown to Col. Preston:

" Dear Brother,
My friend, the Rev'd Mr. Rhea on his way to your distant part called on me and designs to stay some time in Fincastle County. He is well recommended by the Presbytery to which he belongs and I received two letters from ministers belonging to the same body in his favor. He accepted of a call from the congregation of Piney Creek, but was not installed as their minister. He has a large family and cannot so conveniently purchase land for them where he lives, which together with the destitute condition of the Church inclines him to have an inclination to move back if Divine Providence should open a door for his comfortable settlement. He has a view to visit Reed Creek where I apprehend he has some previous invitation. He is a dear friend of mine from old acquaintance. I always found that my Friends were favoured by you. I suppose he will call upon you His son (probably John) is intending to take a Latin School at Reed Creek. I hope if it any way offer to be advantageous to him you will favor the young man. My family insists and desires to be remembered to you and your family and none more than your B'r John Brown
July 26, 1775."

It is during this visit to the Holston Territory that Rev. Joseph Rhea may have first met Robert Preston, his future son in law. Later, in 1776, Robert Preston and Rev. Joseph Rhea would serve together on an expedition against the Cherokees carried on my Col. William Christian during which Rev. Rhea served as one of two chaplains to the expedition. Four years later, in 1780, soon after the death of Rev. Rhea and the subsequent removal of the Rhea family to Sullivan Co., TN, Robert Preston and Rev. Rhea's daughter Margaret married.

1776 Robert was stationed at Fort Vause, now Shawsville, when the entire garrison was captured by the French and Indians. He was one of the men who were on an errand and thus escaped.

1777 a commission from the Masters of William and Mary College in Williamsburg VA was sent to the Washington County Court on April 29th 1777 appointing Robert surveyor of Washington Co. VA. The position of county surveyor was at the time the most lucrative position to be found in the county and was most sought after. Robert along with William Preston of Smithfield had been long actively engaged by Col. James Patton and the Loyal Land Company in surveying and locating grants on one hundred and twenty thousand and eight hundred thousand acres of Company land in Southwest Virginia. For some reason however, the court entered the following order: "Robert Preston, Gent., produced a commission ... it is the opinion of the court that the same should not be received as it is issued by virtue of a prerogative from the Crown of England". Robert appealed the order of the county court to the General Court in Williamsburg which appeal was pending for some time. The disposition of the appeal is unknown however the following appears in the Washington Co. Court records: "Robert Preston, Gent. produced a commission from Thomas Jefferson, Gov. of the Commonwealth of Virginia, being dated the 22nd day of December 1779 appointing him Surveyor of the County of Washington and gave bond with James Dysart (cousin to his wife Margaret Rhea) and Aaron Lewis, his securities, in the sum of 20,000 pounds for the faithful discharge of his office and took the oath of office". He was county surveyor from 1779 to 1831

Robert was a representative of the Loyal Land Company and surveyed and sold all their properties consisting of 800,000 acres of land in Southwest VA. The deed and land survey books, and also his sill shows that he was a very large land owner. He had only two children and he made them both wealthy by his will.

A statement of services performed by Robert Preston during and since the Revolutionary War was given by Mr. Preston in contradiction to a certificate given by Col. Arthur Campbell in favor of Col. Campbell's brother Robert Campbell.

1773 - "In the year 1773 I came to America having relations in it of very respectable character. In 1774 I wrote to my Father then living in Ireland earnestly recommending to him the country of which I had lately become an inhabitant in consequence of which recommendation my parents were induced to remove and arrived in Virginia early in the year 1775 in which state they immediately became resident. From this period I became strongly attached to America, and a zealous supporter of her rights. had perhaps as much real concern for her liberty as any other man, instead of evading the laws of my adopted country as has been represented. I uniformly obeyed her call not only with promptitude, but gave all of --- in my power for the attainment of our just rights and Independence.

1776 - "In the year 1776 I served as a volunteer in the Expedition carried on by Col. William Christian against the Cherokee Indians and had the honor of being appointed commissary of Col. Shelby's regiment, the duties of which station I discharged with fidelity and to the satisfaction of my officers."

1777 - "In 1777 or 1778 a law passed directing a draught of unmarried men. I then resided in the county of Botetourt and was present when said draft took place, and drew for service which service, I performed by substitute in the Continental Army. This circumstance exempted me from all military duty for the term I think of three years."

1778 Robert's sister Jannette married Mathew Rhea, the son of Rev. Joseph Rhea.

1780 - "In February of 1780 I became an inhabitant of the county of Washington and in July of that year served in Capt. Edmonsons company in a tour of duty against the Tories in Carolina which expedition was conducted by Col. Arthur Campbell in person and I was well known to him being frequently in his company. Very soon after my return from this service, perhaps in September of the same year, I was again ordered out against the British and Tories. I prepared myself and proceeded to Watauga, the place appointed for rendezvous. But before we commenced our line of march, Col. William Campbell who commanded, being well acquainted with my peculiar situation, without any application whatever discharged me saying it was unreasonable I should proceed, being only three days married --- I returned home."

1781 - "In the winter of 1781 or spring of 1782 I was again ordered on an expedition against the Cherokee Indians. I immediately equipped myself and with others proceeded down Holstein river to Clouds Creek, nearly an hundred miles from any settlement in the state of Carolina and there remained until discharged by Capt. Hilblard (?) the then commanding it, being found impracticable to carry on the expedition for want of necessaries."

"About this time the American Revolution terminated and gave peace and security to our country which I enjoyed until the year 1790, when by reason of Indian (attacks) committed on the frontier inhabitants of this state, a part of the Militia of Washington County were ordered to be drafted, among whom I was, and performed by substitute although at the same time I was principal surveyor of the county which probably would have exempted me from the service if I had made use of it as an excuse."

"Thus then from the present time to the commencement of the American Revolution I can with pleasure review my conduct having performed all the duties of a well affected citizen during that period."

"The above facts are mostly proven by the affidavits and Certificates of disinterested respectable and worthy Citizens and not by the certificate of a brother---. The Honorable Board will perceive what credit is due to Col. Arthur Campbell's certificate respecting Mr. Robert Campbell and myself by glancing over the above mentioned vouchers and ? to the statement. The credit which ought to be given to the charge contained in Robert Campbells letter and in Col. Arthur Campbells letter will best appear (??) by averting (??) to the order of the county-court of Washington entered into the 16th day of July 1799 and another order of September 1799."

(This is researcher Fred Preston's best interpretation (1997) of Robert's handwritten document. The Carolina referred he presumed was South but the way it was written it looked like a capital A and superscript o. Robert's spelling seemed to be very good but handwriting could have been better.)

1789 at a meeting of the trustees Mr. Preston was ordered by Andrew Russell to prepare particular plats of all the lots of Abington Town that titles had not been made for. The said Russell received 3 1/2 for each plat on delivery to the purchaser for the surveyor's fee. Robert Preston served as a trustee until 1803. Robert Preston Sr. was among the first trustees for the town of Abingdon.

1800-1804 Robert Preston was sheriff of Washington Co. (From History of Southwest Virginia 1746-1786, Washington Co 1777-1870 by Lewis Preston Summers, 1903.)

The following are letters contained in the special collection at William and Mary College in Williamsburg, VA. Transcribed 2000 by researcher and descendant Robert Koontz.

1779 December 20
Certificate from the College of William and Mary appointing Robert Preston surveyor. Signed by James Madison, president of the college. (This is for Col. Robert Sr. soon after he arrived in America - Jr. had not yet arrived.)

1793 May 10

Bill of sale: cloth and yarn made by James Preston (Col. Robert's uncle, father of 'Irish Bob', a woolendraper-EFF), sold to Robert Preston, in Derry. (This may be a bill of sale to Robert Jr. showing title to goods which arrived with him in America this year in July at age 21.)

1793 July 21
Philadelphia
From Robert Preston (cousin "Irish Bob" Jr.- EFF) to Robert Preston: (Col.-EFF)
Cousin Samuel and I are safe arrived. Excellent Captain Hickey, but inhuman mate. Uncle John Davis and Aunt (this appears to be and aunt and uncle to both of them; aunt may be a female Preston, sister of James and John the parents of Irish Bob and Col. Robert-EFF) were well when we left Ireland but is (sic) dead. Your uncle is getting very frail. When we came to town, we met with Cousin Robert Divinport.

1794 June 9
Burnfoot, Londonderry, Ireland
From Alexander Dean [cousin] to Robert Preston: (Col. b 1750-EFF) (Addressed "to the particular care of Mr. Alexander Porter, Wilmantown [?]). Mentions Martha Hustown (Note Samuel Huston mentioned later in 1805), Robert's father (John-EFF) and mother (Eleanor Fairman-EFF) in America, mentions Rebecca, Martha, and Janey in Ireland "I was glad to hear your Walter (Robert's brother) is come a little farther from the Indians."

1794 June 19
Derry, Ireland
From James Preston to Robert Preston (Col. Robert - nephew of James-EFF)
"My Dear Robin" (pet name for Robert.)
My sister Corter(?) died 8 September 1793. Tell Walter (Robert's brother-EFF) I have written to him.

1796 May 20
Elaughmore, Ireland
From James Preston (uncle) to Robert Preston (Col.-EFF)
"You said my Brother and Sister had a sore turn of sickness..." (James' brother John Preston dies in Sept. 1796-EFF) Hope they are better. Mentions "your sister Jenny (Mrs. Matthew Rhea-EFF) and family". I have seen John Hamilton Leatty and his wife. Compliments to John Donnell.

1796 June 13 Derry, Ireland
From James Preston (Robert's uncle-EFF) to Robert Preston (Col.-EFF)
Hope your father has recovered from the palsy (John dies 3months later). Am sending 300 Dublin newspapers.

After 1796 (no date) (Ireland) - (One of those mentioned in the letter, father John Preston, died in 1796)
From Andrew Laird to Robert Preston
Brother James Holmes (Was this Andrew's brother in law, husband of Jennet Holmes who wrote in 1811? - EFF) and family are well. The Kingdom is in confusion -- bloodshed, murder. Gaols full, many transportations. Uncle John Davis Mother's brother (whose mother? Andrew Laird's, or Robert Preston's?) James Holmes and sister (Andrew's sister? - EFF) send love to your father (Robert's father John - EFF), mother [Eleanor Fairman - EFF], brother (Walter-EFF), sister (Janette Rhea-EFF),and their families.

1799 Dec. 26 Robert of Washington Co., VA purchased two tracts of land from James Blount, Thomas Blount, and Willis Blount. The deed in the Williamson Co., TN deed book A-1-21, 22 mentions William Mebane, Edward Harris, James Lincoln, Thomas Talbot, Jenkin Whiteside, James Stead and David Sweat. The record also appears in Washington Co., VA.

1800 May 27 May Ireland
From Alexander and Rebecca Dean to Robert Preston
"Remember us to your brother (Walter-EFF) and Mrs. Preston."

1803 May 30 Ireland
From Alexander Dean and Rebeca Dean to Robert Preston (Col. Robert)
Mentions: Mr and Mrs. Danvenport, Aunt Laird, "Your two old aunts is alive." (Could these be Fairman aunts?-EFF.)

1803 June
(Didn't record sender; Alexander Dean again?)
Aunt Laird's son lives at Aunt Davis (Mrs. John Davis- sister of Col. Robert Preston's father-EFF) . Mentions "Robert McDugall who was killed in your neighborhood."

1803 the Preston's slave "Uncle Rube" died and was buried at Walnut Grove.

1805 May 2 Donegall County
From James (uncle-EFF) and Sarah Preston to Robert Preston (Col. b. 1750-EFF)
"Dear Nephew" Part of my family is with you (son Irish Bob-EFF). "You and your wife's kindness... I experienced your gratitude and affection long e'er you reached America... benefits which they have received." Mentions Alexander. Poor and afflicted condition of James Preston Sr. of Derry: ulcers on his hands and feet, confined to bed for a year. Remember us to Cousin Walter Preston and family; to son and daughter Dennison and family; to Robert and Daughter Preston. (James's) son Alexander. Cousin Sam Huston (married sister of Robert Preston?) and family.

22 May 1805 Donegall County, Ireland
from Aunt Jennet Ferman [= Fairman, this must be sister of Col. Robert's mother, Eleanor Fairmam]
"Dear Nephew" [Col. Robert Preston]
Old aunt interred 12 April. [probably Aunt Margaret, who was 78 in 1803, according to another 1803 letter] sister is blind [whose? Robert's, Aunt Jennett's, or the old Aunt's?]. Your Cousin Jennet's husband died. Mentions "your Cousin Mary and her brother Samuel" (could be cousin Samuel Huston [who married the sister of Robert Preston?] who came with Irish Bob to America in 1793)

6 August 1809 Elaughmore(?), Ireland
From James Preston to Robert Preston
Mentions "Cousin John (actually James' nephew)...and your son Robert"

10 March 1811 Breaheed (Ireland)
From Jennet Holmes[wife of James Holmes? Sister to Andrew Laird? see undated letter later-EFF] to Robert Preston (Col. Robert -EFF)
"Dear Cousin Robert"
My brother Samuel is dead. Aunt Jennet Fairman [Aunt of Col. Robert and sister or sister in law of his mother Eleanor Fairman- EFF] in Drumadoan is dead 16 months ago. My family and I live at Breahed. Brother Andrew (Laird?) is married to Sarah Fairman. They have 2 children, John and Margaret. Our friends in Miltoal: My Uncle and Aunt are dead. Young James is dead.

What is become of your sister Jennet's two children? [Robert's sister married Matthew Rhea in Virginia and had 4 children by the date of this letter - EFF] My husband is dead. Daughter Rebeca died 7 years

10

ago; was married to Robert Johnston and lived but 7 weeks after. My sister Mary sends her love.

1815 and 1819 Londonderry (Co. Donegal-EFF)
There are in the William and Mary College in Williamsburg, VA special collection, letters from Fanny Ellis or Elder to Robert Preston (researcher Mr. Koontz didn't record any information from those letters)

1815 August 25 Elaughmore, Ireland
From James Preston (father of Irish Bob- EFF) to nephew Robert Preston (Col. Robert Preston b. 1750 - EFF).
"That fiend of Satan Thomas Preston...sold my place with his own... Poor Sam will suffer after I am dead and gone." Aunt still alive and well. "My son-in-law William Gilleland intends to ship some of these days." [There were Gillilands in the area of Washington Co. VA about this time - in 1795 a Samuel is married there and in 1805 Mary and an Elizabeth are wed in Washington Co. VA]

1817 May 10
Londonderry (Co. Donegal-EFF).
From James Preston, woolendraper, to Robert Preston
Haven't seen you for 24 years. (Must have been since 1793, when Robert P. bought cloth from him in Derry -- see above.) Son now a "disciple of Bacchus" (i.e., drunkard).

1817 October 6
Franklin (The state of Franklin was declared by those residing in the area of Washington Co. VA and East TN 1784-1788. Could be Franklin TN)
From William P. Gilliland [This must be the son-in-law of James Preston. James Preston was the uncle of Col. Robert Preston. James Preston had written in 1815 that his son in law intended to ship off to America -EFF] to Robert Preston, Walnut Grove
Mentions Mrs. Preston; Aunt Preston; Miss Peggy Rhea; Andrew Dennison and family; Robert G. Preston [this is Irish Bob, William's brother in law - EFF]; Cornall [Colonel] John H. M. Preston [reference to his father in law]; Robert P. Preston; Ferman, Francis [a Fairman?], William McClellan.

1818 (circa) Transcript of letter from Robert Preston to his wife Margaret 'Peggy' Rhea:
In and about this place I have been two weeks tomorrow and have not yet seen one mortal that I would claim a personal acquaintance with. I

am sincerely weary of living in such a way just trying to kill time till Monday next when I hope to get on the road towards Allen County. My letter to John of a former date will inform you of the reasons of my detention: in the mean time I have had the necessary information respecting unfortunate --- gamble. I have also had some late information from L. Derry. I hope I will be enabled --- by next --- Monday to proceed to Allen County and at present I think I shall return home from there, omitting my journey to Tennessee but the appearance of the weather will determine --- in that case when in Allen County. I was three days at my Brothers and did not think proper to go back to him as it would have added about seventy miles to my journey and indeed I think it too long without any addition. I have not seen any of our friends in this Country except Major William Preston. He is in a fair way of recovery. Now my dear Peggy I tell you I am as completely tired of Tavern living as I ever was and have a great and strong desire to be at home with you as when you were in prime of life. I believe age has rather strengthened than reduced my affection for you: your kind hand is the comfort of my age. Your smile --- have been the repository of my inward thoughts and the real friend or comforter in mental distress--- Tell my mother I am well and hope I shall soon see her---
Wishing you health my only love I am
Your affectionate Husband
Robt Preston

(This is the interpretation of Fred Preston (1997) of the handwritten letter. New Castle, Henry Co., both exist in Virginia but not together. Henry Co. and New Castle are located NE of Louisville, KY. Both places where the county name Allen is used, he had Warren (?) County and crossed it out. There is no county by either name in Virginia but both are in Kentucky, Allen Co. on the Tennessee border and Warren Co. just north of that, and both almost directly south of Henry Co. in northern KY. This would be considered frontier country at that time. Robert would have been 67 or 68 at this time and Margaret Rhea Preston, his wife, 61. His brother was Walter Preston, his mother Eleanor Fairman Preston. The Major William Preston was probably the son of Col. William Preston of Smithfield. The John referred to was probably his son Col. John Preston [1781-1864]).

1822 Margaret Rhea Preston, his wife of 45 years, died. Later he would marry again, to the young Sarah Gilleland Dennison. Sarah may have been a cousin. The Preston Papers in the Virginia Historical Society collection contain their prenuptial agreement.

1830 Virginia census he appears as 'Preston Robert snr'. The household has:1 male 5-10, 1 45-50 and one 60-70; two females 30-40. (One woman his wife and one daughter in law Margaret Brown Preston)

1832 The will of Robert Preston Sr. -
I Robert Preston of the County of Washington, and State of VA, being aged and infirm of body but of sound mind and disposing memory, for which I thank God, and calling to mind the uncertainty of human life, and being desirous to dispose of all such worldly estate as it hath pleased God to bless me with, I do hereby make this my last will and Testament in manner and form following, that is to say:

I leave and bequeath to my daughter Jennie Preston, wife of Robert Preston Jr. (his cousin, adopted son and son in law - EFF), my negro woman named 'Kate' and the said Kate's son James. I leave and bequeath to the two sons of Jenny Preston, to wit, Alexander H. Preston and John F. Preston, all of my tract of land lying on Oppossom Creek in Scott County, to be equally divided between the said Alexander R. and John F. Preston.

I leave and bequeath to Alexander R. Preston $200.

I leave and bequeath to my good, kind and loving wife, Sarah G Preston (his first wife Margaret had died 10 years earlier in 1822), my negro boy named Moses. A good horse worth at least $70.00, three cows, her choice out of my stock, one bed, her choice of all the beds in my house and her choice of furniture for said bed, my bureau, one third of my table linen and one-half of the cupboard furniture, one good trunk and all of her wearing clothes. Also 120 acres of land lying on the heard of Locust Branch in Washington County, and adjoining the land of James Anderson and Andrew Dennison.

I leave and bequeath to John Preston (Irish) $300.00.

I leave and bequeath to Robert F. Preston son of John Preston, fifteen shares of stock in the United States Bank with its proceeds.

I give to Edward Latham of Washington, his executors or Administrators in trust for the use and benefit of Margaret Fickle and her issue, my negro woman named Ann, and her three female children and her future Increase; $500 and bed and furniture such as have been common in my house, and a tract of land lying on Dudley's Branch in Lee County containing 278 acres to be appropriated to the use of the said Margaret Fickle and her issue as her and their necessities or interests may require, and I positively require that the said Edward Lathim, his executors or administrators shall so manage the devise here made to him for the use and benefit of the said Margaret Fickle and her issue, that her husband Abram shall at no time have any control over the same nor derive any use or benefit therefrom, and if the said Edward Lathim shall refuse to act as trustee as aforesaid, I hereby authorize my executor herein named, his executors or administrators, to apply to the court of the County of Washinton to have a trustee appointed who shall perform the same duties and exercise the same powers herein required of and vested in the said Edward Lathim.

I leave and bequeath to Robert P. Fickle a horse to be worth $50.00 or $60.00, a new saddle and bridle of good quality, all of which is to be furnished when the said Robert P. Fickle comes to be 18 years of age.

I leave and bequeath to Sarah G. Rhea, formerly Sarah G. Preston, my negro girl named Nancy.

I leave and bequeath to my son John Preston, all the balance of my property whatsoever nature or kind it may be, both real and personal not herein disposed of, and it is my wish and desire that as my estate is in no embarrassment, either by debt or otherwise, that no part thereof shall be valued or sold, and also that my executor shall not be required to give bon and security.
And lastly I do hereby constitute and appoint my son, John Preston executor of this my last will and testament, hereby revoking all other and former wills or testaments by me heretofore made.
In witness whereof I have hereunder to set my hand and affixed my seal this 21st day of November 1832.

Robert Preston (signed and sealed)
Witnesses Joseph Carson, Walter E. Preston, Thomas L. Preston, Edward Lathim.
Probated in court December 23, 1833.

1833 Robert Preston died and was buried in Walnut Grove Church cemetery. His grave is marked by the D.A.R. and by a very large and heavy iron slab with his name molded thereon. Walnut Grove Church is 4 and 1/2 miles east of Bristol on the north side of Lee Highway #11 near Rt. 81 exit 7.

Robert Preston willed his home Walnut Grove to son Col. John Preston who had already married and was living at the Grove which was built in 1802. Col. John Preston deeded it to his oldest son Dr. Robert F. Preston, Robert F. gave it to his two daughters, Mary Winston and Elizabeth Sheffey, Mary inheriting it. At her death, she willed it to Robert F. Sheffey, her nephew, and on his death to his children, Robert P. Sheffey and Margaret Minnick. Robert retained the home place and Margaret the land and a home located near the original Walnut Grove.

WALNUT GROVE
The original 'Walnut Grove' home of Robert Preston was standing in 1937 (WPA notes) but had been weather boarded. It was a long log house with two very large rock chimneys, at each end of the house. The fire places were large and the two mantels downstairs were very tall, one being 7 feet 9 inches wide and 7 feet 4 inches high with a shelf near the top. They were very unusual in design and were the original mantles. The downstairs had paneled wainscoting, and the doors were tongue and grooved by hand.

The framework was put together with wooden pins. Cut, blacksmith nails were used in the building. The floors were made of pine five inches wide and the weatherboarding yellow poplar. The stairway was two flights, open string. There were still 2/3 and 1/2 length strap hinges on the old doors, with brass and iron lock boxes. The oldest part of the house burned about 1864 and most of the house dated from that time.

Today (1995) most of the property had been built over. The plantation fields had been replaced by a shopping center and Super Wal-mart department store. In 2005 the Walnut Grove cemetery at one end of the property and the old Walnut Grove house and log meat-house behind it, still stood. The house was to be moved to another State owned site and the log house demolished as Trammel developers began to built on the last remaining portion of the property.

References:
Much of the story of Robert Preston, including his will, transcribed from the work of the WPA:
Gilliam, Victoria Alice, "Work Progress Administration of Virginia, Statewide Project, Historical Inventory. Field Worker's Report" 1937. Richmond, VA. Copy filed Preston Files, Washington Co., VA Historical Society, Abingdon, VA
.

Letters of the Preston family were from notes taken by descendant Robert Coontz, Jr. at the Special Collections section of the William and

Mary College Library. There letters were written to Robert Preston Sr. from 1793 to 1817 from relatives in Ireland.

Letters, surveys, deeds and other papers of Robert Preston were transcribed from the Preston Papers in the manuscript collection at Virginia Historical Society in Richmond. He married (2) **Sarah G. 'Sally' DENNISON**, b. 1801 in Ireland. Married her older cousin Robert Preston after the 1822 death of his first wife Margaret Rhea Preston.

1860 Virginia census shows her in the Western District of Washington Co. VA in the Abingdon Post Office area.
  Preston, Sarah G. 59, Housekeeper, real estate value $1,500, property $2,000, b. Ireland.
in the same household
  William Caron, 23, Farmer, property value $400, b. VA
  Sarah Carson, 22, housekeeper, b. VA
  Mary Dennison, 58, property value $300, b. Ireland.

He married (1) **Margaret RHEA**, married 28 Sep 1780, b. 27 Jun 1757 in Co. Donegal, Ireland, d. 3 Jun 1822 in Washington Co., VA, buried in Walnut Grove Cemetery Washington Co. VA. Her father was introduced by letter to Col. William Preston, the sponsor of his cousin Robert Preston, by Rev. Brown, a Presbyterian minister and old colleague of Rev. Rhea.

1776 Rev. Joseph Rhea participated in the Col. Christian campaign against the Cherokee. Col. Robert Preston also was on that campaign.

1778 she left Maryland with her mother and family to come to the Holston Territory, arriving in February 1779.

1780 September, she married Robert Preston.

Margaret was instrumental in the establishment of the Walnut Grove Church and eventually organized May 27, 1866. Researcher Fred Preston writes: Walnut Grove was born out of the faith of our earliest pioneers. Its origins are all but lost in early American antiquity. Our best records indicate that the earliest church was a log building, long used also as a school built sometime in the 1780's. In a sketch prepared for a Walnut Grove Cemetery memorial some years ago, Southwest Virginia historian L. P. Summers wrote:

"Sometime prior to 1790, possibly as early as 1781, there was erected on the summit of the hill where the cemetery now is, a large log church which, for many years, was used as a church and school house by the people of the Walnut Grove community. This old church was still standing forty years ago."

Two pioneer women seem to have been particularly instrumental in the founding of the earliest Walnut Grove Church. Margaret Rhea (1757-1822), a minister's daughter, married Robert Preston, Sr. (1750-1833) in September of 1780. Her mother-in-law, Eleanor Fairman Preston (1735-1820) shared her faith. The two women seem soon to have turned to the founding of a church in their community. According to Mr. Summers:

"They are accredited with the establishment of this church and cemetery at Walnut Grove. Both women were exceedingly pious, wonderful women, and exercised a great influence in their day and time."

The land on which the church was built was family estate, belonging to John Preston Sr., and subsequently to Robert Preston Sr. The church took its name from that of the pioneer plantation, "Walnut Grove".

John Fairman Preston taught school in the log church in 1830. Col. John Preston inherited the land and the church and it was mentioned in his will. He died in 1864. A second church was constructed about 1866 but the old log church was still standing. In 1879 there was a fire in the new church building and for a brief time the old log church was used again. In a 1932 "History of Walnut Grove Church", Miss Sydney Preston wrote:

"While it (the new church) was under construction, the congregation moved to the old log church on the hill which had been used for years as a school house. In June 1903, the old log church, which was right much dilapidated, was torn down and where it once stood some of the descendents now sleep."

It was not until 1866 that the Walnut Grove Church was formally chartered as an organized church. Following is the initial entry in the oldest Sessional Record Book. Beaver Creek was the original name of the present Maple Grove Church. "The Walnut Grove Church was organized on the 27th day of May 1866 by the Rev. Thomas Brown and the Rev. James McCain. The following individuals were received as members having been previously dismissed from Beaver Creek and other congregations.

Robt. F. Preston, Mrs. India James, Mrs. Sarah Preston, Robt. C. Craig, John P. Buchanan, Samuel A. Preston, Mrs. E. Buchanan, Edwin Rhea, Miss. N. E. Buchanan, Edward Latham, Wm. P. Wallace, Mrs. Sally Latham, Mrs. Sarah Wallace, Miss Tabitha Latham, Mrs. Susan Rhea, Wiley Carmack, Miss. Susan Rhea, Wm. B. Campbell, Mrs. Ann Preston, Mrs. M. Campbell, Mrs. Fanny Preston, Mrs. M. J. Craig

Some other names mentioned, J. E. Gutherie, Pastor, received the following new members.

July 14, 1918 Robt. Carson Preston by examination
June 13, 1920 Haynes Moffett Whitten by examination
June 13, 1920 Ella Louise Whitten by examination
June 13, 1920 Percy T. Preston Jr. by examination
June 13, 1920 Virginia Wills Preston by examination
June 13, 1920 Irwin Gobble by examination
June 13, 1920 Robin Whitten letter. from Macon, Miss.

By 1961, the city of Bristol had expanded and her mushrooming subdivisions began to envelop the church. The church was much too small also, so in 1961 a new brick church was built. (I presume in approximately the same location. I have been there and the cemetery contains many Prestons and Rheas among others.

The Bristol Association Newsletter, Sept. 2001, Issue 17 reported the following story about Slave cemeteries, as reported by the late Mary Preston Gray.

Robert Preston, master of the large Walnut Grove plantation, was more considerate of his slaves than were most of his contemporaries. For one thing, he allowed them to have a half hour resting period in mid-mornings and again in mid-afternoon. This was an outstanding, charitable practice during a time when most masters required unrelenting daylight to dusk toil of their slaves.

A great oak tree stood at the edge of what was long known as The Indian Hill field. This is the field that now surrounds the Peterbilt Truck building. It was so named because the last Indian seen on the Preston place raced across that field one morning just at daybreak. (This was long after Indians had supposedly abandoned the area). When the slaves were working in that field they retired to the shade of that tree when their twice daily break times came. There fresh water would be brought to them from the Preston home spring. One can imagine how these toil weary slaves looked forward to those eagerly times of refreshment.

One of the highly prized slaves at Walnut Grove was old Rueben, affectionately known as 'Uncle Rube'. He had been a very faithful bondservant of the Preston family long before the move was made to Washington Co., VA. But the time when the aging Uncle Rube was no longer able to continue his usual strenuous labor. He was then given the far less taxing work of looking after the slave children he readily adapted to his new duty. For long hours he patiently played with and looked after the many slave children at Walnut Grove. The Preston home was then surrounded by a grove of ancient and large walnut trees and in summer the shade of these trees made a favorite retreat for Uncle Rube and his 'brood' of children. And he always called these children his 'babies' irregardless of their age. It was long told that he was always grieved when one of them reached fieldwork age (usually around ten years).

Though Uncle Rube had no watch or other means of telling time, some way he could sense when it was time for the field hands to have their breaks under the restin' tree. Then like a pied Piper this old keeper of the children could be seen slowly winding his way up the Indian Hill toward that certain big oak with his brood of babies trailing out behind him. He wanted them to have a little reunion with their parents who they seldom saw in daylight, even during the long days of summer.

He always carried two or three of the youngest babies in his arms while older girls in the group carried the others. And there as always certain to be little crippled Dan perched on uncle Rube's shoulder and holding on to his mane-like hair. Little Dan, then about 3 years old had been born a cripple. He was fortunate to have been born on the Preston plantation. Such children considered to be a potential life long liability had a way of just disappearing on the many plantation of the time. When the time came for the trek up to the restin' tree, little Dan, whose feet were so deformed that he could only crawl under the restin' tree. In season, wild strawberries grew along side the Indian Hill field. As the other children gleefully ran about eagerly picking and eating the luscious berries, uncle Rube would set crippled Dan under the restin' tree and then go pick berries for him.

In late March 1798, crippled Dan became very ill with some kind of infectious disease, likely pneumonia. The Prestons did all they could to save him but to no avail. The child died just before dawn of what would be a windy, by very mild early spring day. The Preston slaves that had died up to that time were buried at a site a short distance from the big oak tree that was the restin' tree, but when crippled Dan died, Uncle Rube remembering how the child had so delighted in meeting with his parent in the shade of the big tree, begged Robert Preston to bury the child there.

To this the master of Walnut Grove agreed. John Preston (later known as Col. John) then 17 years old, used to tell how the kind Uncle Rube wanted to carry the dead child in his arms to the burial site. This request was also granted. Young john would never forget seeing the old and almost feeble slave slowly plodding up the Indian Field hill, his long hair and beard blowing wildly in the strong March winds. The plain little coffin had been carried on ahead and had been placed on the side of the open grave near the big wind tossed oak. The Prestons and slaves stood nearby. This was very unusual. The common practice on most plantations of the time was to dispatch 2 or 3 of the men slaves to buy the dead, while others labored on. Seldom ever did members of the master's family attend a slave burial. The aged Uncle Rube died in 1803. His was the second burial in the new slave burying ground. Over the years, many of the Preston slaves were buried in the Restin' Tree Cemetery. And some say that descendants of these slaves continued to be buried there long after slavery was abolished. The graves were marked by small field stones and all of them, save one, have disappeared. But the old Restin' Tree lives on. It is about 6 feet through and is estimated to be well over 400 years old.

HISTORY OF WALNUT GROVE
The deed history of the Tract has been assembled in 2005 by researchers W. Dale Carter and Wilma M. Smith in their previously unpublished "A History of Robert Preston Walnut Grove Tract"

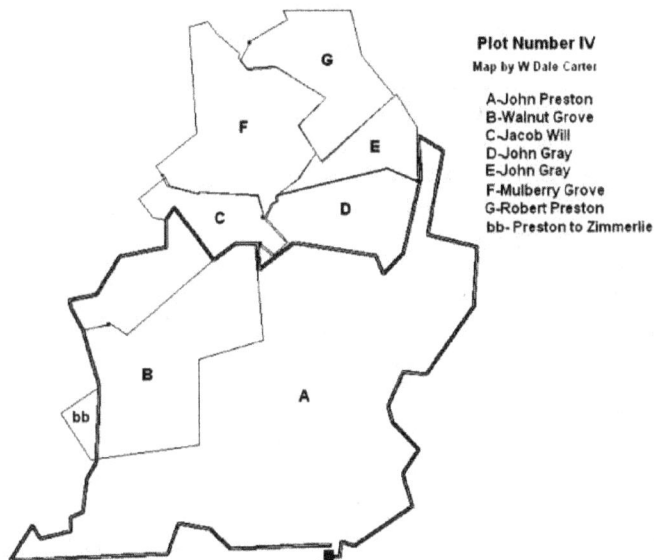

Plot Number IV
Map by W Dale Carter

A-John Preston
B-Walnut Grove
C-Jacob Will
D-John Gray
E-John Gray
F-Mulberry Grove
G-Robert Preston
bb- Preston to Zimmerlie

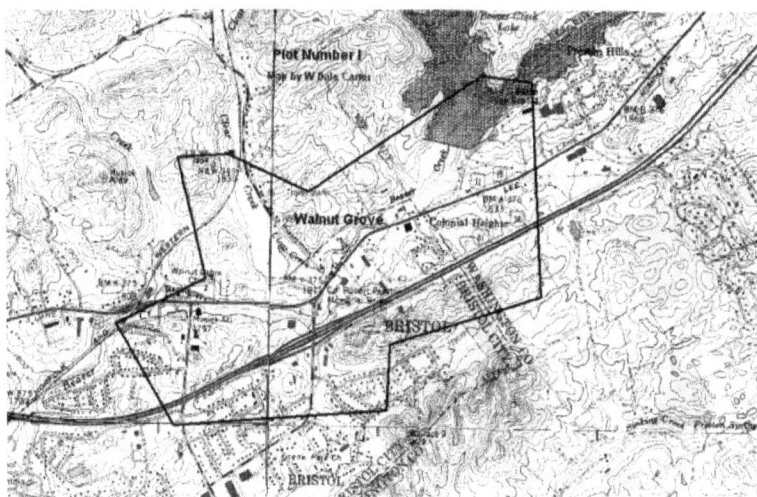

An old house near exit seven of Interstate Highway 81 in Washington County, VA is to be moved because of development of the land the house sits on. The Bristol Historical Association has determined that the house was the home of Robert Preston, an early inhabitant of the country. We have made an attempt to compile a history of the land Robert Preston owned on Beaver Creek and Sinking Creek.

"Long before any permanent settlements were made in Washington County, James Patton, a noted land speculator and other influential men obtained a land grant in 17454 for 120,000 acres from the Colony of Virginia with stipulation that it be located on the west side of the Blue Ridge Mountains and that it be settled by loyal British subjects. In 1748 a party was organized to explore the area on the waters of the Holston and Clinch Rivers. In addition to Patton himself, its more important members were his son-in-law John Buchanan, Charles Campbell, son of John Campbell, Dr. Thomas Walker and most likely the Goldman brothers who acted as pilots or guides. They traveled west as far as present day Kingsport, Tennessee selecting desirable tracts for future surveys."

"In late 1749 and early 1750 James Patton dispatched his son-in-law John Buchanan to go upon the waters of the Holston River and Survey tracts of land selected in the 1748 expedition with the purpose of obtaining land patents. He made several surveys on the waters of Beaver Creek and Sinking Creek. One of those surveys is the site of the Robert Preston House."

"On 19 February 1750 John Buchanan made a survey for 720 acres on Shallow Creek known today as Beaver Creek. No patent resulted from the survey but after Buchanan's death his executors filed for a grant based on the survey of 1750 and the survey was certified in court and the executors of the Buchanan estate obtained a land grant on 23 December 1779 for 720 acres. The grand is recorded in the land office at Richmond in Grant Book B., page 234. Apparently James Buchanan, son of John Buchanan, inherited the land grant and on 13 January 1789 through his attorney, Thomas Madison, sold the grant to Robert Preston. The deed is recorded in Washington County Deed Book 1, page 106. The grant is known as the Walnut Grove tract."

"Robert Preston was the county surveyor in the 1780's and amassed large land holdings in southwest Virginia. On Beaver Creek his land ownership exceeded 6100 acres through land grants and purchases. Adjacent to and including the Walnut Grove tract he owned near 4800 acres. After his death and in his will, the Beaver Creek land was passed on to his son, John Preston. The 4800 acre grant consisted of two tracts surveyed in 1750, several land grants issued after the Revolutionary War plus vacant land adjacent to the land grants. To say the least the land records are a mess. The surveys of the tracts were of poor quality and did not share common property lines. Therefore, after the death of Robert Preston, his son, John, obtained a court order to have his inherited estate resurveyed and a Treasury Warrant issued

22

based on the resurvey and a land grant was issued 1 August 1843 for 4800 acres. The grant is recorded in the land office at Richmond in Grant Book 94, page 706. The old original Walnut Grove survey for 720 acres became part of the 4800 acre grant to John Preston."

"In addition to the 4800 acre grant, Robert Preston also owned a large tract north east of the 4800 acre tract on Beaver Creek. This tract consisted of his land grant issued in 1784, a part of a patent issued to Edmund Pendleton 16 August 1756 and a grant to Walter Preston. Again Preston had the Edmund Pendleton and Walter Preston land resurveyed and a land grant was issued to Robert Preston on 4 October 1820 for 820 acres. This tract is known as the Mulberry Grove Tract. The total Acreage of these two grants is 1362 acres."

"We find only one reference to the home of Robert Preston during the 1780's. In Minute Book 1, page 103, Robert Preston listed entries of 1250 acres of land in Washington County. Of this acreage a 200 acre and 150 acre entry on Beaver Creek is as follows:

Minute Book 1 page 103, 14 August 1780 by virtue of treasury warrant of same date said Robert Preston enters 200 acres of land lying on the northwest side of Beaver Creek joining the lower side of the place Isaac Lebo lived on and extending to the lines of the land Joseph Gray lives on. Robert Preston, surveyor of this county renews the above entries June 9, 1781."

"Minute Book 1, page 103, Robert Preston, surveyor of this county by virtue of a treasury warrant bearing 30 October 1780 enters 150 acres of land on the waters of Beaver Creek and on the south side of the land he lives on and Joining the same beginning at the west end of a large ridge near where John Carmack's mill path crosses the lines of said land thence extending eastward, southward and westward for quantity June 9, 1781."

Mr. Carter's Plot III is a composite showing the Walnut Grove Tract, the Zimmerly grant issued as an assignee of Lebo, the Gray grant and the John Carmack grant giving us the approximate location of the 200 acre entry. In order for it to join Lebo on the lower side and extending to the Gray grant the 200 acre entry must also lay to the south of the Walnut Grove tract. We also know that the 150 acre entry joined the land he lived on south side. Also the lines of the 150 acre entry crossed the path leading to John Carmack's mill. Taking the wording of the entries to be accurate one can only conclude that the first place Robert Preston lived when he came to Washington County in February

23

of 1780 was on his 200 acre entry on the west side of Beaver Creek. On a modern map his first home would have been north of Shakesville, within the city limits of Bristol, Virginia. These entries plus 230 acres, which have not been identified, were surveyed together in 1781 for a 580 acre grant, which atypically was not issued until 1797 and was issued in the name of John Preston Jr.

"While we could not find and entry in the land tax record for 1782, Robert Sr. and his brother Walter are listed in the personal property tax records for Washington County. The 1786 land tax records are the next available and Robert Preston entered 96 and 416 acres of land. The next year he acquired 154 more acres and in 1788 he was charged with the 720 acres of the Beaver Creek land, a portion of which came to be known as Walnut Grove." Mr. Carter and Mrs Smith wrote

"For several years, personal property tax was in the name of John and Robert Preston, and a separate one for Walter. It is not clear if this John was father of Robert and Walter but he was not charged in 1787 tithe table that could indicate he was to old." (John St. was 62 at that time and lived until 1796 - EFF).

"In 1793 the land tax acreage of the Walnut Grove property dropped from 720 to 660 when Preston sold 60 acres to Zimmerlie. In 1798 Robert Preston was charged tax for license for a store. The location of this store is included in the Deed Book 24, page 510, from Robert F. to Col. John Preston. The store tax continued and in 1801 under "retailers of merchandise" he was charged $15. There are many lists and references in the Preston Papers to stores owned by both Robert Preston and his son John."

In 1798 he was listed as doing business as Alexander Porter and Robert Preston. In March 1798 among the entries are "deer skins & cash received 122.1.4, by Iron received Col. James King, 15.5.5, by William Cobb for exchange of horses", and "beeswax, show thread, cream of tarter". In 1809 correspondence indicated Robert and son John were in store business. In 1810 an agreement was entered into between Robert and John Preston and John Preston. John, son of Walter Preston, was to be manager and conductor of business in Lee County. This partnership was to continue for seven years and merchandise was to be received "at Walnut Grove store.

"The first entry in the tax records indicated there were buildings/building on the Walnut Grove tract was 1812. All of Robert's acreage on land tax records was listed along with the location and "improvement" was listed for "Walnut Grove". Also 340 acres, 600 acres, 512 acres and 133 acres were listed as adjacent to that property. The same year Col. John Preston, son of Robert, had an improvement on 600 acres on "Beaver Creek". The 1819 land tax record indicated 300 acres and 340 acres as "Walnut Grove" was Robert's place of residence and John's place of residence was called Beaver Creek. In 1820 a value of $2,000 was established for buildings on his property on the 640 acres designated in tax records as "Walnut Grove". The same year, Col. John was assessed for $2,000 for building on his property also. The value for buildings was a very large amount since very few people in Washington County had buildings of that value. Most of them were from $50, $100 to $400 with only a few valued as high as $400. Over the years, Robert was assessed with small amount for other properties on Beaver Creek."

The researchers noted "The county began listing improvements and buildings in the tax records in 1812 and we know there were buildings on the Walnut Grove tract at that time. The tax record for 1820 strongly suggests that there was a valuable building on his property and most likely this was the frame mansion house he lived in."

"Deed Book 24, Page 196 dated January 1, 1858 indicates that Col. John Preston, mostly out of love and affection for his son Robert F. Preston, deeded 910 ½ acres which included the 300 acres which Robert F. had sold back to John. This included the Walnut Grove tract on which is located the old Robert Preston home. This home continued to be in the Preston and allied families until recent years."

"On 13 January 1789 Preston purchased the Walnut Grove Tract from James Buchanan. The 1820 property tax records show that there was a mansion house located on the Walnut Grove tract valued at $2000. This is no doubt the last residence of Robert Preston. It is logical to assume that Robert Preston would not have built an expensive home on land with no legal title. Therefore, the Preston timber Frame home would have been built after 1789. The first tax record that shows a valuable building on this land was the tax record of 1820 although an improvement was shown in 1812. The homes of Both Robert and John Preston may have been built around the same time."

Children by Margaret RHEA:

+ 5.   i   **John 'Col.' PRESTON** b. 8 Jul 1781.

+ 6.   ii   **Jane 'Jennie' PRESTON** b. 1782.

3. **Walter PRESTON**, (1.John[1]) b. 25 Dec 1756 in Co. Derry, Ireland, d. 9 Aug 1834 in Clark Co., KY, buried in Clark Co. KY. 1775 Walter came to America at the age of 14 (Walter's brother Robert's report says Walter and their parents came to America after him in 1775) with his parents and settled in Washington Co. VA. He was a soldier under Gen. William Campbell in the Revolution. He was Deputy Surveyor of Washington Co. and held other civil offices. Married twice.

This brother of Robert Preston (who served under Edmondson) was a graduate of William and Mary and after the war held many important positions in Washington. He married Annie, daughter of James Montgomery. (See DAR Lineage book 56.)

1808 his first wife died leaving him with children to raise. A year later, he married Letitia, a cousin of his first wife.

He moved to Clark Co. KY with Letitia where they raised five children. Their home and farm was called 'The Rye Patch'. They died and are buried in Clark Co. KY. A number of the 8 children from Walter's first marriage settled in KY.

1810 Kentucky census shows Walter Preston with a young family in Clarke Co. KY: 1 male under 10, 2 males 10-15, one male 25-44; 1 female under 10, 1 from 10-25 and 1 female 25-44. (There are other Washington Co., VA and Sullivan Co., TN names such as John and Lewis Pemberton also enumerated this year in the county.)

1820 the Walter Preston family is enumerated again in Clarke Co. KY. In each of these years 1810 and 1820, there are no other Walter Preston's who appear in the US census records.

He was the Surveyor of Kentucky County, KY; raised a large family most of whom returned to Virginia from Winchester Kentucky. He was the progenitor of the Seven Mile Ford and Bank Prestons.

The Historical Society of Southwest Viginia published a sketch of Walter Preston - Historical Sketches of Southwest Virginia, Publication 17 1984, "the Ten Washington County years, 1776-1786: Walter Preston was born on Christmas day of 1756. He had been appointed a deputy surveyor of Washington County on March 22, 1781, though then only twenty-four. (25) With his two chain carriers, young Preston arrived at Clifton on Monday afternoon, May 12, 1783. He had pushed his work to do so. Preston had begun this tour of surveying on Monday the fifth, completing two surveys that day, two more on Tuesday, four on Wednesday, and five on Thursday. Then rains set in, hard rains, and he had two idle days on Friday and Saturday. Because he had lost so much time, he made two small surveys on Sunday to complete his assignment on the upper Clinch regions of what is today Tazewell County, except for a single survey that he made on the morning of Monday, May 12, 1783. That survey had been for the heirs of James Fowler, deceased, whose co-administrator, as noted above, was Henry Smith. This land was located at the site of the present town of Richlands and termed even then, "the rich lands on the north fork of Clinch." From there he hurried down the well known Hunter's Trace to Clifton. (26)

The Smiths were as delighted to have young Preston, then unmarried, as he was to be there in a civilized home in a savage country, as the area then was. Wild though the setting of Clifton may yet be, let alone what it must have been two hundred years ago, the house was a civilized oasis in the wilderness. Mary James Strother Smith had lived all her life, before coming to the Clinch, in the area of Fredericksburg. Clifton was a very large home, even though the Smith's had only three small children. From an inventory made eighteen years after Preston's visit, we learn that the home had 13 beds, four coverlets, eight blankets, many quilts, dozens of sheets (a rare commodity on the frontier during the Revolution, seventeen slaves, and eleven horses. As already noted in the 1782 tithable list, taken less than year before young Preston's visit, Henry Smith had a herd of 39 cattle and 18 horses. There were also in the home two square walnut tables, a number of looking glasses (a frontier rarity), a drop leaf walnut table, many candlesticks, three fine tablecloths and five "coarse" tablecloths, one and one-half dozen silver spoons, nearly fifty pewter plates, and 750 sheets of writing paper, among other things. In fact, at Smith's death in 1801, his personal property was appraised at $11,000. (27)

When Preston arrived, he and Henry Smith went over the tracts to be surveyed. It was noted that there were two separate settlement tracts to be surveyed - one for the maximum allowed of 400 acres (the original settlement site below Clifton) and the other for 214 acres (the Smithfield tract). Almost two years prior, Henry Smith had received from the Commissioners his two preemption warrants for a thousand acres each, and he was ready to have a number of adjacent tracts up and down the river surveyed to fill out the allowed 2,600 acres, all on the Hunter's Trace except for the Smithfield tract and a few small tracts on Indian Creek. Henry Smith's brother, Daniel, had been a deputy surveyor of Fincastle County, and Henry himself was no mean hand at this. He had in his home instruments of the same type used in that day and exactly three years after Preston's visit, when Russell was struck off, he became surveyor for that entity and so remained until his death when he was succeeded by his only son. This boy, Harry, though only nine in 1783, was fascinated by both Walter Preston and his survey instruments.

On the next day, Tuesday, three surveys were made for Henry Smith. Appropriately enough, they began with the settlement tract site which had been originally surveyed by the Loyal Company's Daniel Smith for 464 acres. Under the 1779 law, this tract could not exceed 400 acres, but it was no problem to chop off sixty-four fringe acres from the tract. Then the next tract below of 410 acres was surveyed and then 140 acres that joined the lower end of the settlement tract and one side of the 410 acre tract. These tracts, charged to the preemption warrants, were about two or three miles downstream from Clifton. The men talked a lot as they worked and work went rather slowly. But, in the evening they rode back to Clifton tired and hungry. (28)

Preston had already told Smith that he would have to go the next morning to the foot of Paint Lick Mountain to survey a tract for John Bristow. This 160 acre tract was soon located and surveyed and the men rode swiftly back to Clifton, the best haven they had seen since they left home, and, in the case of the chain carriers, vastly superior to home. Smith met the men as they rode into Clifton and the group went down by the river and surveyed a tract of 430 acres, the second tract below the settlement tract and west of the earlier-surveyed 410 acre tract. This done, they rode back to Clifton. It had begun to rain. (29)

Since the next day was rainy, they stayed indoors. Henry undoubtedly regaled his guests by telling them of his Long Hunt experience and Mary Smith saw to it that the guests were well supplied with food and drink. None of the men were sorry for this most pleasant interlude. The horses, needless to say, were well cared for in the stables. On Friday, three more tracts were surveyed. These were scattered and not easy to reach. The first was across the river on the south slope of Kent's Ridge. It was surprising, it seemed to the surveyors, that land so far up the mountain would be so good. This tract was 130 acres. From here, they once more crossed the river and went up into House and Barn Mountain and surveyed a fine little tract as a "lick" located in a gap in the north side of that mountain. Then, after this tract of 145 acres, they went to the other side of House and Barn Mountain and surveyed a small tract of 60 acres on Indian Creek. This was located near old U. S. 19, now designated as Route 770. From here, they rode back up Indian Creek and visited the home of Daniel Smith, brother of Henry. Walter

Preston was acquainted with Daniel, who had, as noted, been a surveyor of the area under the Fincastle County days. Daniel was soon to move to Sumner County, Tennessee, but he had another year on the Clinch. He and his wife, Sarah, made young Preston and his men welcome. From here, they rode along the eastern base of House and Barn Mountain to Clifton and a welcome supper. (30)

The next day was Saturday. After their long trip into this mountainous area, the men were tired and, fortunately, it rained. The surveyors also spent Sunday in Clifton. As it happened, Sunday was a beautiful day and Smith and Preston spent much of it talking about many things. When Monday morning came, Preston and his men left. Henry Smith still had about seven or eight hundred acres of his two thousand acres of preemption warrant, including, of course the Clifton tract itself. Smith wanted time to think over exactly where the lines were to run for this, the most important tract in Smith's point of view, to be carved out of the astonishing landscape. Preston had agreed to return the last days of the month. Both men also knew that the tract known today as Smithfield had to be surveyed, but it was twenty miles to the westward and Preston said he would catch it as he and his men started back home early in the coming month. On Monday morning, May 19th, Preston left. By noon he was bury surveying along the base of Paint Lick Mountain. (31)

True to his promise, Walter Preston returned to Clifton. Even more than before, the surveyors were happy to return to Mary Smith's home, such an amazing spot in this rocky wilderness. They arrived about noon on Tuesday, having first surveyed a small tract of 75 acres on both sides of Indian Creek. From that survey, they had gone up the creek past Daniel Smith's cabin and across the rough short cut to Clifton. Smith asked Preston to wait an extra day for the surveys. The weather promised to be better and he wanted to discuss details of the bounds of the Clifton tract with young Preston. (32)

After a day of relative inactivity, the men got on their horses on Friday morning, May 29, 1783, and began their surveys. First, they rode up the river to a small but beautiful piece of land a mile above Clifton. Only 40 acres, it was soon finished. Then came the Clifton survey, which proved to be, when bounded as Henry Smith wished it, 335 acres. They then finished with a tract of 175 acres which began at a corner of the Clifton survey and angled over at the foot of House and Barn Mountain. After this, Preston spent Saturday and Sunday at Clifton. (33)

On Monday, the surveyors rode to the upper reaches of Indian and
Laurel Creeks, east of Richlands, and surveyed three small surveys.
They came back to Clifton, then, for a final stay. Early next morning,
they rode nearly twenty miles toward Abingdon. With them was little
Harry Smith, probably unaware that he was to live out most of his
adult life as chief surveyor of what was subsequently to be his own
county. The boy watched the surveying with much interest and it may
well have been this visit of Preston that gave the needed impetus to
determining the boy's future. Preston and his men, after surveying the
Smithfield tract, bade farewell to the Smith's, father and son, and rode
over the mountain to Abingdon through what is today called Hayter's
Gap. (34)

Virginia Historical Society Sketch References: (26) Washington Co.,
VA Survey Book 1, p. 126, 128, 130, 122 & 136. These pages with
repeats not shown, are given in chronological order in which Preston
surveyed them. (27) Russell Co., VA WB 2, pp 15-24 (28) Washington
Co., VA SB 1, 116, 117 (29) Ibid, 120 & 117 (30) Ibid, 116, 117 (31)
Ibid, various entries, including 131, 132, 159, 160, etc. (32) ibid, 125
(33) ibid, 118 (34) ibid, 133, 135, 119 (35) Fee book, Washington Co.,
VA, 1783-1788, p. 45 (36) Russell Co., VA OB 1, p. 1, 2 & 7 (. He
married (1) **Anne MONTGOMERY**, married 18 Oct 1785, b. 1761 in
Lancaster, PA?, d. 8 Feb 1808. He married (2) **Letitia ROBINSON**,
married 3 Mar 1809, b. 1772, d. 1858 in Clark Co., KY. She was a
cousin of Walter's first wife Anne.
Children by Anne MONTGOMERY:

7. i   **Alexander Montgomery PRESTON**, b. 5 Nov 1786
         in Washington Co., VA, d. 1793 in Abingdon,
         Washington Co. VA.

+ 8. ii   **John Montgomery PRESTON** b. 5 Aug 1788.

+ 9. iii **Mary Robinson PRESTON** b. 10 Feb 1790.

10. iv   **James Montgomery PRESTON**, b. 30 Oct 1791, d.
         11 Apr 1879 in KY. Moved to Kentucky. Died
         unmarried.

+ 11. v   **Robert Robinson PRESTON** b. 21 Oct 1793.

+ 12. vi   **Alexander Montgomery PRESTON** b. 8 Jul 1796.

+ 13. vii **Fairman Holmes PRESTON** b. 13 May 1799.

+ 14.   viii **David Robinson PRESTON** b. 25 Apr 1803.
              Children by Letitia ROBINSON:

   15.   ix   **William PRESTON**, b. 1 Sep 1811, d. 1 Apr 1846.

+ 16.   x   **Gertrude VanLear PRESTON** b. 11 Sep 1811.

   17.   xi   **Samuel PRESTON**, b. 31 May 1813, d. 29 Aug
              1840.

+ 18.   xii **Cyrus Alfred PRESTON** b. 9 Apr 1815.

   19.   xiii **Benjamin Howard PRESTON**, b. 1 Sep 1817. Had
              no children. He married **Orpha BLAIR**, b. ABT
              1817.

4. **Jannette 'Jane' PRESTON**, (1.John[1]) b. 1758 in Walnut Grove,
    Washington Co. VA, d. 1 Nov 1800 in Sullivan Co., TN, buried in
    Weaver Cemetery, Weaver Pike, Sullivan Co. TN. It seems odd that
    her first child's birth appears to be 9 years after their wedding.

    She died fairly young, leaving children as young as 4 years old. She
    married **Matthew RHEA IV**, married 1 Nov 1778 in Virginia, b. 14
    Apr 1755 in Fahan Parrish, Co. Donegal, Ireland, d. 18 Oct 1816 in
    Sullivan Co., TN, buried in Weaver Cemetery in an unmarked grave.
    1769 came to America with his family.

    1776 Jannette Preston's father Robert Preston, and Mathew's father
    Rev. Joseph Rhea were in the Holston Territories together during the
    campaigns against the Cherokees. Matthew was 21 at the time and
    may have accompanied Rev. Rhea to the area and met his future wife
    on the way to that expedition.

    1777 June 15, Mathew was Regimental quartermaster of the 7th VA.

    1778 Sept. he was 2nd Lt. in the VA regiment.

    1778 November he married Jannette Preston.

    1779 February his family followed him south to live nearby on the land
    purchased by his father in Sullivan Co., TN

    1779 July 4, he was a 1st Lt.

1779 promoted to Captain. Served Capt. Joseph Crockett 7th VA Regiment. Served under Gen. Nathaniel Green and fought the British in the Battle of Guilford (N.C.) Courthouse which was the turning point of the Revolutionary War, and at the Battle of Camden SC. General Greene presented him with a handsome sword for "noble conduct and heroic deeds". He was a Major at this time in the 5th VA. Regiment. He served till the close of the war.

1783 Washington Co. VA survey records pg 496 Matthew Rhea - 100 acres Preemption warrant #2390 dated March 7, 1783 - on the waters of Sinking Creek, a north branch of Holston River - line of John Prestons (father-in-law) land and corner of John McCrab's (Matthew's cousin) survey - corner to McNab and William Rhea- on Preston's corner - in the fork of a road.

1783 March 31, Land Warrant 1452.0 - Matthew Rhea assignee acres 2666.66 - years 3 - rank Lt. - Unit Virginia Continental Line.

1792 Letter from his brother-in-law Robert Preston:
Dear Matthew, (brother-in-law Rhea -EFF) With brother James (Matthew's brother - 17 at the time. He may have been studying at Washington College in Abingdon VA this year - EFF), I send your papers with the original statement of your account and it appears there is $16.7.2 3/4 of your money in my hand yet which is ready for you on demand. I would be glad you would come up tomorrow and try what you can do respecting Donnell's affair. I am really ashamed to see him. No doubt he will say, I have been too indulgent to a friend. I hope you will endeavor to prevent such a reflection. A proper statement of the affair is also necessary. You have money lying in the treasury of the U.S. I have some, also; perhaps you can make it convenient to come up tomorrow & ride to Abingdon with me on Monday morning early (which is the time I must start) there to give me a power to receive the money in p a. [power of attorney? - EFF] The county seat must be to it - My love to sisters & cousins & believe me to be with a sincere good wish for your welfare.
Your Bro Robt Preston 27th Octr 1792
NB The bills of sales for the Negroes I have not sent but shall assign them before proper witnesses. R P

Another letter, this from another brother-in-law, addressed to Col. Matthew Rhea, Sullivan County, Tennessee from Walter Preston:
Sept 4th, 1799.
Dear Brother [married to Walter's sister Jane Preston - EFF],

After m-- I obtained a copy of your agreement with -- Todd which caused me to decline the business until I have your sentiments after the perusal of sd copy which you will find enclosed. Mr. Lytle refuses to take cash for his services. I offered him my Bond with good security for the amount. He told me if I had the cash in my pocket and offered payment he would not receive it but would have the one third of the land which is Eight times as much as his pay in cash would amount to, as I am informed the land would sell for 20/ per acre of the common allowance in cash when the business was done was forty dollars per thousand acres. I therefore submit the whole to your own judgment & shall proceed agreeable to future instructions. We are all in a tolerable state of health my wife seems to get better but slow. She is weake & hath great difficulty - - (breath?)thing when she stirs any about. Her -- (Must be child? Anne had given birth to Fariman Preston in May 1799.) grows fast & is a fine brisk boy. I hope with my sister & little cousins are all enjoying the Great blessings of health which may God grant, is the sincere desire of your affectionate brother.
Walter Preston
PS If you wish to write to me before the bearer here of Capt. Montgomery (Walter Preston's father-in-law) returns and can find no safe conveyance put your letter in the Post office to be left in the Lexington P. office- hope to be in about next Christmas if life & health permit. W.P.

Ohio Land office shows, from a Virginia Military Warrant, a Patent to Matthew Rhea. Four sections of land, one dated April 2, 1794, two dated April 24, 1798 and one dated Sept. 24, 1805. Abstract of Revolutionary War Pension File R17386: Virginia - 1/2 pay & Bounty Land Warrant #2451-200. In March 1816 soldier was a resident of Sullivan Co. TN with a wife Martha and children Joseph Robert, Matthew, Margaret Rhea and grandchildren; Jenness and Amy Rhea. In Dec. 1850 soldier's son Matthew Rhea was in Fayette Co. TN and he received Bounty Land Warrant #22548-160-55

Matthew Rhea had a large amount of land in the Ohio country. Virginia discharged it's war obligations partly through the bestowing of Ohio lands on the men who were in the Continental Line of the State of Virginia.

The Rhea Papers in the Tenn. State Library & Archives has substantial correspondence between Matthew, son of Matthew (Rev.) and land developers in Ky and Ohio. One such example is this abstract from the microfilm: " to William Lytle deed of sale of 3 acres, part of 41 acres of a tract entered and surveyed for Matthew Rhea, 1804. On Straight

Creek, #1984, dated Chilicothe, this 9th day of April, 1805. $0.25.5
Signed John Carlisle, Collector of the taxes on the Virginia Army
Lands" and this: "Collectors Office , Chillicothe, October 9th, 1811.
Rec'd of Matthew Rhea, by Joseph N. Couch, four dollars eighty two
cents, being the taxes for the year 1811 on 482 acres of 2nd rate land
entered for Matthew Rhea adjoining Tibbs, No 1982No. of entry 1983.
A.J. William, Collector of 2nd District." Matthew appears on a
Sullivan Co. Tax list 1811-12 showing 187 acres.

1830 Oct. 11th, a note in the microfilm record which simply says "A
letter from Henderson, Ky., about Matthew Rhea's land" at the bottom
is written "N.B. Since writing the within I find from my other ---
Chillicothe printed list that Lt. Rhea did receive or is entitled to receive
2,666 acres in Ohio. This is the 2nd item in this letter. If Patent is had
already for this let me know what Co. it lies in the Va. & ? water
courses & lds (pounds? - EFF) & if for sale, what the very lowest price
may be - , to whom I am to refer in Ohio etc., & I may buy it. J B".
Children:

+ 20.   i   **Joseph McIlwaine RHEA** b. 14 May 1787.

+ 21.   ii   **Robert Preston RHEA** b. 28 Jun 1791.

+ 22.   iii   **Margaret Matilda RHEA** b. ABT 1795.

+ 23.   iv   **Matthew RHEA V.** b. 23 Feb 1796.

Third Generation

5.   **John 'Col.' PRESTON**, (2.Robert[2], 1.John[1]) b. 8 Jul 1781 in
Washington Co., VA, d. 10 Oct 1864 in Walnut Grove, Washington
Co. VA, buried in Walnut Grove Cemetery Washington Co. VA. A
birth announcement for John comes from a letter written by John Rhea,
to his brother, Mathew Rhea, in the Continental Army. Dated 11
October, 1781. 11 October, 1781.
Dear Brother,
Day after tomorrow the troops of this county will march; whether they
go to your camp or not, time only can determine. I am not going with
them. We had news here which is believed, that you have had a hard
battle in your quarter; 24 field officers lost, Colonel Washington
wounded and all his men but twelve lost, but the English extremely
routed. I long to hear the particulars of this action which I expect I will
have from you here at home for I am naturally desirous that you make
your winter quarters with us on this side of the mountain this year. We

all want to see you. If possible, come over this winter, unless you think and resolve to live and die in the Army. You have lost too much time already, but be not in a hurry to resign until you are assured of some other way. We are all well. PEGGY HAS A SON. She and MR. PRESTON are well.

P.S., Come over, let nothing hinder you, 'tis a hard thing if after almost five years constant attendance on the fatigues and Duties of War, you cannot get so much time as to come and see your friends. Report here says that Cornwallis and his army are eating their horses. We expect soon to see you. If you see Colonel Isaac Shelby, who goes commander of our men, esteem him as a gentleman who has shown and approved himself much my good friend.

1799 John graduated from Dickson College, Carlisle PA where he became a member of Union Philosophical Society in 1796. He studied law under St. George Tucker at the College of William and Mary in 1801-02 (Letter from Francis Preston 9 Nov. 1801, WMCP folder 126). Other sources indicate he was also a graduate of Princeton University.

1800 May 21, he was recommended by the Washington Co. Court as an ensign in the 2nd Battalion of the 105th Regiment and the commission was issued July 28, 1800. Less than three months later he was commissioned a captain of the company and on Sept. 22, 1802 he was commissioned major of the 2nd Battalion. He became a colonel of the 105th Regiment on January 19, 1805.

A lawyer by education, he never practiced his profession but was for more than a quarter of a century presiding judge of the county court of Washington Co. VA. He was appointed to the Court on 20 August 1803 and qualified January 17, 1804. He was presiding justice from 1820 until 1852.

John's father Robert built the original 'Walnut Grove' house for John who after his marriage to Margaret Brown Preston in 1802, began 'housekeeping at the Grove. His large family of 14 children were born there. He had inherited his parent's large estate and devoted his life to farming. He was a farmer and from time to time had an interest in a number of mercantile firms in the county and in TN. He is mentioned in the Preston Family Papers - Preston Davie Genealogical Collection, Filson Club, 118 W. Breckenridge St. Louisville, KY 40203. A picture of Col. John Preston appears on page 476 Summers History of Southwest Virginia.

1810 his family was enumerated in the Washington Co., VA census. He was called 'Col. John Preston. Also enumerated along with him were a John Preston and Andrew Diniston (Dennison - probably his cousin).
In John's household were himself age over 45 and a female age 25-44.

1860 Virginia census shows his family in the Clear Branch area of Washington Co., VA.
  John Preston, Col. 79, farmer, real property value $61,760, personal property value $47,860, b. VA
  Elizabeth 45.
This was a amount of property was a sizeable fortune in 1860. Next household is is son Henry's family.

Near the present house (1937 - WPA notes) is an office building which belonged to the original home and it is in a very good state of preservation. Col. Preston being a very large slave holder, it was necessary to have such an office building.

1864 in his will dated April 4, 1861 proved October 24, 1864 John Preston made liberal provision for each of his children. His youngest child was Henry Preston, and in his will he states: To William R. Sheffey, Elizabeth Sheffey, and John P. Sheffey his great-grandchildren (descendants of his oldest daughter Susan) $1000 each to be paid by son Francis when the children came of age. He mentioned he had given land on Walker's Mountain to his son Francis. His great-grandchildren, the children of William C Edmonson and by his granddaughter Susan E. Rhea, were given the one to their father for about $900 each. He mentioned he had conveyed to his son Robert F. the plantation of which he lived and afterward had bought 300 acres of the same land for his own dwelling and that he had given to his son-in-law James L. White and daughter Margaret, both deceased, a variety of property which he confirmed to their heirs. He gave to his son William A. a tract in Lee County, the Wild Cat Valley Place and the Dysart Tract in Wise County and the property bought at a sale and loaned to him by deed in Washington Co. including the Negroes in his possession. To his daughter Ellen F. Sheffey he gave the money owned to him by her husband James W. Sheffey. His sons John Preston of Louisville and Walter E. Preston of Arkansas were to have all the slaves they carried to Arkansas. He gave to his daughter Elizabeth Madison Preston a tract on Beaver Creek containing 765 acres and 100 acres he had lately bought of Robert F. Preston, slaves, one half of the home stock of cattle, horses, sheep, and hogs, and one half of the household and kitchen furniture. To his son Francis he gave a small tract on the north side of Island Road, and land west of Walker's Mountain. His daughter Jane P. Craighead was given land in Sullivan Co. TN at the mouth of Beaver Creek and forty shares of stock of the Exchange Bank of Virginia (and he confirmed slaves already given to her). To his son James T. he gave two tracts in Scott County on the north fork of Clinch. To his son Thomas W. who already received land, Negroes and money, he gave one slave. To his son Henry he gave his place of residence and Henry's place of residence being all the land in his grant of 4800 acres except 62 acres sold to Worley and 610 acres conveyed to son Robert F. on the northwest side of the main road. His grandson John, son of Francis, was given 200 acres on the east end of the home place. His son henry was to have the salves and stock at his place. He stated he did not intend to devise the Walnut Grove meeting house and the graveyard to his daughter Elizabeth M. but gave it to his sons Robert F., William A., Francis , James and Henry as trustees for the use of the Old School Church. He confirmed a Negro girl and her child to his daughter Ellen F. Sheffey. The residue of his estate was given to his son James R. and he named sons William A and James T. as executors.

By codicil dates April 4, 1861 he gave his son Robert F. 200 acres opposite his residence, to his daughter Elizabeth M. 30 shares of stock in Farmers Bank of Virginia and a bond for $1,300 and he gave 15 shares in that bank equally to his granddaughters Mrs. David Cummings, Mrs. Edward M. Campbell and Susan P. White. His library of books was given to sons.

By codicil dated June 17, 1862 he revoked a gift of 100 acres to Elizabeth M. and gave that to Robert F. He also revoked a bequest of a slave to Henry and gave her to James T. Since his son William had died he named his son-in-law James W. Sheffey executor in his place.

Much of the story of John Preston, including his will, transcribed from work: Gilliam, Victoria Alice, "Work Progress Administration of Virginia, Statewide Project, Historical Inventory. Field Worker's Report" 1937. Richmond, VA. Copy filed Preston Files, Washington Co., VA Historical Society, Abingdon, VA. He married **Margaret Brown PRESTON**, married 5 Oct 1802 in Smithfield, Washington Co., VA, b. 23 Feb 1784 in Blacksburg, Montgomery Co., VA, d. 4 May 1843 in Washington Co., VA, buried in Walnut Grove Cemetery Washington Co. VA. She was the 12th child in her family and was born at Smithfield 7 months after the death of her father.

Buried at Walnut Grove Church cemetery, her grave marked by a unique coffin shaped iron cover "Margaret B. Preston wife of JNO Preston Dec'd 4, May 1843; Ag'd 59 yrs."

Children:

+ 24.   i   **Susan Smith PRESTON** b. 17 Jul 1803.

+ 25.   ii   **Robert 'Dr.' Fairman PRESTON** b. 5 Dec 1804.

+ 26.   iii   **Margaret Rhea PRESTON** b. 26 Aug 1806.

+ 27.   iv   **William Alfred PRESTON** b. 21 May 1808.

+ 28.   v   **John PRESTON, Jr.** b. 10 Feb 1811.

+ 29.   vi   **Eleanor Fairman PRESTON** b. 7 Nov 1812.

30.   vii   **Elizabeth Madison PRESTON**, b. 26 Aug 1814 in Washington Co., VA, d. 5 Apr 1865 in Washington Co., VA. Never married. Lived with her father at Walnut Grove.

Gave the land for the Walnut Grove Presbyterian Church to be built upon in Bristol VA.

+ 31.   viii   **Thomas White PRESTON** b. 13 Aug 1816.

32.   ix   **Walter Eugene PRESTON**, b. 28 Jan 1818 in Washington Co., VA, d. 23 Apr 1866 in Phillips Co. ARK?. 1835-37 he studied law at the University of Virginia.

He moved to Phillips Arkansas where he was a planter and a member of the House of Representatives 1848-49 and 1850-51.

He had no children. He married **Frances 'Fannie' HAYES**, b. ABT 1818 in Jackson TN, d. 1891. Married second Lucius L. Battle a physician from Arlington TN.

+ 33.   x   **Francis 'Frank' PRESTON** b. 26 Mar 1822.

+ 34.   xi   **Jane PRESTON** b. 26 Jun 1822.

+ 35.   xii   **James Tecumseh 'Col' PRESTON** b. 1 Apr 1824.

  36.   xiii   **Joseph PRESTON**, b. 1 May 1826 in Washington Co., VA, d. 11 May 1847. Never married.

+ 37.   xiv   **Henry PRESTON** b. 20 Nov 1828.

6.   **Jane 'Jennie' PRESTON**, (2.Robert^2, 1.John^1) b. 1782 in Washington Co., VA, d. 24 Apr 1863 in Washington Co., VA, buried in Walnut Grove Cemetery Washington Co. VA. John Preston in his will left 'to the two sons of Jenny Preston, to-wit, Alexander R. Preston and John F. Preston all of my tract of land lying on Opossum Creek in Scott Co to be equally divided between them'.

Father Robert Preston had large holdings in Virginia and a number of tenants. She married **Robert 'Irish Bob' PRESTON, Jr. Jr.**, married 12 Apr 1798 in Washington Co., VA, b. 1772 in Co. Donegal, Ireland, d. 9 Sep 1858 in Washington Co., VA, buried in Walnut Grove Cemetery Washington Co. VA. Robert was born in Ireland and was brought over to America by his cousin Robert Preston Sr. about 1793. He reports his arrival with cousin Samuel (Houston) in a letter dated July 1793 written from Philadelphia. (A number of letters from family indicate they lived in Co. Donegal, in the vicinity of Derry.)

He was placed in charge of a store which was kept in a log storehouse near the residence of Robert Sheffey on Lee Highway about 4 miles east of Bristol VA.

A few years thereafter he married his 2nd cousin Jane Preston the daughter of his sponsor Robert Preston Sr. The marriage took place in the house which was the residence of Mr. Sheffey.

Robert Sr. located his daughter and her husband on a fine estate called 'Locust Glen', a few miles distant, now on the old Jonesboro Road, near Spring Creek Presbyterian Church. There they built a small log church. They lived happily together for 61 years and left three children.

1797 The following is a transcript of a deed which may be for the property called 'Locust Glen'. (A 'pole is the same as a 'rod' and is equal to 5.5 yards or 16.5 feet.)

James Monroe ~~Esquire, Governor of the Commonwealth of Virginia,
To all to whom these presents shall come, Greeting: Know ye, that by virtue of a Land Office Treasury Warrant, Number two thousand one hundred and fifty seven filed the eighth day of March one thousand seven hundred and ninety seven (1797) there is granted by the said Commonwealth, unto Robert Preston Junior--
A certain Tract or Parcel of Land, containing fifty eight acres by survey bearing date the eight day of March one thousand seven hundred and ninety eight, lying and being in the County of Washington, on the North side of the North Fork of Holstein River, and is bounded as followeth, "to with". Beginning at a white oak, on the bank of the River, and is corner to Wells land, with his line, thence 5 72o, W 184 poles to two black oaks, corner to Mary Wills, Survey, with the lines of the same thence N 30o W 62 poles to a black oak and Chestnut oak near the top of a Piney Knob, S85o W58 poles to a white oak on Petis Morrison's line, with the same, thence N 19o, E 43 poles to a white oak, gum and dogwood, S 83o, E250 poles to the beginning... with its Appurtenances; To Have and to Hold the said Tract or Parcel of Land with its Appurtenances, to the said Robert Preston Junior --- and his Heirs for ever.

In Witness whereof, the said James Monroe ~Esquire, Governor of the Commonwealth of Virginia, hath hereunto set his Hand, and caused the lesser Seal of the said Commonwealth to be affixed at Richmond, on the Fifth day of April in the Year of our Lord, One Thousand Eight hundred and of the Commonwealth the twenty fourth.
Jas Monroe

1810 Robert Preston is enumerated in the Washington Co., VA census - 2 males under 10, 1 10-24, one make 25-44; 1 female under 10, one female 25-44. (On the same page is a John Huston also with a young family, possibly a cousin).

1820 he is shown as 'Preston, Robt Junr' when enumerated on the Washington Co., VA census. This original record has been alphabetized and thus family groups were not readily evident. The enumerator shows 1 male 16-18, one 15-26 and one over 45; two females one over 45; 6 slaves.

1819 Thomas M. Randolph Esq Governor of the Commonwealth of Virginia, To all to whom these presents shall come, Greeting: Know ye, That in conformity with a Survey made the twenty seventh day of January 1819 by virtue of a Land Office Treasury Warrant, Number

5796; issued the 23rd November 1816; There is granted by the said Commonwealth unto Robert Preston Junior ~ A certain Tract or Parcel of Land, containing four and a half acres Situate in the County of Washington on the waters of Spring Creek and on both sides of Jonesborough road and bounded as followeth To wit. Beginning at two black oaks and a chestnut a corner to John Mitchell's land thence with his line S 42 W130 poles to two hickories by a lying black Oak the corner of John Campbell's old survey thence with said Preston's lines N17 E 26 poles to a white Oak and lying chestnut and thence N49 E 106 poles to the Beginning. ~ To Have and to Hold the said Tract or Parcel of Land with its Appurtenances, to the said Robert Preston Jun. -- and his heirs forever. (Transcribed by researcher Fred Preston.)

In Witness whereof, the said Thomas M. Randolf Esq. Governor of the Commonwealth of Virginia, hath hereunto set his Hand, and caused the lesser Seal of the said Commonwealth to be affixed at Richmond, on the first day of July in the Year of our Lord, One Thousand Eight Hundred and Twenty ~ and of the Commonwealth the forty fourth. Th. M. Randolf

1830 Virginia census he is shown as Preston, Robert Jnr. The household had: 1 males 15-20 (John Fairman Preston), 1 50-60 years old; 1 female 40-50.

1833 - Will of Robert Preston, Sr., Son of John Preston of Walnut Grove, VA (father in law, sponsor and adopted father of Robert Preston. father of Jennie Preston)

I, Robert Preston, of the County of Washington, and the State of Virginia, being aged and infirm in body, but of sound mind and disposing memory, for which I thank God, and calling to mind the uncertainty of life and being desirous to dispose of all such worldly estate as it has pleased God to bless me with, I do hereby make this my last Will and Testament in manner and form following, that is to say: I leave and bequeath to my daughter Jennie Preston, wife of Robert Preston, Jr., my negro woman named "Kate", and the said Kate's son, James. I leave and bequeath to the two sons of Jennie Preston, to wit, Alexander R. Preston and John F. Preston, all of my tract of land lying on Opossum Creek in Scott County, to be equally divided between the said Alexander R. and John F. Preston. I leave and bequeath to Alexander R. Preston $200. I leave and bequeath to my good, kind and loving wife, Sarah G. Preston, my negro boy named Moses. A good horse worth at least $70, three cows, her choice out of my stock, one bed, her choice of all the beds in my house and her choice of furniture

for said bed, my bureau, one-third of my table linen and one-half of the cupboard furniture, one good trunk and all of her wearing apparel clothes. Also, 120 acres of land lying on the head of Locust Branch in Washington County, and adjoining the land of James Anderson and Andrew Dennison. I leave and bequeath to John Preston (Irish) $300.00. I leave and bequeath to Robert F. Preston, son of John Preston, fifteen
shares of stock in the United States Bank with its proceeds.

I give to Edward Latham of Washington Co., his Executors or Administrators, in trust for the use and benefit of Margaret Fickle and her issue, my negro woman named Ann and her three female children and her future increase; $500 and bed and furniture such as have been common in my house, and a tract of land lying on Dudley's Branch in Lee County containing 278 acres, to be appropriated to the use of the said Margaret Fickle and her issue as her and their necessities or interests may require, and I positively require that the said Edward Latham, his Executors and Administrators, shall so manage the devise here made to him for the use and benefit of the said Margaret Fickle and her issue, that her husband, Abram, shall at no time have any control over the same nor derive any use or benefit there from, and if the said Edward Latham shall refuse to act as trustee as aforesaid, I hereby authorize my Executor herein named, his Executors and Administrators to apply to the Court of Washington County to have a trustee appointed who shall perform the same duties and exercise the same powers herein required of and vested in the said Edward Latham. I leave and bequeath to Robert P. Fickle a horse to be worth $50 or $60, a new saddle and bridle of good quality, all of which is to be furnished when the said Robert P. Fickle comes to be 18 years of age.

I leave and bequeath to Sara G. Rhea, formerly Sarah G. Preston my negro girl named Nancy.

I leave and bequeath to my son, John Preston, all the balance of my property whatsoever nature or kind it may be, both real and personal and not herein disposed of, and it is my wish and desire that as my estate is in no embarrassment, either by debt or otherwise, that no part thereof shall be valued or sold, and also that my Executor shall not be required to give bond and security. And lastly, I do hereby constitute and appoint my son, John Preston, Executor of this my last Will and Testaments by me heretofore made. In witness whereof I have here unto set my hand and affixed my seal this 21st day of November, 1832.(Signed) Robert Preston, S.S. Witnesses: Jos. Carson, Walter E. Preston,

Thomas L. Preston, Edward Latham.
(The will was probated in Court Dec. 23, 1833.)

Robert Jr. and Jennie organized and were very active in the Spring
Creek Presbyterian Church and were admired and loved by all in the
community. Had six children.

The following are transcripts of letters uncovered by Robert Coontz in
2000 (rcoontz@@compuserve.com). The one of Oct 6, 1817 mentions
a Robert G. Preston, Irish Bob - with a middle name of Gilliland ??? It
is thought, his mother was Sarah Gilliland. "Here are the notes I made
on the letters at William and Mary. There were many others that I
didn't have time to read or couldn't make out - plenty of work still left
for anyone with time to do it."

"The letters made fascinating reading, with references to the
Napoleonic Wars and other historical events. I had to omit all of that in
my note taking to concentrate on names. There may be barely enough
information to figure out how most of the people mentioned fit
together, but it is tricky. An aunt may be either the father's sister or the
mother's sister; her name may be either a maiden name or a married
name. Then there are cousin marriages and the habit of naming every
female Jennet -- which may be the same as Jane."

It would be interesting to try to find some of these people in Irish or
British records. Certainly there is enough information to identify the
ship on which "Irish Bob" Preston (Robert's adopted son) crossed the
Atlantic. At any rate, I hope some of this proves useful to you. Please
let me know if you reach any conclusions. Thanks, Robert Coontz"

20 December 1779 - Certificate from the College of William and Mary
appointing Robert Preston surveyor. Signed by James Madison,
president of the college.

10 May 1793 - Bill of sale: cloth and yarn made by James Preston, sold
to Robert Preston, in Derry. [*Which* Robert Preston?]

21 July 1793 - Philadelphia - From Robert Preston ["Irish Bob"?] to
Robert Preston:
Cousin Samuel and I are safe arrived. Excellent Captain Hickey, but
inhuman mate. Uncle John Davis
and Aunt were well when we left Ireland but is [sic] dead. Your uncle
is getting very frail. When we came to town, we met with Cousin
Robert Divinport.

20 May 1796 - Elaughmore, Ireland
From James Preston to Robert Preston
"You said my Brother and Sister had a sore turn of sickness..."
[Brother = Robert Preston's father?] Hope they are better. Mentions
"your sister Jenny and family". I have seen John Hamilton Leatty and
his wife. Compliments to John Donnell.

30 May 1803 Ireland - From Alexander Dean and Rebeca Dean to
Robert Preston
Mention: Mr and Mrs. Danvenport, Aunt Laird, "Your two old aunts is
alive."

2 May 1805 Donegall County
From James and Sarah Preston to Robert Preston
"Dear Nephew"
Part of my family is with you. "You and your wife's kindness... I
experienced your gratitude and affection long e'er you reached
America... benefits which they have received." Mentions Alexander.
Poor and afflicted condition of James Preston Sr. of Derry: ulcers on
his hands and feet, confined to bed for a year. Remember us to Cousin
Walter Preston and family; to son and daughter Dennison and family;
to Robert and Daughter Preston. [James's] son Alexander. Cousin
Sam Huston and family.

22 May 1805 Donegall County, Ireland - from Aunt Jennet Ferman [=
Fairman]
"Dear Nephew"
Old aunt interred 12 April. [probably Aunt Margaret, who was 78 in
1803, according to another letter] sister [whose? Robert's, Aunt
Jennett's, or the old Aunt's?] is blind. Your Cousin Jennet's husband
died. Mentions "your Cousin Mary and her brother Samuel"

6 October 1817 Franklin [where? Somewhere in the U.S.]
From William P. Gilliland to Robert Preston, Walnut Grove Mentions
Mrs. Preston; Aunt Preston; Miss Peggy Rhea; Andrew Dennison and
family; Robert G. Preston ["G" for "Gilliland"? Is this the "Irish Bob"
Preston who married Robert Preston's daughter Jane?]; Cornall
[Colonel] John H./M. Preston; Robert P.
Preston; Ferman, Francis, William McClellan.

They organized and were very active in the Spring Creek Presbyterian
Church and were admired and loved by all in the community. Had six
childre.

44

The Preston Family of Walnut Grove, Virginia

Children:

38.   i   **James PRESTON**, b. 17 Jan 1799 in Washington Co., VA, d. 1828. He married **Jane COLVILLE**, b. ABT 1799 in VA?.

39.   ii   **Margaret PRESTON**, b. ABT 1801 in Washington Co., VA. Died young.

+ 40. iii **Sarah Jane Gilliland PRESTON** b. 27 Jun 1803.

+ 41. iv **Alexander 'Dr' R. PRESTON** b. 8 Dec 1805.

42.   v   **Fairman PRESTON**, b. 28 Jun 1808 in Washington Co., VA, d. 1811. Died in an accident.

+ 43. vi **John Fairman 'Capt' PRESTON** b. 26 Apr 1811.

8. **John Montgomery PRESTON**, (3.Walter[2], 1.John[1]) b. 5 Aug 1788 in Abingdon, Washington Co. VA, d. 14 Sep 1861. 1818 he married for the first time. He and Ellen had 3 children.

Secondly he married a distant cousin Maria Preston, daughter of Gen. Francis Preston of the Smithfield, VA Prestons.

1850 his family is enumerated in the Virginia census in the Town of Abingdon, Washington Co. VA.
John M. Preston, age 62, real estate valued at $13,000, b. VA
Walter ", age 31, lawyer b. VA
Elizabeth ", 26 b. VA
John M. ",11, b . VA
Chalres H. C. ", 9, b. VA.

Wealthy merchant and first mayor of Abington VA. He married (1) **Eleanor 'Ellen' WILSON**, married 26 Jul 1818 in Washington Co., VA, b. ABT 1788 in VA?. He married (2) **Maria Thornton Carter PRESTON**, married 20 Sep 1837 in Washington Co., VA, b. 26 Aug 1806 in Saltville, Washington Co. VA, d. 18 Oct 1842 in Abingdon, Washington Co. VA, buried in Aspenvale Cemetery, Seven Mile Ford, VA. Second wife of John Preston.
Children by Eleanor 'Ellen' WILSON:

+ 44. i   **Walter PRESTON** b. 18 Jul 1819.

+ 45.   ii   **James Wilson PRESTON** b. 24 Aug 1821.

+ 46.   iii   **Elizabeth Ellen PRESTON** b. 30 Apr 1824.
        Children by Maria Thornton Carter PRESTON:

+ 47.   iv   **John Montgomery PRESTON Jr.** b. 14 Oct 1838.

+ 48.   v   **Charles Henry Campbell PRESTON** b. 12 Sep 1840.

9. **Mary Robinson PRESTON**, (3.Walter^2, 1.John^1) b. 10 Feb 1790 in VA, d. 11 Dec 1856. She married **Chiles COLEMAN**, married 21 Apr 1821, b. 1798 in VA, d. 12 Jan 1853. 1850 Oct. 9th the US census shows the family was living in Boone Co., KY:
 Chiles Coleman 52, farmer, property value $12, 000, b. VA
 Mary Coleman 50, b. VA
 Nancy " 23, b. KY
 Ellen ", 22, b. KY
 James P. ", 20, b. KY
 Robert T. " 18, b. KY
 William Reynolds, 15, b. KY
(All in the same household)

He and Mary had 6 children.
        Children:

+ 49.   i   **Walter Preston COLEMAN** b. 7 Feb 1823.

  50.   ii   **John Preston COLEMAN**, b. 4 Jun 1824 in VA?, d. 17 Jun 1862. He married **Miss SPEARS**, b. ABT 1824.

+ 51.   iii   **Anne Montgomery COLEMAN** b. 16 May 1826.

  52.   iv   **Ellen COLEMAN**, b. 31 Dec 1827 in KY, d. 1876. DId not marry.

+ 53.   v   **James P. COLEMAN** b. 29 Nov 1829.

  54.   vi   **Robert F. COLEMAN**, b. 15 Apr 1832 in KY, d. 18 Feb 1865. Died unmarried.

11. **Robert Robinson PRESTON**, (3.Walter^2, 1.John^1) b. 21 Oct 1793 in VA, d. 5 Mar 1866. 1850 his family is enumerated in the Virginia census in the Town of Abingdon, Washington Co. VA.

Robt. R. Preston age 56, Cashier of E. Bank, real estate valued at $5880 b. VA

Elizabeth 41, b. VA

Mary 18, b. VA

Ann 14, b. VA

Walter 10, b. VA

John 8, b. VA

Amelia 5, b. VA

Thomas 3, b. VA

also in this household, probably brothers of Elizabeth Cummings Preston:

Chas. J. Cummings, 38 Lawyer, b. VA

David C. Cummings, 36, Merchant, b. VA

1860 his family is enumerated in the Virginia census in the Town of Abingdon, Washington Co. VA.

Robert. R. Preston age 66, Cashier of Bank, real estate valued at $12,000, personal property $11,550, b. VA

Elizabeth AM 51, housekeeper, b. VA

Ann M. 25, b. VA

Walter S., 21, student, b. VA

John A., 19, Clerk in Bank, b. VA

Amelia C., 15, b. VA

Thomas W.13, b. VA

Elizabeth C. 8 b. VA. He married **Elizabeth CUMMINGS**, b. 1809 in VA.

Children:

55.   i   **Arthur Cummings PRESTON**, b. ABT 1833 in Washington Co., VA. Died young.

+ 56.   ii   **Mary C. PRESTON** b. 18 Sep 1833.

57.   iii   **Anne Montgomery PRESTON**, b. 27 Mar 1835 in Washington Co., VA, d. 23 Sep 1912. Unmarried.

58.   iv   **James PRESTON**, b. 13 Mar 1837 in Washington Co., VA, d. 19 Aug 1842.

59.   v   **Walter S. PRESTON**, b. 6 Jan 1840 in Washington Co., VA, d. 15 Feb 1910. Served in the C.S.A Army.

1880 he is enumerated in the Federal census in Abingdon, Washington Co., VA with the family of his sister Amelia Preston.

Died unmarried.

60. vi **John A. PRESTON**, b. 3 Jun 1842 in Washington Co., VA, d. 18 Sep 1914. 1860 he was a clerk in a bank. Served in the C.S.A. Army. Died unmarried.

+ 61. vii **Amelia Cummings PRESTON** b. 1 Dec 1844.

+ 62. viii **Elizabeth 'Lizzie' Cummings PRESTON** b. 1 Mar 1852.

+ 63. ix **Thomas Wilson PRESTON** b. 1 Dec 1846.

64. x **Campbell PRESTON**, b. 2 Mar 1852, d. 6 Nov 1854.

12. **Alexander Montgomery PRESTON**, (3.Walter^2, 1.John^1) b. 8 Jul 1796 in KY, d. 1 Aug 1866. He was named after his brother who had died 3 years earlier. It is reported that he married and they went to Kentucky. The 1850 census would indicate the entire family was from Kentucky.

1850 Federal census finds the family enumerated in District No. 2 Clark Co., KY:
Preston, Alexander M., 36 (age does not agree with other records), merchant, property value $3,100, b. KY [remainder of the family is on the next sheet of the census]
Elizabeth Preston 43, b. KY
Mary ", 14 b. KY
Ann ", 12, b. KY
Elizabeth ", 11, b. KY
Samuel ", 9, b. KY
Lucy ", 6, b. KY
Ellen ", 4, b. KY
Alexander ", 2, b. KY
[in the same household]
Packson Bruener, 26, clerk, b. KY
Anna Heinde, 24, b. ? He married **Elizabeth CLARK**, b. 1803 in KY. She and Alexander had 4 children.

Children:

65.   i   **Mary PRESTON**, b. 1836 in KY.

+ 66.   ii   **Anne Montgomery PRESTON** b. 1838.

67.   iii   **Samuel PRESTON**, b. 1841 in KY, d. in TX.

68.   iv   **Lucy PRESTON**, b. 1844 in KY.

69.   v   **Ellen PRESTON**, b. 1846 in KY, b. 1846 in VA?.
Moved to Texas. Never married.

70.   vi   **Alexander PRESTON**, b. 1848 in KY.

71.   vii   **Elizabeth PRESTON**, b. 1849 in KY. Moved to
Texas. Never married.

13.   **Fairman Holmes PRESTON**, (3.Walter[2], 1.John[1]) b. 13 May 1799
in VA, d. 1869. 1830 Virginia Federal census shows the family
enumerated in Abingdon, Washington Co., VA.
  Preston, Fairman H.; 1 male under 5, one 20-30, one 30-40; 1 female
under5, one 20-30.

1850 Federal census of Virginia shows the family enumerated in
Washington Co., VA.
  Preston, F. H. age 51, farmer. Real estate value $10,000. b. VA
  -- S. H., Female, age 47, b. VA
  -- C. C. P. Female age 13, b. VA
  -- John G. male, age 19, clerk, b. VA.

He had 5 children. He married **Sarah 'Sallie' GIBSON**, married 29
Jan 1825, b. 1803 in VA. 1860 Federal census shows a James
Gibson, 48, enumerated in Abingdon, VA two households away from
Sarah's brother in law Robert F. Preston, 66. Both James and Robert
work at a bank. Is James be the brother of Sarah?
  Children:

72.   i   **Ellen PRESTON**, b. ABT 1826 in Washington Co.,
VA.

+ 73.   ii   **Anne Amelia PRESTON** b. 29 Aug 1826.

+ 74.   iii   **Walter PRESTON** b. ABT 1828.

75.   iv   **John G. PRESTON**, b. 1831 in Washington Co., VA. Died young.

76.   v   **Charles PRESTON**, b. 1837 in Washington Co., VA. Died young.

14. **David Robinson PRESTON**, (3.Walter[2], 1.John[1]) b. 25 Apr 1803, d. 5 Mar 1850. He married **Janet CREIGH**, b. ABT 1803 in Lewisburg, WV. She and David had 6 children.

Children:

77.   i   **Thomas PRESTON**, b. ABT 1830 in WVA?. Died young.

78.   ii   **Mary PRESTON**, b. ABT 1832 in WVA?. Died young.

79.   iii   **Fairman PRESTON**, b. ABT 1834 in WVA?.

+ 80.   iv   **Walter Creigh PRESTON** b. ABT 1836.

+ 81.   v   **John A. PRESTON** b. ABT 1838.

+ 82.   vi   **Davidella 'Della' Margaret PRESTON** b. 1 Jul 1846.

16. **Gertrude VanLear PRESTON**, (3.Walter[2], 1.John[1]) b. 11 Sep 1811, d. 9 Apr 1840. Had three children. Died at a young age. She married **Loring REYNOLDS**, married 1 Oct 1833, b. ABT 1811, d. BEF 1840. 1831 to 1836 Loring H. Reynolds is shown in the Illinois Public Land Purchase records as purchaser of 15 pieces of land at various times during those years.

1850 Loring Reynolds does not appear in the Federal census index.
Children:

+ 83.   i   **Letitia Robinson REYNOLDS** b. ABT 1833.

+ 84.   ii   **Gertrude Preston REYNOLDS** b. ABT 1835.

85.   iii   **William Preston REYNOLDS**, b. ABT 1837.

18. **Cyrus Alfred PRESTON**, (3.Walter[2], 1.John[1]) b. 9 Apr 1815.
Married late in life and had 2 children.

1879 Illinois census shows the young family in Planview, Macoupin
Co., IL:
  Preston, Cyrus A. 55, farmer, b. KY.
  -- Mary A, 30, keeping house, farmer, b. PA
  -- Cyrus A., 3, b. IL
  --Annie W., 30, at home, b. KY
(In the same household)
  Motte Annie 3, b. PA
  Foley, John, 22, laborer on farm, b. Ireland. He married **Mary A.
  wife of Cyrus PRESTON**, b. 1850 in PA.
       Children:

    86.   i   **Cyrus A. PRESTON**, b. 1867 in IL.

20. **Joseph McIlwaine RHEA**, (4.Jannette[2], 1.John[1]) b. 14 May 1787 in
Sullivan Co., TN, d. 14 Jun 1860 in Sullivan Co., TN, buried in
Presbyterian Cemetery Sullivan Co. TN. Joseph Rhea at the age of
14 entered Washington College in TN. He graduated in 1805.

1806 he married Catherine.

He served in the War of 1812 as an Orderly Sergeant; was in Canada
as secretary to an officer. When he returned from the war they lived
in Washington and Scott Counties in Virginia then came to the home
place in TN called 'Soldiers Nest' where he lived till he died in 1860.
Kitty died the same year.

He was a farmer and schoolteacher, being highly educated and a great
temperance lecturer. He, being a reformed man, knew the evils of
this curse. He was often urged to accept public offices, but always
declined.

He helped build the 'Pleasant Grove Church' of which he was an Elder
to the time he died. Had eleven children. He married **Catherine
'Kitty' MYERS**, married 1806, b. 28 Jul 1788 in Berkeley Co. VA,
d. 25 Feb 1860 in Sullivan Co., TN, buried in Presbyterian Cemetery
Sullivan Co. TN.
       Children:

+ 87.   i   **Jennet 'Jane' Preston RHEA** b. 1808.

The Preston Family of Walnut Grove, Virginia

88. ii **Eliza Ann RHEA**, b. 3 Jan 1810 in Sullivan Co., TN, d. 4 Jan 1811 in Sullivan Co., TN.

+ 89. iii **Emma RHEA** b. 26 Feb 1811.

90. iv **Matthew RHEA**, b. 12 Aug 1815 in Sullivan Co., TN, d. 1819 in Sullivan Co., TN.

91. v **Robert Charles RHEA**, b. 13 Feb 1817 in Sullivan Co., TN, d. 1818 in Sullivan Co., TN.

+ 92. vi **Margaret RHEA** b. 9 Dec 1818.

93. vii **Samuel Myers RHEA**, b. 18 Oct 1821 in Sullivan Co., TN, d. 17 Oct 1840 in Sullivan Co., TN, buried in Weaver Cemetery, Weaver Pike, Sullivan Co. TN.

+ 94. viii **Eleanor Fairman 'Ellen' RHEA** b. 14 Oct 1828.

+ 95. ix **Walter Preston RHEA** b. 12 Mar 1831.

+ 96. x **Edmund RHEA** b. 9 Feb 1834.

21. **Robert Preston RHEA**, (4.Jannette[2], 1.John[1]) b. 28 Jun 1791 in Bluff City, Sullivan Co., TN, d. 31 Mar 1872 in Sullivan Co., TN, buried in Pleasant Grove Cemetery 'A History of Watauga Co. North Carolina' by John Preston Arthur, pg 340, "R.P Rhea, also born in West Virginia, and a graduate of the Naval Academy at Annapolis, MD. He became a teacher of great note and had the honor of having taught Gen. T. J. (Stonewall) Jackson."

Educated at Princeton. Served in the War of 1812 under Gen. Winfield Scott. Captured by the British, he was a prisoner of war with brother. Kept for one year in Quebec, Canada; put in irons.

After living a while in Virginia, moved to Sullivan Co. TN on the land entered and located by his father lying on East TN and VA Railroad 2 miles east of Bluff City TN (W. L. Rhea - Genealogy of Rhea Family, 1895).

1870 census shows he and Nancy living in Sullivan Co. with children Margaret 38, Mary 35 and Matthew 30 living at home. Real estate value $2500 and personal property $1650.

52

He was a teacher; tutored Stonewall Jackson for West Point (this is recorded on his tombstone).

1873 November 3, the will of Robert Rhea dated 4 Feb. 1871 was proven in Sullivan Co., Tennessee: Wife Nancy ... our 3 children, Margaret Mary R. Matthew Rhea ... Hoping that they may all live together in the old mansion house... 8 children (not named) an equal share in the old tract. 11 acres secured by an entry in two parcels adjacent to the old tract...Stock in East TN and VA Railroad. Exc. son, Robert C Rhea. Wit: N. Long, James D. Rhea.
Signed Robert P. Rhea. He married **Nancy DAVIDSON**, married 1828, b. 3 Mar 1801 in Kentucky, d. 9 Oct 1875 in Sullivan Co., TN, buried in Pleasant Grove Cemetery
Children:

+ 97.   i   **Lucretia Jane RHEA** b. 1828.

+ 98.   ii   **John 'Dr.' Preston RHEA Sr.** b. 20 Jul 1829.

99.   iii   **Josiah Davidson RHEA**, b. ABT 1830 in Sullivan Co., TN.

100.   iv   **Margaret RHEA**, b. 1833 in Sullivan Co., TN.

101.   v   **Mary 'Mollie' R. RHEA**, b. 1835 in Sullivan Co., TN.

+ 102.   vi   **Robert 'Dr.' Campbell RHEA** b. 19 Apr 1837.

103.   vii   **Matthew RHEA**, b. 1838 in Sullivan Co., TN. Served in Comapny F 63rd Tennesee Infantry. He married **Sarah F. RHEA**, b. 1845 in The Elms, Bristol, Sullivan Co, TN, (daughter of James Dysart RHEA) d. 16 Nov 1893 in Blountville, Sullivan Co, TN?.

104.   viii   **Sarah 'Sally' RHEA**, b. 1840 in Sullivan Co., TN. Lived on Lookout Mountain TN. She married **Courtland Columbus JACKSON**, married 12 Feb 1861 in Bluff City, Sullivan Co., TN, b. 28 Jul 1825 in Westerlo, NY, d. 1 Jun 1912. Married at the outbreak of the Civil War. Had 7 children. He was inclined to write poetry. He was a farmer and a teacher at SS mission in Marquis, GA. IGI shows

Courtland with birthplace of Oswego NY and another listing with the same date but born Westerlo, Albany, NY.

22. **Margaret Matilda RHEA**, (4.Jannette[2], 1.John[1]) b. ABT 1795 in Sullivan Co., TN. The following was taken from 'Tennessee Divorces 1797-1858' Gale W. Bamman, C. G. and Debbie W. Spero:

1827 Fickle, Margaret Sullivan Co. TN - The marriage bonds between Margaret and her husband Abram B. Fickle are to be dissolved upon proof that Abram has been convicted as deputy postmaster of taking money out of a letter in the post office. Margaret would then be constituted the sole guardian of their son, Robert P. Fickle. Acts of TN, 1827, p. 196

1829 Fickle, Margaret, Sullivan County TN - Margaret petitioned in 1827 for a divorce from her husband, Abraham B. Fickle, because he had been convicted of taking money out of a letter while acting as assistant or deputy post master in Blountville and had been sentenced to 10 years imprisonment. She didn't get her divorce in 1827, but in December 1827 a law was passed making it lawful for her to file her petition for divorce in Sullivan County and if above charges against Abraham had been carried out she should get her divorce. She wants a divorce and her name to be changed to Margaret Rhea. 150-1829.

Fickle, Margaret 22 August 1831 Sullivan County - Margaret is petitioning for a divorce from her husband, Abraham B. Fickle. She applied for same in 1827, and on 13 December 1827 an act was passed requiring her to file her petition in the circuit court of Sullivan County and prove that Abraham had been convicted as deputy postmaster of taking money out of a letter and was sentenced to two years' imprisonment. She at that time was unable to get her divorce because of decision of Sullivan County Circuit Court. In 1829 she petitioned the legislature again for a divorce, but again the courts refused. She has not seen Abraham for more than 5 years, but has been informed that he lives in Jonesboro and is dissolute. She wants to be separated from him for life so that she can provide for herself and her son. She wants a divorce and to change her name to her former name of Margaret Rhea and her son's name of Robert P. Fickle to Robert Preston Rhea. 150-1831
Witnessed by Samuel Rhea, Justice of the Peace.

Margaret and her young son left Washington Co. and resided in Sullivan Co., TN.

A curious bequest appears in the will of Margaret's uncle Robert Preston Sr. of Washington Co. VA dated Nov. 11, 1832. Certainly a comment on his feelings about Abram.

"I give to Edward Lathan of Washington, his Executors or Administrators in trust for the use and benefit of Margaret Fickle and her issue my negro woman named Ann, and her 3 female children and her future increase; $500 and bed and furniture such as have been common in my house, and a tract of land lying on Dudley's Branch in Lee Co. containing 278 acres, to be appropriated to the use of the said Margaret Fickle and her issue as her and their necessities or interests may require and I positively require that said Edward Latham shall so manage the devise here made to him for the use and benefit of the said Margaret Fickle and her issue and that her husband, Abram shall at no time have any control over the same nor derive any use or benefit there from, and if the said Edward Latham shall refuse to as trustee as aforesaid, I hereby authorize my Executor herein named to apply to the Court of the County of Washington to have a trustee appointed who shall perform the same duties..

I bequeath to Robert P. Fickle (Margaret's son - EFF) a horse to be worth $50...to be furnished when the said Robert P. Fickle come to be 18 years of age.

1840 Sullivan Co. census shows "Fickle, Matilda Margaret, widow, with one son Robert b. 1822, property valued at $1200, cattle, no slaves.

1850 and 1860 Margaret appears on the Sullivan Co. TN census in the residence of Robert Preston Fickle (her son) showing age 66 and 74 respectively. She married **Abram FICKLE**, married 31 May 1822 in Washington Co., VA, b. 1801 in Wythe Co. VA, buried in Greendale VA. Convicted in 1827 of taking money out of a letter in the post office while
acting as deputy postmaster. Sentenced to 10 years imprisonment. An Abram Fickle appears with another wife in the 1870 VA census. Some genealogies of Abram report he died in 1822, but his divorce records
and references to his conviction contradict this.
Children:

+ 105.   i   **Robert Preston FICKLE** b. 1822.

23. **Matthew RHEA V.**, (4.Jannette[2], 1.John[1]) b. 23 Feb 1796 in Sullivan
Co., TN, d. 7 Apr 1870 in Somerville, Fayette Co., TN. Baptized by
Rev. Samuel Doak in 1798 under the old elm tree where his
grandfather Rev. Joseph Rhea preached. Rev. Rhea and Rev. Doak
used a large stone near the great tree for their pulpit. Matthew was
trained like his father and brother John in the classics. He attended
Washington College where he boarded with Dr. Samuel Doak.

The following is a letter from Matthew to his wife Mary Looney
Rhea:
Hardensburg, Ky.
April 17th, 1820
My dear Polly,
I expect you have almost lost patience waiting for a letter. I have
begun to write twice but finding no opportunity to send the letters
soon I stop. With the blessing of Heaven I have had quite a
comfortable journey thus far. Have been on the Wabash San Barton. I
am almost halfway to Lexington. I will go on through Louisville and
Georgetown. I expect (no accident falling) to be at Ohio next
Saturday or Sunday. My spirits are very low for several days at first
but have become quite tolerable, I hope yours are so also. Let pious
reflections be your constant companions, they will give you more
comfort than
any other. Remember me in love to your father Mother, etc. May
heavens best blessings await you and our little infant.
Your loving husband,
Matthew Rhea
Addressed to: Mrs. Matthew Rhea, Columbia, West Tennessee.
Note: Their first child, Margaret, would have been just under 3
months old. Her mother and father would have been Abram Looney
and Elizabeth Gammon. (His parents, Matthew Rhea IV and Jane
Preston Rhea were both dead by this time.)

Letter - Matthew Rhea V to Mary 'Polly' Looney Rhea
Augusta, Ky.
April 29th, 1820
My dear Polly,
I have just received yours of the 12th inst. It affords me a moments
most pleasing employment than I have had since I left home. On the
22nd inst. I crossed the river at this place and have been in Ohio ever
since until this evening. My health has been very good save one or
two days headaches occasioned by getting wet. I expect to be ready to
leave this place in 3 or 4 days for Blountville nine days will be
sufficient for that journey. Should it please a kind providence to aid

my success in business here and at Blountville. I shall have made quite a good trip I am already tired of traveling, but I hope the balance of my way will be more pleasant than the part I have passed. It will never be necessary for you any more to insist on my staying home for should I quit home again I will make journeys scarce with myself The moments are few when the past enjoyments of home and friends are not present to my mind. All the endearing transactions of past felicity constantly flood in upon my recollection and disturb the little composure which I still strive to promote. If Christian faith and fortitude ever were essentially necessary to the happiness of a man, it must be so to him whom necessity drives far from the objects of his love and affection. The thousand trifling incidents which might if permitted, forever debar a return to his home must proclaim his complete dependence on the beneficence of a Creator. Upon receipt of this letter if you write directing to Knoxville, I can get it as I go through that place. I intended to write to your father from this place but as I have nothing worthy of a letter I think it not worth while. Money is scarce and of a very bad quality. I expect I can get enough to answer my purposes but nothing more. My love to the family. May your God be with you conferring his best blessings.
Your affectionate husband
M. Rhea
Mailed 3 May, 1820
Augusta to Mrs. Matthew Rhea, Columbia, West Tennessee

Note: These letters provided by Annie Rhea Bruce. Spelling errors are as the letter was written.

As a surveyor he surveyed the State of TN and made the first map of the State in 1832. This map was highly prized by the Union forces during the war between the states.

The Chickasaw Purchase by Gen. Andrew Jackson and Gov. Isaac Shelby opened up 7 million acres of frontier in Western Tennessee. Because many of Matthew's friends and relatives had been drawn further West, he became interested in the area. About 1834 he took his growing family west. If he left a surveyor, he arrived a teacher.

Sommerville was the county seat of Fayetteville and a female academy was erected here in 1833. Matthew moved to Sommerville to become its President and first teacher. 20 years later the academy became the Somerville Female Institute with a new building. Matthew retained a connection to the institute until 1860 when he retired to his farm near Sommerville where he died in 1870.

He and his family were active in the Sommerville Presbyterian Church. Stained glass windows were placed in the church in the memory of Matthew and Mary Looney Rhea, also one in the memory of his son Lt. Matthew Rhea was killed at the battle of Belmont in the Civil War. He married **Mary 'Polly' LOONEY**, married 13 Dec 1818 in TN, b. 10 Jun 1804 in Sullivan Co., TN, d. 11 Nov 1884 in TN. Shortly after their marriage they moved to Maury Co. TN where they made their
home from 1820 to 1834 and raised 13 children.
Children:

+ 106.   i   **Margaret Jane RHEA** b. 25 Jan 1820.

+ 107.   ii   **Elizabeth Looney RHEA** b. 4 Mar 1822.

   108.   iii   **Ellen Preston RHEA**, b. 15 Feb 1824 in Sullivan Co., TN, d. 21 Jun 1843. Died young. (A sister born the year after her death was said to be named Ellen Preston as well(?)).

+ 109.   iv   **John William RHEA** b. 1828.

+ 110.   v   **Sarah Lucinda RHEA** b. 28 Feb 1828.

+ 111.   vi   **Abram Looney RHEA** b. 25 Feb 1830.

   112.   vii   **Matthew RHEA VI.**, b. 8 Mar 1833 in Sullivan Co., TN, d. 7 Nov 1861 in Belmont, Miss. During the Civil War, Matthew Rhea was a 1st Lt. in Cavalry Co. A, commanding the Confederate company. 'Lieut. Matthew Rhea, of Sommerville, Tennessee, was one of the bravest of the brave who fell at Belmont, in defense of Southern Independence. [Note Belmont was a town and possibly a plantation of the same name in Fayette County, as was Somerville. If this is the one, not one in Miss., then this may have been in a preliminary battle to the Battle of Shiloh, close by.] He has given to the world an exhibition of constancy and courage worthy of the best days of Rome, and which will render his name historical. He wore in the action, an old ancestral sword, which had been presented to his grandfather by General N. Greene, during the

Revolutionary War. Upon the Damascus blade were the words, "Victory or Death". When Lieut. Rhea entered the service, his venerable father took down the sword from its place upon the wall and handed it to him, saying, "My son, let no dishonor befall this sword." The gallant young officer replied, "Father, I know the value of this sword, and will surrender it only with my life." In the beginning of the late action, Lieut. Rhea was ordered to deploy his company as skirmishers, and having advanced some distance from the main body of his regiment, he was suddenly cut off by an overwhelming force of the enemy, who were in ambush awaiting his approach. In an instant, a terrible hand to hand encounter ensued. Several of his comrades stood by him to the last and were cut down. He was shot with a Minnie ball, which entered and fractured his cheek bone, and had sunk exhausted upon his knees, when he was surrounded by the enemy, who demanded his sword. Matthew, waiving his sword in the air uttered these words "Never," said he, "will I surrender this sword to the enemies of my country while I have life to defend myself." A wounded comrade, in describing the scene, says, "The last I saw of Lieut. Rhea, he had discharged his pistols at the enemy, and was upon his knees badly wounded, and desperately defending his life with his sword, while several Federal soldiers were clubbing him with muskets". And, thus, he yielded up his life for the liberties of his country and has made his name immortal. That was his first battle and his last. His sword it is said was placed in the armory in Chicago. (W L Rhea)

The following touching poem is from the pen of Mrs. L. Virginia French. The sword referred to in this poem was presented to Col. Matthew Rhea, the grandfather of Lieut. Matthew Rhea, by General Nathaniel Greene at the Battle of Guilford Courthouse, for gallantry in the field. This historic sword was captured when Lieut. Rhea was killed. The family have made every effort to regain it. On the blade was engraved, "Victory or Death". Lieut. Rhea was the brother of Mrs. Hunsdon Cary and uncle of

Rev. N. M. Long. In memory of Lieut. Matthew
Rhea, who fell bravely fighting for his country in the
Battle of Belmont, November 7, 1861.

"VICTORY OR DEATH"
Poem by Mrs. L. Virginia:
"Old Mississippi's waters gleamed
As in the golden days of yore,
An autumn's torches glowed and burned
Like sunset's glories, on the shore
On hillside green, and peaceful vale,
On distant dome, and shining spire,
The sun's meridian splendor lay
In waves of glowing living fire.
How tranquil all? NAY! See yon shore
Has banners floating far and wide;
And armaments of gallant men
Are moving to the water's side.
They cross the stream--then sound the trump,
Then rolling drum and thrilling fife,
Till red-browed battle's gorgeous pomp
Is blackening in the desperate strife.
They've met the foe! Their banners wave
On high, above the smoke and gloom
Which hangs its shrouding funeral pall
Where manhood sternly makes his tomb,
Where, with his energies immortal
He makes the road to honor straight
And forces open glory's portal
Though standing face to face with fate.
Behold him there--the gallant Rhea,
As on the battle's bloody merge
He waves his relic sword on high--
Loud cheering on the desperate charge--
To "Victory of Death", lead on;
And glorious was the charge they made;
And in his heart he bore the words
Engraven on his battle blade.
Down close the clouds--anon they rise,
They're swept aside; what do we see,
The leader stricken to the plain
Yet fighting still upon his knees--
"Surrender!" Through the iron shower
Come thundering on the swarming hordes;

"Surrender!" "You're in our power"--
Vain, vain, the menace; list his words--
His head erect, his proud lips curled,
And writhing in its haughty scorn,
"No! Never will I yield this sword
Once by my father's father borne."--
Fallen! fallen! Stricken to his knee,
His right arm raised, his forehead bare,
Oh! Tis a gallant sight to see
That quiet grandeur in his air--
Amid the cannon's thundering blare
It was a stern and pallid face,
Yet grandly glorious to behold
And full of that majestic grace
That Grecian heroes wore of old.
They've struck him down! A score of foes
Glare, thirsting for his latest breath.
God's rest by thine, on gallant heart,
Who found both victory and death.
The Southland turns her streaming eyes
To where thy blood baptized her sod--
For her thy glorious sacrifice--
For her thy spirit passed to God.
And thou art gone! The brave, the proud,
With eye of fire and arm of might,
Beneath the sable battle cloud
Thy Spirit passed.   "God speed the right!"
The language of thy latest breath.
God's peace be thine who nobly sought
The arms of "victory or death."
To hero souls of every clime
The record of thy death remains
Engraven on the shaft, which time
Shall rear upon our history's plains.
This Southern land for thee, today,
Will build of loving hearts a shrine,
And every heart will, weeping, say
"Oh! Gallant dead, God's rest be thine."
(written at the General Bedford Forrest home,
November 22, 1881)

Matthew had married a woman 2 years his senior.
They lived in Sommerville. Had no children. He

married **Harriet BEARD**, married 15 Sep 1859, b. ABT 1823 in TN?.

113.　viii　**Mary Annis RHEA**, b. 2 Sep 1835 in Sullivan Co., TN, d. 21 Oct 1844.

114.　ix　**Samuel Doak RHEA**, b. 17 Nov 1837 in Sullivan Co., TN, d. 21 Oct 1843.

115.　x　**Jennet Preston RHEA**, b. 8 Feb 1840 in Sullivan Co., TN, d. 20 Feb 1840.

+ 116.　xi　**Walter Preston RHEA** b. 28 Jul 1841.

+ 117.　xii　**Ellen Preston RHEA** b. 2 Sep 1844.

+ 118.　xiii　**Mary Frances Bell 'Fanny' RHEA** b. 13 Jun 1848.

Fourth Generation

24.　**Susan Smith PRESTON**, (5.John^3, 2.Robert^2, 1.John^1) b. 17 Jul 1803 in Washington Co., VA, d. 2 Nov 1828 in Blountville, Sullivan Co., TN, buried in Blountville Cemetery, Sullivan Co., TN. Notable Southern Fam., Z. Armstrong 1922 notes this wife was Susan Rhea Preston, daughter of Robert and Margaret vs. entry in the Preston Family Bible which I have taken as accurate.

1844 she is mentioned in a letter from Alexander Preston to his nephew Samuel Pretson (in Ireland) - copies at Hist. Soc. Wash. Co., VA. "Col. John Preston's wife died in May... left 12 children, one dead (Susan). Susan, who married J.C.Rhea had 3 children (and she died)". Died 3 months after a birth. She married **Joseph Campbell RHEA**, married 2 1824 in Washington Co., VA, b. 14 Feb 1800 in Sullivan Co., TN, d. 15 Jul 1853 in Pulaski, Giles Co. TN. He was a merchant with John McNabb until 1827.

1831 he moved to Pulaski TN after the death of his first wife Susan.

Col. Rhea purchased land in the city of Pulaski TN. The block which is bordered by Flower Street, South Four Street, Madison Street and almost to South Third Street. This is shown on a map drawn by his son William Rhea, as lot number 374 in 1884. The place was called "Colonial College" and he and his family lived in the house which he had built there. Later, Mary A. Rhea (Aunt Mamie) and her husband

Dr. Sumpter built the large house which was the site of many interesting events. The house faced Madison street and was next to a large house on the corner of Madison and South Third.

A Joseph C. Rhea is mentioned in TN State records: 1832 36 2.1 Giles Co. Union Planter Bank, 1833 38 34.1 Giles Co. Planters Bank of TN

He was a member of the Blountville Presbyterian Church. He did much to persuade his fellow men to lead better lives with his uncle Robert P. Rhea. Often stumped the county making temperance speeches (W. L. Rhea, 1895).

Joseph Campbell Rhea (1800-1853), married twice: First, Susan Rhea Preston (-1828) (daughter of Robert Preston and Margaret (Rhea) Preston); Married second, (1836) Catherine Reynolds (-1857). Joseph Campbell Rhea lived in Sullivan County, Tennessee, until 1841 when he moved to Giles County, Tennessee, where resided until his death. He assisted his cousin, Matthew Rhea, in making the first map of Tennessee. He was colonel in the Tennessee Militia. (Notable Southern Families, Z. Armstrong, Vol ! & II, 1922).
Children:

+ 119. i **Margaret RHEA** b. 1823.

120. ii **William RHEA**, b. 1825 in Sullivan Co., TN, d. 7 Jan 1847 in Monterey, Mexico, buried in Mexico. Graduated from West Point. Cadet from 1841 to 1845. Was commissioned 2nd Lt. in the 6th Infantry. Served on frontier duty at Fort Gibson, Indiana Territory, Oklahoma. In 1845-6 he was transferred to 3rd Infantry by Sept. 21 1846. Was a 1st Lt. in the US Army during the Mexican War. Died of measles while in service in Mexico and was buried there.

+ 121. iii **Susan Elizabeth RHEA** b. 3 Aug 1828.

25. **Robert 'Dr.' Fairman PRESTON**, (5.John[3], 2.Robert[2], 1.John[1]) b. 5 Dec 1804 in Washington Co., VA, d. 7 Jul 1889 in Washington Co., VA. 1824 Robert had attended medical school in Philadelphia. Operated a drug and chemical store there for a time. Mrs. Margaret Sheffey Minnick had in her home a safe which was his medicine chest and a ancient silver mug he owned. (1937 WPA VA report by Victoria Gilliam.)

1860 Virginia census shows the family enumerated on page 331 in the Clear Branch section of the Western District of Washington Co., VA
    Robt F. Preston 55, Farmer, real property value $36,000, personal property $15,000 [quite wealthy for the time] b. VA
    Sarah " 59, b. PA
    Mary " 32 b. VA
    Nancy " 20, personal property value $100, b. VA
The family of Robert's cousin William is enumerated on nearby on the same page of the census.
1860 Virginia census slave schedule shows Robt. F. Preston of Western District of Washington Co. VA with 12 slaves ranging in age from 33 to 9 months old.

Robert's father left him the plantation on which Robert lived and slaves namely: Hary, Viney and her family, Caine and Poly and her family. He was an eminent physician in Philadelphia but retired to his ancestral home in Virginia where he lived until his death. Owned the home place 1833-1889.

1880 the family is enumerated in the Virginia census in Goodson, Washington Co., VA.
    Preston, Robert F. 74, farmer, . VA
    Winston, Edwind 57, son in law, civil engineer, b. VA
    Mary, 51, daughter, keeping house, b. VA
    George, 54, boarder [Edwind's brother? - EFF]
    Black, E. 18, domestic servant

Enumerated as the next household are Robert Sheffey and granddaughter Mary Preston Sheffey. He married **Sarah MARSHALL**, married 5 Dec 1827 in Philadelphia PA, b. 20 Feb 1799 in Philadelphia PA, d. 10 Dec 1866 in Walnut Grove Cemetery Washington Co. VA. Sarah was a Quaker from a prominent Philadelphia family.
                    Children:

122.   i   **Mary Marshal PRESTON**, b. 21 Sep 1828 in Washington Co., VA, d. 5 Jul 1900. Mary was born and later lived with her husband Edmund at 'Walnut Grove

                1870 VA census she is enumerated with her husband in the household of her father.

1880 VA census, her husband no longer appears in the census with her and her father.

Owned the old home place from the time of the death of her father in 1889 until her death in 1900.

Mary's father left her some old silver consisting of a coffee pot, tea pot, water pot, cream pitcher, sugar dish, etc. She gave these to Mrs. Minnick with the request they be left in the family. (1937 WPA VA report by Victoria Gilliam)

1900 she left the home place to her nephew Robert F. Sheffey. She married **Edmund 'Captain' WINSTON**, married 11 Jun 1867, b. 1823 in VA, d. in Washington Co., VA. Surveyed the North and West Railway and much of Bristol. Mary Street in Bristol is named for his wife Mary, and Edmund and Winston Streets are named for himself. Mary Street Methodist Church was named for his wife but the name was later changed to Reynolds Memorial Church.

1870 Federal census shows Mary and Edmond enumerated in Goodson District of Washington Co., VA with her father Robert F. Preston.
  Preston Robert F. 65, farmer, retired M.D., real property value $20,000, personal property $2000, b. VA
  Winston, Mary, 41, keeping house, b. VA
  Winston, Edmond, 47, civil engineer, personal property value $100, b. VA.

123.   ii   **Margaret PRESTON**, b. ABT 1830 in Washington Co., VA, d. ABT 1833. Died when she was 3 years old.

+ 124.   iii   **Elizabeth Virginia PRESTON** b. 4 Jan 1833.

26. **Margaret Rhea PRESTON**, (5.John^3, 2.Robert^2, 1.John^1) b. 26 Aug 1806 in Washington Co., VA, d. 26 Mar 1860 in Abingdon, Washington Co. VA, buried in White Family Cemetery Washington Co. VA. Born at 'Walnut Grove' and died at her home 'Fruit Hill'.

1860 her will dated Feb. 17, 1860, was proved April 16, 1860 in
Washington Co., gave her estate equally to her children and the
children of her deceased daughters Margaret and Jane and gave her
silver plate to her daughter Susan White. Gave a slave to her son
John P., one to the children of Gordon Ogden and Jane his wife, and
one to the children of Wm. Y. C. Humes and Margaret his wife.

Her son James and son-in-law David Cummings were her executors.
She married **James Lowery WHITE**, married 27 Dec 1825 in
Walnut Grove, Washington Co. VA, b. 21 Dec 1804 in Abingdon,
Washington Co. VA, d. 8 Dec 1838 in Washington Co., VA. James
was educated at Transylvania University and settled at 'Fruit Hill' near
Abingdon VA where he resided until his death.

1839 An inventory of his estate, valued at $8073.89, was made March
29, 1839 and returned to the court by Robert R. Preston his
administrator. (Will Book 8, pp. 96-99).
Children:

+ 125.   i   **Elizabeth Wilson WHITE** b. 12 May 1827.

+ 126.   ii   **Margaret Rhea WHITE** b. 1 Jun 1828.

+ 127.   iii   **Jane Conn WHITE** b. ABT 1831.

+ 128.   iv   **John Preston WHITE** b. 7 Mar 1832.

   129.   v   **James Lowery WHITE Jr.**, b. 30 May 1833 in
Washington Co., VA. Served the C.S.A. as Captain
in Company K 37th Virginia Infantry in Stonewall
Jackson's Brigade. He was a student at VMI for 3
years, 1850-53. In
1853 studied in the medical department of the U. of
VA. He continued his
studies at Jefferson Memorial College in Phil. PA.
graduating with and M.D. in
1855. On April 22, 1861 he enter C.S.A. service.
Appointed surgeon. After
the war he practiced in Farmville.
Had no children. He married (1) **Sarah 'Sallie
Taylor PEYTON**, married 22 Jun 1859 in
Washington Co., VA, b. ABT 1832 in Roanoke Co.
VA. She was a cousin of her husband James. He
married (2) **Lelia E. JACKSON**, married 20 Sep

1864 in Farmville, VA, b. ABT 1843 in Farmville, VA.

+ 130. vi **William Young Conn WHITE** b. 1835.

+ 131. vii **Ellen Sheffey WHITE** b. 26 May 1836.

+ 132. viii **Susan Preston WHITE** b. 29 Aug 1838.

27. **William Alfred PRESTON**, (5.John^3, 2.Robert^2, 1.John^1) b. 21 May 1808 in Washington Co., VA, d. 26 May 1862 in Botetourt Co. VA. His father left him land lying in Lee Co. known as Wild Cat Valley place, also John's house in Kingsport TN, also a tract of land lying in Wise Co called the Dysart Tract containing 375 acres.

1836 he was commisioned Justice of the County Court 18 July 1836 and qualified 26 Aug. 1836.

1849 and 1850 he was one of the commisioners to supervise elections. After the death of Martha, secondly married his cousin Elizabeth.

1860 Virginia census his young family is enumerated in Clear Branch, Western District, Washington Co., VA.
  William A. Preston 52, farmer, real property value $25,000, personal property $40,000.
  Elziabeth 29, housekeeper, b. VA
  Alfred 2, b. VA.
  William 1, b. VA. He married (1) **Martha E. WYLEY**, married 15 Sep 1828, b. ABT 1808 in Greeneville, Greene Co., TN, d. in Washington Co., VA, buried in Walnut Grove Cemetery Washington Co. VA. Age 45 at the time of her death. He married (2) **Elizabeth RADFORD**, married 30 Mar 1857 in Botetourt Co. VA, b. 26 Jun 1832 in Bedford Co. VA, d. 8 Feb 1898. She was a cousin of her husband William. She and William lived at 'Greenfield'. After William's death she married John Munford.
  Children by Martha E. WYLEY:

133. i **William Moseley PRESTON**, b. 20 May 1850 in Washington Co., VA. Died young.
        Children by Elizabeth RADFORD:

+ 134. ii **Alfred G. PRESTON** b. 24 Jan 1858.

135. iii **John PRESTON**, b. 23 Jul 1860 in Washington Co., VA. Died young.

136. iv **Robert Moseley PRESTON**, b. 8 Sep 1862 in Washington Co., VA. Died young.

28. **John PRESTON, Jr.**, (5.John[3], 2.Robert[2], 1.John[1]) b. 10 Feb 1811 in Washington Co., VA, d. 1 May 1882 in Ky?ARK?. Student at SC College in 1828 and graduated A.B. in 1830.

1836 after practicing law for a time in Washington Co. VA, he moved to Helena Ark. where he lived for a number of years.

1837 he was appointed judge of the circuit court and in 1838 was a candidate for the Arkansas Legislature.

1840 he again ran for office but was defeated by 2 votes. At one point he lived in Trimble Co.

1870 Federal census shows couple enumerated in Bedford, Trimble Co., KY.
  Preston, John, 50, Lawyer, real estate value $40,000, property value $6,000, b. VA
  " Mary H., 52, housekeeping, b. KY.
  Murphy, Thomas, 75, gardener, b. Ireland.
  Jackson, Catherine, 23, mulatto, house servant, b. KY.
  " Charles, 9/12 mulatto, b. KY
  Green, Tilson, 9, black, b. KY. He married **Mary Howard WICKLIFFE**, married 15 Jan 1852 in Lexington, Fayette Co., KY, b. ABT 1811 in Lexington, Fayette Co., KY, d. 17 Nov 1892 in Louisville, KY. A cousin of husband John. Both she and John died without issue.

1894 a dispute concerning her will resulted in Kentucky Court of Appeals case #23008.
               Children:

137. i **Robert PRESTON**, b. 1860, d. 1860. Died in infancy.

29. **Eleanor Fairman PRESTON**, (5.John[3], 2.Robert[2], 1.John[1]) b. 7 Nov 1812 in Washington Co., VA, d. 10 Jan 1887 in Marion, Smythe Co., VA. Born at "Walnut Grove" in Washington Co. VA.

Notable Southern Families, Volumes I & II
"Eleanor Fairman Preston (-1887), who married (1835) Judge James
Sheffey. Children: (1) Margaret Sheffey (1836-1869), who married
Col. William E. Peters, and had children: James White Sheffey and
William Edgar; (2) John Preston Sheffey (1837-), who married
Josephine Spiller, and had children: (a) Margaret Peters Sheffey
(1865-), (married Percy C. March); (b) Eleanor Fairman Sheffey
(1866-), (married B. F. Buchanan. Children: John Preston Buchanan,
who married and had children: Eleanor Fairman and John Preston
Buchanan II; Josephine Spiller Buchanan; Campbell Buchanan;
Virginia Buchanan; Frank Buchanan; Nellie Buchanan; David
Buchanan); (c) Susie Montgomery Sheffey (1867-), (married Dr. E.
M. Copenhaver. Children: Preston and Elizabeth Marcellus); (d)
Jesephine Spiller Sheffey; (e) James White Sheffey (1871-), (married
Lucy Lee Carlock. Children Lucy Lee, Caroline, James White
Sheffey II, Josephine Spiller White, Eleanor Fairman and Harold
Carlock); (f) Miriam Sheffey; (g) John Preston Sheffey II (1876-),
(married Virginia Harrington. Children: Margaret and Virginia); (3)
Jane Sheffey; (4) Elizabeth Sheffey (1842-1875), who married Maj.
James A. G. Pendleton, and had one child, James Sheffey Pendleton,
(1874-) who married Margaret Fudge, and had children: Albert G.,
Elizabeth and Granville F.; (5) Ellen White Sheffey (1813-1904), who
married Joseph Brainard Rhea, (son of Rev. Samuel Rhea and his
second wife, Martha (Lynn) Rhea). Children under Joseph Brainard
Rhea; (6) Mary Sheffey (1844-1906), who married Col. William E.
Peters, (whose first wife had been her sister, Margaret), and had one
child: Don Preston Peters (1887-), who married Rhetta Ghangh, and
had children: Mary Peters and Don Preston Peters II; (7) Martha
Sheffey (1849-1899), who married Robert J. Preston, M. D., and had
children: (a) Eleanor Fairman Preston (1876-), (married Dr. J. T.
Watkins. Children: James Thomas Watkins II, Robert Sheffey,
William and Sherman); (b) Robert Sheffey Preston (1885-), (married
Alice Reed); (8) Virginia Sheffey (1850-), who married H. B. Haller."

True, noble, Christian woman, managing her home and household
affairs well. A woman full of energy, instilling unto her children
habits of industry and morality. Lived to see all her children grow
married and settled in life and all professing Christians. (W.L.Rhea-
1895)

1884 will dated Nov. 3, was proved Jan 17, 1887 Smythe Co. VA
Will Bk 6 pp. 237-38. She married **James White S. SHEFFEY**,
married 29 Dec 1835 in Washington Co., VA, b. 15 Mar 1813 in

Wythe Co. VA, d. 27 Jun 1876 in Richmond, Henrico Co., VA. Read law at Abington VA and was admitted to the bar at age 21.

After his marriage he moved to Marion VA and from Sept 1850 until his death associated with his son John P. in the practice of law there.

1861 he was a member of the Convention of that year and on 17 April 1861 signed the Ordinance by which Virginia seceded. He was a captain in the home guards during the war and saw some service guarding the bridge and tracks of the VA and TN Railroad.

1870 the Federal census shows the family enumerated in Marion, Smythe Co., VA:
  Sheffey, James W. 56, lawyer, real property value $100,000, personal property $20,000, b. KY.
  -- Ellen F. 56, keeping house, b. VA
  -- Elizabeth, 28, at home, b. VA
  -- Mary 25, at home, b. VA.
  -- Martha 21, at home b. VA.
  -- Virginia 2o at home, b. VA.

1875-76 he represented Smythe Co. in the VA House of Delegates. He was a trustee of Emory and Henry College from 1853 to 1877 and a member of the Board of Visitors of the U. of VA 1863-64.
  Children:

+ 138. i **Margaret SHEFFEY** b. 4 Oct 1836.

+ 139. ii **John Preston SHEFFEY** b. 12 Dec 1837.

  140. iii **Jane Preston SHEFFEY**, b. 31 Aug 1839 in Marion, Smythe Co., VA, d. 11 Nov 1842 in Marion, Smythe Co., VA.

+ 141. iv **Elizabeth Madison SHEFFEY** b. 5 Jan 1842.

+ 142. v **Ellen White SHEFFY** b. 25 Aug 1843.

+ 143. vi **Mary W. SHEFFY** b. 8 Dec 1844.

  144. vii **Celestine SHEFFEY**, b. 12 Apr 1846. Died young.

+ 145. viii **Martha E. SHEFFEY** b. 15 Mar 1849.

146. ix **Virginia Watson SHEFFEY**, b. 17 Aug 1850 in Marion, Smythe Co., VA, d. 31 May 1928 in Richmond, Henrico Co., VA. in 1923 she donated additional land for the Royal Oak Presbyterian Church in Marion. She had no children. She married **Henry Bowen HALLER**, married 9 Nov 1874, b. 1 Apr 1849 in Smythe Co. VA, d. 1 Oct 1915 in Richmond, Henrico Co., VA.

147. x **James W. SHEFFEY**, b. 20 Sep 1851 in VA, d. 4 Sep 1853 in VA. This James Jr. died young, shortly after the birth of his brother Daniel.

148. xi **Daniel SHEFFEY**, b. 29 May 1853 in VA, d. 1 Sep 1854. Died young, a year after his younger brother.

149. xii **James W. SHEFFEYJr.**, b. 1856 in VA. It was reported by researchers that James Jr. died young, just 4 months after the birth of his younger brother Daniel. However, there is a James W. Sheffey Jr. age 24, a clerk in a store, b. VA enumerated in the 1870 census just a short distance from James Sr. in Marion, Smythe Co., VA. It appears he was the younger brother of Daniel, and named for another deceased brother as well as his father.

31. **Thomas White PRESTON**, (5.John^3, 2.Robert^2, 1.John^1) b. 13 Aug 1816 in Washington Co., VA, d. 1 Apr 1862 in Shiloh, TN. 1834 he had entered Georgetown University in Washington D.C. Oct. 22, 1834 and received BA in 1837.

1840 he received his B.Law from U of VA. Practiced law in St. Louis MO with PC Morehead and later moved in 1846 to Memphis.

1860 Federal census shows the family enumerated in Memphis, Shelby Co., TN.
   F. (sic) W. Preston, 40, Attorney at Law, real property value $50,000, personal property value $7,000, b. VA
   Susan ", 30, b. TN [His second wife Susan Maguire]
   David ", 12, b. TN
   Percy ", 9/12 b. TN

During the Civil War he was on the staff of General Albert Sidney Johnston.

1862 he was killled at the battle of Shiloh. He married (1) **Susan Booker MAGUIRE**, b. 12 Jul 1829 in Columbia, Maury Co., TN, d. 7 Aug 1906 in Columbia, Maury Co., TN. Second wife of Thomas Preston. He married (2) **Mary Jane CRAIGHEAD**, married 19 Jun 1845 in Davidson Co. TN, b. 1827 in Nashville, Davidson Co., TN, d. 13 May 1849 in Mississippi Co. ARK. Mary was husband Thomas' first cousin.

Children by Susan Booker MAGUIRE:

150. i **Henry Percy PRESTON**, b. 12 Sep 1859 in TN, d. 31 Aug 1863 in Memphis, Shelby Co., TN. Died as a young boy, just 7 months after his infant brother, and a little over a year after his father was killed at the battle of Shiloh.

151. ii **Thomas W. PRESTON**, b. 12 Nov 1862 in Memphis, Shelby Co., TN, d. 12 Jan 1863 in Memphis, Shelby Co., TN. Born six months after his father's death at the battle of Shiloh; died as an infant the following year as did his oldedr brother, capping a series of tragedies for the young mother Susan M. Preston.

Children by Mary Jane CRAIGHEAD:

152. iii **John PRESTON**, b. 27 Jul 1846 in Nashville, Davidson Co., TN, d. 1 Aug 1846 in Nashville, Davidson Co., TN.

+ 153. iv **David Craighead PRESTON** b. 12 Jan 1849.

33. **Francis 'Frank' PRESTON**, (5.John^3, 2.Robert^2, 1.John^1) b. 26 Mar 1822 in Washington Co., VA, d. 13 Jan 1892 in Washington Co., VA, buried in Walnut Grove Cemetery Washington Co. VA. 1840 he was a student at Caldwell Institute, Greensboro NC and at U of VA 1840-41.

He was a farmer of Montgomery Switch, Washington Co. VA.

1860 Federal census his family was enumerated in the Clear Branch Post Office area of the Western District of Washington Co., VA.

Francis Preston 38, farmner, real property value $40,000, personal property $23,000, b. VA.
-- Robert " 9, b. VA
-- Francis " 7, b. VA
-- John " 2, b. VA.
[Frank's wife Martha had died the previous year.]

1862 April 7 he was mustered into Confederate Service in the Washington Co. VA militia and served 9 days. One wonders about the challenges of the young family when a widowed father goes off to war.

1870 Federal census his family was enumerated in the Abingdon Post Office area of the Goodson Township of Washington Co., VA.
  Preston, Robert, 48, farmer, value of real estate $6,800, personal property $7,700.
-- Robert M. 18, student
-- Francis 16, student
-- John C. 12, attending school, value of real estate $4,000 [It is odd that the enumerater attributed real property to a young person]

1880 Federal census shows Francis enumerated with his growing second family, now married to Martha; living in the Goodson District of Washington Co. VA:
  Preston, Francis 57, Farmer
-- Martha F. 33 wife, keeping house.
-- Francis E. 26, son, farmer.
-- John C. 22 son, student.
-- Mary T. 2, daughter
  Farris, Elizabeth 44, servant, domestic servant
-- Margauriter, 8
-- Willie Ann 5. He married (1) **Martha 'Mattie' Powell FULTON**, b. ABT 1846 in Smythe Co. VA, d. 4 Jul 1927 in Washington Co., VA, buried in Walnut Grove Cemetery Washington Co. VA. Her will dated 6 May 1927 was proved 15 June 1928 (Smythe Co VA will book 10 pp. 361-62). She gave $10,000 equally to Mrs. Annie Preston Wilson, Dr. Robert W. Preston and Mrs. Katherine Preston Ferry. Gave $2500 to establish the Creed Fulton Chair for Christian Education at Emory and Henry College as well as other bequests. He married (2) **Martha Virginia MOFFETT**, married 6 Apr 1851 in Waverly, Loudoun Co. VA, b. 1820 in Landon Co VA, d. 23 Jun 1859 in Washington Co., VA, buried in Walnut Grove Cemetery Washington Co. VA.
Children by Martha 'Mattie' Powell FULTON:

154. i **Mary Taylor PRESTON**, b. 13 Nov 1877 in Washington Co., VA, d. 5 Sep 1894 in Washington Co., VA, buried in Walnut Grove Cemetery Washington Co. VA. A twin.

155. ii **Charles Fulton PRESTON**, b. 13 Nov 1877 in Washington Co., VA, d. 3 Dec 1878 in Washington Co., VA, buried in Walnut Grove Cemetery Washington Co. VA. Mary's twin, he died as an infant.
Children by Martha Virginia MOFFETT:

+ 156. iii **Robert M. PRESTON** b. 23 Mar 1852.

157. iv **Frances E. PRESTON**, b. 12 Dec 1853 in Washington Co., VA, d. 2 Oct 1882 in Washington Co., VA, buried in Walnut Grove Cemetery Washington Co. VA.

158. v **William A. PRESTON**, b. 19 Apr 1855 in Washington Co., VA, d. 11 Aug 1855 in Washington Co., VA, buried in Walnut Grove Cemetery Washington Co. VA.

159. vi **John C. PRESTON**, b. 1858 in Washington Co., VA. Col. John Preston -"to my grandson John, son of Francis, I devise 200 acres lying on the east end of my home place, adjoining the Msrs. Campbells to be laid off as to embrace that portion of land coming to the main road, nearly oppostite the great Hurricane Pond, but should my grandson die before he arrives to the age of 17 years, I devise the same to Francis his father. "John went on to become a physician and practiced in Dade City FL.

34. **Jane PRESTON**, (5.John³, 2.Robert², 1.John¹) b. 26 Jun 1822 in Washington Co., VA, d. in AL. 1860 Federal census shows Jane as head of household, presumably James has passed away leaving her a young but wealthy widow with 6 young children. She is living in McKinley, Marengo Co., AL.
 Craighead, Jane P., 39, farmer, value of real property $109, 200, personal property $138,045, b. VA
 David ", 12, b. AL

John ", 10, b. AL
James ", 9, b. AL
Jane " ,7, b. AL
Preston " 5, b. AL
Thomas " 2, b. AL

1864 after his death, her father John left her "a tract of land lying and being in Sullivan Co TN at the mouth of Beaver Creek. I likewise give her 40 shares of bank stock in the Exchange Bank of VA, unless I dispose of them or the proceeds of them during my lifetime. I likewise give to her any money or slaves (including Lizzy) that I may have given her heretofore." She married (1) **Mr. MARSHALL**, b. ABT 1822 in VA?. Second husband of Jane. No children. She married (2) **James B. CRAIGHEAD**, married 27 Dec 1846, b. 1796 in TN. Marriage and children mentioned in 'Notable Southern Fam.', Z. Armstrong 1922.

1825 Richard C. Bacon of Luneburg Co., VA gave power of attorney to James B. Craighead of Huntsville, AL to sigh and injunction bond to be given by said Richard C. Bacon and others to Germon Y. Stokes, July 25, 1825 [The Valentine Papers, Vol 1-4, 1864-1908, page 466, the Bacon Family].

He was first cousin to his wife Jane.

1850 Federal census shows the family enumerated in Marengo Co., AL:
  Craighead, James B. 54, a Planter, real property value $30,000, b. TN.
  Jane P. ", 30, b. VA.
  David ", son, 3, b. AL.
  John B. " 1/12 b. AL [enumerator wrote 'twins' across John and Elizabeth]
  Elizabeth ", 1/12 b. AL.
              Children by James B. CRAIGHEAD:

160.   i   **David CRAIGHEAD**, b. 1847 in Marengo Co., AL.
            1880 Federal census shows him enumerated in
            Terrell, Kaufman Co., Texas boarding with the
            Lancaster family.
              Craighead, David, 32, boarder, Editor, b. AL, to
            parents from TN and VA.

161.   ii   **Elizabeth CRAIGHEAD**, b. 1 Sep 1850 in Marengo Co., AL.

162.   iii   **John B. CRAIGHEAD**, b. 1 Sep 1850 in Marengo Co., AL. 1880 does not appear in the Federal census index.

+ 163. iv   **Preston CRAIGHEAD** b. 1855.

164.   v   **Jennie CRAIGHEAD**, b. 1857 in Marengo Co., AL.

165.   vi   **Thomas 'Rev.' CRAIGHEAD**, b. 1858 in Marengo Co., AL. He married **Rachel CARTER**, b. 1840 in TN.

35. **James Tecumseh 'Col' PRESTON**, (5.John[3], 2.Robert[2], 1.John[1]) b. 1 Apr 1824 in Washington Co., VA, d. 9 Dec 1883 in Washington Co., VA?, buried in Walnut Grove Cemetery Washington Co. VA. His father John left him two tracts of land in Scott Co.

1840 he was a student at Virginia Military Institute.

During the Mexican War he served as a Lt. in the company of Col. Arthur Cummings.

Studied law and practiced in Abington VA and was later a farmer in Washington Co. VA.

1855 Dec. he was one of the residents appointed in the village of Goodson to patrol the neighborhood.
1860 May 24 he was admitted as a Justice of the Peace of Washington Co. VA

1860.Oct 5 page 334 of the Virginia census shows the family enumerated in the Goodson area of the Western District of Washington Co., VA.
  James T. Preston 35, farmer, real property value $14,000, personal property $11,000.
  Fanny " 33, h. Keeper b. VA
  John " 9, b. VA
  James " 7, b. VA
  Walter " 5, b. VA
  Robert " 3, b. VA

Fanny " 1, b. VA

James was a Col. of militia before the Civil War and active in mustering C.S.A. troops.

Retired near Bristol VA. He married **Frances 'Fannie' RHEA**, married 1 Aug 1850, b. 30 Nov 1825 in Sullivan Co., TN, d. 1888 in Sullivan Co., TN, buried in Walnut Grove Cemetery Washington Co. VA. A refined, educated and handsome lady. Read and studied Latin and Greek with her father. Sabbath school teacher. (W.L.Rhea-1895).
Children:

+ 166. i   **John PRESTON** b. 21 Jul 1851.

+ 167. ii   **James Rhea PRESTON** b. 22 Jan 1853.

  168. iii **Walter Eugene PRESTON**, b. 19 Dec 1854 in Washington Co., VA, d. 28 Jul 1882 in Texas. He was a student at Emory and Henry College 1871-73 and received B.A.
He died unmarried.

+ 169. iv   **Robert Fairman PRESTON** b. 1 Apr 1857.

  170. v   **Frances 'Fanny' Rhea PRESTON**, b. 1859 in Washington Co., VA, d. 1878 in Washington Co., VA, buried in Walnut Grove Cemetery Washington Co. VA. Died as a child.

  171. vi   **Frances 'Frank' McIlwaine PRESTON**, b. 1864 in Washington Co., VA, d. 1907 in Washington Co., VA, buried in Walnut Grove Cemetery Washington Co. VA.

37. **Henry PRESTON**, (5.John[3], 2.Robert[2], 1.John[1]) b. 20 Nov 1828 in Washington Co., VA, d. 17 Jul 1899 in Washington Co., VA, buried in Walnut Grove Cemetery Washington Co. VA. 1852 Henry lived after his marriage that year on Preston land on Sinking Creek until the death of his father at which time he inherited the Home Place. Henry was the last surviving son of Col. John Preston of Walnut Grove. Henry's father made generous provisions for this his youngest son in his 1861 will (proved in 1864). He was devised 4800 acres of Virginia land, "families of slaves: Isaac and Lucy and their family of children; Aggy and sons Ned and George; Mary and her children;

Jane and her children; Andy and Hirshey and their family; Betsy and Clary and her children and Bill. I likewise devise to my said son Henry all of the stack of every kind on my place at my death after fulfilling the foregoing devise. I give to my son Henry the remaining half of my household and kitchen furniture"

1860 October, Virginia census shows Henry and his family in the Clear Branch area of Washington Co., VA.
  Henry Preston 32, farmer, personal property value $18,200, b. VA.
  Ann 27 b. VA
  Mary 7, b.VA
  Margaret 5, b. VA
  Ellen 3, b. VA
  Elizabeth 2, b. VA
  Ann 6/12, b. VA

Henry was a big farmer and slave holder and contributed largely to the support and care of the widows and orphans of the Confederate soldiers and to the needy in the County. During the war he and a brother furnished the Confederate Government with a large number of slaves to aid in ditch and trench building

1899 a newspaper clipping tells of Henry Preston: "Death of Henry Preston Sr., one of Washington Co. VA's most prominent Citizens: Henry Preston Sr. died Monday night at 10 o'clock at his handsome farm home 6 miles east of Bristol. Mr. Preston had been an invalid for 4 years of rheumatism. He is survived by 10 children, 8 daughters and 2 sons, his wife having preceded him a few years... Col. Henry Preston was the last surviving son of Col. John Preston of Walnut Grove. Col. Preston was one of the old time, old school Virginia gentlemen. He was a man of extensive reading and information, having been educated at the University of Virginia. He owned and operated one of the, if not the largest and finest farms in Washington County."

1899 September 18, the will Henry made Sept. 4, 1895 was probated ..I direct that all of my personal property be sold except as to what household and kitchen furniture, books and portraits, silverware, & c. I may have at my decease. As to this I give to my son Henry, the portrait of my father, and to my son, Percy, I give the portrait of my brother Thomas, and to my daughter Cary, I give my silver spoons and cup. The balance of the household and kitchen furniture is not to be appraised, and is to be equally divided among all my children, including my library.

...my entire real estate to be equally divided between them with the following restrictions. However, I devise a portion of my realty that would otherwise go to my son Henry Preston Jr. to his wife and children now living and that may be hereafter born unto them, and not to be subject in any way to the debts of my said son, and in this connection I will and direct that in the division of my lands, the interest hereby and herein devised to the wife and children of my son Henry, shall be so laid off as to embrace the dwelling and building now occupied by them, and to conveniently laid off in connection therewith as far as practicable so as not to do detriment to other interests.

4th. I further direct that the interests of my 6 unmarried daughters in my lands under this will shall be laid off together in one body and so as to embrace my mansion house, said interests to be laid off as compactly as possible so as not to do detriment to the other interests. And I further will and direct that this body of land of said six interests shall not be further divided until three years after my decease, it being the desire of my said six daughters to remain together for said period.

5th. There are certain debts that have been contracted by my son Henry Preston Jr. for my benefits viz: The balance of the Mary Steele note of about $600, the debt due William Sharrett of about $400, the note due Robert Sharrett of about $700, and a debt to William Wilson of about $120. These debts I direct to be paid by my executor out of my estate.

6th. I hereby nominate and appoint Henry Preston Jr., and O. F. Bailey the Executors of this my will.

Given under my hand and seal this 4th day of Sept. 1895. (signed) Henry Preston. Attest: S. P. Legare, A. J. Hensley

Much of the story of Henry Preston transcribed:
Gilliam, Victoria Allice, "Work Progress Administration of Virginia, Statewide Project, Historical Inventory. Field Worker's Report" 1937. Richmond, VA. Copy filed Preston Files, Washington Co., VA Historical Society, Abingdon, VA. He married **Anne Cary CARTER**, married 8 Sep 1852 in Albermarle Co., VA, b. 19 Apr 1833 in Redlands, Abermarle Co VA, d. 12 Jan 1895 in Walnut Grove, Washington Co. VA, buried in Walnut Grove Cemetery Washington Co. VA. 1895 her obituary read: On the morning of the 12th of January 1895 at the hospitable home of Henry Preston, Mrs.

Preston's sweet gentle spirit passed into the paradise of God. She was laid to rest in the Walnut Grove cemetery...born reared and educated in Albermarle Co. of distinguished lineage and refined culture. She was the embodiment of all those graces and virtues that make up the character of true Christian womanhood. She was a direct descendant of President Thomas Jefferson.

Children:

172. i   **Mary Coles PRESTON**, b. 9 Feb 1854 in Washington Co., VA, d. 27 Mar 1914 in Washington Co., VA, buried in Walnut Grove Cemetery Washington Co. VA. 1854 baptized by Rev. Thomas Brown at Walnut Grove Church. Did not marry. Died at The Grove at age 60.

173. ii   **Margaret Brown PRESTON**, b. 9 Sep 1855 in Washington Co., VA, d. 9 May 1926 in Washington Co., VA, buried in Walnut Grove, Washington Co. VA. Her will dated 9 Sept 1916 was proved Washington Co. VA 22 Nov 1926 gave her brother Henry the land left her by her sister Isetta and to her brother Percy her own farm and left her other property to her sisters Ellen and Cary A. Lillinger. She did not marry.

+ 174. iii   **Ellen Bankhead PRESTON** b. 3 Mar 1857.

175. iv   **Elizabeth Madison PRESTON**, b. 5 Oct 1858 in Washington Co., VA, d. 4 Jan 1906. Married her cousin James. Had no children. She married **James White CUMMINGS**, married 18 Jul 1900 in Washington Co., VA, b. 19 Sep 1855 in Washington Co., VA, (son of David Campbell CUMMINGS and Elizabeth Wilson WHITE) d. 9 Jul 1924 in Washington Co., VA, buried in Sinking Spring Cemetery Washington Co. VA. 1877 he graduated from medical department of U. of the City of NY in and was a physician in Abingdon VA. Married first his cousin Elizabeth.

1910 1920 Federal census shows the family enumerated in Abingdon, Washington Co., VA, living on Main St., family no.69.

Cummings, Jas W., 50, (noted M2 -second
marriage), married 3 years, b. VA, physician, general
practice.

-- Fannie, wife, 32, (noted M2 -second marriage
also), married 3 years, 3 chidlren, 2 living, b. VA to
parents from WV and VA.

-- Francis (sic), daughter, 2, b. VA.

-- Jas W. Jr., daughter (sic), 1/12 (1 month - April
19 census), b. VA.

(in the same household)

Smith, Lizzie, cook, black, 20, married, b. VA,
cook, private family.

Summers, S A, boarder, 29, single, b. VA to VA
parents, deputy clerk, county court. (Fannie's brother)

Anderson, Lillian, Nurse, 18, single, b. VA to VA
parents, nurse, private family.

1920 Federal census shows the family enumerated in
Abingdon, Washington Co., VA, living on West
Main St.

Cummings, James W., head, owns home, 69, b. VA
to VA parents, Physician, General Practice.

-- Fannie, wife, 40, b. VA to parents from WV and
VA

-- Frances, daughter, 12, b. VA.

-- Mary, daughter, 10, b. VA.

-- Elizabeth P., 8, b. VA.

Summers, Andrew, brother-in-law, 39, single, b.
VA to parents from WV and VA, Deputy Clerk,
Circuit Court.

1924 his will dated 8 Oct. 1923 was proved 16 July
1924 Washington Co. VA. He gave his estate to his
wife Francis and daughters Frances R., Mary C. and
Eliza Preston Cummings equally. Named Sunshine
Summers executor.

+ 176.   v   **Henry PRESTON Jr.** b. 29 Jul 1861.

   177.   vi **Anne Cary PRESTON**, b. 18 Feb 1863 in
              Washington Co., VA, d. 17 Oct 1931. She married
              Albert Pendelton KILLINGER, married 7 Jun
              1899, b. ABT 1859.

178.   vii   **Jane Craighead PRESTON**, b. 24 Aug 1863 in Washington Co., VA, d. 23 Jan 1907 in Washington Co., VA, buried in Walnut Grove Cemetery Washington Co. VA. Born and died at The Grove.

179.   viii **Isetta Randolph PRESTON**, b. 5 Nov 1865 in Washington Co., VA, d. 18 Jun 1916 in Washington Co., VA, buried in Walnut Grove Cemetery Washington Co. VA. Died unmarried. Born and died at The Grove.

180.   ix   **Eugenia Frances 'Jeanne' PRESTON**, b. 3 1868 in Washington Co., VA, d. 4 Jan 1913 in Abingdon, Washington Co. VA. 1900 Federal census shows the couple enumerated in Abingdon, Washington Co., VA.
          Gibson, Charles, C., head, Dec. 1863, 35, married 10 years, b. VA, farmer.
          -- Eugenia, P., wife, Jan 1868, 32 married 10 years, b. VA.
          Williams, Mary, cook, black, May 1881, 19, single, b. VA.
          -- Clifton, cooks child, black, Jan 1899, 1, single, b. VA. She married **Charles Cummings GIBSON**, married 2 Oct 1889 in Washington Co., VA, b. 14 Dec 1863.

+ 181.   x   **Percy Thomas PRESTON** b. 11 Oct 1875.

40.   **Sarah Jane Gilliland PRESTON**, (6.Jane³, 2.Robert², 1.John¹) b. 27 Jun 1803 in Abingdon, Washington Co. VA, d. 20 Jul 1874 in Sullivan Co., TN, buried in Blountville Cemetery, Sullivan Co., TN. She and her marriage are mentioned in the Nov. 1844 letter of her uncle Alexander Preston in Sevierville TN to his nephew Samuel Preston in Ireland. He writes "Robert P. Rhea married Sarah G. Preston, my niece. Have five children, Joseph, Robert, Jane, Frances and Peggy."

The will of her grandfather Robert Preston Sr. reads 'to Sarah G. Rhea, formerly Sarah G. Preston, my negro girl named Nancy.'

A picture of Sarah still hangs (2001 in the Earhart home at the 'Elms' in Blountville, TN. The photograph is of her at an advanced age and was probably taken in the 1870's.

Her tombstone in Blountville Cemetery reads 'Sarah G. wf of Robert P.' She married **Robert Preston RHEA**, married 17 Oct 1826 in Abingdon, Washington Co. VA, b. 17 Sep 1802 in Back Creek, Sullivan Co TN, d. 26 Mar 1881 in Sullivan Co., TN, buried in Blountville Cemetery, Sullivan Co., TN. Robert P. Rhea was always a citizen of Sullivan Co. TN. He lived and owned the home of his father. There all his children were born and reared. In 1896 it was owned by his oldest son Joseph, living there with his family. This was a very dear spot to all the nieces and nephews who loved to visit his home. He was always lively and cheerful. They would enter heartily and enter into sports and plays, get a crowd together and they would play "Blind Man's Bluff" he being the Blind man.

His school days were spent in the log school house near his father's home. He also went to Washington College, to old Dr. Sam Doak in 1819 and 1820. Came out of school and carried on farming extensively on his land, owned many slaves, forty or fifty, big and little, male and female. They did all kinds of work, belonging to the farm, had a sugar camp where maple sugar and syrup was made. He was kind and good to these slaves, never cruel and they loved and respected him. His wife was a very managing and industrious and energetic woman, up early and late planning her work. She had spinning and weaving carried on, long as they owned these slave in the house. While granny Braden lived there (1828) they spun, wove and made cloth from wool, flax and cotton all raised on the farm (except the cotton) and made up into clothes, blankets, sheets, table linen for the house. It was laborious work to raise the bread meat and grain for so many mouths. That day is all past (1896).

Robert was a high toned honorable citizen, had the esteem and respect of all who knew him. Held co. offices and places of trust though he never sought them. He made a profession of religion and united with the Presbyterian Church in Blountville TN. In that Church his place was never vacant. It was his joy and pleasure to be found in the Sanctuary and to do the work of the Sanctuary. He was and elder in the church for many years until he died. He was a great Temperance lecturer, gave much of his time and attention to this cause, going through his country holding temperance meetings and making speeches. He could always draw a crowd. Along this line he did much good in the way of reforming the drunkard and lifting him up our of the mire. He also much interested in public affairs, helping to

build the East Tennessee. and Georgia. RR. Was one of the Board of
Directors and also one of the thirty, who saved the Charter of the
Road. He was a pure, true man, honest and upright. When
he passed away he was greatly missed by all who knew him. He had
a large circle of relatives and friend. When the last summons came,
he was ready. Had fought and the fight finished his course and was
laid away amid the regrets of a large number of people. (From
"Genealogy of the Rhea Family" by W. L. Rhea, son of Samuel,
1895.)

The Col. John Anderson Townhouse on Lot 26 is one of Blountville's
original dwellings where legend and deed disagree as to its
beginnings. The lot was originally bought by Dr. Elkanah Dulaney
probably as an investment property and the log house there today was
probably built by him for rental purposes. In 1811 he sold lot 26 and
27 to Joshua Miller for 500 dollars. Miller sold lot 26 "including the
house at present occupied by Joshua Russel's family to Robert Rhea
for $300. Robert kept the property for 2 years then sold it to his
brother in law Edward B. Anderson for $600. He may have made
improvements and it was probably he who built the frame rear section
which was at first connected to the log house by a 'dog trot.

1826 Aug. 24, John Scott to Robert Rhea bill of sale; $400; to sell
Rhea one negro man named Lewis. Wit. Joseph Scott, Isaac
McKinley.

1831 June 7, Isaac and Elizabeth Scott bill of sale to Robert Rhea;
$400; sell to Rhea a negro man named Braxton; wit Isaac McKinley.

1837 Mar. 11, John Philips bill of sale to Robert P. Rhea; $23.63;
Philips sells to Rhea, 1 old sorrel mare (now with foal), 2 milk cows.
Wit. Jos. S. Rhea. (Sullivan Co. deed book.)

1850 Sullivan Co. TN census he was a farmer with property valued at
$8000.

1870 after the war, he is enumerated as head of household with wife
Sarah G. and son Joseph and his wife Elizabeth, daughter Jane P.
Vance, living there following the death of Belfor Vance, Delia
Wadkins (keeping house at age 16) and infant Robert Rhea born July
1870. Real estate value $4000
property $2102.

1880 census shows Robert living with his son Joseph and his family.

Children:

182.   i   **Jane Preston RHEA**, b. 1829 in Sullivan Co., TN,
d. AFT 1896. Lively, kind, pleasant and very
industrious. A great comfort to her parents in their
declining years. Her married life with Mr. Vance was
short and spent in VA. She came back to her father's
house to spend her widowhood. Later she married
Audley. They lived a while in Bristol, where he was
selling goods in cousin Joe's store. His health began
failing and they moved to the 'Block House', the old
homestead, then called 'Lucille'. They were both
members of the Presbyterian Ch. (Genealogy of the
Rhea Family, W L Rhea, 1895). She married (1)
Balfour VANCE, b. ABT 1800 in Abingdon,
Washington Co. VA. She married (2) **Audley
ANDERSON**, married 1 Jun 1873, b. 28 Jan 1821 in
Scott Co., VA, d. 18 Dec 1894 in Scott Co., VA. He
was born at the Block House. The Block House
burned while it was occupied by Audley's family. He
built another house on the same place and continued
to then live on the farm at the same spot where the
Block House formerly stood; carried on farming.
When a young man, clerked in the store for his uncle
Samuel Rhea of Blountville. He also sold goods for
his brother Joseph R. Anderson of Bristol. He was
quiet and retiring in disposition, loved his home and
family. His family were all Presbyterians.
(His birth date had been reported as Jan. 28, 1821 and
also as in March 1822 in his obituary.)

Audley Anderson married first Cornelia Alexander
and had six children. The mother died, and he
afterward married Eliza Ryland who died without
children. He again married his cousin Jane Rhea
Vance.

He married the eldest daughter of Col. Dix and Sarah
Graham Alexander. The war ruined his business in
Rodgersville and after the death of his wife there he
moved to Bristol and went into business with his
brother Joseph. He was made deacon in the Bristol
Presbyterian Church. He again married, Eliza Ryland
of Jonesboro. She died leaving no children.

1873 he married Jane Rhea Vance. He bought the old homestead and passed the remaining days of his life. He was made a ruling elder in the church."

1880 Federal census shows the family in Estillville, Scott Co., VA:
Anderson, Audley 58, Farmer, b. VA to parents from VA and TN.
-- Jane P. 52, wife, keeping house, b. TN to parents from TN and VA.
-- Alice C., 20, daughter, at home, b. TN. [daughter from Audley's first marriage - EFF]
-- Audley S., 16 son, works on farm, b. TN. [son from Audley's first marriage - EFF]
Newland, E, black, 40 servant, cannot read or write, b. TN
-- Rebecca, black, 18, servant, cannot read or write, b. TN

1894 the following is a copy of his obituary. "At his residence, 'Block House', or 'Lucille' in VA, at 4 p.m. Sabbath Dec. 3, 1894. Mr. Audley Anderson, departed this life. Blessed day, to enter upon that rest. The subject of this notice, was born on the old Anderson homestead, in Scott Co., VA Mar. 12, 1822. He was the son of Isaac & Margaret Rhea Anderson of Scotch Irish descent. With this death, only four of the twelve children are living (1895). Mr. Anderson descended from a Presbyterian ancestry. As a result of home training, as well as Church training the old Anderson and Rhea families have given to the Church ministers and wives of ministers 28 in number. Before the war Mr. Anderson left his fathers house and embarked in the mercantile in Rodgersville TN. He carried with him his church letter and at once united with the Old School Presbyterian Church at that place having been converted in youth under the ministry of Rev F. A. Ross in Kingsport.

+ 183. ii **Joseph RHEA** b. 12 Dec 1830.

+ 184. iii **Frances 'Frank' Elizabeth RHEA** b. 31 Dec 1832.

+ 185.   iv   **Margaret 'Peggy' Preston RHEA** b. 22 Jun 1835.

  186.   v   **Robert James RHEA**, b. 18 Dec 1837 in Sullivan Co., TN, d. 17 Sep 1864 in Forsyth GA. Youngest son of Robert and Sallie. Born on Back Creek; educated at home in Blountville TN. Rode out every day a distance of four miles to Jefferson Academy. For a while was a student at Emory & Henry College, VA. After that to Maryville College for year or two. War came up, he enlisted in CSA. Was engaged in several battles: Fishing Crk, Shiloh. Was sick, came home with a spell of fever for a year. In 1864 he returned to his Regiment. In battle near Atlanta July 22, 1864 he received a wound and never recovered.

  187.   vi   **Sara Sells RHEA**, b. 1841 in Bristol, Sullivan Co., TN, d. 1934 in Sullivan Co., TN, buried in Blountville Cemetery, Sullivan Co., TN.

41.   **Alexander 'Dr' R. PRESTON**, (6.Jane[3], 2.Robert[2], 1.John[1]) b. 8 Dec 1805 in Washington Co., VA, d. 3 Mar 1874 in Washington Co., VA. Born at "Locust Glen" the home of his father, 5 miles west of Abingdon VA. He received his education at the Abingdon Academy and in medicine at Transylvania College. Practiced medicine in VA until his death.

His family is outlined in a letter Alexander Preston wrote in 1844 (Collection of Washington Co. Historical Society).

1840 Virginia census shows 'Preston Alexander R. ' in Abingdon, Washington Co., VA. In the household: 1 male 30-40; 1 female 20-30.

1850 Virginia census shows the family in the 'Town of Abingdon, Washington Co., VA.
Alex B. Preston age 44, doctor, real estate values 1000, b. VA
Henry S. age 8 b. VA
Robt. A. age 8 b. VA
Mary S. age 6 b. VA
[His wife Sarah had died in 1846. The next family enumerated is that of Robt Preston.]

1860 he was elected to the General Assembly from Washington Co. VA.

1860 Oct census for Virginia shows the family in Abingdon, Washington Co., VA.
   A. R. Preston 54, M.D., real property $55,000, personal property $50, 000, b. VA
   Henry 18, student, b. VA
   Robert, 16, ", b. VA
   Mary 15, b. VA

1870 he was clerk of the Circuit Court in VA.

1870 August page 12 of the Virginia census shows him in Abingdon, Washington Co.., VA:
   Preston, A. R. 69, retired M.D., real estate $25,500, personal property $21,000, b. VA
(in the same household)
   White, John 28, farmer, b. VA
   " Mary, 25 keeping house. VA
   Boyd, Sarah 20, black, domestic, b. VA

. He married **Sarah SMITH**, b. 5 Jun 1815 in Russell Co. VA, d. 26 Jan 1846.
                      Children:

   188.   i   **Henry Smith PRESTON**, b. ABT 1830 in Washington Co., VA.

+ 189.   ii   **Robert A. PRESTON** b. 25 Dec 1842.

43. **John Fairman 'Capt' PRESTON**, (6.Jane³, 2.Robert², 1.John¹) b. 26 Apr 1811 in Washington Co., VA, d. 16 Jan 1875 in Abingdon, Washington Co. VA. Lived on farm in Abington raised their children and died there. Both members of the Presbyterian church.

1860 Oct 10, page 355 of the Virginia census for Washington Co., VA shows the family in the town of Abingdon.
   John F. Preston 49, farmer, value of real estate $29,000, value of personal property $28,000 b. VA
   Nancy " 45, h. Keeper, b. TN
   Nancy " 21 Pupil (?)VA
   Robert " 18, student, b. VA
   Sarah " ,16, Pupil (?) b. VA

James " 14, b. VA
Rhea " 11, b. VA
Jenny ", 5, b. VA
(In the same household)
Jane Preston 80, b. VA [probably John's mother]
Samuel A. Preston 53, Colporteur (?), real property value $13,600, personal property value $250, b. Donegall, Irld. He married **Jane RHEA**, b. 1813 in Blountville, Sullivan Co., TN, d. 4 May 1876 in Abingdon, Washington Co. VA.

Children:

+ 190. i   **Nannie Montgomery PRESTON** b. 4 May 1838.

+ 191. ii   **Robert J. PRESTON** b. 25 Jan 1841.

+ 192. iii **Sarah Elleanor PRESTON** b. 21 Oct 1843.

+ 193. iv   **James Brainerd PRESTON** b. 3 Dec 1845.

+ 194. v   **Samuel Rhea PRESTON** b. 4 Sep 1849.

+ 195. vi   **Jennie Fairman PRESTON** b. 1 Nov 1856.

44. **Walter PRESTON**, (8.John^3, 3.Walter^2, 1.John^1) b. 18 Jul 1819 in Washington Co., VA, d. 1 Nov 1867. 1839 he graduated from Princeton and from Harvard in 1842.

1850 his family is enumerated with his father as head of household in the Virginia census in the Town of Abingdon, Washington Co. VA.
John M. Preston, age 62, real estate valued at $13,000, b. VA
    Walter, age 31, lawyer b. VA
    Elizabeth, 26 b. VA
    John M. 11, b . VA
    Charles H. C. 9, b. VA.

1860 October, Virginia census shows Walter married, living in Abingdon, Washington Co., VA:
    Walter Preston 41, lawyer, real estate value $7000, personal property $3,000, b. VA
    Garnett " 26, H. Keeper, b. VA
    Sallie " 4, b. VA
    William " 2, b. VA
    Elizabeth 8/12, b. VA

1861 he was elected to the Congress of the Confederacy.

Member of the Virginia Legislature and a well known orator and lawyer. Had 4 children. He married **Agatha Garnett PEYTON**, b. 1834 in Roanoke, VA. 1870 Virginia census shows her now as the head of the household. Walter had died in 1867. They are still shown in Abingdon, Washington Co., VA.

Preston A. G. 36, reap property value $10,000, personal property $1,000, b. VA

Sallie P. 13, at home, b. VA

Lizzie, 10, at home, b. VA

Nellie, 8, b. VA

Susan 5, b. VA

Montgomery 4, b. VA

[The dwelling in which Garnett lives, has 18 residents. They other residents range in age from 12 to 98. They do not seem to be related.]

Children:

  196. i **Sarah PRESTON**, b. 1856 in Washington Co., VA.

  197. ii **William PRESTON**, b. 1858 in Washington Co., VA.

+ 198. iii **Elizabeth Arthur PRESTON** b. 1 Feb 1860.

  199. iv **Ellenor Garrett PRESTON**, b. ABT 1862. She married **Rev. TYNING**, b. ABT 1850 in New York, NY.

  200. v **Walter Montgomery PRESTON**, b. ABT 1864 in VA. Unmarried.

  201. vi **Susan Madison PRESTON**, b. ABT 1866 in VA. Unmarried.

45. **James Wilson PRESTON**, (8.John[3], 3.Walter[2], 1.John[1]) b. 24 Aug 1821 in Washington Co., VA, d. 8 Dec 1881. 1880 Federal census of Virginia shows the family enumerated in Abingdon, Washington Co., VA.

Preston, James W. 59, farmer, b. VA

-- Kate 53, at home, b. VA

-- Ellen 30, keeping house, b. VA

--Walter 29, at home, b. VA

-- Margaret 24, at home, b. VA

-- John 22, law student, b. VA
-- Kate 20, at home, b. VA
-- Gillie 13, at home, b. VA
Trigg, Anna, 64 boarder. b. VA
Trig, Connolly, 33 boarder, lawyer, b. VA. He married **Catherine A. GREENWAY**, married 5 Oct 1847, b. 13 Jun 1826 in VA?, d. 2 Jan 1911. 1850 there is only one Greenway family enumerated in Washington Co., VA. Although Kate is 24 and not enumerated with the family, circumstantially it appears these are her parents, John and Margaret Greenway. In this household, as a clerk for the merchant John Greenway, is Samuel Preston, b. Ireland, a cousin of John M. Preston, Kate's husband.

Children:

202. i   **Ellen Wilson PRESTON**, b. 1850 in Washington Co., VA. Died unmarried.

203. ii **Walter G. PRESTON**, b. 1851 in Washington Co., VA. 1870 he is enumerated in the Federal census in Abingdon, Washington Co. VA with his parents, age 19, a student.

      Died unmarried.

204. iii **Margaret Virginia PRESTON**, b. 1856 in Washington Co., VA.

205. iv **John G. PRESTON**, b. 1858 in Washington Co., VA.

206. v   **Nannie Gilbert PRESTON**, b. 1857 in Washington Co., VA.

+ 207. vi **Katherine Greenway PRESTON** b. 18 Jun 1860.

46. **Elizabeth Ellen PRESTON**, (8.John[3], 3.Walter[2], 1.John[1]) b. 30 Apr 1824 in VA, d. 9 Mar 1896. Married Gen. Arthur Cummings. They called their home "Mont Calm" high on a hill in Abington. They had 2 sons. She married **Arthur Campbell CUMMINGS**, married 26 Feb 1852, b. 1 Oct 1822 in VA?, d. 19 Mar 1905.
     Children:

208.   i   **Ellen Wilson CUMMINGS**, b. 27 Apr 1854 in Abingdon, Washington Co. VA, d. 13 Sep 1900.

209.   ii   **John Preston CUMMINGS**, b. 29 Jun 1856, d. 17 Apr 1876.

47.   **John Montgomery PRESTON Jr.**, (8.John[3], 3.Walter[2], 1.John[1]) b. 14 Oct 1838 in Abingdon, Washington Co. VA, d. 27 Sep 1928. Lived at Seven Mile Ford, VA. Had 8 children. He married **Mary Lewis COCHRAN**, married 3 Feb 1864 in Charlottesville, Albemarle Co., VA, b. 21 Oct 1840 in Charlottesville, Albemarle Co., VA, d. 26 Apr 1932.

Children:

+ 210.   i   **Margaret Lynn PRESTON** b. 27 Jul 1865.

211.   ii   **John Montgomery PRESTON III.**, b. 17 Jul 1866 in VA, d. 13 Feb 1951. He married **Sallie MITCHELL**, married 4 Nov 1913, b. ABT 1866.

+ 212.   iii   **Elizabeth Cummings PRESTON** b. 3 Jun 1868.

+ 213.   iv   **Cochran 'Rev.' PRESTON** b. 9 May 1871.

214.   v   **Sarah Buchanan PRESTON**, b. 11 Nov 1873 in VA, d. 24 Feb 1949. 1900 Federal census shows the couple enumerated in Greenville, Greenville Co., SC at 1213 Pendleton St.
   Dean, Alvin H., head Mar 1863, 37, married 2 years, b. SC, lawyer.
   -- Sarah P. wife, Nov 1873, married 2 years, no children, b. VA.

   1930 Federal census shows Sarah enumerated in Greenville, Greenville Co., SC living at 1012 Buncombe Street.
   Dean, Sarah P, head, owns home, value of house $20,000, has radio, age 56, first married at 24, widow, b. VA
   Hickey, Ethel, boarder, 24, b. SC, stenographer, law.
   Abram, Frances, boarder, 24, b. SC. stenographer, textile.

Had no children. She married **Alvin Henry DEAN**, b. 22 Mar 1863 in Spartanburg, SC, d. 18 Aug 1929 in Greenville, SC. He was a lawyer, and mayor of Greenville at the time of his death.

215. vi **Mittie PRESTON**, b. 21 Oct 1875 in VA, d. 21 Oct 1875 in VA.

216. vii **Maria PRESTON**, b. 5 Apr 1878 in VA, d. 24 Jul 1878 in VA.

217. viii **Nelly Cummings PRESTON**, b. 1 Sep 1880 in VA, d. 23 Jun 1966. Wrote and published 2 books, "Hitching Posts for Memories" and "Paths ofGlory".

48. **Charles Henry Campbell PRESTON**, (8.John³, 3.Walter², 1.John¹) b. 12 Sep 1840 in Washington Co., VA, d. 1931. He bore the name of his uncle who had died 8 years earlier in 1832, the younger brother of his mother Maria.

Married 3 times.
1900 the Federal census shows the family located in Licking Hole, Goochland Co., VA.
Preston, Charles, head, 59, widowed, b. VA, Farmer.
-- Blair D. son, Oct 1877, 22, single, b. VA, farm laborer.
-- Susan M., daughter, Aug 1886, 22, b. VA.
-- Catherine L., daughter, Mch 1888 12, . VA.
-- Annie M., daughter, Feb 1890, 10, b. VA. at school.
Taylor, Susan M. , s-in-law, Nov 1769, 30, single, b. VA, house keeper.
Jones Julia, servant, Black, Feb. 1882, 11, single, b. VA.

1920 Federal census shows him in Licking Hole, Goochland Co., VA lving with the family of his daughter Suzie:
  Leake, Louis M., head rents, 30, b. VA to VA parents, Physician and farmer,
  -- Suzie M., wife 32, b. VA.
  -- Andrew K., son, 7, b. VA.
  Preston, Charles H C, father in law, 78, widowed, b. VA.
  -- Hattie D., sister in law, 30, single, b. VA.
  Taylor, Suzie B., aunt, 48, single, b. VA.

1930 Federal census Charles is living in the household of his son in law Louis Lecke in Licking Hole, Goochland Co., VA. He was age

89, a widower. He married (1) **Mary WOODSON**, b. ABT 1840. Had 3 children but their twins died in infancy. He married (2) **Kitty DABNEY**, b. 1836, d. 1881. He married (3) **Lucy Walker TAYLOR**, b. 1849, d. 1893. 1900 census shows Lucy had passed away. Her sister Susan was living with the family and taking care of the house and children.

Children by Mary WOODSON:

218.   i   **Charles Henry Campbell PRESTON Jr.**, b. 21 Jul 1866, d. 1891. Never married.
Children by Kitty DABNEY:

219.   ii   **Blair Dabney PRESTON**, b. 1879, d. 1957. Never married.
Children by Lucy Walker TAYLOR:

+ 220.   iii   **Susan Morris PRESTON** b. 1 Aug 1886.

221.   iv   **Kathryn 'Kitty' Dabney PRESTON**, b. 1 Mar 1888 in VA. 1930 Federal census shows the couple in Licking Hole, Goochland Co., VA living on River Road:
   Anderson, Calvert B. head, owns home, value of property $60,000, age 48, married at 44, b. VA, farmer.
   Kathryn, wife-h, age 42, married at 38, b. VA. She married **Calvert B. ANDERSON**, b. 1882 in VA.

222.   v   **Anne Montgomery PRESTON**, b. 1 Feb 1890 in VA, d. 1906.

223.   vi   **Lucy Taylor PRESTON**, b. ABT 1892. Died in infancy.

49. **Walter Preston COLEMAN**, (9.Mary[3], 3.Walter[2], 1.John[1]) b. 7 Feb 1823 in VA?, d. 10 Jun 1870. He married (1) **Sarah 'Sally' NIELSON**, b. ABT 1823. He married (2) **Fannie BLACK**, married 2 Sep 1851, b. ABT 1823.
Children by Sarah 'Sally' NIELSON:

224.   i   **Martha 'Mattie' Nielson COLEMAN**, b. 1866 in VA?, d. 1871.

225. ii **Ellen Douglas COLEMAN**, b. 1869 in VA?, d. 1869.
Children by Fannie BLACK:

226. iii **Mary COLEMAN**, b. ABT 1852 in VA?.

227. iv **Walter Preston COLEMAN Jr.**, b. ABT 1855 in VA?.

228. v **Samuel COLEMAN**, b. ABT 1857 in VA?.

229. vi **Preston Chiles COLEMAN**, b. ABT 1861 in VA?.

51. **Anne Montgomery COLEMAN**, (9.Mary^3, 3.Walter^2, 1.John^1) b. 16 May 1826 in KY, d. 24 Jul 1889. She married **Mr. JAMES**, married 13 Sep 1860, b. ABT 1826.
Children:

230. i **Robert Coleman JAMES**, b. ABT 1861 in VA?. Never married.

53. **James P. COLEMAN**, (9.Mary^3, 3.Walter^2, 1.John^1) b. 29 Nov 1829 in KY, d. 20 Sep 1873. He married **wife of James COLEMAN**, b. ABT 1829.
Children:

231. i **Anne COLEMAN**, b. ABT 1860.

232. ii **Charles COLEMAN**, b. ABT 1862 in VA?.

233. iii **Mary COLEMAN**, b. ABT 1864 in VA?.

56. **Mary C. PRESTON**, (11.Robert^3, 3.Walter^2, 1.John^1) b. 18 Sep 1833 in Washington Co., VA, d. 22 Jun 1914. 1880 Federal census shows her enumerated in Abingdon VA next to her sister in law Ellen Campbell. Mary and Ellen appear to both be widows with young families.
Campbell, Mary P., 46, keeping house.
-- Ganneth, 18, son, at home, b. VA
-- Mammie T., 16, daughter, at home, b. VA.
-- Robert R., son, at home, b. VA.
(same household)
Perry, Adam, black, 15, servant (there is a servant named Joseph Perry in the home of Ellen Campbell).

Preston, Lizzie, 27, sister, at home.
Campbell, John A., 16, boarder, Tobacconist. She married **Joseph Trigg CAMPBELL**, married 5 Oct 1856, b. ABT 1833, d. BEF 1880.

> *Children:*

234. i   **Garnett CAMPBELL**, b. 26 Jul 1861 in VA, d. 24 Jan 1938. Moved to Abiline TX. His name has also been shown as J.
Garreth Campbell. He married **Grace KENYON**, b. ABT 1861.

235. ii   **Mary Conley CAMPBELL**, b. 10 May 1864 in VA, d. 6 Jun 1942. 1930 Federal census shows her enumerated on Main Street, Abingdon, Washington Co., VA in the household of her brother Robert. She is 65.

     Died unmarried.

236. iii   **Robert Robinson Preston CAMPBELL**, b. 25 Aug 1867 in VA, d. 27 Aug 1952. 1930 Federal census shows the couple enumerated on West Main Street in Abingdon, Washington Co., VA:
   Campbell, Robert R., head, owns home, value $10,000, no radio, age 62, married at 40, b. VA to parents from VA, insurance, life.
   -- Mary B. T., wife-h, age 58, first married at 26, b. MS to parents from VA.
   -- Mary T., sister, age 65, single, b. VA to parents from VA.

     Had no children. He married **Mary Byrd TRIGG**, married 1872, b. 1872 in VA, (daughter of Abram Byrd TRIGG and Susan Preston WHITE) d. 1961. Married Robert, her cousin. They had no children.

61. **Amelia Cummings PRESTON**, (11.Robert^3, 3.Walter^2, 1.John^1) b. 1 Dec 1844 in Washington Co., VA, d. 5 Oct 1921. 1920 Federal census shows her enumerated as a widow age 76 in Abingdon, Washington Co. VA. She married **Robert A. PRESTON**, married 12 Feb 1868, b. 25 Dec 1842 in Washington Co., VA, (son of Alexander 'Dr' R. PRESTON and Sarah SMITH) d. 5 Dec 1916. Served as a

Captain in the Confederate Army and was superintendent of of Washington Co. VA schools.

1880 Federal census shows the family in Abingdon District, Washington Co., VA.
  Preston, Robert A., 37, farmer.
  -- Amelia 35, wife, keeping house.
  -- Alexander R. 11, son
  -- Elizabeth McD,10, daughter
  -- Maggie S. 8, daughter, sick with dysentery.
  -- Robert R. 7 son
  -- Thomas W. 4 son
  -- Mary C. 9/12 August, daughter
  -- Elizabeth 72, mother in law
  -- Walter S. 49 brother in law, farmer
(in the same household)
  Heathe, Elsie, 30. servant, b. VA
  Campbell, Amelia 22, servant, b. VA
  Cotton, James, 24, servant, b. VA

1910 Federal census Washington Co., VA his family appears.
  Preston, Robert, 68, a healer
  -- Amelia 63,
  -- S.R. son 41 and his wife Bessie G. 29,
  -- Maggie 37,
  -- Ann M. 73 sister in law,
  -- Elizabeth 1 1/2
  -- Frank G. 1 1/2 grandchildren.
              Children:

+ 237.   i   **Alexander R. PRESTON** b. 1869.

+ 238.   ii   **Elizabeth 'Lizzie' McDonald PRESTON** b. 26 Mar 1870.

  239.   iii **Margaret Smith PRESTON**, b. 1872 in VA?.

  240.   iv   **Robert Robinson PRESTON**, b. 1873 in Abingdon, Washington Co., VA. Died unmarried.

+ 241.   v   **Thomas Wilson PRESTON** b. 10 Jan 1876.

  242.   vi   **Mary Campbell PRESTON**, b. 1 Aug 1880 in Abingdon, Washington Co., VA.

62. **Elizabeth 'Lizzie' Cummings PRESTON**, (11.Robert[3], 3.Walter[2], 1.John[1]) b. 1 Mar 1852 in Washington Co., VA. She married **Walter Howard LEYBURN**, b. 1 Jul 1852 in Augusta Co., VA. 1900 the Federal census of Virginia shows the family in Waynesoro, Augusta Co., VA on Arch Av.:
    Leyburn, Walter, H. head, b. July 1852, 47, married 13 years, b. VA, parents b. VA, mining engineer
    -- Lizzie, C., wife, Mar 1852, 48, married 13 yers, 4 children, 4 living, b. VA
    -- Bessie, C., daughter, May 1889, 12, b. VA
    -- Jennie P., daughter, Sept 1891, 8, b. VA
    -- Alfred P., son, Feb 1893, b. VA
    -- Nellie C., daughter, Aug 1895, 4 b. VA
    Bonds, Patsey, servant, black, females, July 1845,54, no children, widowed, b. VA.
    Children:

+ 243. i   **Bessie Cloud LEYBURN** b. 1 May 1889.

  244. ii   **Jennie Preston LEYBURN**, b. 1 Sep 1891 in VA, d. 1950. She married **Alex HEIGHT**, b. ABT 1880 in Elmira, NY.

  245. iii **Alfred P. LEYBURN**, b. 1 Feb 1893 in VA, d. 1 May 1959 in Dade Co., FL. Worked in Washington D.C. Died in 1956 leaving 2 daughters one who lived in Washington D.C.

       1959 May the Florida death records indicate the death of Alfred Preston Leyburn. He married **Clarice C. wife of Alfred LEYBURN**, b. 11 Nov 1901, d. 26 Nov 1987 in Broward Co., FL. SS records indicate her last address as Deerfield Beach, Broward Co., FL. SS# issued in 1973 in FL.

  246. iv   **Nelly C. LEYBURN**, b. 1 Aug 1895 in VA. Lived in Washington D.C.

63. **Thomas Wilson PRESTON**, (11.Robert[3], 3.Walter[2], 1.John[1]) b. 1 Dec 1846 in Abingdon, Washington Co. VA. Fought at the Battle of New Market May 15, 1864 with the Cadets of VMI. He was a member of the Class of '67.

1900 Federal census finds the family enumerated in Vicksburg, Warren Co., Mississippi at 106 Adams St.:

Preston, T. W., head, b. Dec. 1846, 53, married 20 years, b. VA, bookkeeper.

-- M. S., wife, b. Mar 1858, 42, married 20 years, 5 children, 5 living. b. MS, parents b. KY and MS.

--Shelby, son, Aug. 1882, 17, b. Missouri, messenger.

-- Nellie C., daughter, July 1887, 13, b. Mississippi, at school.

-- Margareta, daughter, Mar. 1890, 10, b. MS, at school.

-- Elizabeth, daughter, July, 1893, 6, MS.

-- Mirian, D., daughter, June 1895, 4, b. MS. He married **Mary SHELBY**, married 1880, b. 1 Mar 1858 in Huntsville, Madison Co. AL. 1900 Federal census record indicated she was born in Mississippi.

Children:

+ 247. i **Shelby PRESTON** b. 1 Aug 1882.

248. ii **Robert PRESTON**, b. ABT 1883.

249. iii **Nelly C. PRESTON**, b. 1 Jul 1887 in MS.

250. iv **Margaret PRESTON**, b. 1 Mar 1890 in MS. She married **Edward KEIF**, b. ABT 1886.

251. v **Elizabeth PRESTON**, b. 1 Jul 1893 in MS.

252. vi **Miriam D. PRESTON**, b. 1 Jun 1895 in MS.

66. **Anne Montgomery PRESTON**, (12.Alexander[3], 3.Walter[2], 1.John[1]) b. 1838 in KY. Moved to Texas. Married there.

1880 Federal census finds this family in San Antonio, Bexar Co., TX. Anne appears without her husband.

Gillespie, Anne, 40 [probably 42], boarder, seamstress, b. KY to parents from VA.

-- Clayton, 5, son, . TX to parents from GA and KY. She married **Clayton GILLESPIE**, married in TX, b. ABT 1838 in TX?.

Children:

253. i **Clayton GILLESPIE Jr.**, b. 1875 in TX. One report is that he died young.

73. **Anne Amelia PRESTON**, (13.Fairman³, 3.Walter², 1.John¹) b. 29
Aug 1826 in Washington Co., VA, d. 16 Aug 1905. She married
David CUMMINGS, married 18 Apr 1848, b. 18 Apr 1818 in VA?.
1880 his sons are living with David's brother in Caddo Co., LA.
Children:

+ 254.   i   **Robert Carter CUMMINGS** b. 2 1849.

   255.   ii   **Ellen CUMMINGS**, b. 17 Aug 1852 in VA?. Died
young.

   256.   iii   **Fariman Preston CUMMINGS**, b. 22 Mar 1855 in
VA?, d. in LA?. 1880 Federal census of LA shows F.
Preston Cummings enumerated in the household of
his uncle Robert in Caddo Co., LA:
Cummings, Robert C. 65, farmer
-- Robert C. Jr, 21 nephew, farmer
-- F. Preston 25, nephew, farmer

Died young.

   257.   iv   **Mary CUMMINGS**, b. 13 Sep 1860 in VA?, d. in
Knoxville, Knox Co., TN.

74. **Walter PRESTON**, (13.Fairman³, 3.Walter², 1.John¹) b. ABT 1828
in Washington Co., VA. He married **Frances 'Fannie' EVANS**, b.
ABT 1828.
Children:

   258.   i   **Jane Cummings PRESTON**, b. ABT 1860.

80. **Walter Creigh PRESTON**, (14.David³, 3.Walter², 1.John¹) b. ABT
1836 in WVA?. He married **Sybil DAVIS**, b. ABT 1836.
Children:

   259.   i   **Alfred PRESTON**, b. ABT 1872 in WVA?. Served
as a judge in Beckley WV.

Had no children. He married **Blanch BARGER**, b.
ABT 1872.

   260.   ii   **David PRESTON**, b. ABT 1879 in WVA?.

81. **John A. PRESTON**, (14.David³, 3.Walter², 1.John¹) b. ABT 1838 in
WVA?. He married (1) **Sarah 'Sallie' Lewis PRICE**, b. ABT 1838.
He married (2) **Lily DAVIS**, b. ABT 1838.
Children by Sarah 'Sallie' Lewis PRICE:

  261.   i   **Samuel Price PRESTON**, b. ABT 1870 in WVA?.
1920 Federal census shows a Samuel P. Preston
living in Lewisburg, Greenbriar Co., WV, age 40,
married to Elizabeth, with 4 young sons, a lawyer,
general practice.

  262.   ii   **James Montgomery PRESTON**, b. ABT 1872 in
WVA?.
Children by Lily DAVIS:

  263.   iii   **John A. PRESTON Jr.**, b. ABT 1874.

  264.   iv   **Walter Creigh PRESTON**, b. ABT 1874. Lived in
Cincinnatti OH.

82. **Davidella 'Della' Margaret PRESTON**, (14.David³, 3.Walter²,
1.John¹) b. 1 Jul 1846 in W. VA, d. ABT 1930. She was born in
1851, apparently after the death of her father.

1910 Federal census shows her name as Margaret. This is clearly her
family listed in Tappahannock, VA with her husband of 34 years and
many of her children listed with her. It also shows her born in W.
VA.

After her husband Thomas' death she moved to Richmond VA to live
with her daughter.

1930 Federal census shows Della as a widow now living in
Richmond, Clay Ward, Henrico Co., VA residence at 915 Ward St.:
  Wright, Della P, head, owns home, value $7,500, widow, b. WVA to
parents from VA.
  -- Jeannette, daughter, single, 45, b. VA, Manager's Private
Secretary, Fertilizer Works.
  Hesterhauser, Lucy W., roomer, single, 31, b. VA, teacher, public
school. She married **Thomas Roane Barnes 'T.R.B.' WRIGHT**,
married 1874, b. 1 Feb 1843 in Tappahannonck, Essex Co., VA, d.
1914. 1850 Virginia Federal census of November shows Thomas
enumerated with his parents in the Town of Tappahannock, Essex
Co., VA.

William A. Wright 57, lawyer, real estate value $7,700, b. VA.
Charlotte ", 40, b. VA.
William ", 19, b. VA
Charlotte ", 16, b. VA
Maria ",13, b. VA.
Thomas ", 11, b. VA.
Edward ", 8, b. VA.
Martha ", 6, b. VA.

Historical recount of an event during Thom's service during the Civil War::
"And just at this time T. R. B. Wright who was then a private in the Essex Sharpshooters, seeing our flag fall, ran and seized it and carried it to the front, calling to the men to follow. Ah, Tom, Sergeant Jasper did not perform as brave and act as that, but the men couldn't follow. Had they attempted it, without an interposition of Providence, not one would have been left to tell the tale, and God alone spared your life" Captain Albert Reynolds, Company F, 55th Regiment.
Chancellorsville Southern Historical Society Papers, Vol. XXIV, Richmond, VA, January-December, 1896 (From Richmond Dispatch, Feb. 7, 1897.)

1870 Federal census shows Thomas as head of household in Millers Tavern, Essex Co., VA:
   Wright, Thos R. B. (clearly written) 29, Attny at Law, real estate value $3,000, property $250, b. VA
   -- Charlotte, 60, keeping house, real estate value $3,000, property $500, b. VA.
   -- Mattie H. 22, without occupation, real estate value $3,000, no value for property, b. VA.

1880 Federal census of Virginia shows the young family enumerated in Tappahannock, Essex Co., VA:
   Wright Thor B. (sic - clearly Thor) 40, Atty at Law, b. VA to VA parents.
   " Della D. 28, wife, keeping house, b. VA to VA parents.
   " Preston, 2, son, at home, b. VA.
   " Ella D., 10/12, July daughter, at home, b. VA.

1888-1889 Chatiagne's Virginia Gazetteer and Business Directory shows TRB Wright as one of four attorneys listed in the town of Tappahannock VA. The population of the town was 794 at the time.

1900 Federal census shows the family living on Water Lane in Tappahannock, Essex Co., VA (the house on Water lane was Thomas' family's home from the 1850's:
  Wright, T. R. B., head, Feb 1843, married 26 years, b. VA, Judge.
  -- Della P., wife, July 1846, 53, married 26 years, 6 children, 6 living, b. VA.
  -- Jeanette C., daughter, May 1880, 20, single, b. VA.
  -- Chartie B., daughter, July 1882, 17, single, b. VA.
  -- Della, daughter, Apr 1886, 14, single, b. VA.
  -- T. R. B. Jr., son, Oct 1888, 11, single, b. VA.
  -- Wm. A, son, Mar 1890, 10, single, b. VA.

1904 TRB Wright is listed as the Commanders of the Confederate Veterans organization of Grand Camp Wright-Lane, located in Tappahannock, VA.

1910 Federal census shows the family again in Tappahannock VA. Oddly, Della's name is now shown as Margaret, wife of 34 years to Thomas.
Wright, Thoams R. B., head, 69, b. VA, lawyer, Distict Judge, owns home.
Margaret, wife, married 34 years, 6 children, 6 liviing, b. WVA to parents from WVA.
Jeanette, daughter 30, single, b. VA, Teacher, music.
Charlotte, daughter, 28, single, b. VA, Teacher, at home.
Della, daughter, 24, b. VA, Teacher, Private School.
Thos. R., son, 21, single, b. VA, machinist, Cas--- factory
WIlliam, son, 18, b. VA
(Son Preston had now gone to the oil fields of California.)
The Ronae-Wright-Trible House of 1850 is on the walking tour route of Tappahannock, at the corner of Water Lane and Duke Street in the center of the town a block from the Rappahannock River. It is a brick Georgian mansion built about 1850 by Dr. Lawrence Roane and was a private home in 2005.
Children:

+ 265. i   **Preston WRIGHT** b. 1878.

  266. ii   **Della D. WRIGHT**, b. 1 Jul 1879 in Tappahannonck, Essex Co., VA.

  267. iii   **Jeannette Creigh WRIGHT**, b. 1 May 1880 in Tappahannonck, Essex Co., VA.

268. iv **Charlotte B. 'Charlie' WRIGHT**, b. 1 Jul 1882 in Tappahannonck, Essex Co., VA.

269. v **Thomas Roane Barnes WRIGHT, Jr.**, b. 1 Oct 1888 in Tappahannonck, Essex Co., VA.

270. vi **William Alfred WRIGHT**, b. 1 Mar 1890 in Tappahannonck, Essex Co., VA.

83. **Letitia Robinson REYNOLDS**, (16.Gertrude^3, 3.Walter^2, 1.John^1) b. ABT 1833. She married **Frederick Oscar MERRIWEATHER**, b. 1 Oct 1833 in KY.
Children:

271. i **Stella MERRIWEATHER**, b. 1856.

272. ii **Gertrude V. L. MERRIWEATHER**, b. 2 Sep 1858 in IL.

273. iii **Alfred Preston MERRIWEATHER**, b. 2 Jul 1862 in IL.

+ 274. iv **Guy MERRIWEATHER** b. 19 Jan 1871.

275. v **Frank MERRIWEATHER**, b. ABT 1878 in IL.

84. **Gertrude Preston REYNOLDS**, (16.Gertrude^3, 3.Walter^2, 1.John^1) b. ABT 1835. She married **Malcolm Braeme STUART**, married 1 Sep 1859, b. ABT 1835.
Children:

276. i **Letitia STUART**, b. ABT 1865.

277. ii **William STUART**, b. ABT 1867.

278. iii **Walter STUART**, b. ABT 1869.

279. iv **Willis STUART**, b. ABT 1871.

280. v **Gertrude STUART**, b. ABT 1873.

87. **Jennet 'Jane' Preston RHEA**, (20.Joseph^3, 4.Jannette^2, 1.John^1) b. 1808 in Sullivan Co., TN, d. 28 May 1884 in Texas Co., MO. 1860 Jennet sold the farm and with four of her children moved by covered

wagon in to Texas Co. MO. There she bought land from Samuel Hughes.

1884 when she died she left 4 children, 10 grand children and 1 great grand child. She married **Elkanah WOLFORD**, married 15 Sep 1831 in Sullivan Co., TN, b. 29 Aug 1806 in Sullivan Co., TN, d. 18 Dec 1842 in Sullivan Co., TN, buried in Old Wolford Cemetery Blountville TN. 1830 Bought land in Sullivan Co. TN and Jennet sold the same land in 1860 (Deed book 11 pp. 225/6 and book 12 p. 38)

1842 Elkanah died leaving Jannette and five children to raise. She never remarried but lived on the farm for 20 years.
Children:

+ 281. i **Joseph Rhea WOLFORD** b. 18 Apr 1834.

   282. ii **Catherine 'Kitty' WOLFORD**, b. 13 Mar 1837 in Sullivan Co., TN, d. 21 Aug 1867 in Texas Co. Missouri. Twin of Margaret.

   283. iii **Margaret Jane WOLFORD**, b. 13 Mar 1837 in Sullivan Co., TN, d. 29 Nov 1915 in Marion, Williamson Co., IL. She was a twin of Catherine.

        1860 Margaret kept a diary of the trip from Sullivan Co. TN to Texas Co. MO marking their progress as far as Richland Co. Illinois. She was 23 when the family moved west. Margaret Jane's diary transcribed with its unique spellings:

        "Sullivan Co. TN. Left the old native home the 12th day of Sept. '60 destine for Mo. To cairnes camp ground and camped the night.
19th thence across the north fork River to old Mr. Cleak's and there eat dinner. Thence through Estilville west of there some miles to an old still house and there camped with solum thoughts of the night before impressed upon our minds.
20th thence to Col. Neal's and eat dinner. Thence to Patinsville. Here struck Towel's Mountain. Across it camped at the foot of it at Stickleyville, a beautiful place, Lea Co.

21 from there we struck Walling's ridge, thence to Jonesville and on to the widow Ewings and there camped in a beautiful grove of oaks.

22nd thence to Mrs. Daughety's and eat dinner in the Towel's Valley thence to Mr. Hoskins. Here encamped for Sabbath and 23rd in the bend of the creek in full view of Cumberlin Mountain. Thence past Ealy's Store in Knox Co. Ky and to Cumberlin Gap. Here eat dinner at Dickenson's Thence to the log mountains. Camped at them in a store.

25th thence to Cumberlin River 3 miles from it and eat dinner. Thence through Mersburg (Now Middlesboro) 6 mile west there camped in a beautiful water scarce.

26th Thence through Barbrasville west 8 miles and eat dinner in desert place well calculated make people homesick. Thence to Lorrel Co Ky to and old horse mile an there camped.

27th thence 3 miles through London 3 miles west and eat dinner at a smith shop and store. Thence west. Heard some rain that night.. Nothing hurt.

28th thence 5 miles to big rock castle River in Rock Castle Co. Ky to Mrs. Hackney's and eat dinner. Thence through Mt Vernon on mile and a half east and camped in a swamp where we had to lay down fence rails to put beds on. Traveled until 8 o'clock to get any place to get water.

29th thence 11 miles to the crab orchard and eat dinner. Here we struck the turnpike to Lincoln Co Ky.

Thence through the walnut flat west some 5 mile and here camped over Sabbath in one mile of Stanford in a nice green lot. A wet day the 30th Sabbath.

October 1 1860 thence through Stanford 12 miles through Danville, a beautiful town in Boilan Co. Ky thence 5 miles and eat dinner. Thence into mercer Co Ky 5 miles to Haredsburg. Thence 4 miles and camped upon the narrow bank of the pike. Buggies running all night thick by the side of clever folks.

2nd thence Edwards thence Salvicy. Here the annual fare going on. Thence 5 miles to Anderson Ky Ripleyville. 3 miles to Laranceburg. One mile and eat dinner. Thence rough and ready thence 7 mile into Franklin Co and camped near an old brickyard.

3rd thence through Andersonville. Thence Shelby Co Clayville. Thence Shelbyville 3 mile and eat dinner at a toll gate. Thence Simosnville. Thence Boston Jefferson Co and camped at Mr. Nelson's.
4th Thence Middleton thence through Louisville across the Ohio into New Albina (New Albany). Floid Co Indiana thence Moreesburg and camped.
5th thence Soleno, thence Greenville. Thence Harrison CO to a beautiful swamp grove and eat dinner.
Thence Palming thence Fredricksburg, thence Blue River Washington Co, 2 mile and camped.
6th thence Hartinsburg, thence Orange Co. thence Chambersburg thence 2 mile and eat dinner. Thence 5 miles and camped over Sabbath. 7th beautiful place. 8th thence Lost River down it mile and eat dinner. Thence Maron Co. 8 miles and camped (tonight our dog was stoled)
9th thence East fork of White River foryed (Forded?) thence Mt Pleasant thence Davis Co. 3 mile and eat dinner near an old pond. Thence Knox Co Washington. Thence west fork of White River forged. 8 mile and eat dinner. Thence Vinvannes and cross the Wabash River into Ill and camped near the bank near the river.
11th thence Lawrence Co. Ill. thence Laranceville some mile and eat dinner, thence through Prairiation west some miles and camped in a prairie and bought firewood tonight.
12 thence Richland Co. through Olney west of it and eat dinner. Thence Nobel west 4 miles and camped at old MR. Barkers.
Signed
Margaret J. Wolford."

Lived in the same house as her mother in Texas Co. until Martha died; then moved to the home of her niece Jennie Wolford Hughes, Marion Ill and died there. She never married.

+ 284. iv **William Owen WOLFORD** b. 17 Dec 1838.

285. v **Martha E. WOLFORD**, b. 22 May 1841 in Sullivan Co., TN, d. 8 Jun 1909 in Texas Co. Missouri.

89. **Emma RHEA**, (20.Joseph^3, 4.Jannette^2, 1.John^1) b. 26 Feb 1811 in Sullivan Co., TN, d. 11 Jun 1887 in Sullivan Co., TN?. She married **Pharoh RILEY**, b. ABT 1810 in TN?.
   Children:

   286. i   **Ann Myers RILEY**, b. 1 Jul 1837 in Bluff City, Sullivan Co., TN, d. 1879 in Sullivan Co., TN?. Left 5 children when she died (W. L.. Rhea manuscript - Genealogy of Rhea Family, 1895).

92. **Margaret RHEA**, (20.Joseph^3, 4.Jannette^2, 1.John^1) b. 9 Dec 1818 in Sullivan Co., TN, d. 1 Mar 1895 in Sullivan Co., TN. She married **Joseph HODGE**, b. ABT 1820 in TN?.
   Children:

   287. i   **Robert Bruce HODGE**, b. ABT 1850 in Sullivan Co., TN, d. in Pulaski TN?. Preaching at Brick Church, Pulaski TN - 1895 (WL Rhea).

   288. ii   **J. Frank HODGE**, b. ABT 1852 in Sullivan Co., TN.

   289. iii **Anderson HODGE**, b. ABT 1854 in Sullivan Co., TN.

   290. iv   **Rhea HODGE**, b. ABT 1856 in Sullivan Co., TN.

   291. v   **Ellen HODGE**, b. ABT 1858 in Sullivan Co., TN.

   292. vi   **Laura HODGE**, b. ABT 1860 in Sullivan Co., TN. She married **C. W. BELL**, b. ABT 1860 in TN?.

94. **Eleanor Fairman 'Ellen' RHEA**, (20.Joseph^3, 4.Jannette^2, 1.John^1) b. 14 Oct 1828 in Sullivan Co., TN, d. in Bluff City TN?. She married **John MILLARD**, married 20 Nov 1851 in Sullivan Co., TN, b. 1829 in Sullivan Co., TN. Had 8 children, 3 died in infancy. (W.L.Rhea-1895)

1870 Federal census shows John and Ellen living in Sullivan Co. with four children and Elizabeth Rhea 46. His real estate valued at $2000 and personal property $850.
   Children:

293. i **Marshall Wallace MILLARD**, b. 20 Jan 1853 in Sullivan Co., TN. 1877 Graduated from King College, Bristol TN and from Union Theological Seminary in 1880. Spent four years in Texas preaching, 10 years in Tennessee.

Had 7 children. Lived in Bethsada, Williamson Co. TN (W.L.Rhea-1895). He married **Ellen C. NORTON**, married 1879 in Prince Edward Co. VA, b. ABT 1855 in VA?.

+ 294. ii **Joseph Rhea MILLARD** b. 24 Jan 1856.

295. iii **Jennet Rhea MILLARD**, b. 27 Jun 1862 in Sullivan Co., TN. She married **George L. F. FLEENOR**, married 1880 in Sullivan Co., TN?, b. ABT 1860 in Sullivan Co., TN. 1895 lived Island Mills TN. Had one daughter age 11 in 1895. (W. L. Rhea - 1895).

296. iv **Nancy Margaret MILLARD**, b. 26 Jul 1866 in Sullivan Co., TN.

297. v **James Abia MILLARD**, b. 5 May 1871 in Sullivan Co., TN.

95. **Walter Preston RHEA**, (20.Joseph[3], 4.Jannette[2], 1.John[1]) b. 12 Mar 1831 in Sullivan Co., TN, d. 9 Nov 1897 in Salem Fulton Co., AR, buried in Salem Cemetery, Salem, Fulton Co. AR. Walter was born in Sullivan Co. TN the tenth child in the family. He was educated in the common schools of his native state and at Maryville College. Graduation from Maryville College end his formal schooling but he was a natural student and continued to study and learn until the day of his death.

1855 he was married to Miss Sarah Piles who was born in TN. They became the parents of 10 children.

He served the C. S. A. under Col. Fulkerson as 1st Lt. in Co. F 63rd TN Infantry. Served 3 years in the Civil War under General Longstreet.

1866 he brought his family to Arkansas and soon settled in Salem. The potentials were impressive to him.

1869 Mr. Rhea bought the old Pow Cochran home which is located an eighth of a mile southeast of Salem Cemetery. This was the Rhea family home for many years and might have remained the family home if he had not become afflicted with asthma and felt the need for a home at a higher elevation. He lived his last days on the hill east and south of town.

1866 he had come to Fulton County at an opportune time.. The county was short of men with qualifications which would enable them to take care of County business. He ran for the office of County Clerk in 1874, was elected and served for 10 years. The country deed records are full of documents with his signature. He had been a Democrat in his political views and always interested in the cause of education. He and his family were members of the Presbyterian church.

1870 Federal census shows the family enumerated in Franklin, Fulton Co., Arkansas;
  Rhea, W P (Edmund had been written and then written over), 40, Merchant, real property $950, personal property $1413, b. TN.
  " Sarah, 35, Housekeeper, b. TN
  " Sarah, 13, b. TN
  " Charles 11, b. TN
  " Joseph 9, b. TN.
  " Lillie 5, b. TN.
  " Edmund, 3, born Ark (Thee first child b. in AR)
  Pile, G. C., 28, clerk, b. TN. (Sarah's brother)
The birthplaces of the children in the census would indicate the family came to Arkansas between 1865 and 1867.

He engaged in the mercantile business with two partners, R. A. Robbins and Arch Northcutt. He invested in the county. He became the owner of 600 acres of fertile river bottom land and a large amount of valuable town property. Because of ill health, he retired from active management of his business and farming in 1882. Several of his children and his son-in-law Rufus Robbins were active in the mercantile business in Salem for many years. (From 'Biographical and Historical Memoirs of Northeast Arkansas', Goodspeed Publishing, Chicago, Nashville, 1889.)

1994 Lula Burton had 2 post cards from Joseph Rhea Wolford calling him Jannet Rhea Wolford's brother. She also had a letter from W. Rhea to Margaret and Martha Wolford after Joseph Rhea's death in 1896 (Joseph and Walter were 1st cousins). He was in Washington

Co. AR each time. In 1867 he had removed to Salem AR. He had 6 boys and 2 girls. He married **Sarah Jane PYLE**, married 1858, b. 30 Sep 1836 in Sullivan Co., TN, d. 21 Oct 1915 in Salem Fulton Co., AR. George and Priscilla Snodgrass Pyle had a daughter of this name born about the the same time. No confirmation yet if she is the same person as the wife of Walter Rhea.

    Children:

+ 298.   i   **Laura Ella RHEA** b. 1856.

  299.   ii   **David Charles RHEA**, b. 1858 in TN?. He married **Miss RIPTOE**, b. ABT 1858 in TN?.

+ 300.   iii   **Joseph Matthew RHEA** b. 1862.

+ 301.   iv   **Margaret Lillian RHEA** b. 1862.

  302.   v   **Elizabeth Eleanor RHEA**, b. 1 Jun 1865 in ARK. She apprears in the 1900 census living with her uncle Joseph Hodge, husband of Margaret Rhea, in Sullivan Co. TN. She married **E. N. KEIGER**, b. ABT 1868 in TN?.

  303.   vi   **Edmond George RHEA**, b. ABT 1866 in TN?. Did not marry.

+ 304.   vii   **Oscar Lee RHEA** b. 3 Jun 1876.

  305.   viii   **Kitty RHEA**, b. ABT 1877 in TN?. Died young.

+ 306.   ix   **Holmes Gans RHEA** b. 1878.

96. **Edmund RHEA**, (20.Joseph[3], 4.Jannette[2], 1.John[1]) b. 9 Feb 1834 in Sullivan Co., TN, d. in Blythville, AR. 1860 was in Arkansas. 1870 Arkansas census birth dates of children would indicate he lived in Missouri from 1854 to 1860 before he came to Arkansas.

Married 3 times. Represented his county in the Ark. legislature for 2 terms.

1870 Federal census shows an E. D. Rhea in Fulton Co., AR. He is enumerated in the same country as Walter Preston Rhea - presumably his brother.

Rhea, E. D., 36, farmer, value of real property $1000, personal property $500, b. TN.
" Helana, 38, Housekeeper, b. TN.
" James, 16, farmer, b. MO.
" Mary, 10, b. MO.
" Charles, 10, b. MO.

1880 Federal census shows an E. D. Rhea as a physician now in Chickasawba Township of Mississippi Co., ARK. There are 3 doctors enumerated on this page of the census.
Rhea, E. D. 45, M. D., b. TN to parents from TN and MD.
-- Sarah E., 25, wife, keeping house, b. AR to parents from MO and OH.
-- Wisper (?), 5/12, son, b. AR. (June 1 census date)

1910 Federal census shows him with another wife, in Blythville, Chickasawba Township of Mississippi Co., ARK.
Rhea, Edmund D., head, Feb 1836, 64, married 15 years, b. TN to parents from TN and MD, physician.
-- Fannie, wife, July 1846, 54, married 15 years, 0 children, 0 living, b. TN to parents from SC.
-- Maggie W., daughter, 17, Sept 1882, 17, b. AR to parents from TN and TN, school teacher. He married (1) **Helana wife of Edmund RHEA**. He married (2) **Sarah E. wife of Edmund RHEA**, b. 1857 in AR, d. ABT 1882. 1882 she gave birth to Margaret. She may have died soon thereafter. By 1885 Edmund Rhea had married his third wife.

Children by Helana wife of Edmund RHEA:

307.   i   **James RHEA**, b. 1854 in MO.

308.   ii   **Mary RHEA**, b. 1860 in MO.

309.   iii **Charles RHEA**, b. 1860 in MO.
             Children by Sarah E. wife of Edmund RHEA:

310.   iv **Margaret 'Maggie' RHEA**, b. 1 Jul 1882 in Mississippi Co., AR.

97. **Lucretia Jane RHEA**, (21.Robert[3], 4.Jannette[2], 1.John[1]) b. 1828 in Sullivan Co., TN. She married **James Gray RIVERS**, b. ABT 1810 in Boone Co. NC. Subj: Re: Rivers Rhea
Date: 10/13/2004 9:40:15 AM Eastern Daylight Time
From: "Lona" <ldills2653@@comcast.net>

To: <DrEdFoley@@aol.com>
Sent from the Internet (Details)

All my data on the family has come from someone else or online
genealogy sites but seems to be accurate as far as I can tell. Dr.
James Rivers is in the Sullivan Co., TN census of 1840 with his
parents and siblings. I believe James Rivers was born around 1827
(probably in Virginia where the family lived for several years) and
came to Sullivan Co., TN with his parents just before the 1840
census. I think he must surely have still been living with his parents
in the 1850 census but not real sure and then by 1860 he is married
and living in Carter Co., TN where he shows up in the 1860 census
with his wife. I assume they were in Watauga Co., NC by 1870 and
know he was there in the census of 1880. The parents for James
Rivers are Samuel Rivers and Rebecca Grey who married in
Southampton Co., VA where a marriage license is recorded. This is
also verified by a record that was printed in "A History of Watauga
County, North Carolina--Sketches of Prominent Families, Part 7 by
John Preston Arthur", that states, "Dr. James Grey Rivers was a son
of Samuel and Rebecca Rivers, who were Virginians by birth. Dr.
James Rivers married Miss Lucretia Jane Rhea." So all my data was
verified with this information. It is beyond this Samuel Rivers that I
have my road block. I had always thought that Samuel was of the
Virginia branch of Rivers' but this book information also mentioned
the heavy silver ladle and the name Horace Rivers. Do you know
who this Dr. and Mrs. Murray of North Carolina might be? Would
she be the daughter of James and Lucretia Jane Rivers? I have never
come across a Horace Rivers and wonder about this book data. All
the Horace Rivers' came into South Carolina and settled. If our James
Rivers descends from this South Carolina branch of Rivers' I guess
Samuel could have just gone to Southampton Co. Va and there met
and married Rebecca Grey. This is what I need to prove. But if you
have no Rivers data I don't guess either of us will solve this road
block but thanks for getting back to me. I love doing genealogy but it
really can be very addictive. Have a great day. Lona.

Children:

311.   i   **Robert RIVERS**, b. ABT 1840 in NC?. Editor of
           the Wautuga Democrat, Boone Co., NC.

312.   ii **James RIVERS Jr.**, b. ABT 1842.

313.   iii **Addie RIVERS**, b. ABT 1844.

+ 314. iv **Nannie Robert RIVERS** b. ABT 1846.

98. **John 'Dr.' Preston RHEA Sr.**, (21.Robert^3, 4.Jannette^2, 1.John^1) b. 20 Jul 1829 in Clarke Co. WV, d. 13 Mar 1896 in Sullivan Co., TN, buried in Pleasant Grove Cemetery A country doctor. Sergeant in Reserve Corps during the War. Was the First Master of the Masonic Lodge at Zollicoffer (Bluff City).

1870 census shows his property valued at $2100 - no real estate. Appears on list of doctors in Sullivan Co.; shows he was certified in Dec. 2

1889 which may have been the first year of county certification.

His family bible was sold at auction Mar. 1989 and bought by Jane Rhea Hyder Clayton, 1845 S. Palmetto Av, S. Daytona, FL 32019. 904-767-5725. He married **Matilda Ann LONGACRE**, married 10 Aug 1857, b. 19 Feb 1834 in Sullivan Co., TN, d. 5 Mar 1922 in Bluff City, Sullivan Co., TN, buried in Pleasant Grove Cemetery Her death appears in the Sullivan Co. death records; shows father Joseph Longacre and mother 'Ann'(?).

1922 obituary - Funeral services for Mrs. Matilda Longacre Rhea who died at her home near Bluff City Wed., were conducted at Pleasant Grove. Mrs. Rhea belonged to one of the oldest families of Sullivan County. Her ancestors came to this section from Ireland with the early pioneers. She was born in 1834 and united with the Presbyterian Church at Pleasant Grove while a young girl. In 1858 she married Dr. John Preston Rhea, in which union ten children were born, five of whom are still living. Her husband died 26 years ago.

Besides her 5 children she is survived by 17 grandchildren and 6 great grandchildren. She also leaves one brother J. E. Longacre of California and one sister, Mrs Amanda Holbert of Missouri.
Children:

315. i **Mary Rebecca RHEA**, b. 10 May 1858 in Wantauga Co., NC, d. 1 Mar 1902 in Sullivan Co., TN, buried in Pleasant Grove Cem. 1880 Soundex shows she was born in NC. Rhea family bible show only she and sister Nancy were born in Watauga Co. NC.

1900 Federal census shows the family enumerated in Civil District 20, Sullivan Co., TN.

Burkey Elbert J. head, Oct. 1852, 47, married 17 years, b. TN to TN parents, merchant.

-- Mary, wife, Mary 1858, 42, married 17 years, 1 child, 1 living (the ones look like 7's) b. TN.

-- Mary M., daughter, Feb 1889, 11, single, b. TN. (in the same household)

Rhea, John P., B in Law, Feb 1892, 28, single, b. TN, School teacher.

Goodman, Sarah, boarder, Dec 1879, 20, single, b. TN, servant. She married **Elbert J. BURKEY**, married 25 Oct 1882, b. ABT 1860 in Sullivan Co., TN?.

316. ii **Nancy Melissa RHEA**, b. 8 Jan 1860 in Wantauga Co., NC, d. 4 Mar 1864.

317. iii **Matthew Belmont RHEA**, b. 20 Jan 1862 in Bluff City, Sullivan Co., TN, d. 17 May 1896 in Sullivan Co., TN?, buried in Pleasant Grove Cem. Sullivan Co. TN. Probably named for his cousin Matthew Rhea VI who died heroically in battle at Belmont, Mississippi a few months before this Matthew's birth. He married **Sallie RHEA**, b. ABT 1862.

318. iv **Robert Orestes RHEA**, b. 3 May 1864 in Bluff City, Sullivan Co., TN, d. 28 Dec 1938 in Bristol, Sullivan Co., TN, buried in Weaver Cem., Weaver Pike, Sullivan Co. TN. 1900 Federal census shows Robert's household included 4 children and his mother, sister Maggie and Nora and bother John .

1910 mother Matilda and Nora enumerated next door.

He, Barsha and children appears in a photo on page 65 of 'Sullivan Co. Pictorial History, 1999.

1920 census Sullivan Co. 3rd Civil District. #32 he, Margaret, 4 children. Farmer.

1938 obituary - Following a brief service at the home of 400 Holborn street this morning, funeral services will be held at 11:00 at the Weavers church for Robert Rhea, 74, who died last night after an illness of two years. Mr. Rhea was the son of Dr. J. P. Rhea and Mrs. Matilda Longacre Rhea, of Bluff City and had been a life long member of the Presbyterian church at Weavers. He came to Bristol 10 years ago. Surviving are his widow, Mrs. Margaret Barsha Rhea and two sons and three daughters. (Dec. 28, 1938). He married **Barsheba Margaret 'Maggie' GAMMON**, married 1 Aug 1888, b. 7 Oct 1867 in Sullivan Co., TN, d. 14 Nov 1945 in Sullivan Co., TN?, buried in Weaver Cem., Weaver Pike, Sullivan Co. TN. Her tombstone reads 'Wife of Robert O. Rhea'.

Census shows both her parents were born TN. 1940 city directory shows her as widow of Robert O. living at 400 Holburn in Bristol TN. Her name appears in the family bible of George and Barsheba Gammon. From this association it is assumed this was their daughter.

Obituary - Mrs. Robert Rhea Dies at Home Here. Death Follows Illness of Nine Years: Was Mother of Karl Rhea. Mrs. Margaret Barsha Gammon Rhea, mother of Karl O. Rhea, adjutant of the Hackler-Wood Post of the American Legion, died at 4:30 o'clock yesterday afternoon at her home at 400 Holborn St. She had been in declining health for the past nine years. Mrs. Rhea, wife of the late Robert O. Rhea, united with the Presbyterian church in childhood and had lived a faithful and devout Christian life. Surviving are five children.

319. v   **Nancy 'Nannie' C. RHEA**, b. 1866 in Sullivan Co., TN.

+ 320. vi   **Nancy Kalla RHEA** b. 10 Oct 1866.

+ 321. vii   **Joseph Addison Longacre 'Dr.' RHEA** b. 23 Mar 1869.

+ 322. viii   **John 'Dr.' Preston RHEA Jr. Jr.** b. 6 Feb 1872.

+ 323. ix   **Margaret 'Maggie' A. RHEA** b. 7 Jun 1874.

+ 324.   x   **Josiah Edward 'Ned' RHEA** b. 10 Jan 1877.

325.   xi   **Norah Matilda RHEA**, b. 2 Oct 1878 in Bluff City, Sullivan Co., TN, d. 28 Feb 1941. 1900 census shows her living with Brother Robert and 1910 shows her still single (31) living next door from Robert with mother Matilda.

1920 census shows her as a public school teacher. Her mother Matilda 'Ray' is enumerated with Nora and her husband George. She married **George Oliver GAMMON**, married 28 Jun 1911, b. 25 Jun 1875 in Blountville, Sullivan Co., TN, d. 30 Jul 1958. His name appears in the family bible of George Gammon (b. 1832).

He also appears in the family bible of John P. and Matilda Longacre Rhea whose daughter he married. There is an entry for George's mother and father in this Rhea bible as well. (Owned by Jane Rhea Hyder Clatyon, Daytona FL.)

1920 Sullivan Co. census shows he, wife Nora and mother in law Matilda in 1st Civil Dist.

1945 he was living in Gardner, FL.

326.   xii   **Matilda I. RHEA**, b. 1879 in Sullivan Co., TN.

102.   **Robert 'Dr.' Campbell RHEA**, (21.Robert[3], 4.Jannette[2], 1.John[1]) b. 19 Apr 1837 in Sullivan Co., TN, d. 3 Nov 1911 in Johnson Co., TN. 'The McQueen Family of Johnson County, Tennessee' by Carl B. Neal written in 1958 contains a collection of interviews but has no documentation of facts. "Margaret Caroline McQueen, born 5-10-1846, died 10-16-1930, married Dr. Robert Campbell Rhea shortly after the Civil War, about 1867. He was born 4-19-1837 and died 11-3-1911. There are 4 branches of the Rhea family, the Preston Rheas, the Muddy Creek Rheas, the Snapp Rheas and the Breden Rheas. Dr. Robert C. belonged to the Preston Rhea branch. Several Rheas are listed as having been in what is now Sullivan Co. TN prior to 1785. One John Rhea, son of Joseph Rhea a Presbyterian minister was later a member of Congress. A Robert Campbell is reported to have lived in NE Tenn. prior to 1785.

Dr. Rhea was a medical student at the time he was married. He practiced at Shouns later, all his life. Several years after the Civil War he restored the old McQueen home and he and his family lived there until he died and the home has been occupied by him and his descendants ever since it was restored. He also appears in Hamilton Co. TN in East TN Civil War records in the Rescue Corps."

This and other family details passed along in 1998 from Lessa McQueen Alkire, lalkire@@brightok.net, http://www.familytreemaker.com/users/a/l/k/Lessa-M-Alkire. He married **Margaret Caroline MCQUEEN**, b. 10 May 1846 in Johnson Co., TN, d. 16 Oct 1930 in Johnson Co., TN.
Children:

+ 327.   i   **Samuel Robert RHEA** b. 22 Mar 1868.

+ 328.   ii   **Mary Elizabeth RHEA** b. 21 Nov 1869.

+ 329.   iii **Nancy Martitia 'Titia' RHEA** b. 1870.

  330.   iv   **Margaret Belle RHEA**, b. 1873 in Sullivan Co., TN, d. 25 Jul 1941 in Shouns, Johnson Co., TN, buried in Shouns Cem., Johnson Co., TN. Obituary - Shouns TN - July 21 - Miss Margaret Rhea, daughter of the late Dr. and Mrs. G. (sic) C. Rhea of Shouns, died at her home at 10pm Saturday. Death was attributed to a heart ailment.

  331.   v   **Francis Preston RHEA**, b. ABT 1875 in TN. Unmarried. Died in an auto wreck.

  332.   vi   **John Wayne RHEA**, b. ABT 1877 in TN. Died young.

  333.   vii **Charles Caldwell RHEA**, b. ABT 1879 in TN.

  334.   viii **Eleanor Campbell RHEA**, b. 1883 in TN. She was an Alumna of Salem College and was teaching school in Mountain City TN when she married Clayton. 1941 they were living in Mountain City, TN. She married **William Elliott Clayton WRIGHT**, married 11 Jun 1913, b. 1879 in Washington Co., VA, d. 1958 in Johnson Co., TN. Born near Damascus VA.

He came to Johnson Co. TN about 1898 and engaged in merchandising, originally with his brother and nephews. Acquired the general store Silver Lake Mercantile Co. When Highway 91 was relocated, he moved the store in 1935 to the relocated road in a rock building he had built. Also bought land in Ackerson Creek which he farmed. He also engaged in the lumber business. Attended Emory and Henry College.

1930 Federal census shows the family enumerated in District 1, Johnson Co., TN, living on Laurel Road. Their names in the federal index are misspelled making locating them difficult. Enumeration district No 46-1, sheet No. 1 A 147.
   Wright William C, head, owns home, has radio, 51, married at 35, b. VA to VA parents, Retail merchant, dry goods.
   -- Elenor (sic) C., wife-h, 44, married at 27, b. TN to parents from VA and TN.
   -- Charles McQu-- (smudged), son, 13, single, b. TN.

335.   ix   **Buelah Carolyn RHEA**, b. 1890 in TN. She lived in the old McQueen-Rhea home in Shouns. She married **Clyde HODGE**, b. ABT 1890. He worked as a journalist in Johnson City, TN.

336.   x   **Edwin Bruce RHEA**, b. 1904 in TN, d. 1946.

105.   **Robert Preston FICKLE**, (22.Margaret³, 4.Jannette², 1.John¹) b. 1822 in Washington Co., VA?, d. 23 Nov 1895 in Sullivan Co., TN, buried in Blountville Cemetery, Sullivan Co., TN. A genealogy of the Fickle family was written and is in the family files at the Blountville TN library. It contains many erroneous references and has omitted many facts, primarily related to the conviction of Abram Fickle for theft. However, other facts which pertain to more direct knowledge of the author are of interest and are reported here.

1822 he was born, the only son of Abram Fickle and Margaret Rhea Fickle. "His name was chosen with great concern. Preston was the family name of Margaret's illustrious grandfather, James P. Preston, the 15th Governor of Virginia, (This was actually not a near relative

- EFF) serving one term 1815-1819. (This was actually James Patton Preston son of Wm. Preston of the Smithfield Prestons whose relationship to the Walnut Grove Prestons has not yet been established. There are however associated.) She chose Robert because of her brother Robert Preston. The name "Preston" would be handed on down for three more generations of Fickles. A few years after Abram's death (he is buried at Reuben's Place, now the Bowman property near Greendale Virginia) Margaret and her young son Robert left Washington County, Virginia and resided in Sullivan County, Tennessee". At the age 28 Robert married Mary Elizabeth Chamberlain, who was born September 27, 1831.

1850 their marriage took place on October 30. Robert and Mary would have nine children born to them during their 44 year marriage. Robert was employed in the clerical department of the Blountville Courthouse. He was for 6 years Chairman of the Chancery Court. He was to survive the shelling of the courthouse during the Civil War. However, many rare documents and records were lost when the courthouse burned. As part of his duties, Robert was authorized to make subsistence payments to released prisoners of the county. He was a Lt. in the reserve Corps for the C. S. A."

He was very active in the masonry. He held the office of Post Master in the Blountville lodge of 8 years. (One may note the irony of this when reading about his father's imprisonment for theft from the post - EFF). At his funeral he was buried with Masonic honors and 7 lodges were represented in the procession. In that period of time only a few lodges were in existence, therefore this indicates that many people were present from all parts of the country.

1888 Dec. 29 he is reported as suffering from asthma. (Bristol Courier).

At the time of his death on November 23, 1895, he was the Blountville Postmaster. Both he and his wife, Mary Elizabeth are buried in the Blountville Cemetery. He was a man of great popularity and was considered as one of Sullivan County's best citizens. Records show Robert Fickle was also a slave owner.

He was a "Man of good mind and retentive of general information on all topics of the day. Could tell what he knew and loved to tell it. A great historian of both ancient and modern history. (W. L. Rhea - 1895)

From notes by Jacquie Dishner 1997, 422 Hwy, 75, Blountville, TN 37617, as well as from 'Families and History of Sullivan Co., TN 1779-1992' Published 1992 and references to him by Oliver Taylor in his book 'Historic Sullivan', Bristol Press, 1909. He married **Mary Elizabeth CHAMBERLAIN**, married 30 Oct 1850, b. 27 Sep 1831 in Washington Co., TN, d. 1894 in Sullivan Co., TN?. Daughter of the widow who married Col. Abram McLellan.

Children:

+ 337.   i   **Oscar FICKLE** b. 27 Oct 1852.

  338.   ii   **John Preston FICKLE**, b. 2 May 1853 in TN, d. 21 Mar 1862 in TN.

+ 339.   iii   **Lincoln Rhea FICKLE** b. 23 Sep 1855.

+ 340.   iv   **Samuel Bruce FICKLE** b. 18 Oct 1857.

+ 341.   v   **Margaret Laura FICKLE** b. 24 Jan 1860.

  342.   vi   **Mary Francis FICKLE**, b. 1 Oct 1862 in TN, d. 15 Aug 1863 in TN.

+ 343.   vii   **Jane 'Jennie' Preston FICKLE** b. 13 Oct 1864.

  344.   viii   **Robert 'Lee' FICKLE**, b. 3 May 1867 in Sullivan Co., TN. Never married.

106. **Margaret Jane RHEA**, (23.Matthew[3], 4.Jannette[2], 1.John[1]) b. 25 Jan 1820 in Sullivan Co., TN, d. 17 May 1880 in Sullivan Co., TN, buried in Pleasant Grove Cem. Sullivan Co. TN. When her husband Col. Long died, Margaret married her cousin James D. Rhea. Margaret's sister Elizabeth married James D.'s brother John Rhea. She married (1) **Nicholas M. 'Col.' LONG**, married 21 Jul 1848 in Fayette Co., TN, b. ABT 1820 in TN?. He was a civil engineer and soldier in the Seminole War. Later an attorney. She married (2) **James Dysart RHEA**, married 28 Oct 1858, b. 4 Jul 1802 in Sullivan Co., TN, d. 29 Nov 1886 in Bluff City, Sullivan Co., TN, buried in Pleasant Grove Cem. Born on his father William's farm, now owned by the Earharts (2005). Lived to be an old man. Chose profession of law and spent his last years farming. Was an elder in Presb. Church. After selling his farm to John Earhart he moved to Bluff city.

Lived in the Stonehouse on the north side of the river with one of his married daughters.

1850 census shows him with property worth $10,000.
Children by Nicholas M. 'Col.' LONG:

+ 345.   i   **Nicholas M. LONG Jr.** b. 27 Jul 1849.
Children by James Dysart RHEA:

  346.   ii   **Matthew Belmont RHEA**, b. 22 Feb 1863 in Sullivan Co., TN, d. 27 May 1863 in Sullivan Co., TN?, buried in Pleasant Grove Cem. Probably named for his uncle Matthew Rhea who was killed in the Civil War at Mississippi just 15 months before this Matthew's birth.

107. **Elizabeth Looney RHEA**, (23.Matthew[3], 4.Jannette[2], 1.John[1]) b. 4 Mar 1822 in Maury Co. TN, d. 8 Jun 1892 in Somerville, Fayette Co., TN. One source shows her as born in Maury Co. TN. She and John were first cousins once removed. She was the daughter of John's first cousin Matthew Rhea. She remained in Jonesboro until the Civil War was ended and then with her children ages 7 to 23 years, moved to Fayette Co. TN. Her elder son William was already there. Her parents had gone to Fayette Co. in 1834.

In her later years she made her home with son William. She married **John RHEA**, married 22 Dec 1840 in Fayette Co., TN, b. 31 May 1810 in Sullivan Co., TN, d. 24 Aug 1862 in Jonesboro, Washington Co., TN. 1847 he was a member of the Paperville Presbyterian Church. He and Elizabeth were dismissed from the church on Apr. 15, 1851 to join the Jonesboro church.

1850 Federal census for TN shows him as farmer. In 1850 the family moved to Jonesboro TN.

He died in the Civil War at age 50. (Another source notes d. March 24, 1862.) The family is mentioned in Notable Southern Families., Z. Armstrong 1922.
Children:

  347.   i   **Mary Elizabeth RHEA**, b. 1840 in Sullivan Co., TN, d. 27 Nov 1876. Never married.

348.   ii   **William Abram RHEA**, b. 30 May 1844 in Jonesboro, Washington Co., TN, d. 24 Mar 1921 in Memphis, Shelby Co., TN, buried in Somerville City Cemetery, Somerville TN. He and Mollie bought the Whitfield property, known as Bellview and lived there until Mollie's death. For many years he served as county surveyor. He bought land in Somerville on South Main St. which he later sold to the County Board of education for a girls dormitory for public schools. Later he married again and lived in Memphis. Died at his home in Memphis 15 years after 2nd marriage.

Served the C.S.A. in the war.

Notable Southern Families., Z. Armstrong 1922 incorrectly notes his death in 1869. He married (1) **Mary 'Mollie' Rhea IRVIN**, married 11 Feb 1869 in Dancyville, Haywood Co., TN, b. 6 Jan 1846 in TN?, d. 19 Dec 1896 in Somerville, Fayette Co., TN. Had 7 children with William A. Rhea. Died at her home in Somerville. He married (2) **Louise Smith EDMONDSON**, married 1901, b. 1857 in VA, (daughter of William Campbell EDMONDSON and Susan Elizabeth RHEA) d. 1934 in Memphis, Shelby Co., TN, buried in Somerville City Cemetery, Somerville TN. Upon her death, left many things to her nephew Walter Rhea. Some sterling silver and an old photo of 'Aunt Lulu' and William in their Memphis yard was in the possession of Anne Rhea Bruce 2002.

+ 349.   iii   **Matthew Robert RHEA** b. 5 Jul 1846.

+ 350.   iv   **James Samuel RHEA** b. 11 Feb 1849.

351.   v   **Sarah Frances 'Fanny' RHEA**, b. 6 Sep 1853 in Jonesboro, Washington Co., TN, d. 1924 in Memphis, Shelby Co., TN. She married **Henry Harrison LEWIS**, married 1875, b. ABT 1850 in TN?. Had 5 children.

352.   vi   **John Rufus Wells RHEA Jr.**, b. 30 Sep 1855 in Jonesboro, Washington Co., TN, d. 9 Mar 1917.

After the death of his first wife, he married her sister. He married (1) **Rebecca Jane 'Tillie' LOCKETT**, b. 22 Jul 1859 in TN?, d. 31 Dec 1901. He married (2) **Margaret Elnor LOCKETT**, married 11 Mar 1903 in Somerville, Fayette Co., TN, b. 13 Nov 1863, d. 5 May 1945. The 'Family Record of F. H. Lockett (her father) in the John Rufus Wells Rhea Bible states that a girl was born to John and Margaret.

353. vii **Walter RHEA**, b. 1858 in Sullivan Co., TN, d. 11 Sep 1876.

354. viii **Lucinda Harriet RHEA**, b. 1858 in Sullivan Co., TN, d. 10 Jan 1884. Her gravestone is reported to read Lucy R. Rhea.

109. **John William RHEA**, (23.Matthew^3, 4.Jannette^2, 1.John^1) b. 1828 in Sullivan Co., TN, d. 1873 in Memphis, Shelby Co., TN. A John William, son of Mathew and Mary appears in 1850 census in Fayette Co. TN.

1873 died of yellow fever at his home in Memphis. He married **Stalia G. PORTER**, married 12 Apr 1860, b. ABT 1828 in TN?, d. 1929.

Children:

355. i **Annie RHEA**, b. ABT 1861 in TN?.

356. ii **William RHEA**, b. ABT 1863 in Memphis TN?.

+ 357. iii **Pearl RHEA** b. ABT 1865.

358. iv **Lillian RHEA**, b. ABT 1967 in TN?.

110. **Sarah Lucinda RHEA**, (23.Matthew^3, 4.Jannette^2, 1.John^1) b. 28 Feb 1828 in Maury Co. TN, d. 25 Aug 1892. She married **S. Alexander MILLER**, married 28 Aug 1849, b. 1 Oct 1823, d. 28 Jan 1903.

Children:

359. i **Mary Jane MILLER**, b. 6 Mar 1846, d. 31 Dec 1927.

+ 360. ii **S. A. MILLER Jr.** b. 24 Jan 1850.

111. **Abram Looney RHEA**, (23.Matthew^3, 4.Jannette^2, 1.John^1) b. 25 Feb 1830 in Maury Co. TN, d. 9 Sep 1912 in Maury Co. TN. 1853 graduated from Memphis Medical College in Memphis in 1853. Student of surgery in Philadelphia PA in that same year.

Private in Co. B 13th TN in C.S.A. infantry under Col. Vaughn. After fighting at Shiloh for 2 days was made surgeon in which place he served till close of the war.

Mace Gray, in transcription of William Rhea's genealogy of the Rhea family, notes he died in Maury Co. TN although the family lived in Whiteville, Hardeman Co. TN. He married **Emma CROSS**, married 10 Nov 1869, b. 28 Apr 1846 in TN?, d. 7 Dec 1927 in Whiteville, Hardeman Co. TN.
     Children:

   361. i   **Matthew D. RHEA**, b. ABT 1860 in TN?.

   362. ii   **William RHEA**, b. ABT 1862 in TN?.

+ 363. iii   **Jennie Lou RHEA** b. 3 Dec 1874.

+ 364. iv   **Richard Cary RHEA** b. 1877.

   365. v   **Frank Preston RHEA**, b. 14 Oct 1879 in TN?.

   366. vi   **Ellen C. 'Nellie' RHEA**, b. 1881 in TN?. She married **E. L. STEWART**, b. ABT 1881.

+ 367. vii   **Elizabeth 'Lizzie' RHEA** b. 1883.

   368. viii **Ruby F. RHEA**, b. 14 Jan 1889 in TN?, d. 18 Jan 1914. She married **Charles DUNCAN**, b. 9 Nov 1887, d. 6 Feb 1955.

116. **Walter Preston RHEA**, (23.Matthew^3, 4.Jannette^2, 1.John^1) b. 28 Jul 1841 in Sullivan Co., TN, d. 30 Nov 1880. Too young to join at the beginning of the war, in 1863 he raised a cavalry company and was mustered into the 14th TN Co A. Later, Captain of 4th Tenn Cavalry.

1880 he died leaving Jennie with a young family; his youngest son was only one year old. He married **Jane 'Jennie' Bowen**

EDMONDSON, married 29 Jun 1870, b. 1 Oct 1852 in VA, (daughter of William Campbell EDMONDSON and Susan Elizabeth RHEA) d. 1 Jul 1919. She and her husband were third cousins once removed.

Children:

+ 369. i   **Hugh Preston RHEA** b. 1 May 1871.

    370. ii   **William Edmondson RHEA**, b. 1 Mar 1873 in TN?, d. 1910 in Cahttanooga TN?.

+ 371. iii   **Susan Brown 'Susie' RHEA** b. 1 Feb 1875.

+ 372. iv   **Mary Looney 'Mamie' RHEA** b. 1877.

+ 373. v   **Walter Preston RHEA Jr.** b. 1879.

117. **Ellen Preston RHEA**, (23.Matthew^3, 4.Jannette^2, 1.John^1) b. 2 Sep 1844 in Sullivan Co., TN, d. in Memphis TN?. DAR #4081. She married **Hudson CARY**, married 1 May 1866, b. ABT 1844 in Marshall Co. MS.

Children:

    374. i   **Miles Fairfax CARY**, b. ABT 1868 in TN.

    375. ii   **Marion CARY**, b. 12 Sep 1869 in TN?, d. 12 Aug 1870.

    376. iii   **Rhea Preston CARY**, b. 1871 in TN. Marriage mentioned in Notable Southern Families, Z. Armstrong 1922. She married **Charles EWING**, b. ABT 1871 in TN?.

+ 377. iv   **Eleanor Marion 'Nellie' CARY** b. 22 Dec 1884.

    378. v   **Hudson Fairfax CARY**, b. ABT 1886 in TN.

118. **Mary Frances Bell 'Fanny' RHEA**, (23.Matthew^3, 4.Jannette^2, 1.John^1) b. 13 Jun 1848 in Sullivan Co., TN, d. 12 Apr 1927 in Somerville, Fayette Co., TN. This family is mentioned in 'Notable Southern Families'. She married **James Taylor RHEA**, married 20 May 1875, b. 17 Jun 1847 in The Elms, Bristol, Sullivan Co, TN, (son of James Dysart RHEA) d. 5 Jul 1914 in Somerville, Fayette Co., TN. James was in the Tennessee Reserve Corps for C.S.A.

during the war. In 1863 he enlisted in Witchers Company of Owen White's battalion on Home Guards C.S.A. and served till the end of the War. He participated in affairs at Hamilton's Ridge, Carters Station, and Russelville in Eastern TN.

1867 he joined the Presbyterian Church

1869-1873 he attended Kings College.

1875 he married his third cousin.

Engaged in farming until 1900.

He was killed at home by his neighbor through a mistake (per Mace Gray).

Obituary - James T. Rhea Victim Accidental Shooting. Brother of Mrs. B. W. Norvell and Mrs. B. G. McDowell of This City. Mrs. B. W. Norvell and Mrs. B. G. McDowell received information this week of the accidental killing of their brother James T. Rhea, a prominent banker of Somerville, TN. He formerly lived in Bristol having been educated at King College. A dispatch from Somerville to Nashville Tennesseean says: James T. Rhea prominent lumberman, president of the Somerville Bank and Trust Company and holder of large farm lands in this county, was accidentally killed in the rear yard of his home at 9 o'clock last night. The fatal shot was fired by J. N. Pulliam whose premises adjoin those of the dead man. Mr. Pulliam, thinking he heard someone around his chicken house went to his rear porch and fired three shots with the intention of frightening away the robber. After firing the shots, and he heard no more noise, Mr. Pulliam thought himself mistaken and returned to his room. He thought no more of the matter until a commotion was started when the body was discovered. The discovery was made by Mrs. Rhea who becoming uneasy when her husband did not return and went into the yard to look for him. As was his custom, he made the rounds of his premises before retiring. One hour had elapsed when his body was found. One of the three shots fired by Mr. Pulliam had taken effect, striking Mr. Rhea on the base of his brain. According to physicians, death was instantaneous.

Mr. Rhea leaves four children; Howard M. Rhea, connected with the bureau of chemistry department of agriculture, Washington D.C., James D. Rhea an attorney of Memphis; Rev. Alfred T. Rhea,

127

Presbyterian minister of Augusta ARK; and Mrs. J. E. Crawford f
Williston, this county.

Children:

379.　i　　**James W. RHEA**, b. 2 Mar 1876 in TN, d. 10 Jul
　　　　　　1876 in TN. Died as an infant.

+ 380.　ii　　**Alfred Long RHEA** b. 5 Dec 1878.

381.　iii　　**Mary Ellen RHEA**, b. 1 Sep 1882 in TN, d. 14 Jan
　　　　　　1949 in Somerville, Fayette Co., TN. She married
　　　　　　John Kerr CRAWFORD Jr., married 1907 in
　　　　　　Somerville, Fayette Co., TN, b. 10 Dec 1877 in
　　　　　　Williston, Fayette Co. TN, d. 7 Aug 1936 in
　　　　　　Somerville, Fayette Co., TN. Family mentioned in
　　　　　　Notable Southern Families, Z. Armstrong 1922.

　　　　　　They lived in Williston, TN.

382.　iv　　**James Dysart RHEA**, b. 12 Nov 1887 in Somerville,
　　　　　　Fayette Co., TN, d. 22 Oct 1931 in Nashville,
　　　　　　Davidson Co., TN. A native of Sommerville, he left
　　　　　　Sommerville to attend law school at Cumberland
　　　　　　University and practiced at Memphis until the
　　　　　　outbreak of trouble with Mexico.

　　　　　　He was a member of the Chickasaw Guards at the
　　　　　　time and was ordered with that unit to the border. He
　　　　　　returned to Memphis with a 2nd Lt.'s commission and
　　　　　　shortly thereafter World War I began. He went to
　　　　　　Fort Oglethorpe and with a captain's commission was
　　　　　　acting major in the 6th Division when it was ordered
　　　　　　to France. The division was abroad 7 months but
　　　　　　Captain Rhea was confined to the hospital with
　　　　　　influenza much of the time and never reached the
　　　　　　front. After the war he was continuously in
　　　　　　Government service.

　　　　　　1917 he married Miss Jennie Hearn. They lived at
　　　　　　3709 Meadowbrook Av. in Nashville. He was a chief
　　　　　　estate tax officer of the Nashville division , United
　　　　　　States Internal Revenue Service for the last 6 years of
　　　　　　his life.

1931 although he had not been in exceptionally good health for 2 years, he was apparently unaware of an impending illness when on Saturday afternoon he took his two sons George Hearn Rhea 10, and Bunn Sumpter Rhea 4, to see the Vanderbilt-Tulane football game. He was very ill Sunday morning and was taken to Barr's Infirmary where he died of pneumonia with complications at age 45. His obituary appeared in the Nashville Tennessean October 30.

At the time of his death he held a commission as a 1st Lt. in the 55th field artillery and was a member of the personal staff of General Robert Travis, commander of all filed artillery units attached to the 30th Division. He married **Jessie Florence HEARN**, b. 16 Sep 1890 in Nashville, Davidson Co., TN, d. 25 Feb 1978 in Nashville, Davidson Co., TN.

383.   v   **Howard Matthew RHEA**, b. 22 Jan 1889 in TN, d. 24 Feb 1958. Worked with the bureau of chemistry department of agriculture, Washington, DC. He married **Wilhelmina Blackman LITTERER**, married 11 Jun 1913, b. 15 Sep 1892, d. 3 Oct 1978.

384.   vi   **Abel RHEA**, b. 22 Jan 1890, d. 5 Jul 1891. Died as an infant.

Fifth Generation

119. **Margaret RHEA**, (24.Susan[4], 5.John[3], 2.Robert[2], 1.John[1]) b. 1823 in Sullivan Co., TN, d. BEF 1855. She was the first wife of Ezra Sheffey. (Second he married her cousin Elizabeth Preston.) Her marriage is mentioned in an 1844 letter from Alexander Preston to his nephew Samuel Preston in Ireland. "Margaret was married last spring to a Mr. Sheffy". Wash. Co., VA Hist. Society. She married **Ezra Nuckolls SHEFFEY**, married 1844, b. 13 Jul 1824 in Wythe Co. VA, d. 13 Feb 1891 in Washington Co., VA, buried in Walnut Grove Cem. Washington Co. VA. He was born in Ivanhoe VA and died at home in Washington Co., VA. He had married at the age of 20 Miss Margaret P. Rhea. They had 4 children.

1855 his first wife died.

After Margaret's death, he married her cousin Elizabeth Preston. Together with his first wife, he had 5 children.

Dr. Sheffy connected himself to the Presbyterian Church at the age of 19 and was Superintendent of a Sunday School for 48 consecutive years. From the age of 19 he was a faithful servant of the church. His time, talents, means, influence and example were consecrated to the promotion of its beast interest. With a conscience void of offense towards God and man, a zeal intelligent and guided by divine truth, he executed the duties of his office.

1880 he and his family are enumerated in the Virginia census in the Goodson District of Washington Co., VA. Three Sheffey families, those of Ezra, and sons Robert and Charles are the households adjacent to Robert F. Preston the patriarch,
Sheffey, E. N., 55, dentist. b. VA, father born VA, mother Bavaria.
Elizabeth V. 45, keeping house
Henry S. 19, son, farmer
Sarah M. 16, daughter
Mauise (?) M. 11, daughter
Anne C. P. 8, daughter,
Hams, David, 48, black, servant
Boyd, Sallie A. 26, white, servant

During his declining years, though at times subjected to extreme suffering, his chamber was the scene of patience and calm resignation rarely exhibited.

The writer remembers Dr. Sheffey a man of decided discretion and prudence. Unassuming and modest, he has given to us and his surviving friends, a striking example of what can be accomplished by an earnest and conscientious member of the church. Being a man of great amiability of disposition, generous to a fault, and exceedingly affectionate, he went faithfully forward as a Christian and let his light shine." (In memorium, written by W.L.C. Copy in vertical files, Washington Co., VA Historical Society.)
Children:

385. i **William SHEFFEY**, b. ABT 1850 in TN?VA?.

386. ii **Elizabeth SHEFFEY**, b. ABT 1852 in TN?VA?.

387. iii **John Preston SHEFFEY**, b. ABT 1854 in TN?VA?.

121. **Susan Elizabeth RHEA**, (24.Susan[4], 5.John[3], 2.Robert[2], 1.John[1]) b. 3 Aug 1828 in Sullivan Co., TN, d. 13 Apr 1860. She married **William Campbell EDMONDSON**, married 3 Aug 1848 in Marion, Smythe Co., VA, b. 28 May 1816 in Abingdon, Washington Co. VA, d. 15 Jul 1883 in Washington Co., VA, buried in Glade Springs Cem. Washington Co. VA. 1864 April 16, he enlisted as a private in the 6th Battalion of Virginia Reserves, C.S.A. and served as ordinance sergeant. He was the grandson of Revolutionary War Col. William Edmondson.

1880 Federal census shows William enumerated in the Glade Spring district of Washington Co., VA with his second wife Sarah and their 3 children.
Edmondson, William C., 64, farmer, b. VA
-- Sarah A., wife, Keeping Home, b. VA.
-- Clara, 16, daughter, at home, b. VA
-- William C., 14, son, at home, b. VA.
-- Rees T.(?), 12, son, at home, b . VA.
Children:

388.   i   **John Preston EDMONDSON**, b. 1851 in VA, d. 1910 in TN?. An attorney and Judge in the Shelby Co. TN area until his death in 1910. (researcher Anne Bruce - 1997). He married (1) **Flora HUMPHIA**, b. ABT 1850 in Somerville, Fayette Co., TN. Died when only son died (W.L.Rhea-1895). He married (2) **Mary GRAHAM**, b. ABT 1850 in Memphis, Shelby Co., TN, d. 1901.

+ 389.   ii   **Jane 'Jennie' Bowen EDMONDSON** b. 1 Oct 1852.

390.   iii   **Louise Smith EDMONDSON**, b. 1857 in VA, d. 1934 in Memphis, Shelby Co., TN, buried in Somerville City Cemetery, Somerville TN. Upon her death, left many things to her nephew Walter Rhea. Some sterling silver and an old photo of 'Aunt Lulu' and William in their Memphis yard was in the possession of Anne Rhea Bruce 2002. She married **William Abram RHEA**, married 1901, b. 30 May 1844 in Jonesboro, Washington Co., TN, (son of John RHEA and Elizabeth Looney RHEA) d. 24 Mar 1921 in Memphis, Shelby Co., TN, buried in Somerville City Cemetery, Somerville TN. He and Mollie bought the Whitfield property, known as

Bellview and lived there until Mollie's death. For many years he served as county surveyor. He bought land in Somerville on South Main St. which he later sold to the County Board of education for a girls dormitory for public schools. Later he married again and lived in Memphis. Died at his home in Memphis 15 years after 2nd marriage.

Served the C.S.A. in the war.

Notable Southern Families., Z. Armstrong 1922 incorrectly notes his death in 1869.

124. **Elizabeth Virginia PRESTON**, (25.Robert[4], 5.John[3], 2.Robert[2], 1.John[1]) b. 4 Jan 1833 in Washington Co., VA, d. 5 May 1897. She was the second wife of Ezra N. Sheffey. She married **Ezra Nuckolls SHEFFEY**, married 5 Sep 1855, b. 13 Jul 1824 in Wythe Co. VA, d. 13 Feb 1891 in Washington Co., VA, buried in Walnut Grove Cem. Washington Co. VA. He was born in Ivanhoe VA and died at home in Washington Co., VA. He had married at the age of 20 Miss Margaret P. Rhea. They had 4 children.

1855 his first wife died.

After Margaret's death, he married her cousin Elizabeth Preston. Together with his first wife, he had 5 children.

Dr. Sheffy connected himself to the Presbyterian Church at the age of 19 and was Superintendent of a Sunday School for 48 consecutive years. From the age of 19 he was a faithful servant of the church. His time, talents, means, influence and example were consecrated to the promotion of its beast interest. With a conscience void of offense towards God and man, a zeal intelligent and guided by divine truth, he executed the duties of his office.

1880 he and his family are enumerated in the Virginia census in the Goodson District of Washington Co., VA. Three Sheffey families, those of Ezra, and sons Robert and Charles are the households adjacent to Robert F. Preston the patriarch,
 Sheffey, E. N., 55, dentist. b. VA, father born VA, mother Bavaria.
 Elizabeth V. 45, keeping house
 Henry S. 19, son, farmer
 Sarah M. 16, daughter
 Mauise (?) M. 11, daughter

Anne C. P. 8, daughter,
Hams, David, 48, black, servant
Boyd, Sallie A. 26, white, servant

During his declining years, though at times subjected to extreme suffering, his chamber was the scene of patience and calm resignation rarely exhibited.

The writer remembers Dr. Sheffey a man of decided discretion and prudence. Unassuming and modest, he has given to us and his surviving friends, a striking example of what can be accomplished by an earnest and conscientious member of the church. Being a man of great amiability of disposition, generous to a fault, and exceedingly affectionate, he went faithfully forward as a Christian and let his light shine." (In memorium, written by W.L.C. Copy in vertical files, Washington Co., VA Historical Society.)
Children:

+ 391.   i   **Robert Fairman SHEFFEY** b. 24 Jun 1856.

+ 392.   ii **Henry L. SHEFFEY** b. 1859.

+ 393.   iii **Charles Marshall SHEFFEY** b. 1858.

  394.   iv **Sarah M. SHEFFEY**, b. 1864 in Washington Co., VA. She married **Mr. RIDDLE**, b. ABT 1862 in VA?.

  395.   v   **Anne C. P. SHEFFEY**, b. 1872 in Washington Co., VA.

125. **Elizabeth Wilson WHITE**, (26.Margaret^4, 5.John^3, 2.Robert^2, 1.John^1) b. 12 May 1827 in Washington Co., VA, d. 9 Jul 1905 in Washington Co., VA, buried in Sinking Spring Cem. Washington Co. VA. She married **David Campbell CUMMINGS**, married 7 Jun 1854 in Washington Co., VA, b. 23 May 1812 in Washington Co., VA, d. 17 Feb 1900 in Washington Co., VA, buried in Sinking Spring Cem. Washington Co. VA. 1865 to 1869 he was clerk of the Circuit Superior Court of Law and Chancery of Washington Co. VA.
Children:

+ 396.   i   **James White CUMMINGS** b. 19 Sep 1855.

+ 397. ii   **Robert Preston CUMMINGS** b. 8 Feb 1857.

   398. iii   **David Campbell CUMMINGS Jr.**, b. 23 Jun 1861 in Abingdon, Washington Co. VA, d. 24 Apr 1913. A judge for Washington Co. VA court. Died unmarried.

126. **Margaret Rhea WHITE**, (26.Margaret[4], 5.John[3], 2.Robert[2], 1.John[1]) b. 1 Jun 1828 in Washington Co., VA. She married **William Young Conn 'General' HUMES**, married 10 Aug 1854 in Washington Co., VA, b. 1 May 1830 in Abingdon, Washington Co. VA, d. 11 Sep 1882 in Huntsville AL. 1848-51 he was a student at Virginia Military Institute and then read law. Began to practice in Knoxville.

1858 he moved to Memphis.

1861 he enlisted in the C.S.A. on May 13 as 1st Lt. in Capt. Smith Bankhead's CP, TN light Artillery, C.S.A. He was transferred to another company as Captain on Nov. 23 1861 and taken prisoner at Island No. 10 April 1862. Exchanged from Johnson's Island OH Nov. 1862. May 15 1863 he was promoted to Major of Artillery on Gen. Wheeler's staff. Appointed Brigadier General Nov. 17, 1863. Later a lawyer in Memphis.

1880 Federal census shows the family enumerated in Memphis, Shelby Co., TN.
  Humes, Wm Y C, 48, Lawyer, b. VA to VA parents.
  -- Sallie A., 40, wife, b. Miss., to parents from Miss. and VA.
  -- Newton, W., 21, son, RR Clerk, b. VA to parents born in VA.
(note mothers birthplace - son from 1st marriage.)
  -- Lizzie N., 15, daughter, school, b. TN to parents from VA.
  -- Matta S. 13, daughter, school, b. TN to parents from VA.
  -- Young, 11, son, school, , b. TN to parents from VA.
  Cogswoll, M., mulatto, 38, cook, b. VA
  -- Lizzie, mulatto, 14, b. servant, VA.
  White, Solomon, 29, Butler, Waiter, b. VA.
       Children:

   399. i   **James Lowery HUMES**, b. ABT 1856 in TN?.

   400. ii   **Newton HUMES**, b. 1859 in TN.

127. **Jane Conn WHITE**, (26.Margaret[4], 5.John[3], 2.Robert[2], 1.John[1]) b. ABT 1831 in Washington Co., VA. Jane and John had two sons. She married **John Gordon OGDEN**, b. ABT 1829 in VA?, d. in Mo?. He was a clerk in his father's mercantile firm in Abingdon VA and later a farmer near Warrensburg MO about 1856.

1860 Federal census shows John and his young sons enumerated next to his father in Warrensburg Township, Johnson Co., MO. Jane does not appear in the Missouri census.
  Elias Ogden, 63, Farmer, real estate $10,000, property $2,000, b. VA.
  Mariah, L, 52, b. VA
  Mary S., 21, b. VA
  F. V. (male) 20, b. VA
  Henry, W., 18, b. VA.
  Beverly, J. 14, b. VA
  Louisa, 12, b. VA
  Newton, 10, b. VA.
  John G. Ogden, 30, farmer, real estate $10,000, property $7,400, b. VA. (His 3 family members are shown as a separate family unit by the enumerator.)
  James W. , 6, b. VA.
  Gordon, 4, b. MO.

1861 June 20, he was elected 1st Lt. of Co. E 3rd Regmt. of Inf. 8th Div. of Missouri State Guard, C.S.A. Resigned command on Nov. 23, 1861 and on Aug 1 1862 enlisted as a private in Co. D. Jackman's MO. Inf. (later 16th MO. Inf.) and served until the surrender under Gen. E. Kirby Smith at New Orleans May 26, 1865.
                    Children:

   401.   i   **James OGDEN**, b. 1854 in MO.

   402.   ii   **Preston OGDEN**, b. ABT 1858.

   403.   iii **Gordon OGDEN**, b. 1856 in MO.

128. **John Preston WHITE**, (26.Margaret[4], 5.John[3], 2.Robert[2], 1.John[1]) b. 7 Mar 1832 in Washington Co., VA, d. 16 Jan 1905 in Austin, Travis Co., TX. He graduated from Emory and Henry College in 1850 and studied law at the University of Virginia 1850-51. 1852-3 he visited Texas for his health. 1853 he was admitted to the bar. Married in 1853 to his cousin. He settled in Sequin, TX in 1855.

1856 he and had their first child, born in Virginia in April.

1861October 19, he was enrolled in Company E 6th Texas Infantry C.S.A. and on October 30 mustered in having been elected Captain by his men. He was taken prisoner on Jan 11, 1863 at Arkansas Post, Ark. and sent to Camp Chase, Ohio and Fort Delaware, Delaware until exchanged on April 29, 1863. In that year he was ordered to report to General E. Kirby Smith in the Trans-Mississippi Department and was thereafter absent from his company.

1864 he was displaced as an officer on the consolidation of regiments and in this year ran for District Judge but was not elected. In September 1864 he was in command at San Antonio, TX. He had acted as ordnance officer in Gen. Bernard E. Bee's division in winter of 1863-64; was at one time on the staff of Gen. Steele and also was engaged under Gen. Harry Hays in endeavoring to collect the scattered troops belonging to commands east of the Mississippi River. He continued to serve until the surrender of the troops under General Smith in 1865.

After the War, he was elected mayor and appointed District Judge in 1874. He was elected Presiding Judge.

1892 he resigned to become reporter to the Court of Criminal Appeals, in which capacity he served until his death.

1900 Federal census shows his family enumerated in Austin City, Travis Co., TX, living at 305 East Eighth St.:
  White, John P. head, Mar 1832, 68, married 47 years, b. VA
  -- Anne S. wife, Feb 1836, 64, married 47 years, 5 children, 5 living, b. SC to parents from VA and SC.
  --James L., son, Apr. 1856 44, widower, b. TX, lawyer.
  -- Walter L. son, Jan 1870 30, single, b. TX, lawyer.
  -- Louis M., son, Feb 1872, 28 single, b. TX, dentist.
  -- Bessie L., daughter, July 1873, 26, b. TX
  Crenshaw, Mary W., daughter, Mar 1868, 32, Married 7 years, 2 children, 2 living, b. TX
  Johnson, Ida, servant, July 1873, 26, single, b. Sweden, cook, immigrated 1870, 20 (?) years in the US. He married **Annie Stuart LEWIS**, married 7 Sep 1853 in Albemarle Co., VA, b. 1 Feb 1836 in SC, d. in Austin TX?. It has been noted she was from Texas, a granddaughter of Mary Preston Lewis
of Sweet Springs WVA. She and John were cousins.
  Children:

+ 404. i **James Lewis WHITE** b. 1 Apr 1856.

+ 405. ii **Annie Lewis WHITE** b. 12 Apr 1861.

+ 406. iii **Mary Magdelene WHITE** b. 1 Mar 1868.

   407. iv **Walter Lewis WHITE**, b. 1870 in TX, d. 1927.
1900 Federal census shows him living with his
parents in Austin TX at age 30, single, a lawyer.

+ 408. v **Montgomery Lewis WHITE** b. 1871.

   409. vi **Louis Milton WHITE**, b. FEB 1872 in TX, d. 1893.
Had no children.

   410. vii **Bessie Lelia WHITE**, b. 1 Jul 1873 in TX, d. 1944.

130. **William Young Conn WHITE**, (26.Margaret[4], 5.John[3], 2.Robert[2],
1.John[1]) b. 1835 in Washington Co., VA?, d. 13 Oct 1904 in
Baltimore, MD, buried in Sinking Spring Cem. Washington Co. VA.
1853-56 he was a student at Virginia Military Institute.

1861 April 22, he became Captain of Co B, 37th Infantry of VA and
served until April 1862. He was with the medical Dept. He enlisted
March 1864 as a private in Co. D 1st VA Cavalry and served until
the end of the war.

He was a physician and farmer of "Fruit Hill" near Abingdon, VA.

1873 he was elected a Fellow of the Medical Society of Virginia. He
married **Elizabeth Campbell CARTER**, b. 1847 in Russell Co.
VA, d. 1922 in Washington Co., VA, buried in Sinking Spring
Cem. Washington Co. VA. 1922 her will was dated Nov 6, 1915;
proved March 22, 1922 Washington Co. VA will book 32 pp. 36-37.
Gave $500 and a promissory note she held to her son Stuart White
and the remainder of her estate to her daughter Pauline Mason.
      Children:

   411. i **Stuart WHITE**, b. 1870 in Washington Co., VA?.
Went to California and married Emily.

1920 Federal census shows he and his wife
enumerated in Santa Monica, Los Angeles Co., CA
living at 151 Hill St.:
  White, Stuart, head, 46, b. VA tpo VA parents,
works Gen. ncui?, Studio.
  -- Emma (?), wife, 46, b. IN, to parents from MD
and OH.

Had 2 children. He married **Emily or Emma WEST**,
b. ABT 1870 in IN.

412.   ii   **Pauline Campbell WHITE**, b. 1871 in Washington
Co., VA?. She and Thomas had no children. She
married **Thomas Hill MASON**, b. ABT 1871 in WV,
d. 1920.

131. **Ellen Sheffey WHITE**, (26.Margaret[4], 5.John[3], 2.Robert[2], 1.John[1])
b. 26 May 1836 in Washington Co., VA, d. 13 Jul 1912. Born at
'Fruit Hill' in Washington Co. VA.

1880 Federal census shows Ellen S. Campbell as head of household
in Abingdon, Washington Co., VA, following the death of her
husband in 1878.
Campbell, Ellen S., 444, keeping house, b. VA.
-- Daniel T., 22, son, law student, b. VA.
-- Maggie P., 17, daughter, at home, b. VA.
-- Bessie C., 14, daughter, at home, b. VA.
-- Susan T., 12, daughter, at home, b. VA.
-- William W., 10, son, works - Mountain(?) Tobacco Factory (this
is June 1880).
-- Frank, 8, son, b. VA.
-- Jn Preston, 6, son, b. VA.
-- Malcolm, 4, son, b. VA.
Ogden, James W., 24, boarder, Druggist, b. VA.
Perry, Joseph, black, 17, Servant, b. VA. She married **Edward
McDonald CAMPBELL**, married 29 Apr 1857 in Washington Co.,
VA, b. 31 Oct 1825 in Washington Co., VA, d. 11 Jun 1878 in
Warm Springs NC. Born at "Halls Bottom" in Washington Co. VA.

He was appointed surgeon of the 1st Reg. of Cavalry C.S.A. at
Harpers Ferry VA. 19 June 1861 he was ordered to report to the
37th VA Inf. He served until 14 May 1862 when he resigned on
account of physical incapacitation.

Graduated from Jefferson Medical College Phil. PA and was a physician in Abingdon VA for more than 35 years.

1878 his will dated was written 30 May 1878 and proved 27 June 1878 Washington Co. VA. Gave his
wife interest in Wise Co. property and part of "Halls Bottom".
Children:

413. i   **Daniel Trigg CAMPBELL**, b. 20 Jan 1858 in Abingdon, Washington Co. VA, d. 11 Apr 1920 in Bonham, Fannin Co., TX.

414. ii   **Edward Donald CAMPBELL**, b. 4 May 1861 in Abingdon, Washington Co. VA, d. 25 Sep 1871. Died young, killed by an accidental gun shot.

+ 415. iii **Margaret Preston CAMPBELL** b. 23 Mar 1863.

416. iv **Josephine Trigg CAMPBELL**, b. 23 Sep 1864 in Abingdon, Washington Co. VA, d. 4 Aug 1865. Died young.

+ 417. v   **Bessie Cummings CAMPBELL** b. 1 Mar 1866.

+ 418. vi **Sussie Trigg CAMPBELL** b. 3 Mar 1868.

+ 419. vii **William White CAMPBELL** b. 18 Oct 1869.

+ 420. viii **Frank CAMPBELL** b. 22 Aug 1871.

421. ix **James White CAMPBELL**, b. ABT 1873 in Washington Co., VA?.

+ 422. x   **Preston White CAMPBELL** b. 24 Jan 1874.

423. xi **Malcolm CAMPBELL**, b. 10 Jul 1875 in Abingdon, Washington Co. VA, d. 1 Jun 1947 in New York City, NY. Marriage mentioned in Notable Southern Families., Z. Armstrong 1922.

Served 1 year on Local Draft Board in New York City during WWI. Later was in active service at Camp Syracuse. During the influenza epidemic, was put in charge of Irving Hospital in Syracuse. Later transferred to Fort Ethan Allen where he was discharged.

Had no children. He married **Charlotte Luella BRADER**, married 6 Jan 1913, b. ABT 1875 in VA?.

132. **Susan Preston WHITE**, (26.Margaret[4], 5.John[3], 2.Robert[2], 1.John[1]) b. 29 Aug 1838 in Washington Co., VA, d. 19 Jun 1908. She and Abram had two children.

1880 Federal census shows a Susan enumerated in Abingdon, Washington Co., VA, perhaps a widow, living in the household of Thomas Trigg (brother in law?):
  Trigg, Thomas, 39, Bank Clerk.
  -- Frances, 54, sister, keeping house.
  -- Sally, 48, sister, at home.
  -- Anne, 40, sister, at home.
  Trigg, Susan, 40, Boarder, Boarder, b. VA to VA parents.
  -- Mary, 8, daughter, b. VA to VA parents.
(There are also two mulatto servants and 4 young mulatto children in the household.) She married **Abram Byrd TRIGG**, married 26 Sep 1867 in Washington Co., VA, b. 3 1836 in Abingdon, Washington Co. VA, d. 22 Sep 1878 in Greenville, Washington Co. MS. 1861 April 22 he enlisted 1861 as a private in Co. K 37th VA Inf, C.S.A. as a private. Was wounded 9 Aug. 1862 at Cedar Run and served until the surrender at Appomattox Court House. He was a merchant in Greenville, Miss. after the war.
    Children:

424. i **Mary Byrd TRIGG**, b. 1872 in VA, d. 1961.
Married Robert, her cousin. They had no children.
She married **Robert Robinson Preston CAMPBELL**, married 1872, b. 25 Aug 1867 in VA, (son of Joseph Trigg CAMPBELL and Mary C. PRESTON) d. 27 Aug 1952. 1930 Federal census shows the couple enumerated on West Main Street in Abingdon, Washington Co., VA:
  Campbell, Robert R., head, owns home, value $10,000, no radio, age 62, married at 40, b. VA to parents from VA, insurance, life.
  -- Mary B. T., wife-h, age 58, first married at 26, b. MS to parents from VA.
  -- Mary T., sister, age 65, single, b. VA to parents from VA.

Had no children.

425.   ii   **Margaret Preston TRIGG**, b. ABT 1874.

134. **Alfred G. PRESTON**, (27.William^4, 5.John^3, 2.Robert^2, 1.John^1) b. 24 Jan 1858 in Washington Co., VA, d. 22 Jun 1933 in Botetourt Co., VA. 1874-76 he was a student at Hampden-Sydney College and at Emory and Henry College 1875-77. He was one of the founders of the Chi-Psi fraternity at Hampden-Sydney.

At age of 19 he became the owner of "Greenfield" where he lived the remainder of his life.

He was elected justice of the peace of Botetourt Co. at age 21. Was chairman of county Democratic committee for many years. Commissioner of Revenue for 14 years.

1889-90 represented the county in VA House of Delegates. Had 11 children.

1900 Federal census shows the family living in the Amsterdam District of Botetourt Co., VA:
Preston, Albert head, Jan 1858 42, married 14 years, b. VA farmer.
-- Alice, wife, Nov 1865, 34, married 14 years, 9 children, 8 living, b. VA
-- Frank B. son, Mar 1887, 13, single, b. VA.
-- Lucy A., daughter, Aug 1889, 12, b. VA.
-- Susan B., daughter, Dec 1892, 7, b. VA.
-- John W. B., son, Mar 1896, 6, b. VA.
-- Mary M. daughter, Nov. 1898, 1 b. VA
-- ??aid C. son, Apr 1900, 2/12, b. VA. He married **Alice Murrell BROCKENBROUGH**, married 28 Oct 1885 in Botetourt Co. VA, b. 14 Nov 1865 in Lynchburg, Campbell Co., VA, d. 3 Apr 1936 in Botetourt Co. VA. Married at "Glen Alpine Farms", Bedford Co. VA. Died at "Greenfield".
Children:

426.   i   **William Alfred PRESTON**, b. 9 Nov 1886. Died unmarried.

+ 427.   ii   **Frank Brockenbrough PRESTON** b. 15 Mar 1888.

+ 428.   iii   **Lucy Alice PRESTON** b. 21 Aug 1889.

429. iv **Elizabeth Radford PRESTON**, b. 23 Apr 1891 in VA. Died young.

+ 430. v **Susan Radford PRESTON** b. 30 Dec 1892.

+ 431. vi **John Brockenbrough PRESTON** b. 6 Mar 1894.

+ 432. vii **Annie Beale PRESTON** b. 12 Aug 1897.

+ 433. viii **Mary PRESTON** b. 17 Nov 1898.

434. ix **Channing PRESTON**, b. 6 Apr 1900 in Botetourt Co., VA.

435. x **Robert PRESTON**, b. 6 Apr 1902 in Botetourt Co., VA. Lived in Wilmington Delaware. Did not marry.

436. xi **David PRESTON**, b. 1905 in Botetourt Co., VA. Lived at the ancestral home 'Greenfield'.

138. **Margaret SHEFFEY**, (29.Eleanor[4], 5.John[3], 2.Robert[2], 1.John[1]) b. 4 Oct 1836 in Marion, Smythe Co., VA, d. 29 Aug 1869. She married **William Elisha 'Col.' PETERS**, married 8 Sep 1858 in Smythe Co. VA, b. 18 Aug 1829 in Bedford Co. VA, d. 22 Mar 1906 in Charlottesville, Albemarle Co., VA. Married Mary after the death of her sister Margaret.

1845-48 attended New London Academy in Bedford Co. VA and was a student at Emory and
Henry College 1845-48 and the U of VA 1850-53.

1853 to 1861 he was a professor of Latin at Emory and Henry except 1856-58 when he attended lectures at the U. of Berlin.

1861 he is listed as private 17 April 1861 in the service. He was elected 1st Lt of Cavalry Co. of 50th Reg. Later in 1861 appointed adjutant of Gen. Floyd's Brig.; Nov. 1861 Lt. Col.

1862 May, he was Colonel of 21st VA Cavalry. Wounded at Moorfield WV.

1880 Federal census shows the family in the 13th District of Albemarle Co., VA:

Peters, William E., 51, Prof of Latin, b. VA.
-- Mary D. 32, wife, Keeping House, b. VA.
-- James W., 16, son, attending school, b. VA.
-- William E. 10 son, b. VA.
-- Don Preston, 2, b. VA.
Jones, Mary, black, 42, cook, b. VA.
Young, William, black, 22, servant, Diningroom Svt., b. VA.

1930 Federal census shows the family enumerated at the University
of Virginia, Charlottesville District, Albemarle Co., VA. There are
five students in the same home as the three members of the family.
  Peters, William E., Aug 1829, 70, married 27 years, b. VA, Prof of
Latin.
-- Mary S. wife, Dec 1844, 55, married 27 years, 1 child (sic) i
living, b. VA
-- Don P, son July 1877, 22, single, b. VA, medical student.
            Children:

    437. i   **James White Sheffy PETERS**, b. 28 Apr 1864 in
              VA, d. AFT 1910 in Kansas City, Jackson Co., MO.
              1910 Federal census shows him enumerated in
              Kansas City, Jackson Co., MO:
                Peters, James W. S., boarder, 45, single, b. VA to
                VA parents, lawyer, law office.

    438. ii **William Edgar PETERS**, b. 15 Aug 1869 in VA.

139. **John Preston SHEFFEY**, (29.Eleanor[4], 5.John[3], 2.Robert[2], 1.John[1])
      b. 12 Dec 1837 in Marion, Smythe Co., VA, d. 20 Aug 1905 in
      Marion, Smythe Co., VA. Marriage mentioned in Notable Southern
      Families., Z. Armstrong 1922.

Was Captain of a Virginia Co. for the C.S.A. during the Civil War.

1858 He attended Emory and Henry College and graduated with
honors. Studied law at U. of VA.

1859 he began practice in Marion VA with his father.

1861 May 25 he enlisted as 1st Lt Co. A 8th VA Cavalry. C.S.A.
and May 14, 1862 appointed Captain of the Co. Captured at
Moorfield WV and sent to Camp Chase OH until exchange at end of
the war.

1870 the Federal census shows him enumerated not far from his father and brother James Jr. in Marion, Smythe Co., VA:
Sheffey, John P. 32, lawyer, real property value $3,700, personal property value $6,000, b. VA
-- Josaphine (sic), 29, at home, b. VA.
-- Eleanor, 4, b. VA
-- Susan M. 3, b. VA
Margaret P., 2, b. VA
-- Josaphine 7/12, b. VA

1893-4 served in the Virginia House of Delegates. He was also a Circuit Court Judge.

1900 Federal census shows the family in Marion, Smyth Co., VA:
Sheffey, Jno. P. head, Dec. 1837, 62, married 26 years, b. VA, lawyer.
" Josephine, wife, Mar. 1840, 60, married 26 years, 7 children, 7 living, b. VA
" Josephine, daughter, Feb 1870, single, b. VA
" James White, son, Sept 1871, 28, single, b. VA.
" Miriam, daughter, Feb. 1874, 26, single, b. VA.
" Jno. P. Jr., son, Nov. 1876, 23, single, b. VA. He married **Josephine SPILLER**, married 19 Jun 1863 in Wytheville VA, b. 31 Mar 1840 in Wythe Co. VA, d. 19 Nov 1904. 1860 Federal census shows her enumerated in Wytheville, Wythe Co., VA with her well off, perhaps widowed mother.
Susan Spiller, 50, no employment, real estate value $40,000, property $26,000, b.VA.
Jane ", 23, property value $6,000, b. VA.
Josaphine (sic) ", 20, b. VA.
Lucy, 17, b. VA.
Frank, 15, b. VA.
William, 14, b. VA.
Robert, 10, b. VA.

Children:

+ 439.   i   **Margaret Peters SHEFFEY** b. 1 Oct 1868.

+ 440.   ii   **Eleanor Fairman SHEFFEY** b. 11 Jul 1866.

+ 441.   iii   **Susan 'Susie' Montgomery SHEFFEY** b. 12 Aug 1867.

442. iv **Josephine Spiller SHEFFEY**, b. 25 Feb 1870 in Marion, Smythe Co., VA, d. ABT 1927.

+ 443. v **James White SHEFFEY** b. 13 Sep 1871.

444. vi **Miraim SHEFFEY**, b. 1 Feb 1874 in Marion, Smythe Co., VA.

+ 445. vii **John Preston SHEFFEY Jr.** b. 1 Nov 1876.

141. **Elizabeth Madison SHEFFEY**, (29.Eleanor[4], 5.John[3], 2.Robert[2], 1.John[1]) b. 5 Jan 1842 in Marion, Smythe Co., VA, d. 10 May 1875 in Marion, Smythe Co., VA. She married **James Albert Gallatin 'Maj. PENDLETON**, married 24 Oct 1872 in Smythe Co. VA, b. 20 Feb 1836 in Smythe Co. VA, d. 2 Mar 1901 in Smythe Co. VA. 1861 he was captain of the Smyth Blues which on 18 April 1861 entered C.S.A. service as Co. D 4th VA Infantry. 1861 July, he was at Manassas.

1862 January he was promoted to Major and commanded the regiment at the battle of Kernstown. After 18 months his health failed and he was discharged. He was a lawyer in Smyth Co.

1875 he served as Superintendent of Schools.

1901 his will dated Feb. 8, 1901 was proved March 4, 1901 in Smyth Co., will bk. 7 pp. 497-98.
    Children:

+ 446. i **James Sheffey PENDLETON** b. 1 Nov 1874.

142. **Ellen White SHEFFY**, (29.Eleanor[4], 5.John[3], 2.Robert[2], 1.John[1]) b. 25 Aug 1843 in Marion, Smythe Co., VA, d. 8 Jan 1905 in Marion, Smythe Co., VA. Died after a long spell of sickness. She married **Joseph Brainard RHEA**, married 10 Oct 1866 in Marion, Smythe Co., VA, b. 8 Apr 1838 in Blountville, Sullivan Co., TN, d. 7 Jul 1902 in Smythe Co. VA. Served C.S.A in Co. A 60th TN Cavalry Regiment. Captured by the Yankees near Bristol Dec. 1864 and confined to Camp Chase, Ohio until May 1865.

Sold goods with brother John until 1872 when he moved with his family to Marion Virginia.

1900 Federal census shows Joseph and family enumerated in
Marion, Smyth Co., VA
  Rhea, Joseph B., head, Mch 1838, 62, married 34 years, b. TN to
parents from TN, merchant and farmer.
  " Ellen, wife, Aug. 1843, 56, married 34 years, 4 children, 3 living,
b. VA to parents from VA.
  Adams, Eleanor, daughter, Aug 1871, 28, widow, 2 children, 2
living, b. VA.
  " Charles L., g son, Dec. 1896, 3, b. TN to parents from MD and
VA.
  " Brainard R., g son, July 1898, 1, b. TN to parents from MD and
VA.

1907 Joseph was found dead in his bed.
            Children:

> 447.   i   **James White Sheffey RHEA**, b. 6 Jun 1869 in VA?,
>   d. 9 Apr 1917. Was a prominent educator. Never
>   married. Taught at the University School in
>   Memphis.
>
> + 448.   ii   **Eleanor Lynn RHEA** b. 7 Aug 1871.
>
> + 449.   iii **Margaret Preston RHEA** b. 22 Jan 1876.
>
> 450.   iv   **Virginia Sheffey RHEA**, b. 28 Jul 1880 in VA?, d. 9
>   Nov 1883. Died in infancy.

143. **Mary W. SHEFFY**, (29.Eleanor[4], 5.John[3], 2.Robert[2], 1.John[1]) b. 8
Dec 1844 in Marion, Smythe Co., VA, d. 1906 in Charlottesville,
Albemarle Co., VA. Married her sister Margaret's widower.
Margaret had died at the age of 32, 4 years before Mary's marriage.
She married **William Elisha 'Col.' PETERS**, married 14 Jul 1873
in Smythe Co. VA, b. 18 Aug 1829 in Bedford Co. VA, d. 22 Mar
1906 in Charlottesville, Albemarle Co., VA. Married Mary after the
death of her sister Margaret.

1845-48 attended New London Academy in Bedford Co. VA and
was a student at Emory and   Henry College 1845-48 and the U of
VA 1850-53.

1853 to 1861 he was a professor of Latin at Emory and Henry except
1856-58 when he attended lectures at the U. of Berlin.

1861 he is listed as private 17 April 1861 in the service. He was elected 1st Lt of Cavalry Co. of 50th Reg. Later in 1861 appointed adjutant of Gen. Floyd's Brig.; Nov. 1861 Lt. Col.

1862 May, he was Colonel of 21st VA Cavalry. Wounded at Moorfield WV.

1880 Federal census shows the family in the 13th District of Albemarle Co., VA:
  Peters, William E., 51, Prof of Latin, b. VA.
  -- Mary D. 32, wife, Keeping House, b. VA.
  -- James W., 16, son, attending school, b. VA.
  -- William E. 10 son, b. VA.
  -- Don Preston, 2, b. VA.
  Jones, Mary, black, 42, cook, b. VA.
  Young, William, black, 22, servant, Diningroom Svt., b. VA.

1930 Federal census shows the family enumerated at the University of Virginia, Charlottesville District, Albemarle Co., VA. There are five students in the same home as the three members of the family.
  Peters, William E., Aug 1829, 70, married 27 years, b. VA, Prof of Latin.
  -- Mary S. wife, Dec 1844, 55, married 27 years, 1 child (sic) i living, b. VA
  -- Don P, son July 1877, 22, single, b. VA, medical student.
  Children:

  451. i   **James W. PETERS**, b. 1868 in VA.

  452. ii **William E. PETERS**, b. 1870 in VA.

+ 453. iii **Don Preston PETERS** b. 1 Dec 1877.

145. **Martha E. SHEFFEY**, (29.Eleanor[4], 5.John[3], 2.Robert[2], 1.John[1]) b. 15 Mar 1849 in Marion, Smythe Co., VA, d. 4 Nov 1898 in Baltimore Co. MD. She married **Robert J. PRESTON**, married 19 Oct 1875 in Smythe Co. VA, b. 25 Jan 1841 in Washington Co., VA, (son of John Fairman 'Capt' PRESTON and Jane RHEA) d. 20 Aug 1906 in Lewiston NY. Born at 'Locust Glen' near Abingdon.

1859-61 he had attended Abingdon Academy and Emory and Henry College.

Joined Capt. James Campbell's Co. C.S.A. and was elected 1st Lt. When ordered to Richmond he resigned. May 25, 1861 enlisted as private in Co. K 37th VA Inf. until Sept. 9, 1862. Re-enlisted June 15, 1863 in Co. C. 21st VA Cavalry.

Practiced medicine in NY, Abingdon VA and Marion VA. Successful and noted physician in Marion.

1880 Federal census shows the family enumerated in Abingdon, Washington Co., VA family #190.
  Preston, Robert J, 39, Physician, b. VA to VA parents.
  -- Martha E., 30, wife, keeping house, b. VA to VA parents.
  -- Eleanor F., 4, daughter, b. VA to VA parents.
(in the same household)
  Mead, Violet, mulatto, 18, servant, b. VA to VA parents.
  -- Alsie, black, 11, servant, b. VA to VA parents.

1888 Robert was Superintendent of the Southwestern State Hospital.

1900 Federal census shows Robert living at the Southwestern State Hospital in Marion, Smyth Co., VA. Martha had passed away.
  Preston, Robert, superintendent, Jan. 1841, widowed, b VA to VA parents, Physician. His daughter Eleanor is not enumerated with him either. Son Robert S. Preston, age 14, is enumerated at Hampton-Sidney College.
    Children:

+ 454.   i   **Eleanor Fairman PRESTON** b. 11 Aug 1873.

+ 455.   ii   **Robert Sheffey PRESTON II.** b. 30 Jul 1885.

153. **David Craighead PRESTON**, (31.Thomas[4], 5.John[3], 2.Robert[2], 1.John[1]) b. 12 Jan 1849 in Nashville, Davidson Co., TN. 1866-68 studied for 2 years at KY Military Institute. He was a Railroad Contractor and lived in Nashville.

1880 Federal census shows him living in Nashville, Davidson Co., TN at 35 North High Street, with the family of his cousin Thomas Craighead. David C. Preston, 31, 'cousin', a Rail Road Contractor, b. Arkansas, to parents born in Virginia and Tennessee.

1900 Federal census shows what appears to be David enumerated in Chicago, Cook Co., IL married with a family.

Preston, David C. head, July 1851, age 48, married 12 years, b. TN to father from KY and mother from TN, a Civil Engineer. [The information is not a perfect match, but there are no other David Prestons in the earlier census records born in TN, the occupation is consistent with his earlier training, and the middle initial 'C' would make this an unlikely coincidence.]
-- Maria F. wife, Jan 1859, 41, married 12 years, 4 children, 3 living, b. TN
-- Wm. H., son, Mar 1890, 10, b. IL.
-- Hattie, daughter, June 1893, 5, b. IL
-- May W. daughter, Feb 1895, 5, b. IL
Pederson, Frida, servant, Nov. 1894, 25, b. Sweden. He married **Maria F. wife of David PRESTON**, b. 1859 in TN.
Children:

456.   i   **William H. PRESTON**, b. 1 Mar 1890 in IL.

457.   ii   **Hattie PRESTON**, b. 1 Jun 1893 in IL.

458.   iii   **May W. PRESTON**, b. 1 Feb 1895 in IL.

156.   **Robert M. PRESTON**, (33.Francis[4], 5.John[3], 2.Robert[2], 1.John[1]) b. 23 Mar 1852 in Washington Co., VA, d. 27 Feb 1906 in Leesburg, Loudoun Co. VA, buried in Union Cem. Leesburg VA. Robert was an officer at the People's Bank of Leesburg. They had 5 children.

1900 Federal census shows the family enumerated in Leesburg, Loudon Co., VA
Preston, Robert M, head, Mar 1853, b. VA, bank clerk.
-- Hattie A. wife, June 1853, b. VA
-- Anne, daughter, Mar 1887 19, single b. VA.
-- Robert W. son, Aug 1888 11, single b. VA.
-- Katherine, daughter, Feb 1892, 8, single b. VA.
Curtis, Herbert N, boarder, April 1855, 45, single, b. MA, bookkeeper
Aldridge, Anne, sister in law, Apr 1853, 47, single, b. VA. He married **Harriet West ALDRIDGE**, married 6 Apr 1880 in Loudoun Co. VA, b. 23 Jun 1858, d. 5 Feb 1916 in Leesburg, Loudoun Co. VA, buried in Union Cem. Leesburg VA. 1910 Federal census shows her enumerated as the head of the household, as Robert had passed away in 1908. She is living on Berry Street in Leesburg, Loudon Co., VA. Only one daughter is at home, but she is now also living with two of her Aldridge sisters.

Preston, Harriet West, 52, widow, 3 children, 3 living, b. VA, own means [note under employment]
-- Catherine G., daughter 17, single, b. VA
Aldridge, Virginia, sister 58, single, b. VA
-- Anne, sister, 56, single, b. VA
Children Anne and Robert do not appear enumerated under the name Preston in Leesburg in 1910. These two siblings appear in 1920 in South Carolina.

Children:

+ 459.   i   **Anne PRESTON** b. 1 Mar 1887.

  460.   ii   **Robert W. PRESTON**, b. 1 Aug 1888 in VA.

  461.   iii   **Katherine PRESTON**, b. 1 Feb 1892 in VA.

163. **Preston CRAIGHEAD**, (34.Jane^4, 5.John^3, 2.Robert^2, 1.John^1) b. 1855 in Marengo Co., AL. 1880 Federal census shows Preston now head of the household, enumerated in Marion, Perry Co., AL
Craighead, Preston 25, Clerk in Store, b. AL
-- Fannie, 23, wife, b. AL to parents from VA and AL.
-- Jane 60, mother, keeping house, b. VA, to parents from Ireland.
-- Jennie, 20, sister, boarding, b. AL.
-- Thomas, 22, brother, Minister, b. AL.
-- James, 28, brother, boarding, Frail Health [noted by enumerator] b. AL.

1910 Federal census shows Preston enumerated with his children in Uniontown, Perry Co., AL living on East Street:
Craighead, Preston, head, 55, married 30 years, b. AL, farmer.
-- Fannie S. wife, 53, married 30 years, 8 children, 6 living, b. AL
--Blanche, S. daughter, 23, single, b. AL.
--Fannie R., daughter, 22, single, b. AL.
--Joseph W. son, 19, single, b. AL.
--Haywood, son, 17, b. AL.
--Vernon, daughter, 15, single, b. AL.

1920 Federal census shows Preston enumerated in Dayton, Marengo Co., AL with only his son.
Craighead, Preston, head, owns home, free of mortgage, age 60, farmer.
-- Hayward, son, 28, single, b. AL, Salesman, Retail Store.
Preston's wife Fannie is enumerated with other members of the family at their home on East St. in Uniontown. The census for these

two areas was done 3 days apart. Haywood is actually enumerated again in Uniontown on the 9th of January.

Craighead, Fannie, head, age 62, married, b. AL
-- Blanche, daughter, 38, single, b. AL, teacher, Kindergarten.
-- Fannie, daughter, 32, single, b. AL
-- Haywood, son, 27, single, b. AL, merchant, general.
-- Jeanne, daughter, 23, single, b. AL.

Only son Joseph could not be found in the 1920 census index. He married **Fannie wife of Preston CRAIGHEAD**, b. 1857 in AL.

Children:

+ 462. i **Hayward CRAIGHEAD** b. 1892.

463. ii **Blanche CRAIGHEAD**, b. 1887 in Marengo Co., AL. 1930 Federal census shows Blanche as head of household with her two sisters, all unmarried, living at the family home on East St., Uniontown, Marengo Co., AL.   None of them are working.

464. iii **Fannie CRAIGHEAD**, b. 1888 in Marengo Co., AL. 1930 unmarried living with her two sisters at the family home in Uniontown, Al.

465. iv **Joseph W. CRAIGHEAD**, b. 1891 in Marengo Co., AL.

466. v **Vernon CRAIGHEAD**, b. 1895 in Marengo Co., AL. 1930 unmarried living with her two sisters at the family home in Uniontown, Al.

467. vi **Preston A. CRAIGHEAD Jr.**, b. 1896 in Marengo Co., AL. 1930 Federal census he is enumerated in the Faundale section of Marengo Co., AL with his wife. He is a dairy farmer. He married **Hattie wife of Preston CRAIGHEAD**, b. 1898 in AL.

166. **John PRESTON**, (35.James[4], 5.John[3], 2.Robert[2], 1.John[1]) b. 21 Jul 1851 in Washington Co., VA, d. 27 Jun 1938 in Austin, Travis Co., TX. 1906 President and Superintendent of TX State Lunatic Asylum till 1925.

1871-72 he was a student at U of VA and received his M.D. He also graduated from Belleveue Hosp. Med. College in New York City 1873 and began practice in Washington Co. VA.

1876 he married a cousin whose family had moved to Texas from Virginia 20 years before..

1878 he moved to TX and located in Seguin.

1880 Federal census shows John enumerated with the family of his father in law who had also removed to Texas more than 15 years before. They were living in Seguin, Guadalupe Co., TX
  White, Preston 48, Judge
  -- Annie 45, wife, keeping house
  -- Jul? 15, son, at school b. TX
  -- Mary Mag 13, daughter, at home b. TX
  -- Walter 11, son, at school, b. TX
  -- Lewis 10, son at school, b. TX
  -- Bessie 9 daughter, at home, b. TX
  -- Caroline, 30, mulatto, servant, house, b. VA
Preston, John 29, son in law, physician, b. VA
  -- Annie, daughter, at house, b. TX
  -- Walter grandson 2/12, b. TX.

1887 he was appointed 1st Asst. Physician at TX Lunatic Asylum at Austin. Supt. of N. TX Hosp. for the insane in 1890 and then Supt. of the TX State Epileptic Colony at Abilene.

1910 the Federal census shows the family enumerated at the State Lunatic Asylum at Austin in Travis Co., Texas where Dr. Preston is the superintendent.
  Preston, John, head, 58, married 31 years, b. VA, Superintendent, Institution
  -- A. L. wife, 49 married 31 years, 7 children, 7 living, b. TX.
  -- Fannie, daughter, 20, single, b. TX.
  -- Robert W. son 18, single, b. TX.
  -- Annie L. daughter, 12, single, b.TX
  -- Margarette, daughter, 5, single, b. TX.

1920 Federal census shows the family at the home in Austin, with daughters Fannie, Annie and Margaret single living at home.

1930 Federal census shows John and Annie living in Austin, Travis Co., TX:
  Preston, John, head, owns home, value $20,000, the family has a radio, age 78, married at 28, not employed.

Annice (sic) wife, 68, married at 18, b. TX. He married **Annie Lewis WHITE**, married 16 Apr 1876, b. 12 Apr 1861 in Seguin, Guadalupe Co., TX, (daughter of John Preston WHITE and Annie Stuart LEWIS) d. 27 Nov 1946.

Children:

+ 468.   i   **Walter White PRESTON** b. 18 Apr 1880.

+ 469.   ii   **John Lewis PRESTON** b. 24 Mar 1883.

470.   iii   **James Rhea PRESTON**, b. 1885 in Seguin, Guadalupe Co., TX.

471.   iv   **Frances 'Fannie' Rhea PRESTON**, b. 1890 in Travis Co., TX. 1930 Federal census shows her at home with her parents at the State Asylum in Austin, Travis Co., TX. The enumerator notes she is 29, and a teacher.

472.   v   **Robert White PRESTON**, b. 1892 in Travis Co., TX. Served in Quartermasters Department, Camp McArthur Texas during WWI.

473.   vi   **Annie Lewis PRESTON**, b. 1898 in Travis Co., TX.

474.   vii   **Margaret Lynn PRESTON**, b. 1904 in Travis Co., TX.

167. **James Rhea PRESTON**, (35.James[4], 5.John[3], 2.Robert[2], 1.John[1]) b. 22 Jan 1853 in Washington Co., VA, d. 3 Apr 1922 in Jackson, Miss. Born at "Walnut Grove". Superintendent of schools in Mississippi.

1871-73 he was a student at Geo. Washington U. and later at Emory and Henry College and there received A.M. degree.

1874 he moved to Mississippi as a teacher.

While Superintendent of Water Valley schools he was chosen by the legislature to be State Superintendent - an office he held from 1886-96.

1896 he was a graduate student at U. of Edinburgh. 1898 he founded Stanton College at Natchez Mississippi and Belhave College which burned in 1910.

1920 Federal census he was enumerated in Kingston Precinct, Adams Co., Mississippi at Natchez and Woodville Road:
  Preston, James R., head, rents, age 65, b. VA to parents from VA and TN, farmer, general farm.
  -- Elizabeth V., wife, 44, b. LA to parents from MS and LA.
  -- Elizabeth M., daughter, 16, b. MS
  -- Frances R., daughter, 15, b. MS.
  -- James R., Junior, son, 13, b. MS
He composed the State motto "Virtue et Armis". He married **Elizabeth Alice VAUGHAN**, married 18 Dec 1902 in Natchez, Miss., b. 1 May 1875 in Clinton LA, d. 2 Jun 1972 in Jackson, Miss.
          Children:

    475.   i   **Elizabeth McIlwaine PRESTON**, b. 1904 in MS. Lived in Highland Park, IL. She married **Kenneth KRAFT**, b. ABT 1903.

    476.   ii   **Frances Rhea PRESTON**, b. 1905 in MS. Lived in Mississippi. She married **Henry P. MILLS**, b. ABT 1905.

    477.   iii **James Rhea PRESTON Jr.**, b. 1907 in MS.

169. **Robert Fairman PRESTON**, (35.James[4], 5.John[3], 2.Robert[2], 1.John[1]) b. 1 Apr 1857 in Washington Co., VA, d. 16 Oct 1928 in Washington Co., VA?, buried in Walnut Grove Cem. Washington Co. VA. Was a lawyer; lived in VA (W. L. Rhea manuscript, Sullivan Co., TN Public Library - 1895).

1930 Federal census shows the family living in the Goodson area of Washington Co., VA on Bristol Washington Highway:
  Preston, Robert F., father, owns home, free of mortgage, age 62, married, b. VA, farmer, retired.
  -- Lizzie, wife age 50, b. VA, teacher, public schools.
  -- Arthur, son, age 23, b. VA
  -- Lucy, daughter, age 18, b. VA
  -- Eleanor, daughter, age 16, b. VA
  -- Fannie Rhea daughter, 12, b. VA
  -- Robert, son, age 10, b. VA
[in same household]

Childers, Bruce, servant, black, 45, divorced, b. VA cook, house.
Campbell, Mary, cousin, age 50, single, b. VA, teacher, public
schools. He married **Elizabeth 'Lizzie' McDonald PRESTON**,
married 12 Feb 1896 in Washington Co., VA, b. 26 Mar 1870 in
Abingdon, Washington Co., VA, (daughter of Robert A. PRESTON
and Amelia Cummings PRESTON) d. 3 May 1934 in Washington
Co., VA, buried in Walnut Grove Cem. Washington Co. VA.
Married her cousin Robert.

Children:

478.　i　**Arthur Cummings PRESTON**, b. 1897 in
Washington Co., VA.

479.　ii　**Frances McIlwaine PRESTON**, b. ABT 1898 in
Washington Co., VA.

480.　iii　**Mildred C. PRESTON**, b. ABT 1900 in Washington
Co., VA.

481.　iv　**Lucy PRESTON**, b. 1902 in Washington Co., VA,
d. 1965.

482.　v　**Eleanor Fairman PRESTON**, b. 1904 in
Washington Co., VA. Married and moved to Florida.
She married **William SIMPSON**, b. ABT 1904.

483.　vi　**Frances 'Fannie' Rhea PRESTON**, b. 1908 in
Washington Co., VA, d. 1971.

484.　vii　**Robert Fairman PRESTON**, b. 1910 in
Washington Co., VA. He married **Corinne HELMS**,
b. ABT 1910.

174.　**Ellen Bankhead PRESTON**, (37.Henry^4, 5.John^3, 2.Robert^2,
1.John^1) b. 3 Mar 1857 in Washington Co., VA, d. 3 Mar 1923.
They had 2 children. She married **Otway Giles BAILEY**, married
24 Apr 1889 in Washington Co., VA, b. 25 May 1854 in Amherst
Co., VA, d. 1930 in Waugh, Amherst Co. VA. 1876-79 he was a
student at Virginia Military Institute. For many years was a civil
engineer.

1900 Federal census shows the family in Pedlar, Amherst Co., VA.
Bailey, O. G., head, May 1854, 46 married 11 years, b. VA, farmer.

-- Ellen, wife, Mar 1859, 41, married 11 years, 2 children, 2 living, b. VA
  -- Preston, son May 1891, 9, b. VA.
  -- Otway, son Jan 1895, 5, b. VA.

Served as Superintendent of Schools for Amherst Co. VA. 1910-14 he was collector for Internal Revenue at Lynchburg VA.

After his retirement he lived at Waugh, VA.

1920 Federal census shows the family at 1114 Bedford Av., Lynchburg City, Campbell Co., VA.
  Bailey, Otway G., head, owns home free of mortgage, 64, b. VA, agent, life insurance.
  -- Ellen P. wife, 62, b. VA
  -- Otway G. son, 25, single, b. VA. [no employment noted]

1930 he is living with the family of his son OG Jr. in Madison, Cumberland Co., VA.
Children:

+ 485.   i   **Preston Henry BAILEY** b. 25 May 1891.

+ 486.   ii   **Otway Giles BAILEY, Jr.** b. 20 Jan 1895.

176. **Henry PRESTON Jr.**, (37.Henry[4], 5.John[3], 2.Robert[2], 1.John[1]) b. 29 Jul 1861 in Washington Co., VA, d. 14 Dec 1921 in Abingdon, Washington Co. VA, buried in Walnut Grove Cem. Washington Co. VA. 1920 Federal census shows the family enumerated in the Goodson District of Washington Co., VA:
  Preston, Henry, head, owns home free of mortgage, 58, b. VA, farmer.
  -- Nellie, wife, 56, b. VA
  -- Hanley, daughter, 28, singe, b. VA.
  -- Sidney, daughter, 28, single, b. VA.
  -- Hal, son, 24, single, b. VA.
  -- Anna, daughter, 26, single, b. VA, teacher, graded school.
  -- Caron, son, 17, single, b. VA. He married **Mary 'Nellie' Helen CARSON**, married 16 Dec 1890, b. 13 Nov 1863 in Halls Bottom, Washington Co. VA, d. 17 Oct 1959 in Washington Co., VA, buried in Walnut Grove Cem. Washington Co. VA. Daughter of R P Carson and Maria Aston.
Children:

487. i **Sidney PRESTON**, b. 4 Sep 1885 in Washington Co., VA, d. 5 Oct 1938 in Washington Co., VA, buried in Walnut Grove Cem. Washington Co. VA. A twin of Henley.

488. ii **Henley PRESTON**, b. 4 Sep 1891 in Washington Co., VA, d. 1 Nov 1970 in Washington Co., VA, buried in Walnut Grove Cem. Washington Co. VA.

+ 489. iii **Henry PRESTON III** b. 27 Jun 1895.

490. iv **Robert Carson PRESTON**, b. 10 Sep 1902 in Washington Co., VA, d. 5 Jul 1941 in Washington Co., VA, buried in Walnut Grove Cem. Washington Co. VA. He was hit and killed by a car in front of is home.

491. v **Anne Carter PRESTON**, b. 16 Jun 1904 in Washington Co., VA.

181. **Percy Thomas PRESTON**, (37.Henry[4], 5.John[3], 2.Robert[2], 1.John[1]) b. 11 Oct 1875 in Washington Co., VA, d. 2 Apr 1941 in Washington Co., VA, buried in Walnut Grove Cem. Washington Co. VA. Percy was the youngest child of Henry and Anne Preston.

1910 the family is enumerated in the Virginia census in Goodson District, Washington Co, VA.
 Preston, Percy 34, married 4 years, b. VA, home farm
 -- Corinne, wife 35, married 4 years, 2 children, 2 living, b. VA
 -- Virginia W. daughter, 3, b. VA
 -- Percy L. (or T) Jr., son 10/12, b. VA
 Wills, Virginia, mother in law, widowed, age 71, 8 children, 5 living, b. TN, parents b. VA

1920 the family is enumerated again in the Virginia census in Goodson District, Washington Co, VA. Daughter Elizabeth 6 b. VA now is listed. Sister Margaret Preston 63 and mother in law Virginia Willis, now 82 are living with the family. A black servant John Mason 46, is recorded as their cook.

1930 the family is enumerated again in the Virginia census in Goodson District, Washington Co, VA. Son Percy Jr. now 20 and daughter Elizabeth 16 (incorrectly noted as son) are living at home. Brother in law James Willis age 57 b. VA, is the only other one living in the household. He married **Corinne Roane WILLS**, married 7 Sep 1905 in Clifford VA, b. 1 Apr 1875 in Amherst Co., VA, d. 28 Jul 1952 in Washington Co., VA, buried in Walnut Grove Cem. Washington Co. VA. 1937 statement made to the WPA researcher by Mrs. Percey Preston, wife of the then owner of the Preston house off Lee Highway, called Walnut Grove, relative to the transfer of the property:

"The old house on the site of the present house was frame about the size of the present home, as the kitchen chimney now used belonged to the house which was burned. no one seems positive as to the year the house was burned - it was either 1860 or 1861. Mr Preston's father (Col. John) must have spent his last years with his son Henry."

"Mr. Henry Preston left the home and about 600 acres of land to his single daughters Mary Coles, Margaret Brown, Jane Craighead and Isaetta R. Preston. Jane died in 1907, leaving her share to the three other girls. Shortly afterwards the girls decided to divide the property. Mary Coles, the oldest of the children, got the home and 150 acres of land. Her will was not legal, so the heirs, Ellen B. Baily, Anne Cary Killinger, Henry and Percy Preston, put the property up for sale and Percy bought out the other heirs." Signed Corinne Wills Preston (WPA Virginia 1937 report - Preston files of Washington Co., VA Historical Society.)

> *Children:*

492.   i   **Virginia PRESTON**, b. 19 Nov 1907 in Washington Co., VA. She married **Albert WILSON**, married 6 Jun 1925, b. ABT 1907.

493.   ii   **Percy Thomas PRESTON**, b. 15 Jun 1909 in Washington Co., VA. Lived in Lowry Hills, Bristol, VA. He married **Mary Margaret CARTER**, married 6 Sep 1933, b. ABT 1909.

494.   iii   **Elizabeth Madison PRESTON**, b. 13 May 1913 in Washington Co., VA, d. 28 Jun 1991 in Washington Co., VA, buried in Walnut Grove Cem. Washington Co. VA. She married **Kyle Roosevelt FARRIS**, married 28 Dec 1940, b. 30 May 1910, d. 30 Apr 1971 in Washington Co., VA?, buried in Walnut Grove Cem. Washington Co. VA. Son of Dr. and Alice C. Farris.

183. **Joseph RHEA**, (40.Sarah[4], 6.Jane[3], 2.Robert[2], 1.John[1]) b. 12 Dec 1830 in Virginia, d. 13 Aug 1909 in Sullivan Co., TN, buried in Blountville Cemetery, Sullivan Co., TN. Born at the home of his father and grand father, on Back Creek, Sullivan Co., Joseph Rhea's education was limited, only attending school in the log school house then near home. Not withstanding these limited opportunities he has a strong good mind and well stored with knowledge on all subjects. Showed great love for books and reading, read a great deal, retained it, could talk about it fluently, dare say, we'd have made a brilliant man.

After he was grown he had to take the management of the farm & colored people on it. Had to do this until the commencement of the war, at which time he enlisted as a soldier in the Confederate Army, went into it, was in several battles, but escaped all danger. All his comrades say he was a splendid soldier, always at his post, ready for duty, brave and fearless. Served in Company G 19th Tennessee Infantry.

After the War, returned to his father's house, found things in a dilapidated condition; the slaves all gone. All had left the old plantation but one family. The farm was much worn out by long and continued cultivation. But amid these discouraging features, Joseph faltered not; he buckled on the harness, put his shoulders to the that which with renewed strength and energy, determined, by divine help to bring things up again succeed, which he did. All the children were born and raised on the Old Homestead of his father R. P. Rhea. These children have been a great comfort and very helpful to their parents. They are bright, quick, have habits of neatness, good quiet dispositions, industry. The boys are musical in their tastes, play the violin banjo and are mechanical - make what they want. One of them told me this fall he intended to make a "bicycle" before another year. Cousin Jo' is very entertaining, loves to talk and laugh, tell anecdotes very fond of his kindred.
('Genealogy of the Rhea Family by W. L. Rhea , 1895)

1870 census shows he and Eliza Ann living on the farm with his father Robert Rhea. Joseph died at the age of 79 in the 4th District in Sullivan Co., Tennessee. The county records note senility as the cause.

1880 Federal census the family is enumerated in Civil District 4 of Sullivan Co., TN:

159

Rhea, Joseph 49, farmer, b. TN to TN parents.
-- Eliza, 42 wife, keeping house, b. VA to VA parents.
-- Robert E. 10, son at home, b. TN.
-- Alexander P., 9, son, at home, b. TN.
-- Joseph A. 7, son, at home, b. TN.
-- Sallie, 5, daughter, at home, b. TN

1900 Federal census the family is enumerated in Civil District 4 of
Sullivan Co., TN:
Rhea, Joseph, head 3 c, Dec 1830, 69, married 31 years, b. TN ,
farmer.
Eliza A., wife, Dec 1836, 63, 3 children, 3 living, b. VA.
Robert E., son, July 1864, 36, single, b. TN, farmer.
Lady, S., daughter, Oct 1874, 25, single, b. TN.
John, son, Sept 1878, 21, single, b. TN, farmer.

1910 Joseph died intestate and Robert E. was appointed
administrator on March 23, 1910. Final distribution in 1911 widow
- E. A. Rhea $268, Mrs. Margaret Bullard $15, Ladie S. Rhea $15.
(Margaret had married Chester Bullard.) He married **Eliza Ann
EARHART**, b. 25 Dec 1835 in Virginia, d. 26 May 1919 in
Sullivan Co., TN, buried in Blountville Cemetery, Sullivan Co., TN.
Children:

+ 495.　i　**Robert Earhart RHEA** b. 12 Jul 1870.

　496.　ii　**Alexander Preston RHEA**, b. 30 Oct 1870 in
Blountville, Sullivan Co., TN, d. 24 May 1944 in
Blountville, Sullivan Co., TN, buried in Blountville
Cemetery, Sullivan Co., TN. Born at 'Old Ireland',
the family home in Sullivan Co., TN. With the
exception of 25 years spent in Texas, he lived his
entire life in Sullivan Co. TN.

He was a lifelong member of the Presbyterian
Church. For a number of years and at the time of his
death he was bookkeeper for the Barrow-Scott
Milling Company.

1930 Federal census shows him enumerated in
Bristol, 17th Civil District, Sullivan Co., TN with his
siblings ilving at 314 Taylor Street.
Rhea, Alex P., head, owns home, valued $3,500, has
radio, single, 59, b. TN, bookkeeper, flour mill.

-- Ladie S., sister, single, 54, b. TN, no employment.
-- John, brother, single, 50, b. TN, no employment.
Bullard, Margaret, sister, 52, widow, b. TN.

497.   iii   **Joseph Anderson RHEA**, b. 1873 in Sullivan Co.,
TN. He married **Bess AKARD**, b. ABT 1873.

498.   iv   **Ladie Sarah 'Sallie' RHEA**, b. 15 Oct 1874 in
Sullivan Co., TN. 1910 she was living in household
of brother Robert with their mother as well.

1930 Federal census she is enumerated in the
household headed by her brother Alex Rhea, living at
314 Taylor St. Bristol, TN.

+ 499.   v   **Margaret Davis RHEA** b. 1 Oct 1876.

500.   vi   **John RHEA**, b. 1 Sep 1878 in Sullivan Co., TN, d.
15 Feb 1939 in Blountville, Sullivan Co., TN.
Obituary - John Rhea well known in the city, died
unexpectedly at his home at 334 Taylor St. at 12:30
am yesterday. He had been in declining health all
winter, but recently had seemed much improved. He
walked to the business section of the city on Monday
and apparently was in his usual health. About
12:30 am he arose and shortly afterwards fell dead.
Mr. Rhea was born and reared at 'Old Ireland' the
ancestral Rhea homestead on Back Creek. He never
married.

184.   **Frances 'Frank' Elizabeth RHEA**, (40.Sarah[4], 6.Jane[3], 2.Robert[2],
1.John[1]) b. 31 Dec 1832 in Sullivan Co., TN, d. 4 Nov 1870 in
Blountville, Sullivan Co., TN, buried in Blountville Cemetery,
Sullivan Co., TN. Born at the old home on Back Creek. When old
enough to go away to school she went to Jonesboro for 3 or 4 years.
She was invited up to the Female Academy in Blountville to open a
school. First payment received was a $5 gold piece from Tom
Holley for his daughter. Collected money every month. Taught
from 1852 to 1856 at which time the school closed due to an
outbreak of scarlet fever in town (W. L. Rhea-1895).

1870 census she was enumerated as head of household with her five
young children. Her property valued at $744. She would die within
the year. She married **Theodoric Bland RHEA**, married 1856, b.

21 Jun 1833 in Sullivan Co., TN, d. 15 Nov 1868 in Sullivan Co., TN, buried in Blountville Cemetery, Sullivan Co., TN. He died two years before his wife. When she died in 1870 the children were sent to live with Frances' younger sister Margaret and husband John T. Earhart, until they were old enough to follow the oldest Robert to Texas. In 1870 the oldest was only a young teen, the youngest 8.
Children:

+ 501. i   **Elizabeth 'Bettie' Dysart RHEA** b. 1856.

  502. ii   **Joe RHEA**, b. ABT 1857 in Sullivan Co., TN. Moved to NY. Sold insurance for Southland Co.

+ 503. iii **Robert Preston RHEA** b. 6 Mar 1859.

+ 504. iv   **James Theodoric RHEA** b. 11 Jun 1860.

+ 505. v   **Sarah 'Sally' Gilleland RHEA** b. 1 Mar 1862.

185. **Margaret 'Peggy' Preston RHEA**, (40.Sarah[4], 6.Jane[3], 2.Robert[2], 1.John[1]) b. 22 Jun 1835 in Sullivan Co., TN, d. 25 Feb 1913 in Sullivan Co., TN, buried in Blountville Cemetery, Sullivan Co., TN. Rhea siblings married Earhart siblings. A number of pictures of Margaret have been found. One shows her and her sister together in advanced age. Margaret is wearing a cameo with the likeness of her husband John as a young man. Lived on the Rhea family homestead, the Elms. She married **John Taylor EARHART**, married 21 May 1862 in Sullivan Co., TN, b. 31 Mar 1826 in Blacksburg, Montgomery Co., VA, d. 25 Mar 1896 in Sullivan Co., TN, buried in Blountville Cemetery, Sullivan Co., TN. 1860 Federal census in October shows the family enumerated under the spelling 'Earheart' in Blacksburg, Montgomery Co., VA.
  George Earheart (sic), 66, farmer, value of real estate $31,500, personal property $27,500, b. VA.
  Nancy, 58, b. VA
  Henry, 26, farmer, b. VA.
  Elizabeth, 18, b. VA.
  (next household is son John.)
  John T. Earheart, 33, Farmer, value of real estate $10,000, personal property $2,000, b. VA.

The family story goes that John Earhart did not want to stay on the family farm in Blacksburg VA raising horses so he took his inheritance in gold and headed for Texas. On the way he passed through Sullivan County and was pleased with the area. He continued to Texas but soon returned to Tennessee with his horse and saddlebags with his gold. (A story from James O. Bouton's childhood tales). There in Sullivan County he stopped and spent the night at Margaret's father's house. While on this trip he was pleased with and purchased the farm on Beaver Creek from James D. Rhea, known as the farm of James' father William Rhea. (This original Earhart farmstead is still (1995) in the family. Some of the Rhea/Earhart land has been sold out of the family and included the land where the Bristol Speedway has been built. The property had been sold to John at $.50/acre).

There at the Rhea's in Blountville John also had met the young lady Peggy; thus his interest in his farm increased, his visits more frequent and the young lady more attractive. Once when visiting the Rheas he found Robert, her youngest brother, lying low with fever. He went into the sick room, took charge of him, and proved himself a faithful and efficient nurse. This kindness rather more fully developed him in the estimation of the family. He continued his visits, now more especially to the young lady. Soon they agreed to link these distances and the time fixed to marry. They married and moved over on the Creek to his farm. There they lived; all their children were born there.

1870 census shows John Aerhart (sic) and Margaret (Peggy) with children of the following ages Charles B. 6, Sarah 4, Robert R. 3, Joseph age 6 months. They were enumerated next to father-in-law Robert Preston Rhea's family. John's real estate was valued at $6200 and property $1787.

1871 Nov 6, John T. Earhart, Jacob Smith, William. R. Anderson and Rhea Anderson post Guardian Bond for guardianship of Edward and Margaret Smith, minor children of Margaret Smith, decd. (Sullivan Co. Exect. Admin and Guardian Bonds pg. 99)

1880 Federal census shows James F. Rhea, nephew living with John's family. This would actually be James Theodoric Rhea, the orphan of Frances and Thedoric Rhea. The Earharts had taken the two younger children of Theodoric Rhea into the household on the death of their mother 'Frankie' at the age of 38. These children eventually followed their brother Robert to Texas.

Jan. 3, 1888 the Bristol Courier reported - John T. Earhart has received a letter, as I am informed, that his sister-in-law at Pulaski

VA is dead. Jan. 10, 1888 it was reported that John T. Earhart's son, Joseph and Joseph Rhea's son Robert (Robert Earhart Rhea - John's nephew who was born in 1870, 8 years after John married Margaret Rhea) have entered as students at Holston Institute.

He was an elder in the Blountville church for a number of years. He was a fine farmer, kept everything in nice order around him. He felt he was declining in health the last year or two. He lived getting ready for his last sickness which was rather short and his death sooner than expected. When it came he was ready, consoled by his children, all were around him when he fell "asleep in Jesus". John died Wednesday night March 25, 1896 aged 70 years. He left wife and six children. Mr. Carson conducted his funeral in church and he was buried on the cemetery on the hill. ('Genealogy of the Rhea Family by W L Rhea, 1895).
Children:

506.　i　**Charles Balfour EARHART I.**, b. ABT 1860 in Blountville, Sullivan Co., TN, d. ABT 1860 in Blountville, Sullivan Co., TN. The family story was that he drowned in the creek next to the family home. A brother was later named for him. Dates of marriage and births of the other children do not fit well with this story though.

507.　ii　**Robert R. EARHART**, b. 1 May 1863 in Sullivan Co., TN, d. 31 Jul 1915 in Sullivan Co., TN, buried in Blountville Cemetery, Sullivan Co., TN. No children living with them in 1900 census.

　　　1915 Aug. 1, Obituary: Bristol: R R Earhart, 47 yr, pioneer businessman committed suicide at 529 Ala. by cutting his throat. Survived by brothers Joseph, Chas. John H.; sisters Mrs. Ed Carter, Mrs. Maggie Fain, Arizona. 1913 Bristol City Directory showed him as proprietor of Earhart Furniture at 617 State Street. He married **Maime Bell POWELL**, b. 1 Jul 1871 in Sullivan Co., TN, d. 9 Jul 1920 in Sullivan Co., TN, buried in Blountville Cemetery, Sullivan Co., TN. 1920 Obituary - Mrs. Robert Earhart wife of the late Robert Earhart of the city, died at St. Luke's Hospital yesterday morning at 10 o'clock after an operation for acute indigestion. Mrs. Earhart became ill Sunday, but it was not considered serious until Thursday, when it was realized that she would have to undergo and operation. She was immediately taken to St. Luke's Hospital where the operation was performed the same afternoon, and she died the following morning.

Mr. and Mrs. Earhart came to the city about 20 years ago where Mr. Earhart engaged in the furniture business until his death about 5 years ago. She was formerly Miss Mammie Powell. She wa a member of the Central Presbyterian Church and made many friends in this City. She is survived by two sisters, Miss Mattie Powell with whom she had been living, and Mrs. N. L. Warlick of Jonesboro TN.

+ 508.   iii   **Charles Balfer EARHART II.** b. 23 Nov 1864.

+ 509.   iv   **Sarah Ella EARHART** b. 1866.

+ 510.   v   **Joseph Preston EARHART** b. 1 Dec 1869.

+ 511.   vi   **Margaret Jane 'Maggie' EARHART** b. 1872.

  512.   vii   **John Henry EARHART**, b. 1 Mar 1874 in Bristol, Sullivan Co., TN, d. 17 Aug 1940 in Sullivan Co., TN, buried in Blountville Cemetery, Sullivan Co., TN. 1940 obituary - John Henry Earhart Is Victim of Stroke. John Henry Earhart 66, well known farmer of the Thomas Bridge section of Sullivan Co. died Saturday morning at 11:45 at Kings Mountain Memorial Hospital having suffered a paralytic stroke a few days ago. He was the son of the late John T. and Margaret Preston Earhart, pioneer settlers.

Mr. Earhart is survived by his wife Mrs. Francis (sic) Earhart, and the following children: Mrs. Marion I. Harmon of Erwin and Clarence, William and John Howard Earhart. Also surviving is one sister Mrs. Maggie Earhart Fain of Norris, TN.

189.   **Robert A. PRESTON**, (41.Alexander[4], 6.Jane[3], 2.Robert[2], 1.John[1]) (See marriage to number 61.)

190. **Nannie Montgomery PRESTON**, (43.John[4], 6.Jane[3], 2.Robert[2], 1.John[1]) b. 4 May 1838 in Washington Co., VA, d. 13 Jun 1906. She married **John 'Col.' Calhoun SUMMERS**, married 1866, b. 1 Feb 1839 in Union WVA, d. 19 Jun 1907. During the time this country was in its infancy, John's G-father killed the Indian chief 'Sunshine Arrow' so he called his 8th child by that name in honor of the chief. John was the captain of the "Monroe Invincibles", Company A, 3rd Virginia Regiment, and a major and Lt. Col. of the 60th Virginia Infantry. He and Nannie had 10 children. (From researcher Fred Preston 2005.)

1880 Federal Virginia census shows the family enumerated in Goodson District of Washington Co., VA.
  Summers, John C. 39, lawyer, b. VA, parents b. VA.
  -- Nannie M. 40, wife, keeping house, b. VA, parents b. VA and TN.
  -- Lewis P., 12 son, attending school.
  -- Olivia W. 9, daughter, b. VA
  --Robert J. 7, son, b. VA
  --Jennie P. 5, daughter, b. VA
  --Nannie M. 4, daughter, b. VA
  --Fanny R. 2, daughter, b. VA
  --Sunshine 1, son, b. VA

1900 Federal Virginia census again shows the family enumerated in Goodson District of Washington Co., VA. John's birth and birth place information is different. The ink on this census page is badly smudged.
  Summers, John C., Feb 1841, 59, married 34 years, b. W. Virginia to parents born in Ohio.
  -- Nannie M., wife, May 1849, 60, married 34 years, 10 children, 8 living, b. VA to parents from Virginia.
  -- Robert J., son, Oct 1874, 26, b. VA
  -- Nannie M, daughter, June 1877, 22, single, b. VA
  -- Sunshine A., son, Jan 1880, 15, b. VA
  -- John C., son, Mar 1884, 15, b. VA.
            Children:

+ 513.   i   **Lewis Preston SUMMERS** b. 2 Nov 1868.

+ 514.   ii   **John Fairman SUMMERS** b. ABT 1870.

  515.   iii **Olivia Weit SUMMERS**, b. ABT 1874 in Abingdon, Washington Co., VA.

+ 516.   iv   **Robert James SUMMERS** b. 1 Oct 1874.

517.   v   **Nannie America SUMMERS**, b. 1 Jun 1877 in Abingdon, Washington Co., VA.

518.   vi   **Jennie Pinkney SUMMERS**, b. ABT 1878 in Abingdon, Washington Co., VA. She married **George Thomas MITCHELL**, married 16 Sep 1888, b. 17 May 1865 in Sullivan Co., TN, d. 17 May 1897 in Sullivan Co., TN, buried in Pyle Cemetery, Kingsport, TN.

519.   vii   **Sunshine Andrew SUMMERS**, b. 1880 in Abingdon, Washington Co., VA. 1910, 1920 and 1930 Federal census records show Andrew living with the family of his sister Fannie Clark Summers on Main Street, Abingdon, VA. 1910 and 1920 records show he was Deputy Clerk for the County Court and then the Circuit Court; 1930 manager for Edwin(?) and Sons Motor Co.

+ 520.   viii   **Fannie Rhea SUMMERS** b. 1881.

521.   ix   **Von Moltke SUMMERS**, b. ABT 1884 in Abingdon, Washington Co., VA.

+ 522.   x   **John Carlisle SUMMERS** b. 1 Mar 1887.

191.   **Robert J. PRESTON**, (43.John[4], 6.Jane[3], 2.Robert[2], 1.John[1]) (See marriage to number 145.)

192.   **Sarah Elleanor PRESTON**, (43.John[4], 6.Jane[3], 2.Robert[2], 1.John[1]) b. 21 Oct 1843 in Washington Co., VA, d. 22 Jun 1927 in Bristol, Sullivan Co., TN. She married **David 'Col.' Flournoy BAILEY**, married 29 Feb 1872 in Washington Co., VA, b. 23 Jan 1845 in Charlotte Co. VA, d. 30 Oct 1922 in Bristol, Washington Co., VA. After his father died, Dave Bailey's mother taught school in Louisa Co. VA to support herself and her children (perhaps 3). Her son Dave was her pupil. One day she overheard him planning to run away and join the Confederate Army. She cut the oil cloth off the kitchen table and cut a hole in the center of it for him to stick his head through and use it as a rain slicker. She was too poor to give him anything else but her blessing. (Note: oilcloth was light canvas

onto one side of which was bonded a white thin, flexible, slick surface that was waterproof and easily cleaned by a soapy dishrag) (From Bailey Byers Aug. 13, 1990).

Another anecdote from Bailey Byers, who heard it from the lips of is grandfather, David Bailey. It happened in the Bailey's Crossroads area, where he and some fellow soldiers had become separated from their main body and had lain down to rest on a hot Summer day. They suddenly saw some soldiers nearby. They engaged in a shouting match, and then began to shoot at each other. The two groups closed with each other for hand to hand combat and in the fray David grabbed the muzzle of an opposing soldier's rifle. The rifle went off, sending a fragment through David's hand between the thumb and palm. The two groups disengaged and David's group resumed the search for their main body. En-route they rested again by a creek into which David dipped his hand in order to ease the pain. He either fainted or fell asleep. He was awaken by a woman who claimed to own the land, and who had come to scold the soldiers. She stopped fussing when she saw that they were hurt. David had undone his neckerchief and dragged it through the hole in his hand, thus cleaning out a great deal of septic mess that had been softened by the creek water. The woman bandaged David's hand and gave him some buttermilk to drink and watermelon to eat. The group resumed the search for their main body, finding them at Munson's Hill (now part of the 7-corners area of VA.) David Bailey's hand was crippled for the rest of his life. Some 60 years after this incident (in the early 1920's) Dave and his wife came to live and die at Alcova. He had Bailey Byers drive him around the Bailey's crossroads area to locate the actual sites of this incident.

He came to Bristol before the war and after there resided. Learned the art of printing at the Bristol News and at one time owned and edited the paper. Studied law at Cumberland U., Lebanon TN

1869 in July he began the practice of the profession of law.

1879-80 he represented the County in the VA legislature and was chairman of the Judiciary committee.

1881-85 he was a State Senator.

1920 Federal census shows David and Eleanor enumerated in the home of their son in law, William Tillar in Emporia, Greeneville

Co., VA, living on Church Street. David F. is 75, a lawyer, and Eleanor F. is age 76.

Children:

523. i **Nannie Louise Montgomery BAILEY**, b. ABT 1872 in Sullivan Co., TN?.

+ 524. ii **Jane Rhea BAILEY** b. 15 Dec 1872.

+ 525. iii **Julia Flourney BAILEY** b. 20 Feb 1874.

+ 526. iv **Martha Preston BAILEY** b. 25 Jun 1876.

527. v **Robert Preston BAILEY**, b. ABT 1878 in Sullivan Co., TN?.

528. vi **David Ellar BAILEY**, b. 1879 in Washington Co., VA. 1880 he is enumerated in the household of uncle James Preston, age 1. Called 'neice' in that Virginia U.S. census.

193. **James Brainerd PRESTON**, (43.John[4], 6.Jane[3], 2.Robert[2], 1.John[1]) b. 3 Dec 1845 in Washington Co., VA, d. 21 Oct 1922. His home was 'Locust Glen' 20 miles west of Abington VA. He was a farmer.

He was a freshman at VA Military Institute in during the Civil War and fought with the cadet battalion in the Battle of New Market. A monument by the drill field at VMI in Lexington VA lists the names of those
who fought and includes a number of Prestons. 257 cadets were on the field on Mar 15, 1864 at New Market. 10 were killed, 45 wounded. They youngest was 15, the oldest 25. He and his cousin Thomas W. Preston were in the class of '67.

1880 Virginia census shows him enumerated in Goodson District of Washington Co., VA.
 Preston, James, 33, farmer, b. VA
 -- Jennie F. 23, sister, keeping house, b. VA
 Bailey, David E. 1, niece (sic), b. VA
 Worley, Thursey , mulatto, 18, servant, domestic servant, b. VA

1900 Federal census shows James living in the household of his brother in law Thomas Newman and sister Jennie's family at 411 Russell St., Bristol, VA.

Newman, Thomas, head Nov. 1844, 56, married 8 years, b. VA, asst. agent, RR.

-- Jennie F. wife, Nov 1856, 43, b. VA.

Newman, Arol m, son, Nov 1899, 20, b. VA.

Preston James B., b-in-law, Dec. 1845, 54, widower, b. VA, stock dealer.

-- Seaton T, step nephew, Mar 1892, 8, b. TN.

1930 Federal census shows James living in the household of his brother in law Thomas Newman and sister Jennie at 411 Spencer St., Bristol, VA, age 74. He married **Harriett 'Hattie' Bryan TINSLEY**, married 20 Oct 1890, b. 18 Feb 1861 in Richmond, Henrico Co., VA, d. 1 Jul 1898.

> *Children:*

+ 529.   i   **Seaton Tinsley PRESTON** b. 29 Mar 1892.

194. **Samuel Rhea PRESTON**, (43.John[4], 6.Jane[3], 2.Robert[2], 1.John[1]) b. 4 Sep 1849 in Washington Co., VA, d. 1929 in Decatur, GA. (Fairman Cumming November 23, 2005 phone conversation Foley from Decatur GA with Ed Foley)
He was born in 1849 at Locust Glen, Washington Co. He is only in the family diary when he turns about 5 years old when they write what are we going to do with his crib now that he is grown.

The youngest son of Irish Bob, John Fairman Preston I (Samuel's older brother) kept the farm going. His next oldest brother James also had been there. I just found a letter to James at Locust Glen in Abingdon Virginia. It seems to come from New York State and was written right after John Fairman Preston died. It is all about investments in a mine and what should be do with this investment and that he shouldn't have died without tending to this investment and now you are going to have to tend to it. This does have a lot about the business of John expecting James to take care of the business. There are other letters that Samuel Rhea Preston wrote.

The next oldest brother of Samuel was James. He lived into the 1920's. He was probably a civil war veteran. We have just come across and unsigned civil war 15-page essay in this group of letters written by somebody. It is extremely well written and looks like school essay written in about 1869 about what it was like to face McClellan in the mountains of West Virginia. I read it just once and I left it in Montreat with someone who is collecting things of that period.

John Fairman Preston writes at age over 60, that we hear that so and so is over at Saltville Virginia, I guess I better join the war. He is writing this in March 1865. Then his son Samuel Rhea Preston, who is quite literate, writes in it "I guess we'll have to sell the slaves." I am sorry to have said that, but that is what is says - a 15-year-old boy writes that. I have a book of poems that was a prize dated April 1863. The award was just a few days after the battle of Chancellorsville. They would not have heard of the battle yet. I am not sure what school he had gone to win the prize. He used an 1863 yearbook of the US Dept of Agriculture as a scrapbook. He put his itinerary of his trip to Fernandina in it for instance. He was in the first graduating class of King College in Bristol TN. He gave the oration.

My grandfather started at King and transferred to Furman because his father had moved to Greenville SC. He actually moved to a church and then started this women's seminary.

My great grandfather (Samuel Rhea Preston) was not an effective minister in some respects. He was very emotional and very tedious. I actually have some sermons from many sides of my family, and I think it is better that he became a teacher and founded this college.

His first pastorate was at Fermandina, Florida. They moved after only about a year, fortunate to have an appointment in Athens.

He stayed in Athens about 3 years and then to another town in the valley just north of Abingdon. They were in Athens in 1876 and stayed until 1879. He went to Columbia Theological Seminary for 3 years, 1872-74. I just found the notebook that he had when he arrived there.

After serving in Athens TN, his next in Blacksburg, then to Wytheville VA, then came down to Bristol.

1880 Federal census of Virginia shows the family in Blacksburg, Montgomery Co., VA.
  Preston, S. R. 30, Minister of Gospel, b. VA to parents from VA and TN.
  -- Ida, 26, wife, Keeping House, b. SC to parents from PA and NJ.
  -- John (written in afterward) Fariman, 5, son, b. FL to parents from VA and SC.

-- Samuel (then written in) Rhea, 3, son, b. SC to parents from VA and SC.

-- Mary Floy, 1, daughter, b. TN to parents from VA and SC.
Battle, Judy, black, 30, servant, b. VA.

(Fairman Preston continues) My grandmother once told me that he (John Fairman Preston) taught himself to read at about 4 years old. I have just come across a number of essays he wrote when he 10 years old. It is really nice to read these in my grandfather's handwriting what he wrote in 1885. Supposedly he was in Sunday School with the woman who became the second Mrs. Woodrow Wilson.

1900 the South Carolina US census showed the family in Greenville City, Greenville Co. SC living on Main St.:
Preston, Samuel Rhea, head b. Sept 1849, age 50, married 25 years, b. VA, parents . VA and TN, Minister, rents house.

-- Ida, wife b. Jan. 1854, age 46, married 25 years, 8 children, 7 living, b. SC, parents b. NJ.

-- John Fairman, son b. Apr 1875, age 25, b. FL, student.

-- Samuel Rhea, son, b. Mar 1877, age 23, b. SC, stenographer oil mill.

-- James Brainerd, son b. May 1892, age 18, b. VA, student.

-- Nathan Bachman, son, b. Aug 1887, age 12, b. VA,

-- Ida S., daughter, b. Sept 1889, age 10, b. VA, student.

-- Jenn N., daughter, b. Oct 1897, age 2, b. SC.

-- Mary S. m-in- law, b. 1820, age 80, widow, 7 children, 4 living, b. NJ, parents b. NJ.

-- Eugenia D. s [sister]-in-law, b. Sept 1859, 41, single, b. SC, parents b. NJ. Matron - college.

1920 Federal census of Virginia shows the family living in Richmond, Henrico Co., VA at 318 Seminary Avenue in household #11 headed by John F. Preston (his son).
Preston, Samuel, father in law (sic), 70, b. VA to parents from VA and TN, not employed.

-- Ida S., mother in law, 65, b. SC to parents from NJ.

--Florence, sister in law, 40, single, b. TN to parents from VA and SC, teacher, high school.

--Janey, sister in law, 22, single, b. SC to parents from VA and SC, no employment.
Loodwin, Olvier, servant, black, 78,k widowed, b. NC, cook, private family. He married **Ida SUTPHEN**, married 30 Jun 1874 in Columbia, Edgefield Co., SC, b. 6 Jan 1854 in Columbia, Edgefield Co., SC, d. 1 Jun 1930 in Bristol, Sullivan Co., TN. Ida's father was

John Christopher Sutphen; the guy was a native of NJ and his family goes back to 1651 to the first Dutch Settlements in NY. John C. Sutphen's mother was a Bye, but when her first husband died, the youngest son was put out as an apprentice with a relative and he didn't like it and ran away. Found a wife in NY and went south to Columbia SC. Ida grew up in Columbia.

Ida Sutphen was from Columbia SC and lived near the Wilson family while Woodrow Wilson's father taught at Columbia Seminary. Ida Sutphen Preston knew the Wilsons and went to tea at the White House while she was living in Baltimore about 1919. She went down to visit them just once. Only a childhood friend could to that. She was a few years older than Wilson, and my mother said probably taught him piano lessons.

There is a bullet from one of Sherman's troops guns that she dug out of the wall of her bedroom. My mother knew her grandmother and her grandmother taught her to sew and this bullet is in Ida Sutphen Prestons sewing box.

This daughter of John Christopher Sutphen married a seminary student. The seminary was in Columbia.

Ida's mother lived with her daughter and Samuel Rhea Preston for a while at the end of her life. She didn't die there, but lived with them in Greenville and is in a picture of the family taken at Chicora College.

1930 Federal census of South Carolina shows Ida living with the family of her daughter Ida S. P. Warden in Greenville SC at 16 Daniel(?) Street.
   I)Preston, Ida S., mother in law, 76, widowed, married at 20, b. SC to parents from PA and NJ.
Children:

+ 530.   i   **John Fairman PRESTON** b. 1 Apr 1875.

+ 531.   ii   **Samuel Rhea PRESTON, Jr.** b. 22 Mar 1877.

   532.   iii   **Robert James PRESTON**, b. ABT 1878 in Bristol, Sullivan Co., TN.

   533.   iv   **Mary Florence PRESTON**, b. 1 May 1879 in Bristol, Sullivan Co., TN.

+ 534.   v   **James Brainard PRESTON** b. 27 May 1882.

535.   vi   **Nathan Bachman PRESTON**, b. 10 Oct 1887 in VA, d. 18 Jan 1967 in Decatur, GA. He was an essential oils salesman for Magnus, Mabbee, Rehnard at one time.

               1930 Federal census of Knoxville, Knox Co., TN showed the couple living at 2657 Magnolia Avenue, Knoxville TN:
Preston, Nathan B., head, rents, $55/month, 42 married at 31, b. VA to parents from VA and SC, Manager (rental), Trust Co.
-- Ethel S., wife-h, 33, married at 22, b. TN to parents from TN. He married **Ethel S. 'Spiffy' wife of Nathan PRESTON**, b. 1896, d. 1953.

+ 536.   vii   **Ida Sutphen PRESTON** b. 16 Sep 1889.

537.   viii   **Jane 'Jennie' F. Newman PRESTON**, b. 27 Oct 1897 in Greenville, SC, d. 1 May 1973 in Decatur, GA. She attended Agnes Scott College. She was a professor of English Literature. She never married.

195. **Jennie Fairman PRESTON**, (43.John[4], 6.Jane[3], 2.Robert[2], 1.John[1]) b. 1 Nov 1856 in Washington Co., VA, d. 1910 in Blountville, Sullivan Co., TN. 1900 Federal census shows the family at 411 Russell St., Bristol, VA. Jennie's widowed brother and his son are living with them.
  Newman, Thomas, head Nov. 1844, 56, married 8 years, b. VA, asst. agent, RR.
-- Jennie F. wife, Nov 1856, 43, b. VA.
Newman, Arol, son, Nov 1899, 20, b. VA.
  Preston James B., b-in-law, Dec. 1845, 54, widower, b. VA, stock dealer.
-- Seaton T, step nephew, Mar 1892, 8, b. TN.

1910 Federal census shows the couple at 411 Spencer St., Bristol, VA (same house number as 1900, different street name). Jennie's brother James is living with them.

1910 the Will of. Jennie Preston Newman. Recorded in Will Book #3 page 481, Blountville, TN. May 16, 1910.

I will and bequeath to my husband, T. J. Newman, my house and lot on Windsor Avenue, also my personal property his lifetime. My son, Carol Newman, my diamond pin and amethyst brooch. Seaton, my nephew, to have my piano, my mahogany bureau and my books. Carol to have some books which I will give to him. My large mirror to Floy, also my cameo and coral jewelry to Two. The Oak set of furniture, also the Walnut set, to go to Carol. My Walnut set and bedding to go to Seaton. Black leather furniture to go to Seaton. Mahogany sofa to go to Seaton.

If my husband should be dead at the time of my demise, it is my wish that my house and lot on Windsor Avenue should be sold and after defraying my funeral expenses the remainder to be divided between J. B., Seaton, Carol and Jennef.

12 gilt band custard cups, which were my mother's, to be divided six each to my nieces Janie Bailey Byars and Julia Flournoy Tillar. Mattie Bailey Price to have one gilt band pickle dish and one white one. My daughter Carrie F. Newman to have hand painted bon bon dish, cut glass vase, green salad bowl, red celery dish, hand painted cake plate. Seaton to have loving cup and hand painted china, also cut glass tumblers, carafe. Carrie to have cut glass celery dish.

(Signed) Jennie Preston Newman

May 17th 1910.

I add this amendment to my will. At the death of my husband, Mr. T. J. Newman, my house and lot on Windsor Avenue I will and bequeath to J. B. and Seaton Preston. Carol and Jennef, to have $50 (Fifty Dollars) each out of any money left from my estate. Seaton is to have my diamond ring. Carol the stick pin at my death.

(Signed) Jennie P. Newman

Carrie to have the Walnut sideboard. Seaton to have my china press. Floy to have 1 doz. gilt band soup plates. Jennef 1 doz. gilt band soup plates. All my property not mentioned in will to go to Seaton.

(Signed) Jennie Preston Newman

Researcher Fred Preston notes in 2005: Commentary: I just came into possession of this will and it was significant to me because the living Newmans have no record of Jennie Preston, wife of T. J. Newman. According to their genealogy Thomas James Newman married Alda Roper, daughter of Benjamin Roper, in 1876. I now have proof that Jennie Fairman Preston was married to T. J. Newman in 1900 in Bristol, VA. (Letter written by my father when he was 8 years old, Oct. 17th, 1900 in Bristol.) Question is when did they get married.

Characters mentioned in the will that I can place: Seaton was my father. He was probably very close to Jennie because his mother, Harriet Tinsley Preston died when he was 6 years old. J. B. would be my fathers father, James Brainerd Preston. Carol Newman was the son of T. J. Newman. Carrie F. Newman would be Carolyn Fain Newman, Carol Newmans wife. Carol and Carrie had four children but the first was born in 1910, the year this will was recorded, thus they were not mentioned. Janie Bailey Byars would be Jane Rhea Bailey who married Joseph Cloyd Byars. They lived in Bristol for a time but both died at the Old Deery Inn in Blountville, TN. Julia Flournoy Tillar was Julia Flournoy Bailey who married William Thomas Tillar. Mattie Bailey Price was Martha Preston Bailey who married Judge John W. Price. She married **Thomas James NEWMAN**, b. 1 Mar 1844 in Wytheville VA, d. 1924.
Children:

+ 538.　i　**Carol Montgomery NEWMAN** b. 1879.

198.　**Elizabeth Arthur PRESTON**, (44.Walter[4], 8.John[3], 3.Walter[2], 1.John[1]) b. 1 Feb 1860 in Washington Co., VA. Another researcher showed her name as Elizabeth Cummings Preston. She married **George William WARD Jr.**, married 10 Dec 1878 in Knoxville, TN, b. 31 Jul 1847 in Winchester VA, d. 2 1897 in Washington Co., VA. Educated at Virginia Military Institute. He studied law at U. of VA.

1864 May, fought at Newmarket.

1872 licensed in law and settled at Springfield MO. Came to Abington 1874.

Edited 'Abington Virginian'.

1880 elected County Judge. Later Commonwealth attorney and elected Judge again. Died of pneumonia.
Children:

539.   i   **George William WARD III. JR.**, b. ABT 1880 in VA?. Died unmarried.

540.   ii   **Rosalle Garnett WARD**, b. ABT 1880 in VA?. She married and moved to Western PA. She married **Mr. ANDERSON**.

207. **Katherine Greenway PRESTON**, (45.James[4], 8.John[3], 3.Walter[2], 1.John[1]) b. 18 Jun 1860 in Washington Co., VA, d. 24 Jun 1942 in Abingdon, Washington Co. VA, buried in Sinking Spring Cem. Washington Co. VA. She married **John James STUART**, married 3 1889, b. 15 Apr 1860 in VA?, d. 13 Jul 1939 in Abingdon, Washington Co. VA, buried in Sinking Spring Cem. Washington Co. VA. Had five children.

1910 Federal census of Virginia shows the family enumerated in the Abingdon District of Washington Co., VA
  Stuart, John J. head, 50 married at 21, b. VA, Attorney, practices law.
  -- Kate G. wife, 49 married at 21, 6 children, 5 living, b. VA
  -- William A. son, 20, b. VA
  -- Katherine G. daughter, 18, b. VA
  -- Henry C. son, 17, b. VA
  -- Walter P son, 14, b. VA
  -- Margaret P. daughter 12, b. VA

1930 Federal census of Virginia shows the couple enumerated in Abingdon, Washington Co., VA.
  Stuart, John J., head, owns house, house value $8000, have no radio, age 70, married at 29, bl. VA, Judge of Circuit Court.
  -- Kate G. wife, age 69, married at 28, b. VA.
       Children:

+ 541.   i   **William Alexander STUART** b. 24 Oct 1889.

+ 542.   ii   **Katherine Greenway STUART** b. 1890.

+ 543.   iii **Henry Carter STUART** b. 1892.

    544.   iv   **Carter STUART**, b. 1893 in Washington Co., VA.

    545.   v   **Margaret Preston STUART**, b. 1896 in Washington Co., VA. Moved to Hartford

Connecticut. Had 5 children. She married **Berkeley COX**, b. ABT 1897 in Richmond, Henrico Co., VA.

546.　vi　**Walter Preston STUART**, b. 1898 in Washington Co., VA. Lived in Saltville, VA.

210.　**Margaret Lynn PRESTON**, (47.John^4, 8.John^3, 3.Walter^2, 1.John^1) b. 27 Jul 1865 in VA, d. 16 Jul 1949. At one time lived in Chattanooga TN.

1920 Federal census shows the family in Logan Store Township, Rutherford Co., NC.
　Woods, Thomas E P, head, 45, b. TN to TN parents, principal, prep school.
　-- Marguarete L P, wife, 54, b. VA to VA parents, Matron (?), West Mu--- school
　-- Zellu (?), daughter, 16, single, b. TN to parents from TN and Indiana.
　-- Eward (?), son, 14, b. TN to parents from TN and Indiana.
The census clearly notes that the mother of these children was born in Indiana, but Margaret was clearly noted on the census as having been born in Virginia. The dates of their birth predate the marriage of Thomas and Margaret, so these were probably step children of Margaret's. She married **Thomas 'Rev. T. E. P.' WOODS**, married 26 Aug 1909, b. 1875.
　　Children:

547.　i　**Zellu WOODS**, b. 1904 in TN.

548.　ii　**Eward WOODS**, b. 1906.

212.　**Elizabeth Cummings PRESTON**, (47.John^4, 8.John^3, 3.Walter^2, 1.John^1) b. 3 Jun 1868, d. 28 Aug 1956. Had 4 children. She married **Robert GRAY IV.**, married 4 Sep 1895 in Seven Mile Ford, VA, b. 10 Mar 1859, d. 13 Oct 1932.
　　Children:

549.　i　**Mary Preston GRAY**, b. 2 Aug 1896 in VA. Author of the book titled "The Family Tree" about the Preston family. She lived in Bristol VA and dedicated her life to family genealogy. She was active throughout her life. Unmarried.

+ 550.　ii　**Anne Montgomery GRAY** b. 22 Mar 1898.

+ 551.   iii   **Robert Asher GRAY V.** b. 1 Sep 1900.

552.   iv   **John Montgomery Preston GRAY**, b. 16 Jun 1902, d. 10 Sep 1947. Died unmarried.

213.   **Cochran 'Rev.' PRESTON**, (47.John[4], 8.John[3], 3.Walter[2], 1.John[1]) b. 9 May 1871 in VA, d. 12 May 1935. 1920 Federal census shows the family enumerated at Charlotte Court House township in Roanoke Co., VA, living on Main Street.
Preston Cochran, head, rents, 48, b. VA, clergyman, pastor.
-- Virginia, G., wife 42, b. WV to parents from VA.
-- Elinor, G., daughter, 16, b. VA
-- John M., son, 13, b. VA. He married **Virginia GRAHAM**, b. 1878 in WV.
Children:

553.   i   **Ellinor Graham PRESTON**, b. 5 Jun 1903 in VA.

+ 554.   ii   **John Montgomery PRESTON** b. 4 Jul 1906.

220.   **Susan Morris PRESTON**, (48.Charles[4], 8.John[3], 3.Walter[2], 1.John[1]) b. 1 Aug 1886 in VA. She married **Louis 'Dr.' LEAKE**, b. 1880 in VA. 1930 Federal census shows the family enumerated in Licking Hole, Goochland Co., VA.
Lecke, Louis K., head, owns home, has radio, age 50, 31 when first married, b. VA, Treasurer, County.
-- Susie M., Wife-H, 44, married at 27, b. VA
-- Andrew K., son, 18, single, b. VA.
-- Walter, brother, 48, single, b. VA
-- Charles L., brother, 46, single, b. VA
Preston, Charles, H., Father in law, 89, widower, b. VA
Taylor, Susie, aunt, 60, single, b. VA
Swindell, Frederick nephew, 16, single, b. VA
Wetson, William, lodger, servant, age 46, single, b. VA.
Children:

555.   i   **Andrew K. LEAKE**, b. 1912.

237.   **Alexander R. PRESTON**, (61.Amelia[4], 11.Robert[3], 3.Walter[2], 1.John[1]) b. 1869 in Abingdon, Washington Co., VA, d. BEF 1930. He and his family lived in Washington D.C.

1910 he and his family appear in in the census living with his parents. He is noted as employed in insurance.

1930 Federal census his wife appears as a widow in Bristol, Washington Co., VA. He married **Bessie GORDON**, b. 1879. 1930 Federal census shows family in Bristol, Washington Co., VA. She is a widow - using name Gibson. They live at 506 Moore St. Bristol, VA.

Gibson (It is not 'Gordon'), Bessie P., head, renting, age 49, widow, first married at 20, b. VA, parents b. VA, works Real Estate.

Preston, Frank, G. son, age 22, b. VA, salesman, real estate.

-- Elizabeth G., daughter, 21, b. VA, Stenographic, Printing.

-- Martha M., daughter, 19, b. VA

-- Alexander R., son, 17, single, b. VA.

Children:

556.   i   **Robert PRESTON**, b. ABT 1900 in VA.

557.   ii   **Elizabeth G. PRESTON**, b. 1909 in VA.

558.   iii **Frank G. PRESTON**, b. 1908 in VA.

559.   iv **Martha M. PRESTON**, b. 1911 in VA.

560.   v   **Alexander R. PRESTON**, b. 1913 in VA.

238. **Elizabeth 'Lizzie' McDonald PRESTON**, (61.Amelia[4], 11.Robert[3], 3.Walter[2], 1.John[1]) (See marriage to number 169.)

241. **Thomas Wilson PRESTON**, (61.Amelia[4], 11.Robert[3], 3.Walter[2], 1.John[1]) b. 10 Jan 1876 in Abingdon, Washington Co., VA, d. 15 Jan 1955 in Bristol, Sullivan Co., TN. 1948 article in the local paper by Robert Loving in his column The Local Angle.

'T W Preston's Career Interesting and Useful'
Born in Abingdon to a prominent family. His father had little schooling by took advantage of every opportunity to educate himself and became a master in time in the use of the English language. He was superintendents of the Washington Co., VA Schools for 16 years. His father, a Captain in the Confederate Army, was captured at Chancellorsville and while a prisoner at Fort Delaware wrote poetry of a high literacy quality and memorized the entire New Testament and Psalms.

The economic panic near the end of the last century forced T. W. Preston to lave Abingdon Academy at the age of 14 and go to work. Like his father before him, he studied all his life, especially subjects to improve his composition and command of the English language.

His first job was copying records in the clerk's office in Abingdon and in 1894 he entered the general insurance business 'on his own'. Two years later he went to NYC to accept a job as bookkeeper with the American Gramophone Company. He came to Bristol on September 22, 1898 and recalls that it was 'the night that Pendleton's livery stable burned to the ground. I stopped at the old St. Lawrence Hotel and awoke in the night when the flames lit up my room. The livery stable was on the bank of the creek on Lee St. and I remember that some fine horses perished in the fire'.

Preston started his business career in George L. Carter's office in the Anderson building on State St. At that time, Carter controlled both the Virginia Iron and Coke Co and the V&SW Railroad. "The first winter I was here the mud on State St. was actually 6 to 8 inches deep" he said. "Some wag at our office painted a sign reading 'Ferry every 15 minutes' and stuck it in the street in front of the office".

1901 he bought the small J. L. King Printing Company which operated with 3 job presses and 3 employees on the second floor of the building at 15 Sixth St. 48 years later, King Printing Company has 48 employees in its modern plant on Shelby St. and it has expanded from a business of less than $8,000 a year to a volume of approximately $250,000 a year.

1901 he was married in 1901 to Florence Blair of Wytheville, VA. They have 3 children, Blair Preston, Bristol; Mrs. Henry Farley (Sarah) of Salisbury NC, and Mrs. William M. Eaves (Amelia) of Asheville, NC.

1910 Federal census shows the family enumerated in Bristol City, Washington Co., VA at 308 Oak St.:
  Preston, Thomas W. head, age 34, married 8 years, b. VA, manager at printing office.
  -- Florence B. wife, age 33, married 8 years, 2 children, 2 living, b. VA
  -- Blair T., son age 7 b. VA
  -- Amelia, daughter, age 5, b. VA
(in same household)

Anderson, Maude, boarder, age 23, single, b. VA, teacher at public school.
-- Ben F., boarder, age 17, single, b. VA, binder at printing company.

Along about 1908 he published Oliver Taylor's 'Historic Sullivan and then became interested in gathering for himself additional historic data on the Bristol region. Through the intervening years he has contributed numerous articles to newspapers and historic publications and his books and pamphlets include 'Historic Sketches of the Holston Valley', the compiled 'Speeches of Famous Southwest Virginians'; 'Old Virginia Newspapers' and two booklets in the series 'The Story of Bristol'. He is a member of the Virginia Historical Society and the Washington County Historical Society.

He has been keen on hobbies all his life and owns one of the finest autograph collections in the nation and also has a splendid stamp collection which includes complete envelopes with stamps from all over the world in twelve volumes.

1930 Federal census shows the family in Bristol City, Washington Co. VA at 412 Spencer St.:
   Preston, Thomas W., head, owns home, real estate value $15,000, age 54, married at 25, b. VA works Printing
   -- Florence B. wife, age 53, married at 24, b. VA.
   -- Amelia C., daughter, age 25, single, stenographic
   --Sara P. daughter, age 13
   -- Ruth adopted, age 14
   Phipps, J. McKinney Jr., roomer, age 42, secretary, country club.

1937 he was elected to the Bristol VA council, he became mayor almost immediately. During his administration the municipal accomplishments have included creation of the housing authority; extension of the city limits; building of a high school; purchasing of a city owned electrical distribution system and securing of TVA power and opening of the Highland View section of the City. He has been a member of the Central Presbyterian Church since 1901 and has been an elder of the church for 30 years. His other activities and affiliations include former treasurer and board member of King College; on board and former manager of Sullins College; YMCA treasurer about 20 years; former member of Bristol VA school board, and Rotary Club member 30 years. He married **Florence B. BLAIR**, b. 1877 in Wytheville VA.
         Children:

561.   i   **Amelia C. PRESTON**, b. 1905 in Washington Co., VA. Married and lived in Bristol VA. She married **William M. EAVES**, b. ABT 1900 in Asheville, Buncombe Co., NC.

+ 562.   ii   **Frank Blair PRESTON** b. 1903.

+ 563.   iii   **Sarah Pierce PRESTON** b. ABT 1906.

243. **Bessie Cloud LEYBURN**, (62.Elizabeth[4], 11.Robert[3], 3.Walter[2], 1.John[1]) b. 1 May 1889 in VA. Married and her husband was stationed in China. She married **Rev. DOUGLAS**, b. ABT 1880. Stationed in China for a time. Rev. Douglas was a Presbyterian Minister.

Children:

564.   i   **Bessie Leyburn DOUGLAS**, b. ABT 1910. Lived in Florida.

247. **Shelby PRESTON**, (63.Thomas[4], 11.Robert[3], 3.Walter[2], 1.John[1]) b. 1 Aug 1882 in MO. 1930 Federal census finds the family enumerated in Memphis, Shelby Co., TN at 195 South Barksdale St.:

Preston, Shelby, head, owns home, value $6,200, has a radio, age 47, married at 24, b. Missouri to parents b. VA and Mississippi, sales manager, woodworking place.

-- Mary P. wife, age 43, married at 20 b. MO to parents b. VA and MS.

-- Shelby Jr., son, 16, b. Mississippi. He married **Mary wife of Shelby PRESTON**, b. 1886 in MS.

Children:

565.   i   **Shelby PRESTON**, b. 1914 in MS.

254. **Robert Carter CUMMINGS**, (73.Anne[4], 13.Fairman[3], 3.Walter[2], 1.John[1]) b. 2 1849, d. 24 Sep 1904. 1880 Federal census of LA shows F. Preston Cummings enumerated in the household of his uncle Robert in Caddo Co., LA:

Cummings, Robert C. 65, farmer

-- Robert C. Jr, 21 nephew, farmer

-- F. Preston 25, nephew, farmer. He married **Lydia COVETTE**, married 4 Sep 1889, b. 16 Feb 1867, d. 4 May 1917.

Children:

566.   i   **Preston Covett CUMMINGS**, b. 23 Jun 1890 in VA?, d. 18 Aug 1895.

567.   ii   **Hazel CUMMINGS**, b. 25 Aug 1892.

+ 568.   iii   **Mary CUMMINGS** b. 9 Jun 1894.

569.   iv   **Martha 'Mattie' Strother CUMMINGS**, b. 2 Nov 1897.

570.   v   **David Carter CUMMINGS**, b. 19 Jul 1900 in VA?.

265.   **Preston WRIGHT**, (82.Davidella[4], 14.David[3], 3.Walter[2], 1.John[1]) b. 1878 in Tappahannonck, Essex Co., VA. 1910 Federal Census shows Preston enumerated in the oil fields of California, living with his young wife in a boarding house on Boarding House Road, 13 Township, Kern Co., CA:
   Wright, Preston, head age 32, married 2 years, b. VA to VA parents, Superintendent, Oil Well.
   -- Ann P., wife, 22, married 2 years, 1 child, 1 living, b. NY to NY father and English mother.
(no children are enumerated with them here.)

   1920 Federal census shows the family in Roseville, Placer Co., CA at 200 Placer St.:
Wright, Preston, head, Rents, age 40, b. VA, Theatrical Mgr, Theatre.
   -- Anne A., wife, 30, b. NY to father from NY and mother from Ireland?
   -- Marlene A. (?), daughter, 8, b. CA to parents from VA and NY.
He married **Anne A. wife of Preston WRIGHT**, b. 1890 in NY.
     Children:

571.   i   **Marlene WRIGHT**, b. 1912 in CA.

274.   **Guy MERRIWEATHER**, (83.Letitia[4], 16.Gertrude[3], 3.Walter[2], 1.John[1]) b. 19 Jan 1871 in IL. He married **Jessie L. BROWN**, married 8 Nov 1889, b. 1873 in MO.
     Children:

572.   i   **Hazel MERRIWEATHER**, b. 1 May 1891 in MO.

281. **Joseph Rhea WOLFORD**, (87.Jennet[4], 20.Joseph[3], 4.Jannette[2], 1.John[1]) b. 18 Apr 1834 in Sullivan Co., TN, d. 31 Aug 1895 in Texas Co MO, buried in Big Creek Cem. Texas Co. MO. 1880 Federal census shows the family enumerated in Piney Township, Texas Co., MO:
Wolfrod (sic), Joseph 46, farmer, b. TN.
-- Sarah, 36, wife keeping house, b. TN.
-- William H., 16, son, at home, b. MO.
-- Margaret, 13, daughter, at home, b. MO
-- Rodney R., 1, son, b. MO.

1895 he died 3 weeks after he was stricken with a stoke. He married **Sarah Ann Carrigan WALKER**, married 30 May 1861 in Salem Fulton Co., AR, b. 20 Jun 1844 in Hawkins Co. TN, d. 14 Nov 1922 in Purdin, Linn Co MO, buried in Purdin Cem. Purdin, Linn Co. Missouri.

Children:

573. i **Louise Jennet WOLFORD**, b. 9 Aug 1862 in Texas Co. Missouri, d. 18 Aug 1863 in Texas Co. Missouri.

574. ii **William Henry WOLFORD**, b. 30 Apr 1864 in Texas Co. Missouri, d. 9 Jul 1890 in Texas Co. Missouri. Died of typhoid fever.

575. iii **Margaret Alice WOLFORD**, b. 30 Apr 1867 in Texas Co. Missouri, d. 26 Aug 1955 in Little Rock, Pulaski Co., AR. After the death of her second husband George, she lived near her children in Cartney and Little Rock ARK. She married **George HARMON**, b. ABT 1849 in Mo?, d. 1918 in Purdin, Linn Co MO. Died in 1918 in the influenza epidemic.

576. iv **Elkanah Walker WOLFORD**, b. 1 Dec 1869 in Texas Co. Missouri, d. 18 Jan 1870 in Texas Co. Missouri.

577. v **Grace WOLFORD**, b. 18 Jan 1879 in Texas Co. Missouri, d. 18 Jan 1879 in Texas Co. Missouri. Stillborn.

578.   vi   **Rodney Ross WOLFORD**, b. 18 May 1879 in Texas Co. Missouri, d. 23 Oct 1940 in Texas Co MO. Twin of Grace.

Started the Wolford Monument Company in Houston Mo. with his brother Howard. Worked together until 1921. His grandson operated the business in 1992. Elected Judge of Texas Co. Court and served a number of years.

579.   vii   **Lettie Escott WOLFORD**, b. 28 Feb 1883 in Texas Co., Missouri, d. 20 Aug 1949 in Manhattan, Riley Co., KS. Attended Nagle School and Houston Business College graduating in 1908.

1914 Moved to Linn Co. MO after her marriage. Living in Purdin in 1949. After the berry season went to visit daughter in Manhattan KS where she died of a heart attack.

580.   viii   **Howard Frank WOLFORD**, b. 24 Feb 1886 in Texas Co. Missouri, d. 30 Jun 1960 in Batesville, Independence Co AR. With his brother started Wolford Monument Co. in Houston MO.

1913 Moved to Nevada MO to work a quarry for marble.

1921 moved his family to Cartney ARK. There the family lived in a tent house for a few weeks until they built a regular house.

1928 they moved to Guion ARK to be near the quarry and remained there until 1933 when they move to Batesville 20 miles away for the better schools. Supplied the marble for the famed Lincoln Cenotaph in the Lincoln Monument, Oak Ridge Cem. Springfield IL. (Abe buried behind the stone).

284.   **William Owen WOLFORD**, (87.Jennet[4], 20.Joseph[3], 4.Jannette[2], 1.John[1]) b. 17 Dec 1838 in Sullivan Co., TN, d. 27 Jun 1917 in Springfield, Greene Co., MO, buried in Maple Grove Cem. Springfield MO. Served in Co F 63rd Reg. TN Infantry. Captured at Shiloh. He married **Alice Odell WALKER**, b. 9 Jul 1849 in

Independence Co. ARK, d. 1912 in Springfield, Greene Co., MO, buried in Maple Grove Cem. Springfield MO. She was the sister of Sarah who married William's brother Joseph Wolford.

Children:

581. i   **Ida Lee WOLFORD**, b. 10 Jul 1873 in Springfield, Greene Co., MO, d. 1955 in Springfield, Greene Co., MO. Never married.

582. ii   **Thomas White WOLFORD**, b. 22 Sep 1875 in Texas Co. Missouri, d. 1960 in Springfield, Greene Co., MO. Worked installing cooling systems in US and Canada. Fell in 1932 and was permanently disabled. Retired and lived as a semi-invalid for over 30 years.

         No children by either marriage. He married (1) **Bird WATERMAN**, married 22 Sep 1901, b. ABT 1875 in Mo?, d. ABT 1914. He married (2) **Ertie MCFALL**, married 19 Feb 1914, b. 4 Jul 1892 in Mo?.

583. iii   **Charles Ross WOLFORD**, b. 26 Jan 1878 in Texas Co. Missouri, d. 1921 in St. Joseph MO. Never married. Served in WWI. While serving in France doing construction he fell and crushed his skull. He was discharged from the Army on full disability with a silver plate in his head. He lived at home a few years before he became violent and had to be placed in the State Hospital for the Insane, St Joseph MO. He died there.

584. iv   **Lula Preston WOLFORD**, b. 22 Nov 1881 in Missouri, d. 1966 in Springfield, Greene Co., MO. Never married.

294. **Joseph Rhea MILLARD**, (94.Eleanor[4], 20.Joseph[3], 4.Jannette[2], 1.John[1]) b. 24 Jan 1856 in Sullivan Co., TN. 1885 he graduated from King College in Bristol, and from Theological Seminary, Columbia SC in 1888.

Minister and pastor of Richburg Church, Richburg SC. (W. L.. Rhea -1895)

1900 Federal census shows the couple enumerated at Kings Mountain, Cleveland Co., NC:
Millard, Joseph R., head, Jan 1856, 44, married 11 years, b. TN to TN parents, Preacher.
-- Annie L., Oct. 1868, 36, married 11 years, 1 child, none living, b. SC to SC parents. He married **Anna Lee ELLIOTT**, married 1889, b. 1 Oct 1868 in Chester Co. SC.

Children:

585.   i   **J. R. M. MILLARD**, b. 1890 in SC?, d. 1 Dec 1894.

298.   **Laura Ella RHEA**, (95.Walter[4], 20.Joseph[3], 4.Jannette[2], 1.John[1]) b. 1856 in TN, d. 1944 in Salem, Fulton Co., AR, buried in Salem Cemetery, Salem, Fulton Co. AR. She married **Rufus A. ROBBINS**, married 1882 in Salem Fulton Co., AR, b. 1852 in Izard Co. AR, d. 1920 in Salem, Fulton Co., AR, buried in Salem Cemetery, Salem, Fulton Co. AR. Attended an academy in Philadelphia ARK.

Entered the mercantile pursuit as a clerk in a store in Batesville ARK. Remained there 10 years and then went to Salem.

1882 he married Laura, the daughter of his employer. They had 6 children.

1883 became a member of the Walter Preston Rhea firm.

He was a merchant in Salem the rest of his active life in a multi-story stone building across from the corner of the Court House square. The name Robbins is carved in the stone of building but is obscured by repeated painting. He was a Methodist.

1910 Federal census shows the family enumerated in Benton Township, Fulton Co., AR:
  Robins, Rufus A., head, 58, married 26 years, b. AR to VA parents, Optician.
  -- Laura, E., wife, 54, married 26 years, 7 children, 6 living, b. TN to TN parents.
  -- Bernese (sic), daughter, 20, single, B. AR, teacher, public school.
  -- Irma, daughter, 18, single, b. AR.
  -- Neill R., son, 16, single, b. AR.
  -- Pauline, daughter, 12, single, b. AR.
  -- Gerald, son, 9, b. AR.

Children:

586. i **Maude E. ROBBINS**, b. 1 Sep 1883 in Fulton Co. AR.

587. ii **Bernice Preston ROBBINS**, b. 1 Oct 1888 in Fulton Co. AR. A cousin remembered that Bernice lived in Chicago - never married.

588. iii **Irma ROBBINS**, b. 1 Nov 1891 in Fulton Co. AR.

589. iv **Lillian ROBBINS**, b. ABT 1892 in Fulton Co. AR. Died in infancy.

590. v **Neil R. ROBBINS**, b. 1 Mar 1894 in Fulton Co. AR.

591. vi **Sarah ROBBINS**, b. ABT 1896 in AR?.

592. vii **Pauline Elizabeth ROBBINS**, b. 1 Jul 1897 in Fulton Co. AR, d. in Salem Cemetery, Salem, Fulton Co. AR. A cousin remembers that Pauline lived in Chicago. She married **Mr. TRACY**, b. ABT 1890 in ARK?.

593. viii **Elizabeth ROBBINS**, b. ABT 1900 in AR?.

594. ix **Alfred Gerald ROBBINS**, b. ABT 1902 in AR?. A cousin remembers that Gerald lived in Little Rock at one time.

300. **Joseph Matthew RHEA**, (95.Walter[4], 20.Joseph[3], 4.Jannette[2], 1.John[1]) b. 1862 in Sullivan Co., TN. He married **Alice POWELL**, b. ABT 1862 in TN?.
Children:

595. i **Preston RHEA**, b. ABT 1890 in TN?.

596. ii **David RHEA**, b. ABT 1892 in TN?.

597. iii **Samuel RHEA**, b. ABT 1894 in TN?.

598. iv **Virginia RHEA**, b. ABT 1896 in TN?.

301. **Margaret Lillian RHEA**, (95.Walter[4], 20.Joseph[3], 4.Jannette[2],
      1.John[1]) b. 1862 in TN?. She married **A. W. ELLIS**, b. ABT 1862
      in TN?.

> *Children:*

    599.   i   **Eula Maude Rhea ELLIS**, b. ABT 1890 in TN?.

    600.   ii   **Margaret Lee Rhea ELLIS**, b. ABT 1892 in TN?.

304. **Oscar Lee RHEA**, (95.Walter[4], 20.Joseph[3], 4.Jannette[2], 1.John[1]) b.
      3 Jun 1876 in Salem, Fulton Co., AR, d. 23 Feb 1925 in Salem,
      Fulton Co., AR, buried in Salem Cemetery, Salem, Fulton Co. AR.
      Oscar Lee carried on with his father's merchandising business. At
      one time owned most modern hardware store in North Arkansas.
      He had bought the old B. F. Castleberry home and remodeled it. His
      brother in law Rufus Robins was also a merchant in Salem.

He was frail and ill with tuberculosis when he died en route to a
treatment center in Texas. After his death, his son Orion tried to
continue the business but was not successful. Heavy debts due to
destruction of his store and heavy damage to the home by tornadoes
were too much.

1910 Federal census shows the family enumerated in Salem, Benton
Township, Fulton Co., AR:
  Rhea, Oscar L., head, 33, married 9 years, b. AR, merchant,
general store.
  -- Virginia A., wife, 27, married 9 years, 3 children, 2 living, b. AR
to parents from TN.
  -- Orion, son, 8, b. AR.
  -- Lucille, daughter, 5, b. AR. He married (1) **Jennie RAND**,
married 23 May 1901 in Wild Cherry AR, b. 19 Dec 1881 in Salem,
Fulton Co., AR, d. 12 Oct 1919 in Salem, Fulton Co., AR, buried in
Salem Cemetery, Salem, Fulton Co. AR. The Methodist Church in
Salem has a leaded glass window inscribed "In Memory
of O. L. and Jennie Rhea".
Did leaving children aged 4 to 17. He married (2) **Lula Jane
ALBRIGHT**, married 26 Dec 1920, b. ABT 1900. Married Oscar
Lee a widower with four children, a year after the death of
his first wife.

> *Children by Jennie RAND:*

    601.   i   **Orion Rand RHEA**, b. 1902 in TN?, d. 1988.
                  Never married.

602. ii **Mildred Lucille RHEA**, b. 1904 in TN?, d. 1921.

603. iii **Anne Laura RHEA**, b. 1909, d. 1909. Died at the age of 1 month.

+ 604. iv **Walter Preston RHEA** b. 13 Mar 1915.
Children by Lula Jane ALBRIGHT:

+ 605. v **Sara Lee RHEA** b. 24 Jul 1923.

306. **Holmes Gans RHEA**, (95.Walter[4], 20.Joseph[3], 4.Jannette[2], 1.John[1]) b. 1878 in AR. 1930 Federal census shows the family living in Grandfield, Tillman Co., OK living at 102 East First St.:
Rhea, Holmes, G., head, rents, $47/month, no radio, age 52, first married at age 26, b. AR to TN parents, manager, laundry.
-- Ethel A., wife 42, first married at 29 (13 years prior, but not to Holmes per children's birthplaces), b. AR to parents from GA and AR.
--Edwin K, son, 16, single, b. OK, to parents from AR and TX (Ethel is not his mother.)
-- Aura L., daughter, 12, b. OK to parents from AR.
-- Joe N., daughter, 7, b OK to parents from AR.
(next page of census)
-- Dorothy, M, daughter, 5 9/12, b. OK to parents from AR. He married (1) **Ethel WATERS**, b. 1888 in AR. He married (2) **Jesse WELLS**, b. ABT 1878 in TN?, d. 1915.
Children by Ethel WATERS:

606. i **Ana Lois RHEA**, b. 1918 in OK.

607. ii **Joe N. RHEA**, b. 1923 in OK.

608. iii **Dorothy M. RHEA**, b. 1924 in OK.
Children by Jesse WELLS:

609. iv **Lelia RHEA**, b. ABT 1905 in TN?. She married **Mr. PUCKETT**, b. ABT 1905.

+ 610. v **Hugh Gans RHEA** b. ABT 1907.

611. vi **Edwin K. RHEA**, b. 1915 in OK.

314. **Nannie Robert RIVERS**, (97.Lucretia[4], 21.Robert[3], 4.Jannette[2], 1.John[1]) b. ABT 1846. He married **Sarah JOWNEY**, b. ABT 1846.
   Children:

       612.   i   **Relms RIVERS**, b. ABT 1870.

       613.   ii   **Robert RIVERS**, b. ABT 1872.

       614.   iii   **James RIVERS**, b. ABT 1874.

320. **Nancy Kalla RHEA**, (98.John[4], 21.Robert[3], 4.Jannette[2], 1.John[1]) b. 10 Oct 1866 in Bluff City, Sullivan Co., TN, d. 25 Oct 1936. Lived in Fall Branch, TN. She married **Eli WARREN**, married 14 Nov 1898, b. ABT 1866.
   Children:

       615.   i   **Cecil Rhea WARREN**, b. ABT 1890.

       616.   ii   **Clair King WARREN**, b. ABT 1892.

       617.   iii   **Earnest Glenolyn WARREN**, b. ABT 1894.

       618.   iv   **Eric Lynn WARREN**, b. ABT 1896.

321. **Joseph Addison Longacre 'Dr.' RHEA**, (98.John[4], 21.Robert[3], 4.Jannette[2], 1.John[1]) b. 23 Mar 1869 in Bluff City, Sullivan Co., TN, d. 14 Oct 1948 in Abingdon, Washington Co. VA, buried in Morning View Cem., Bluff City, TN. The Rhea bible owned by Jean Rhea Clayton of Daytona FL, notes his dates of birth, death and marriage. It does not name his wife. Joseph and Emma appear with children in a photograph on page 66 of 'Sullivan Co. Pictorial History, 1999.

   1948 obituary - Dr. Rhea Rites at Bluff City. Funeral services for Dr. J. A. L. Rhea, 79, Bluff City TN, dentist who died at 2pm on Friday in the George Ben Johnston Hospital in Abingdon, will be conducted at the Presbyterian Church in Bluff City. Dr. Rhea is survived by his widow, Mrs. Emma Rhea, one son, Hal Rhea of Bluff City, and one daughter, Mrs. J. Hampton Hyder of Elizabeth TN,; one sister Mrs. Norah Gammon of Gardner, FL and two grandchildren, Marjorie Hyder and Jane Rhea Hyder. He married **Emma MILLS**, married 14 Sep 1898, b. ABT 1869.
   Children:

+ 619.   i   **Gladys RHEA** b. ABT 1902.

   620.   ii   **Hal Preston RHEA**, b. 1905 in Sullivan Co., TN, d. 6 Nov 1988 in Bluff City, Sullivan Co., TN. He married (1) **Blanche REED**, b. ABT 1905. He married (2) **Bertha wife of Hal RHEA**, b. ABT 1900.

322. **John 'Dr.' Preston RHEA Jr. Jr.**, (98.John[4], 21.Robert[3], 4.Jannette[2], 1.John[1]) b. 6 Feb 1872 in Bluff City, Sullivan Co., TN, d. 27 Jul 1915 in Sullivan Co., TN, buried in Weaver Cem., Weaver Pike, Sullivan Co. TN. 1900 Sullivan Co., TN Federal census he was shown living in the home of Elbert J. Burkey, his brother-in-law. John was a noted to be a School Teacher by the enumerator.

1902 graduated from U. of Chattanooga Medical School.

1903 April 7, Certified M.D.

Master of the Masonic lodge at Zollicoffer; a renowned checkers player.

Death record show cause as Bright's disease; another record shows fall from second story window as cause of death. He had lived at Emmett, TN. He married **Ada Texanna CARMACK**, married 20 Aug 1902, b. 10 Jul 1878 in Paperville TN, d. 4 Jan 1924 in Bristol, Sullivan Co., TN, buried in Weaver Cem., Weaver Pike, Sullivan Co. TN. 1910 census reports she and both her parents were born in Va.

She taught until her marriage to Dr. Rhea. They had 3 children. Following her husband's death, she move her children to Bristol TN were she lived the remainder of her years.
          Children:

   621.   i   **Matthew Wendell RHEA**, b. 1904 in Sullivan Co., TN, buried in Weaver Cem., Weaver Pike, Sullivan Co. TN. He married **Margaret JOHNSON**, b. ABT 1904.

   622.   ii   **Mary Beuloxia RHEA**, b. 1907 in Sullivan Co., TN, d. 14 Dec 1984 in Abingdon, Washington Co. VA, buried in Weaver Cem., Weaver Pike, Sullivan

Co. TN. 1940 Beuloxia M. is listed in the Bristol TN City directory - Teacher - residence 1112 Florida Av.

1924 obituary - Mary Beuloxia Rhea, 78, of Highlands Retirement Village in Abingdon hospital. She was a lifelong resident of the Bristol area and taught schools in Piney Flats, Blountville and Bristol. Survivors include one sister Mrs. Claude Buckles, Bristol, and 1 niece Mrs. Robert C. Hersch, Maxton, NC. She married **Edward BLEVINS**, b. ABT 1907.

+ 623.   iii   **Eva Preston RHEA** b. 25 Feb 1910.

323.   **Margaret 'Maggie' A. RHEA**, (98.John[4], 21.Robert[3], 4.Jannette[2], 1.John[1]) b. 7 Jun 1874 in Bluff City, Sullivan Co., TN, d. 26 Jan 1917 in Sullivan Co., TN. Brother J A L Rhea was appointed administrator of her estate. She married **Elija F. DYKES**, married 28 Aug 1901, b. 18 Feb 1872 in Fall Branch, TN, d. 6 Jun 1913.
Children:

624.   i   **Elihu Rhea DYKES**, b. 1902, d. 1902. Died young.

324.   **Josiah Edward 'Ned' RHEA**, (98.John[4], 21.Robert[3], 4.Jannette[2], 1.John[1]) b. 10 Jan 1877 in Bluff City, Sullivan Co., TN, d. 4 Aug 1944 in Panama City, Bay Co., FL, buried in Greenwood Cem., St. Andrews, FL. This family was being researched in 1998 by Evanda Rhea Sallinger of FL, sallinger@@panacom.com.
The Rhea family bible notes his marriage in 1899 but did not show who his wife was.

1899 his marriage appears in the Marriage Record Log of Johnathan Hugh Carrier, Justice of the Peace 1889-1906. He is shown as J.E. Rhea, she as Miss Nannie V. Jackson in Mr. Carrier's log.

Lived in Piney Flats, TN. Was living at the home of his son when he died in 1944. He married **Nancy Virginia 'Nannie' JACKSON**, married 11 Mar 1899 in Sullivan Co., TN, b. 26 Dec 1871, d. 31 Mar 1930 in Fl. Received an A.B from Adelphi College in Garden City NY.

Nannie was a school teacher who taught in a one-room schoolhouse on Lookout Mountain, TN.

Moved to Florida about 1922 and taught chemistry at a high school in Panama City, Florida.
Children:

+ 625.   i   **Lysle Edward RHEA** b. 1 May 1906.

+ 626.   ii   **Gwendolyn Preston RHEA** b. 17 May 1907.

327.   **Samuel Robert RHEA**, (102.Robert[4], 21.Robert[3], 4.Jannette[2], 1.John[1]) b. 22 Mar 1868 in TN, d. 28 Sep 1930. Practiced medicine and lived in the old McQueen-Rhea home.

Lived in Chloride, AZ. He married **Nellie HENDRICKSON**, married in Chloride, AZ, b. ABT 1868 in TN(?). Her name has also been noted as Henderson in the transcription by Mace Gray of W. L. Rhea's 'Genealogy of the Rhea Family'.
Children:

627.   i   **Caroline RHEA**, b. ABT 1900 in Sullivan Co., TN?.

628.   ii   **Robert Randolph RHEA**, b. ABT 1902 in Sullivan Co., TN?.

629.   iii   **Margaret RHEA**, b. ABT 1904 in Sullivan Co., TN?.

328.   **Mary Elizabeth RHEA**, (102.Robert[4], 21.Robert[3], 4.Jannette[2], 1.John[1]) b. 21 Nov 1869 in TN, d. 16 May 1924. She married **Joseph Smythe DONNELLY**, b. 30 Dec 1869 in Mountain City, TN, d. 12 Mar 1915 in Shouns, Johnson Co., TN.
Children:

630.   i   **Irene DONNELLY**, b. 1897 in Sullivan Co., TN?, d. 1978. She married **Robert Wiely SUTHERLAND**, b. 1890, d. 1966.

631.   ii   **Harrison Rhea DONNELLY**, b. 1899 in Sullivan Co., TN?, d. 1926.

632.   iii   **Margaret Edith DONNELLY**, b. 1900 in Sullivan Co., TN?, d. 1986. She married **William Young HILL**, b. 1900, d. 1978.

329. **Nancy Martitia 'Titia' RHEA**, (102.Robert[4], 21.Robert[3],
4.Jannette[2], 1.John[1]) b. 1870 in Shouns, Johnson Co., TN, d. 10 Oct
1942 in Blountville, Sullivan Co., TN. Obituary - Mrs. C. M.
Dulaney, widow of the late Dr. Meigs Dulaney, died at her home,
Medical Grove, near Blountville at 5:30 o'clock yesterday
afternoon. Her death came suddenly, she having become ill early
yesterday morning. She was a member of one of the most prominent
and best known families in this section. She married **Charles 'Dr.'
Meigs DULANEY**, married in Blountville, Sullivan Co., TN, b.
1868 in Sullivan Co., TN, d. 3 Oct 1932 in Blountville, Sullivan Co.,
TN. Owned and occupied the old 'Medical Grove' residence in
Blountville TN.

1920 Federal census shows the family enumerated in the 5th Civil
District of Sullivan Co., TN. Note the nicknames reported to the
enumerator:
    Dulaney, Meigs C., head owns home free of mortgage, 50, b. TN,
farmer, general farm.
    -- Titia, wife, 46, b. TN.
    -- Charles, son, 18, single, b. TN, farm laborer.
    -- Robert, son, 16, single, b. TN.
    -- Billy, son, 13, b. TN.
    -- Mary, daughter, 11, b. TN.
    -- John, son, 9, b. TN.
    -- Laura, daughter, 6, b. TN.
    -- James, son, 4 4/12, b. TN.

1930 Federal census Mr. Dulaney's name is indexed as 'Mays' and
his wife Martina. They reside on Kingsport Highway, 5th Civil
District, Sullivan Co., TN. Brother Nat T., also a physician, is
enumerated as the next household:
    Dulaney, Migs (sic) M, head, owns home, real estate value $5000,
60, married first at 30, b. TN, physician medical, general practice.
    -- Martina, wife -h, 50, married first at 21, b. TN
    -- Mary, daughter, 22, single, b. TN
    -- John, son, 19, single, b. TN
    -- Laura, daughter, 16, b. TN
    -- James, son, 14, single, b. TN

Obituary - Dr. Charles Meigs Dulaney, one of the best known
physicians in Sullivan County, died at five o'clock yesterday
afternoon at his home, Medical Grove, near Blountville.
Death came suddenly, though Dr. Dulaney had been seriously ill for
a week and had worked for a number of years handicapped by

failing health. Dr. Dulaney was by heredity a physician, though the first years of his active life were spent in civil and mining engineering. It was while teaching chemistry in the TN Medical College that he graduated in medicine and located to Medical Grove, one of the fourth generation to practice from the same homestead which has a history unique in the annals of medicine.

In 1786 Dr. William Elkanah Dulaney built the brick home that is now known as Medical Grove and since 1798 until the present, Dr. Dulaney has answered the call of the sick and afflicted from this homestead. Dr. Charles Meigs Dulaney was a namesake of Dr. Charles Meigs, one of the greatest medical teachers of his time.

He was the son of Dr. N. T. Dulaney Sr. who died at Medical grove in 1910, and his grandmother was a Taylor of Happy Valley TN. Since he began the practice of medicine, Dr. Dulaney spent his entire life in his profession. He was the modern representative of the old family doctor, who looked upon the relief of suffering as his first duty. Suffering did not harden his nature, but made him gentle. He gave prescriptions and often the money to buy the medicine and went at any hour of the day or night, braving any weather to aid patients regardless of their ability to pay. He was a brother of Dr. Nat Dulaney of Bristol, Dr. Henry Dulaney of Sawtelle, CA and Mrs. J. B. Converse and Miss Ollie Dulaney of Houston TX.
Children:

+ 633. i **Charles Meigs DULANEY, Jr.** b. 1902.

+ 634. ii **Robert Nathaniel DULANEY** b. 21 Nov 1903.

+ 635. iii **William Davis DULANEY** b. 1907.

  636. iv **Mary Elizabeth DULANEY**, b. 1909 in Sullivan Co., TN. 1942 she was living in Houston TX. She married **J. L. DAVIS**, b. ABT 1899.

  637. v **John Campbell DULANEY**, b. 1911 in Sullivan Co., TN, d. 4 May 1936 in Memphis, Shelby Co., TN, buried in Blountville Cemetery, Sullivan Co., TN. 1936 obituary - Funeral services for John Campbell Dulaney 25, who died in Memphis at 10 o'clock Saturday night, will be held at 11 o'clock Tuesday morning in the Presbyterian Church at Blountville.

Death came to Mr. Dulaney after an illness of five weeks. He underwent an operation on Easter Sunday. His mother Mrs. Meigs Dulaney of Blountville and his brother Dr. Charles Dulaney of Bristol went to Memphis by plane Saturday afternoon and were at his bedside when he died. Mr. Dulaney was born at Blountville Feb. 5, 1911 and received his high school education at Blountville High School. He enrolled in and graduated from Tusculum College and then entered the University of TN School of Medicine at Memphis. He was a member of the graduating class of the college and would have received his degree in June.

He was a member of the board of deacons of the Blountville Presbyterian Church. Mr. Dulaney was married to Miss Helen Dawson of Marked Tree, Ark in September 1933. He met Miss Dawson who was the technician in the Baptist Hospital at Memphis, when he entered school at Memphis. His wife survives him, together with his mother Mrs. Meigs Dulaney, 4 brothers and 2 sisters. His father Sr. Meigs Dulaney one of Sullivan County's most prominent physicians, died in October 1932. He married **Helen DAWSON**, married 1 Sep 1933, b. ABT 1911 in Marked Tree, AR.

638. vi **Laura DULANEY**, b. 1914 in Sullivan Co., TN. 1958 she was living in Bristol, TN. She married **Berkely RUCKER**, b. ABT 1903.

639. vii **James Rhea DULANEY**, b. 1 Sep 1919 in Sullivan Co., TN.

337. **Oscar FICKLE**, (105.Robert[4], 22.Margaret[3], 4.Jannette[2], 1.John[1]) b. 27 Oct 1852 in Sullivan Co., TN. He married **Elizabeth Ann MILLARD**, b. 1853 in Sullivan Co., TN.
Children:

+ 640. i **Alice Laura FICKLE** b. 1 Dec 1878.

641. ii **Maude FICKLE**, b. 22 Dec 1881 in Sullivan Co., TN.

642. iii **Robert FICKLE**, b. 1883 in Sullivan Co., TN.

339. **Lincoln Rhea FICKLE**, (105.Robert[4], 22.Margaret[3], 4.Jannette[2], 1.John[1]) b. 23 Sep 1855 in Sullivan Co., TN. He married **Mary MILLARD**, b. 1857 in Sullivan Co., TN. Sister of Elizabeth Millard.

Children:

643. i **Mary FICKLE**, b. in Sullivan Co., TN.

644. ii **Linnie FICKLE**, b. ABT 1882 in Sullivan Co., TN.

645. iii **Rhea FICKLE**, b. ABT 1884 in Sullivan Co., TN.

646. iv **Preston FICKLE**, b. ABT 1886 in Sullivan Co., TN.

340. **Samuel Bruce FICKLE**, (105.Robert[4], 22.Margaret[3], 4.Jannette[2], 1.John[1]) b. 18 Oct 1857 in Sullivan Co., TN, d. 2 May 1938 in Sullivan Co., TN, buried in Muddy Creek Cem., Sullivan Co. TN. Married at 25. He was a teacher at Devault's School house. Settled on a farm along the north bank of the Holston River. Served as a part time speaker in the Methodist Church and took part in the meetings that were held at Bond's campground.

Had 13 children. Died at his home on Muddy Creek after an illness of several months. He married **Ellen Akard 'Miss Sis' CROSS**, married 6 Aug 1882 in Sullivan Co., TN, b. 24 Jul 1862 in Sullivan Co., TN, d. 15 Oct 1949 in Sullivan Co., TN, buried in Muddy Creek Cem., Sullivan Co. TN. Lived at the mouth of Muddy Creek in the same house in which her father William had lived. Buried at Muddy Creek Baptist Church Cemetery.

She and her children appear in a photo on page 63 of 'Sullivan Co. Pictorial History', 1999. She had been taken to CA in 1944 by her son and spent some time there with the family.

Children:

647. i **Cora Glen FICKLE**, b. 1 Jul 1883 in Sullivan Co., TN, d. 18 Oct 1908 in Blountville, Sullivan Co., TN, buried in Muddy Creek Cem., Sullivan Co. TN. Never married. She was only 25 when she died of tuberculosis. She had been caring for some sick neighbors and contracted the disease from them.

648. ii **Frances 'Fannie' Blake FICKLE**, b. 27 Mar 1885 in Sullivan Co., TN, d. 27 Mar 1974 in Sullivan Co., TN, buried in Muddy Creek Cem., Sullivan Co. TN. She was a schoolteacher. She raised Janes Naff and Haskew Jr. (her brothers) and loved to quilt. She served many years as the superintendent of the Sunday school at Hulls Chapel United Methodist Church. She never married. She was 89 years old when she died on her birthday.

649. iii **William Preston FICKLE**, b. 8 Jun 1886 in Sullivan Co., TN, d. 21 Aug 1947 in CA, buried in Fairhaven Cem., Santa Ana, CA. Married and moved to California where he lived for many years. He died from a heart attack.

The following is contain in a biography written by one of his children.
"June 8th, 1886 is the birthplace of my father. William Preston Fickle, better known as Will. According to stories told by his mother, Ellen and sister Fanny. Will was a very energetic youngster as he grew up. He was always a 'busy boy'. Two of his projects were his partnership in a small grocery store with Mr. Cooper, his future brother in law's father, and his job as a roving dairyman that went from farm to farm purchasing cheese and milk products that were surplus from the farm's own needs.

1907 Will left home and came to California. A young man of 21, Will was hired as a farm worker by the Thomas Strain Ranch northwest of Placentia, CA. This was not challenging for an ambitious Will so he traveled to Kneeland CA and was hired as a logger by the Hammond Lumber Co. Making 2 dollars per day was good money in 1908 so Will sent for his brother Marvin to come West. While employed by Hammond Co. Will and Marvin filed under the Homestead Act and claimed 160 acre tracts of forest land. The land was in Humboldt Co., near Eureka, CA. My family visited the area in 1950. It was covered with fir trees and tan oak and was on the Mad River Big Bend area. After my father's death, the land was sold.

1910 Will and Marvin came to the Bakersfield area where an oil boom was underway. Both were employed by an oil company near Oildale CA. Making more money than he did as a logger, and less strenuous work, Will wrote to another brother, Naff, and he made plans to join will and Marvin. When Naff's mother heard about the plan she was very upset. She knew Naff was not physically strong and had a history of illness. She said "If you go to CA I'll never see you again". Bug Naff wanted to go. He borrowed his train fare from Mrs. Gross and was on his way West.

1910 the boys received word their sister had died. Then Naff became seriously ill. He was concerned that he might not live and wrote a card to his benefactor Mrs. Gross, to let her know he was very sick. He mailed the card on July 5th. It arrived in TN after his death, which was on the 6th. It was just 2 1/2 months after his 17 year old sister's death. The brothers returned to TN with their brother's body in early July. Will stayed in TN for 2 months. (During this period) Will and Bell were married in a civil ceremony by Rev. Houts. Will was 24 years old and Belle was just a few days shy of her 18th birthday. Will and Belle stayed in TN for one month and left for CA on Sept. 9th. The newly married Will and Bell came back to Oildale CA and resumed his work in the oil fields. Moving into quarters at the lease. Bell was employed as the cook and housekeeper.

1912 will was able to be transferred back to Placentia CA area where he had first worked in CA. He was now working for the Standard Oil Co. at the Murphy-Coyote Plant. One of his first jobs was working on an exploratory well. that was drilled on land now occupied by Angel Stadium in Anaheim CA.

1914 Will located 6 and 8/10ths acres of land at the corner of North St. and Blue Gum St. about 4 miles from Anaheim and 3 miles from Placentia. It cost $1800, about $250 per acre. That April, Will and a

Chinese worker planted over 500 Valencia orange
trees on the 6.8 acres. The fist year the trees were
watered from a horse drawn wagon with a tank and
hose. He continued to work in the oil fields full time
and the rest of the time on his orange grove.

1918 Will was able to harvest his first orange crop.
He bought his first tractor, a Fordson. HE was also
able to employ a part time worker for the orchard.
later in the years, Will was called up in the draft for
the first World War even though he was a the father
of 3 by then. He reported to the station in
Fullerton only to learn that the war was nearly over
and his services would not be needed.

1919 Will and Belle had their 4th child and
purchased their first brand new automobile, a
Huppmobile. It was a large touring car.

1923 purchased 3 five acre parcels and one nine acre
parcel of vacant land. Also purchased their second
car, a 9 passenger Studebaker with jump seats. He
used his vacation from Standard Oil Co. to plant
orange trees on new his new land. The home was
added on to and more children were added in the
coming years.

1928 Bell with her sister Kate Poe of Bakersfield
made the train trip back to Piney Flats, TN. Belle's
sister Virginia Hanchar came out to CA to baby sit
the 5 children still at home. Will would wait another
year to return to his home in TN. In 1929 when he
went alone to see his mother and family in Piney
Flats, nineteen years had elapsed since he had last
seen his mother.

1930 to 1936 during the depression years Will was
fortunate to still be working for Standard Oil. His
son had grown into their teens and did much of the
ranch work. The 2 daughters were in college and
orange crops were paying off each year.

1935 Will bought a new Doge sedan for the long
awaited trip back to TN. In July of that year Bell

discovered that she had a cancerous lump in her breast. However, she wanted to make the trip before surgery. It would be her last trip to see her mother and family in TN.

1938 was one of the worst freezes in VA history, froze the orange crop and damaged many trees. More expenses were incurred as Belle's condition worsened.

1942 Will retired from Standard Oil. In the early 40's Will brought his mother Ellen to visit in CA. After all the years of hearing about Will's home, orchards and children she came to see for herself. Later, Will's sister Fanny would also come out to CA. In 1942 he made his 4th trip back to TN. Three of his children, Juanita, Aulba and Lowell traveled with him. In this year he remarried, a widow, Mrs. McKittrick. This marriage lasted but a year, ending in divorce.

1944 he harvested one of his biggest crops. After many years of indebtedness from 1937 to 1939, crop losses due to floods, freezes, and windstorms, Will received over $43,000 for is total crops.

1945 he made his last trip home to TN. This time he flew in an airplane.

1947, Just 19 days before his death from a heart attack, he married another widow, Mrs. Opal Fisher. He left a large ranch home that he occupied for the previous 33 years and a second home in the town of Anaheim. The day of his death Will had gotten on the roof of his garage to install a small TV aerial. He ate a hearty dinner with a piece of caramel pie for dessert. He went to bed at 9pm and expired at 12:08 on August 21st, 1947. Will was 61 years and 2 months and 13 days old.

Will gained the reputation of being one of the most industrious men and a workaholic. He planted 4 orchards of oranges, organized the Goodwin Mutual Water Co., and was an officer, was on the board of Orange Co.'s pioneer water company, Yorba

Irrigation Co., was a stockholder in the Golden State Water Co., and was active in the Atwood community where he plated eucalyptus trees for protective windbreaks for his neighbors orchards as well as his. He married (1) **Mrs. MCKITTRICK**, b. ABT 1886. He married (2) **Hannah Belle HATCHER**, married 8 Aug 1910, b. 15 Aug 1892, d. 13 Jul 1939.

650.　iv　**John Naff FICKLE**, b. 11 Jul 1889 in Sullivan Co., TN, d. 6 Jul 1910 in Oildale CA, buried in Muddy Creek Cem., Sullivan Co. TN. Moved to California in 1909. Died the next year at age 20. Never married. It is thought he may have contracted TB from his sister Cora. He was sick when he left for California to join his brothers who were working there in the oil fields.

651.　v　**Marvin Diggs 'Doc' FICKLE**, b. 11 Aug 1891 in Sullivan Co., TN, d. 21 Feb 1974 in Sullivan Co., TN, buried in Blountville Cemetery, Sullivan Co., TN. Lived most of their married lives in Taft California. He and some of his brothers worked in the oil fields in California. After retirement in 60's they returned to Sullivan Co. TN. No children. Worked in the oil fields of South America for some time in the early 30's with his brother Haskew. He died of prostate cancer. He married **Sarah 'Sally' Lavine COOPER**, married 29 Apr 1939, b. 5 Dec 1905 in Sullivan Co., TN, d. 17 Jul 1989. Sister of Ina's Fickle's husband and Lonna's husband.

652.　vi　**Anna May FICKLE**, b. 16 May 1893 in Sullivan Co., TN, d. 21 Apr 1910. Died young just 18 months after her sister Cora and two months after her brother Naff.

653.　vii　**Ada Jennie Lee FICKLE**, b. 3 Feb 1895 in Sullivan Co., TN, d. 2 Feb 1997 in Bluff City, Sullivan Co., TN, buried in Muddy Creek Cem., Sullivan Co. TN. Last surviving child of Samuel and Ellen. She married and had 4 sons. She died of heart and kidney failure short of her 102nd birthday. Resided at 295 Sycamore Dr. at the time of her death. Survived by one son Billy. She married **Thomas STIDHAM**,

married 3 Oct 1913, b. 21 May 1893 in TN, d. 27
Nov 1944. 1930 Federal census index has misspelled
Thomas' name making it difficult to locate their
records. The family is enumerated in District 3,
Sullivan Co., TN

Stidam, Tohmas N. (sic), head, owns home 38,
married at 21, b. TN, farmer.
-- Ada L., wife-h, 35, married at 18, b. TN.
-- Arlie ., son, 13, b. TN.
-- Kenneth P., 11, b. TN.
-- Hall D., son, 3 4/12, b. TN (April census).
-- Billie P., son, 6/12. b. TN

He and his son Arlie died within 4 days of each other.

+ 654. viii **Beulah Grace FICKLE** b. 18 May 1896.

655. ix **Mary Eliza FICKLE**, b. 27 May 1898 in TN, d. 30
Nov 1899 in Sullivan Co., TN, buried in Old
Wheelers Ch. Cem. Blountville, TN. Died at age 18
months of pneumonia. It is said she was not named
until she died. Her family called her 'Little Sis'.
(Kim Smalley, 1997).

656. x **Lovick Pierce 'Toy' FICKLE**, b. 27 Jul 1899 in TN,
d. 5 Jul 1967, buried in Muddy Creek Cem., Sullivan
Co. TN. Was know to most as Toy. He married
twice but had no children. He is buried with his first
wife. He married (1) **Josie Pet JONES**, married 22
Oct 1929, b. 9 Apr 1908 in TN?, d. 1 Nov 1959,
buried in Muddy Creek Cem., Sullivan Co. TN. He
married (2) **Etta Mottern HARTSOG**, married 9
Feb 1961, b. 2 Jan 1907 in Ashe Co., NC, d. 5 May
1996 in Johnson City, Washington Co., TN. Resided
in Sullivan Co. until she moved to Appalachian
Village in 1974. Retired from Bristol Memorial
Hospital. After the death of her husband Toy, she
lived in Johnson City, TN.

657. xi **Ina Jean FICKLE**, b. 16 Aug 1901 in Sullivan Co.,
TN, d. 28 Apr 1983, buried in Blountville Cemetery,
Sullivan Co., TN. She married **Perry Carson
COOPER**, married 17 Aug 1921, b. 6 Jun 1902 in
Sullivan Co., TN, d. 1 Mar 1982.

+ 658.   xii   **Haskew Devault 'Hass' FICKLE** b. 1 Feb 1903.

659.   xiii   **Lonna Pet FICKLE**, b. 10 Jan 1904 in TN, d. 22 Jun 1991 in Sullivan Co., TN?, buried in Tri-Cities Memory Garden, Blountville TN. Three Fickle siblings married Cooper siblings. She died of a blood disorder. She married **Carl Lee COOPER**, married 8 Jul 1923, b. 11 May 1908 in Sullivan Co., TN, d. 1 Jun 1976 in Sullivan Co., TN. Brother of Perry and Sally. Perry had married Lonna's sister Ina. Carl and Lonna developed 'Carlonna' a farm which pastured prize cattle. Carl was also supervisor at the Kingsport Press and retired after serving there 45 years.

341.   **Margaret Laura FICKLE**, (105.Robert[4], 22.Margaret[3], 4.Jannette[2], 1.John[1]) b. 24 Jan 1860 in Sullivan Co., TN. She married **Charles JONES**, b. ABT 1860 in TN. Brother of Rev. Sam Jones, the Methodist Revivalist. (W.L.Rhea-1895).
Children:

660.   i   **Samuel JONES**, b. ABT 1890 in Sullivan Co., TN.

661.   ii   **Francis JONES**, b. ABT 1892 in TN.

662.   iii   **Annie Laura JONES**, b. ABT 1894 in TN.

343.   **Jane 'Jennie' Preston FICKLE**, (105.Robert[4], 22.Margaret[3], 4.Jannette[2], 1.John[1]) b. 13 Oct 1864 in TN. She married **Edward KENNEY**, b. ABT 1864 in TN?.
Children:

663.   i   **Mary KENNEY**, b. ABT 1895 in TN.

664.   ii   **Robert Preston KENNEY**, b. ABT 1897 in TN.

665.   iii   **Kyle Edward KENNEY**, b. ABT 1899 in TN.

345.   **Nicholas M. LONG Jr.**, (106.Margaret[4], 23.Matthew[3], 4.Jannette[2], 1.John[1]) b. 27 Jul 1849 in TN, d. in Memphis TN?. Pastor of Stangers Church in Memphis, TN for 25 years. He married **Shirley WILSON**, b. ABT 1849 in TN?.
Children:

666.   i   **Richard LONG**, b. ABT 1880 in TN?.

667.   ii   **Margaret Rhea LONG**, b. ABT 1882 in TN?.

668.   iii **Shirley Wilson LONG**, b. ABT 1884 in TN?.

669.   iv   **Walter Preston LONG**, b. 1889 in TN?.

670.   v   **Phelps W. LONG**, b. 1891 in TN?.

671.   vi   **Frances M. LONG**, b. ABT 1893 in TN?.

672.   vii **Emma Law LONG**, b. ABT 1895 in TN?.

349.   **Matthew Robert RHEA**, (107.Elizabeth[4], 23.Matthew[3], 4.Jannette[2], 1.John[1]) b. 5 Jul 1846 in Bristol, Washington Co., VA, d. 21 Aug 1902 in Somerville, Fayette Co., TN, buried in Somerville, Fayette Co., TN. Moved with his family from Virginia to Sullivan Co. TN by 1847 where his parents are listed as members of the Paperville Presbyterian Church and then to Jonesboro TN about 1850.

1863 he joined Lt. W. W. Blair's Co., Local Defense Troops in Jonesboro on June 20. This company was also known as the 'Young Rebels of Jonesboro'. These forces were later incorporated into McKenzies 5th Regiment of the TN Cavalry. It is thought he was paroled at Newton, NC about April 19, 1865.

1865 or 1866 he came with his widowed mother and siblings to Somerville, TN.

1902 obituary from the Sommerville TN newspaper 22 August 1902 read:
Born in Virginia near Bristol in July 1846 he was in his 57th year of age when he passed from earth. His father and family moved from Virginia in 1850 to Jonesboro TN where his father died in 1863. He with his mother and the rest of the family moved to Sommerville in 1865 and has resided in this county ever since except about 18 months in Florida. He was united in marriage in Sommerville Dec. 14 1870 with Mid Annie Tucker. Four children were born of this marriage, 3 of whom, two sons and one daughter, with the wife and mother survive to lament the death of a kind, loving father.

He joined the Presbyterian church in this place many years ago. For a number of years prior to his removal to Florida, he was an elder in that church, and on his return to Sommerville was elected deacon which office he held at the time of his death. He was consistent Christian, loved his church and ever faithful and prompt in his attendance upon services.

He died at his home in Sommerville at 8:30 on the morning August 21, 1902. His death resulted from an accident with which he met about a year ago. While unloading lumber he fell from a box car injuring his kidneys and setting up Hematuria. He had been quite sick for two months and about two weeks since was taken to Roger's Springs hoping that a sojourn there might prove beneficial. For a day or two he seemed to improve but after that grew worse and it was thought advisable to bring him home. He returned home on the evening of the 13th and despite the best medical attention and constant careful tender nursing of his family and friends gradually grew weaker until the end came. His death cast a mantle of sorrow over the whole community.

His funeral was at 9:00 conducted at the Presbyterian church by pastor .J T. Rothrock. He married **Anna Adelade 'Addie' TUCKER**, married 14 Dec 1870 in Somerville, Fayette Co., TN, b. 22 Jul 1850 in Somerville, Fayette Co., TN, d. 10 Jun 1938 in Memphis, Shelby Co., TN, buried in Somerville, Fayette Co., TN. Lived with son Edward's family until she died. Buried beside her husband.

Children:

673.   i   **Thomas Tucker RHEA**, b. 8 Oct 1872 in TN?, d. 18 Aug 1944. He lived in Memphis. Had no children. He married **Susan Mae THOMSON**, married 2 1908 in Beaman, Pettis Co., MO, b. 14 Apr 1874 in TN?, d. 22 Sep 1948 in Sedalia, Pettis Co. MO. Her wedding took place at the Thompson home 'Orchardwod Place' with Rev. F. Y. Campbell officiating.

674.   ii   **John William RHEA**, b. 22 Jul 1874 in Somerville, Fayette Co., TN, d. 28 Sep 1874 in Somerville, Fayette Co., TN. Died as an infant.

+ 675.   iii   **Lucy Mary 'Lula Mae' RHEA** b. 9 Aug 1876.

+ 676. iv **Edward Francis RHEA** b. 30 Jan 1878.

350. **James Samuel RHEA**, (107.Elizabeth[4], 23.Matthew[3], 4.Jannette[2], 1.John[1]) b. 11 Feb 1849 in Jonesboro, Washington Co., TN, d. 18 Sep 1898 in Somerville, Fayette Co., TN, buried in Somerville City Cemetery, Somerville TN. Came to Fayette Co. with his mother and other members of his family after the Civil War. He lived the remainder of his life in District 4 except for a year in Ocala FL in 1894. He was a farmer and owned a cotton gin and saw mill. The old home place was there. He married **Fannie Bell TROTTER**, married 24 Feb 1880, b. 27 Aug 1860 in TN?, d. 28 Jan 1928.
Children:

677. i **Benjamin Edward RHEA**, b. 23 Jan 1881 in Fayette Co., TN, d. 20 Apr 1923. Lived his whole life on the farm where he was born. He married **Cleo ARNOLD**, b. ABT 1880.

678. ii **Matthew William RHEA**, b. 20 Jan 1883 in Fayette Co., TN, d. 8 Oct 1884.

+ 679. iii **James Wilson RHEA** b. 20 Jan 1883.

+ 680. iv **John Edmondson RHEA** b. 1885.

+ 681. v **Sarah Bell RHEA** b. 9 Aug 1889.

+ 682. vi **William Abraham RHEA** b. 27 Jul 1891.

683. vii **Hundson Cary RHEA**, b. 15 Feb 1894 in TN?, d. 1895 in Ocala, Marion Co., FL.

684. viii **Mary Elizabeth RHEA**, b. 1 Sep 1896 in TN?, d. 16 Feb 1984. She married **Raymond Gill MCFADDEN**, married 3 Jan 1929, b. 7 Oct 1891, d. 23 Apr 1980.

685. ix **Robert Henry RHEA**, b. 1 Sep 1896 in TN?, d. 1 1955. He married (1) **Louise wife fo Robert Henry RHEA**, b. ABT 1896. He married (2) **Cora wife of Robert Henry RHEA**, b. ABT 1899.

357. **Pearl RHEA**, (109.John[4], 23.Matthew[3], 4.Jannette[2], 1.John[1]) b.
ABT 1865 in TN?. She and her husband lived in Memphis. She
married **Robert L. MORRIS**, b. ABT 1865.
Children:

    686.   i   **Staley MORRIS**, b. ABT 1890.

360. **S. A. MILLER Jr.**, (110.Sarah[4], 23.Matthew[3], 4.Jannette[2], 1.John[1])
b. 24 Jan 1850, d. 14 Sep 1896. He married **Annie wife of S. A.
MILLER**, b. 1848, d. 1920.
Children:

    687.   i   **Allie Frank MILLER**, b. 17 Aug 1890, d. 23 Jun
        1891.

363. **Jennie Lou RHEA**, (111.Abram[4], 23.Matthew[3], 4.Jannette[2],
1.John[1]) b. 3 Dec 1874 in TN?, d. 21 Dec 1917. She married
George T. WEBB, b. ABT 1874 in TN?.
Children:

    688.   i   **Abram Rhea WEBB**, b. ABT 1900 in TN?.

    689.   ii   **Virginia WEBB**, b. ABT 1902 in TN?.

364. **Richard Cary RHEA**, (111.Abram[4], 23.Matthew[3], 4.Jannette[2],
1.John[1]) b. 1877 in TN?, d. 1933, buried in Whiteville, Hardeman
Co. TN. Researcher Robert Rhea shows Richard died 1961 in
Memphis TN and carried the middle name Cross. He married **Mattie
Lou HAZELWOOD**, b. 1879 in Whiteville, Hardeman Co. TN, d.
1933 in Whiteville, Hardeman Co. TN. Had one son from her
marriage to Mr. Anderson.
Children:

+ 690.   i   **Louise RHEA** b. 1907.

    691.   ii   **Richard Cary RHEA Jr.**, b. ABT 1912 in TN?. He
        married **Hugh C. WISEMAN**, b. ABT 1912.

367. **Elizabeth 'Lizzie' RHEA**, (111.Abram[4], 23.Matthew[3], 4.Jannette[2],
1.John[1]) b. 1883 in TN?, d. 1940. She married **Gaston Harvey
RHODES**, b. ABT 1883 in TN?.
Children:

692.   i   **Albert Harvey RHODES**, b. ABT 1905 in TN?. He married **Della Gwynn WEBB**, b. ABT 1905.

369. **Hugh Preston RHEA**, (116.Walter[4], 23.Matthew[3], 4.Jannette[2], 1.John[1]) b. 1 May 1871 in TN?, d. 1901 in Oakland FLA. He married **Louise BROWN**, b. ABT 1871 in TN?.
Children:

693.   i   **Hugh Preston RHEA Jr.**, b. ABT 1895 in TN?.

371. **Susan Brown 'Susie' RHEA**, (116.Walter[4], 23.Matthew[3], 4.Jannette[2], 1.John[1]) b. 1 Feb 1875 in TN?, d. 1 Mar 1950 in Pulaski TN?. She married **Thomas BUFORD**, b. 1 Jul 1871 in TN?, d. 1 Oct 1949.
Children:

694.   i   **John Edmondson BUFORD**, b. 12 May 1896 in TN?, d. 2 Mar 1897. He married **Alma wife of John BUFORD**, b. ABT 1896.

695.   ii   **Clara May BUFORD**, b. ABT 1902 in TN?. She married **Howard HOOVER**, b. ABT 1900.

696.   iii **Thomas Edmondson BUFORD**, b. ABT 1906 in TN?.

372. **Mary Looney 'Mamie' RHEA**, (116.Walter[4], 23.Matthew[3], 4.Jannette[2], 1.John[1]) b. 1877 in TN?. She married **Lunnsford Y. WILLIAMSON**, b. ABT 1877 in TN?. Notable Southern Fam., Z. Armstrong 1922 - Rhea.
Children:

697.   i   **Jean Rhea WILLIAMSON**, b. ABT 1900 in TN?.

373. **Walter Preston RHEA Jr.**, (116.Walter[4], 23.Matthew[3], 4.Jannette[2], 1.John[1]) b. 1879 in Somerville, Fayette Co., TN, d. 1940 in Memphis, Shelby Co., TN. Captain in the A.E.F in Frances during WWI. He was gassed and shell shocked. He served with the Tennessee Rainbow Div. which was actually the Tennessee National Guard, and later became the Rainbow Div.

1940 he died in a VA hospital. He married (1) **June GROVE**, b. ABT 1888, d. 4 Mar 1982 in Memphis, Shelby Co., TN. He married (2) **Lola May 'Mazie' SALE**, married 26 Aug 1903 in Tipton Co.

TN, b. 7 May 1877 in Covington, Tipton Co. TN, d. 4 Aug 1920, buried in Covington, Tipton Co. TN.

Children by Lola May 'Mazie' SALE:

+ 698. i **Walter Preston RHEA III** b. 20 Jan 1909.

+ 699. ii **Henry Sale 'Hal' RHEA** b. 1912.

377. **Eleanor Marion 'Nellie' CARY**, (117.Ellen[4], 23.Matthew[3], 4.Jannette[2], 1.John[1]) b. 22 Dec 1884 in TN. She married **Samuel Earnest RAGLAND**, married 14 Jun 1902, b. ABT 1884 in TN?.
Children:

+ 700. i **Eleanor Marion RAGLAND** b. 8 Jun 1907.

701. ii **Mary Elizabeth RAGLAND**, b. 26 Aug 1912 in TN?. She married **Bayard BOYLE**, b. ABT 1912.

+ 702. iii **Fairfax Cary RAGLAND** b. 15 May 1914.

380. **Alfred Long RHEA**, (118.Mary[4], 23.Matthew[3], 4.Jannette[2], 1.John[1]) b. 5 Dec 1878 in Somerville, Fayette Co., TN, d. 22 Jul 1925. Lived in Mississippi and in Augusta, Arkansas. He married **Mary Armstrong WAUCHOPE**, b. 25 Jun 1884 in WV, d. 8 May 1948. She was from Richmond VA.

1930 Federal census shows her as a widow with a large family in Somerville, Fayette Co., TN. She has three other family boarding in her home, including the family of Herman Butts, her relatives. Rhea, Mary, head, owns home, value $4,000, 45, widowed, first married at 22, b. TN to TN parents.
James, son, 21, single, b. TN, salesman, drug company.
Katharina, daughter, single, 18, b. TN
Frances, daughter, single, 15, b. TN.
Ellen, daughter, 12, b. TN.
Josephine, daughter, 8, b. TN.
Children:

703. i **James Taylor RHEA**, b. 29 Apr 1908 in Somerville, Fayette Co., TN, d. 11 Sep 1961 in Gallatin, Sumner Co., TN. He married **Louise RALSTON**, married 28 Dec 1933 in Coahoma, Coahoma Co., MS, b. 4 Feb 1907, d. 10 Aug 1988.

704. ii **Katherine Wauchope RHEA**, b. 5 Jul 1911 in Waupanucka OK, d. 1 Sep 1998. She married **Mayes Lyle WEBB**, married 11 Sep 1934, b. 2 Oct 1905 in Whiteville, Hardeman Co. TN.

+ 705. iii **Mary Frances RHEA** b. 1914.

+ 706. iv **Ellen Preston RHEA** b. 31 Dec 1918.

707. v **Josephine Wauchope RHEA**, b. 5 Jul 1921 in Somerville, Fayette Co., TN. She married **William Allen THOMAS**, b. 17 Feb 1922.

Sixth Generation

389. **Jane 'Jennie' Bowen EDMONDSON**, (121.Susan^5, 24.Susan^4, 5.John^3, 2.Robert^2, 1.John^1) (See marriage to number 116.)

391. **Robert Fairman SHEFFEY**, (124.Elizabeth^5, 25.Robert^4, 5.John^3, 2.Robert^2, 1.John^1) b. 24 Jun 1856 in Washington Co., VA, d. 8 Jul 1935 in Washington Co., VA, buried in Walnut Grove Cem. Washington Co. VA. 1900 he inherited Walnut Grove home place from his aunt Mary Preston Winston. He owned it from 1900 until the year of his death in 1935.

1900 June the Virginia census shows the family enumerated in the Goodson District of Washington Co., VA.
   Sheffey, Robert head of house, b. July 1856, married 20 years, b. VA, farmer
   Mary M. wife b. Oct. 1856, married 20 years, 3 children, 3 living, b. VA
   Maggie, M., daughter b. Feby. 1881, 19
   Pearl O., daughter b. May 1884, age 16,
   Robert P. son b. June 1891, age 8
   Carmack, Sally, sister in law, b. June 1874, 25 [in 1910 and 1920 'Aunt Sallie will be enumerated in the household of Robert P. - 1910 before is marriage and 1920 after his marriage.]
   Winston, Mary, aunt, b. 1828, age 71, no children.

1910 Federal census of Washington Co., VA there is a Robert F. Sheffey b. 1856 in VA living in Sullivan Co., TN with a young family, wife Anna W. b. VA, age 25, married 5 years with 3 children.

1920 a Robert appears in Washington Co., VA with a young family living at 19 Elmn (sic) St., Bristol City VA. [Bristol City is halfway in Sullivan Co., TN and halfway in Washington Co., VA.]
   Sheffey, Robert [no middle initial] age 63 [b. 1856], laborer at tannery (?), b. VA
   Sallie, wife, age 53 b. VA
   Carmack, May, step daughter, age 16, b. VA
   Cora, step daughter, age 1, b. VA
   James, step son, age 21, married, b. VA
   Ethel, step daughter, age 18, married. b. VA

1930 a Robert appears in the Virginia census in the King Town suburb of Bristol VA, Washington Co., VA
   Sheffey, Robert H. [F.? hard to read] 73, first married at age 21, b. VA
   Sallie I., wife, age 63, first married at age 31, b. VA.
   Mary C. daughter, age 25, single.

Robert Sheffey had two surviving children, Robert P. Sheffey and Mrs. Margaret Sheffey Minnick. His son inherited Walnut Grove. He married **Mary CARMACK**, married 1879, b. ABT 1856 in VA?. 1900 Washington Co., VA census shows her sister Sally living with the Sheffey family.
                    Children:

+ 708.   i   **Margaret 'Maggie' M. SHEFFEY** b. 1 Feb 1880.

      709.   ii   **Pearl O. SHEFFEY**, b. 1884.

+ 710.   iii   **Robert P. SHEFFEY Jr.** b. 1886.

392. **Henry L. SHEFFEY**, (124.Elizabeth[5], 25.Robert[4], 5.John[3], 2.Robert[2], 1.John[1]) b. 1859 in Washington Co., VA, d. 1939. Marriage mentioned in Notable Southern Fam., Z. Armstrong 1922.

1910 Federal census shows Henry's family enumerated next to that of John Fulkerson, possibly his brother in law, in Civil District 6 of Sullivan Co., TN.
   Sheffey, Henry L., 49, married 29 years, b. VA, farmer.
   -- Faithan (sic), wife, 50, married 20 years, 7 children, 6 living, b. TN to parents from TN.
   -- Walter, son, 25, married 8/12, b. VA, farmer.
   -- Fannie, daughter, 23, b. VA
   -- Francis (sic) daughter, 32, b. VA

-- Nola, daughter, 6, b. TN
-- Nettie, daughter in law, age not given, b. TN to TN parents. He
married **Faith 'Fatha' D. FULKERSON**, b. 1859 in TN, d. 1938.
1880 Federal census shows her name clearly as Fatha Fulkershon 19,
enumerated in the household of her parents Abraham and Eliza in
Carter Co., TN.

Children:

+ 711.　i　**Walter A. SHEFFEY** b. 1885.

　712.　ii　**Fannie SHEFFEY**, b. 1887 in VA.

　713.　iii　**Frances SHEFFEY**, b. 1889 in VA.

　714.　iv　**Nola SHEFFEY**, b. 1906 in VA.

393.　**Charles Marshall SHEFFEY**, (124.Elizabeth[5], 25.Robert[4], 5.John[3],
2.Robert[2], 1.John[1]) b. 1858 in Washington Co., VA. Marriage
mentioned in Notable Southern Families, Z. Armstrong 1922.

1880 the young family is enumerated in the Virginia census in the
Goodson District, Washington Co., VA. His father and brother
Robert are enumerated as nearby households.
Sheffey, Charles M. 22, farmer, b. VA
Carrie H. 20, wife, keeping house. b. VA
Minnie (?) W., 1 daughter. He married **Carrie WINSTON**, b. ABT
1860 in VA?.

Children:

　715.　i　**Minnie (?) W. SHEFFEY**, b. 1879 in Washington
　　　　　Co., VA.

396.　**James White CUMMINGS**, (125.Elizabeth[5], 26.Margaret[4],
5.John[3], 2.Robert[2], 1.John[1]) b. 19 Sep 1855 in Washington Co., VA,
d. 9 Jul 1924 in Washington Co., VA, buried in Sinking Spring Cem.
Washington Co. VA. 1877 he graduated from medical department
of U. of the City of NY in and was a physician in Abingdon VA.
Married first his cousin Elizabeth.

1910 1920 Federal census shows the family enumerated in
Abingdon, Washington Co., VA, living on Main St., family no.69.
Cummings, Jas W., 50, (noted M2 -second marriage), married 3
years, b. VA, physician, general practice.

-- Fannie, wife, 32, (noted M2 -second marriage also), married 3 years, 3 children, 2 living, b. VA to parents from WV and VA.

-- Francis (sic), daughter, 2, b. VA.

-- Jas W. Jr., daughter (sic), 1/12 (1 month - April 19 census), b. VA.

(in the same household)

Smith, Lizzie, cook, black, 20, married, b. VA, cook, private family.

Summers, S A, boarder, 29, single, b. VA to VA parents, deputy clerk, county court. (Fannie's brother)

Anderson, Lillian, Nurse, 18, single, b. VA to VA parents, nurse, private family.

1920 Federal census shows the family enumerated in Abingdon, Washington Co., VA, living on West Main St.

Cummings, James W., head, owns home, 69, b. VA to VA parents, Physician, General Practice.

-- Fannie, wife, 40, b. VA to parents from WV and VA

-- Frances, daughter, 12, b. VA.

-- Mary, daughter, 10, b. VA.

-- Elizabeth P., 8, b. VA.

Summers, Andrew, brother-in-law, 39, single, b. VA to parents from WV and VA, Deputy Clerk, Circuit Court.

1924 his will dated 8 Oct. 1923 was proved 16 July 1924 Washington Co. VA. He gave his estate to his wife Francis and daughters Frances R., Mary C. and Eliza Preston Cummings equally. Named Sunshine Summers executor. He married (1) **Elizabeth Madison PRESTON**, married 18 Jul 1900 in Washington Co., VA, b. 5 Oct 1858 in Washington Co., VA, (daughter of Henry PRESTON and Anne Cary CARTER) d. 4 Jan 1906. Married her cousin James. Had no children. He married (2) **Fannie Rhea SUMMERS**, married 1907, b. 1881 in Abingdon, Washington Co., VA, (daughter of John 'Col.' Calhoun SUMMERS and Nannie Montgomery PRESTON). 1920 census of VA shows Andrew Summers, brother in law, living with the family. He is born to West Virginia father and Virginia mother, and is 1 years younger than "Fannie S." and is later shown in 1930 to be her brother. She is called Fannie Clark in some records, but is from this census information shown to be a Summers.

1930 Federal census of Virginia shows more detail of her connection to the Summers family, with her brother's unique full name appearing as Sunshine A. Summers, who was the son of John C.

Summers. Fannie is now head of the household after the passing of her second husband in 1924. They are shown still living on West Main Street, Abingdon, Washington Co., VA.

Cummings, Fannie S., head, owns home, value $10,000, has radio, 52, widowed, married 19 years, b. VA to parents from WV and VA.

-- Mary C., daughter, 20, single, b. VA.

-- Eliza P., daughter, 18, single, b. VA. (The enumerator notes she is a lawyer in general practice but this was probably intended to be the entry for the resident of the household on line 41 below her)

Moore, Eldridge H., Son in Law, 27, married at 23, b. TN to TN parents, employment - none.

-- Frances C., daughter, 22, married at 17, b. VA.

-- Eldridge H. Jun., gr son, 11/12 (April 9 census date), b. VA

Summers, Sunshine A., brother, 49, single, b. VA to parents from WV and VA, Manager, Edwin (?) & Son Motor Co.

.

Children by Fannie Rhea SUMMERS:

+ 716.   i   **Frances CUMMINGS** b. 1908.

    717.   ii   **Mary Campbell CUMMINGS**, b. 1910 in Washington Co., VA. She married **Mr. WILLETS**, b. ABT 1890.

    718.   iii   **Elizabeth Preston CUMMINGS**, b. 1912 in Washington Co., VA.

    719.   iv   **James White CUMMINGS, Jr.**, b. 1 Mar 1910 in Washington Co., VA, d. BEF 1920.

397. **Robert Preston CUMMINGS**, (125.Elizabeth[5], 26.Margaret[4], 5.John[3], 2.Robert[2], 1.John[1]) b. 8 Feb 1857 in Washington Co., VA?. He married **Susie KELLAR**, b. ABT 1858 in VA?.
    Children:

    720.   i   **Arthur Campbell CUMMINGS**, b. ABT 1890 in VA?.

404. **James Lewis WHITE**, (128.John[5], 26.Margaret[4], 5.John[3], 2.Robert[2], 1.John[1]) b. 1 Apr 1856 in VA. He was the only one of his siblings to be born in Virginia. Before 1856 his father had come to Texas, however his parents clearly state on the 1900 Texas census that he was born in Virginia. Could James' mother have gone to stay with his father's relatives for the birth? James' daughter Anne

would note in the 1910 and later census that James was born in Texas, contrary to what he and his parents reported in earlier censuses.

1880 Federal census shows James enumerated in Austin, Travis Co., TX as a boarder with his young family living at 15 Peach St., age 24, a Clerk in the Court of Appeals.
White, James, 24, boarder, Clerk Court of Appeals, b. VA to VA parents.
-- Ellen 23, boarder, b. VA to parents from VA.
-- Anne, 4/12 (Feb), b. TX to parents from VA.
1900 Federal census shows James L., 44 , a widower, living with his parents in Austin TX. He is a lawyer. Neither of his children are enumerated with him in this household. Daughter Anne is not yet married, as her future husband is a border at school in Charlottesville VA at this time in June 1900. He married **Ellen Douglas CLARK**, b. 1857 in Washington Co., VA, d. BEF 1900.
Children:

+ 721.   i   **Annie Preston WHITE** b. 1 Feb 1880.

+ 722.   ii   **Colin Clarke WHITE** b. 1884.

405. **Annie Lewis WHITE**, (128.John[5], 26.Margaret[4], 5.John[3], 2.Robert[2], 1.John[1]) (See marriage to number 166.)

406. **Mary Magdelene WHITE**, (128.John[5], 26.Margaret[4], 5.John[3], 2.Robert[2], 1.John[1]) b. 1 Mar 1868 in TX, d. 1927. 1900 Federal census shows her enumerated at the home of her father in Austin, showing she has had 7 children, 2 children are living, but they are not enumerated with her in this home. The enumerated shows her as married, not widowed.

1920 Federal census shows her as had of household in Austin, Travis Co., TX, living at 104 West 30th St.:
 Crenshaw, Mary R (?) head, 51, widow
 -- Ben M. son, 34, single, b. TX, fireman, city hall.
 -- Margaret, -- 25, single b. TX, teacher, public schools. She married **Benjamin Mills CRENSHAW**, b. ABT 1867 in VA?, d. BEF 1900.
Children:

723.   i   **Benjamin Mills CRENSHAW Jr.**, b. 1886 in TX. Captain during WWI. Served in France, was

wounded and gassed. He remained in the Army until the Armistice was signed.

724. ii   **Margaret White CRENSHAW**, b. 1895 in TX.

408. **Montgomery Lewis WHITE**, (128.John[5], 26.Margaret[4], 5.John[3], 2.Robert[2], 1.John[1]) b. 1871 in TX, d. 1916. 1910 Federal census shows the family in Austin, Travis Co., TX, living at 2110 Rio Grande:

White, M. L., hear, 35, married 6 years, b. TX, works as Pre Pr (?) in Mfg.

-- Mary Belle, wife 36m married 6 years, 1 child, 1 living, b. TX to TX parents.

-- Louis, son 5, b. TX

[same household]

Erieckison (sic), Hulda, servant, 25, b. Sweden to Swedish parents, cook at Residence. He married **Mary Bell NELSON**, married 1903, b. 1879 in Sweden. 1900 Federal census shows her at b. in Texas. 20 years later she herself is head of the household and the enumerator notes she was born in Sweden. (Note, M. Lewis White's family had a Swedish servant when he was young and the family had one in the household in 1910.)

1930 Federal census shows her as widowed, living at 2610 Rio Grand Rd., Austin TX.

White, M. L. Mrs. head of house, owns home, no mortgage, age 41, widow, b. Sweden to Swedish parents.

-- Lewis, son, 15, single, b. TX.

Children:

725. i   **Lewis Nelson WHITE**, b. 1905 in TX.

415. **Margaret Preston CAMPBELL**, (131.Ellen[5], 26.Margaret[4], 5.John[3], 2.Robert[2], 1.John[1]) b. 23 Mar 1863 in Abingdon, Washington Co. VA, d. 18 Mar 1938. She married **Laurens W. 'Col.' YOUMANS,** married 18 Nov 1886 in Abingdon, Washington Co. VA, b. ABT 1863 in VA?, d. 16 Feb 1908 in Atlanta, GA. Another source shows his death in Hampton Co. SC. His name also appears as Youmens.

Children:

726. i   **MacDonald Campbell YOUMANS**, b. 26 Aug 1887 in VA?, d. 1 Aug 1969. During WWI entered service

as a private. His 2nd Lt. commission reached him as the Armistice was signed.

727. ii **Margaret Preston YOUMANS**, b. 21 Jun 1889 in VA?. She married **Joseph William COX**, b. ABT 1889.

+ 728. iii **Lucille YOUMANS** b. 20 Dec 1891.

417. **Bessie Cummings CAMPBELL**, (131.Ellen[5], 26.Margaret[4], 5.John[3], 2.Robert[2], 1.John[1]) b. 1 Mar 1866 in Abingdon, Washington Co. VA. She resided in Baton Rouge LA. She married **Henry Ramsey LENOIR**, married 31 Oct 1889 in Lenoir City, TN, b. 1864 in Lenoir City, TN, d. 1934.
    Children:

729. i **Ellen White LENOIR**, b. 1890 in VA?.

730. ii **Virginia Ballard LENOIR**, b. 1894 in VA?. She married **Wyatt H. STOVER**, b. ABT 1890 in VA?.

731. iii **Edward Campbell LENOIR**, b. 1896 in VA?. During WWI was a Sergeant in 105th Trench Mortar Battery, a unit of the 30 Division (Old Hickory Division). Served in France. His unit was sent to the front with another division where they were used as shock troops when not using their trench mortars. Was at the front when the Armistice was signed. Was sent to Luxembourg as part of the Army of Occupation. After arriving in France he was offered an opportunity to go to OTC but preferred going to the front. (Notable Southern Families, Z. Armstrong 1922).

418. **Sussie Trigg CAMPBELL**, (131.Ellen[5], 26.Margaret[4], 5.John[3], 2.Robert[2], 1.John[1]) b. 3 Mar 1868 in Abingdon, Washington Co. VA, d. 1957. She resided in Farmville, Prince Edward Co., VA. She married **Edwin Elisha HUNDLEY**, married 2 Jan 1895, b. ABT 1868 in Prince Edward Co. VA.
    Children:

732. i **Elizabeth Estes HUNDLEY**, b. 1895.

733. ii   **Campbell HUNDLEY**, b. 1896 in Washington Co., VA?.

734. iii   **Margaret Preston HUNDLEY**, b. 1898 in Washington Co., VA?.

735. iv   **Frances Edmumds HUNDLEY**, b. 1902 in Washington Co., VA?.

419. **William White CAMPBELL**, (131.Ellen^5, 26.Margaret^4, 5.John^3, 2.Robert^2, 1.John^1) b. 18 Oct 1869 in Abingdon, Washington Co. VA. 1947 he lived in Shreveport, LA. He married **Hallie MCCRACKEN**, married 14 Jun 1899, b. ABT 1869 in Washington Co., VA?.

Children:

736. i   **Mary Ellen CAMPBELL**, b. 26 Jun 1904 in Washington Co., VA?, d. 1 Aug 1992. She married **James GAIENNIE**, b. 30 Dec 1898, d. 1 Aug 1992 in LA.

420. **Frank CAMPBELL**, (131.Ellen^5, 26.Margaret^4, 5.John^3, 2.Robert^2, 1.John^1) b. 22 Aug 1871 in Abingdon, Washington Co. VA, d. 23 Oct 1945 in Bonham, Fannin Co., TX. He married **Sarah 'Sallie' JOUETT**, married 28 Oct 1896 in Bonham, Fannin Co., TX, b. 28 Nov 1871 in Bonham, Fannin Co., TX, d. 7 May 1964 in Plainview, Hale Co., TX, buried 9 May 1964 in Bonham, Fannin Co., TX. Graduated from Martha Washington College in Abingdon, VA, where she received the award for excellence in every medium of art. Her portraits and tapestry received much favorable comment. She was a member of the First Presbyterian Church of Bohnam.

Children:

737. i   **John Jouett CAMPBELL**, b. 12 Aug 1897 in TX, d. 7 Feb 1970 in Terrell, Kaufman Co., TX. He married **Hope BROWNLEE**, b. 26 Apr 1896, d. 14 Jan 1990 in Dallas, Dallas Co., TX.

738. ii   **Ellen Frances CAMPBELL**, b. 6 Aug 1901 in TX.

+ 739. iii   **Malcolm McDonald CAMPBELL** b. 4 Oct 1904.

422. **Preston White CAMPBELL**, (131.Ellen^5, 26.Margaret^4, 5.John^3, 2.Robert^2, 1.John^1) b. 24 Jan 1874 in Washington Co., VA, d. 2 Jul

1954. 1920 Federal census shows the young family enumerated on West Main St, Abingdon, VA.
Campbell, Preston W., 45, b. VA to VA parents, Judge, Circuit Court.
-- Louise H., wife 28, b. VA to VA parents.
-- Preston W. Jr., son, 4 4/12 (as of January 1920 census date), b. VA.
-- Edward M., son, 2 6/12, b. VA
-- Volney H., son, 9/12, b. VA

1927-31 Justice of the State Supreme Court.

1930 Federal census shows the family enumerated on Main Street in Abingdon, Washington Co., VA in the household next to his brother Robert:
Campbell, Preston W., head, owns home, value $20,000, no radio, age 56, married first at 39, b. VA, Judge, Supreme Court.
  -- Louise E. H., wife-h., age 38, married at 22, b. VA to VA parents.
  -- Preston W., Jr., son, 14, b. VA
  -- Malcomb E., son, 12, b. VA.
  -- Volney, H., son, age 11, b. VA.

1931-40 Chief Justice of the Virginia Supreme court. He married **Louise Elwood HOWARD**, married 9 Apr 1914, b. 22 Jun 1891 in Lynchburg, VA, d. 17 Aug 1956.
Children:

  740.   i   **Preston White CAMPBELL**, b. 21 Sep 1915 in Abingdon, Washington Co. VA, d. 23 May 1944 in Europe. He married **Nancy McGuire PATTERSON**, b. ABT 1900 in Bristol, Washington Co., VA.

+ 741.   ii   **Edward Malcolm CAMPBELL** b. 20 Jun 1917.

  742.   iii   **Volney CAMPBELL**, b. 30 Mar 1919 in Abingdon, Washington Co. VA, d. 1967. He married **Ellen Meade WILSON**, married 28 Nov 1942 in Marion, Smythe Co., VA, b. ABT 1919.

427. **Frank Brockenbrough PRESTON**, (134.Alfred[5], 27.William[4], 5.John[3], 2.Robert[2], 1.John[1]) b. 15 Mar 1888 in VA. He married **Margaret Kent JONES**, b. ABT 1888 in LA.

Children:

743. i **Margaret Kent PRESTON**, b. ABT 1920.

428. **Lucy Alice PRESTON**, (134.Alfred[5], 27.William[4], 5.John[3], 2.Robert[2], 1.John[1]) b. 21 Aug 1889 in VA. Lived in Charlottesville VA. She married **William P. MOORE**, b. ABT 1889.
    Children:

744. i **Alfred Preston MOORE**, b. ABT 1920.

745. ii **William P. MOORE Jr.**, b. ABT 1922.

430. **Susan Radford PRESTON**, (134.Alfred[5], 27.William[4], 5.John[3], 2.Robert[2], 1.John[1]) b. 30 Dec 1892 in VA. Moved to Wilmington Delaware. She married **William J. ROBINSON**, b. ABT 1892.
    Children:

746. i **William J. ROBINSON Jr.**, b. ABT 1925.

747. ii **Alfred Preston ROBINSON**, b. ABT 1927.

431. **John Brockenbrough PRESTON**, (134.Alfred[5], 27.William[4], 5.John[3], 2.Robert[2], 1.John[1]) b. 6 Mar 1894 in VA. He married **Gertrude MCCONNELL**, b. ABT 1894.
    Children:

748. i **John Brockenborough PRESTON Jr.**, b. ABT 1932, d. 7 Jun 1978.

749. ii **Jane Deval PRESTON**, b. ABT 1934. Lived in Troutville, VA.

750. iii **Ann PRESTON**, b. ABT 1936.

432. **Annie Beale PRESTON**, (134.Alfred[5], 27.William[4], 5.John[3], 2.Robert[2], 1.John[1]) b. 12 Aug 1897 in VA. Lived in Charlotte, NC.

1930 Federal census shows the family enumerated in Paris, Bourbon Co., KY:
Didier, Darcy C. head, rents $30/month, 37 married at 26, b. VA to parents from VA and MD, President of Cannery.
-- Anna P., wife, 29, married at 24, b. VA.

-- Charles P., son, 10, b. VA. She married **Darcy C. DIDIER**, b. ABT 1897. His name has been reported as Henry D'Arcy Didier. He appears in the 1930 census as Darcy C. Didier.
Children:

751.   i   **Charles Peel DIDIER**, b. 1920 in VA.

433. **Mary PRESTON**, (134.Alfred[5], 27.William[4], 5.John[3], 2.Robert[2], 1.John[1]) b. 17 Nov 1898 in Botetourt Co., VA. Lived in Salem, VA. She married **Evan W. LINDSAY**, b. ABT 1898.
Children:

752.   i   **Annie Beale LINDSAY**, b. ABT 1925.

439. **Margaret Peters SHEFFEY**, (139.John[5], 29.Eleanor[4], 5.John[3], 2.Robert[2], 1.John[1]) b. 1 Oct 1868 in Marion, Smythe Co., VA. She married **Percy Cochran MARCH**, b. 1 Dec 1863 in OH. Percy was named after his father's (Rufus Pierce March) commanding officer during the Civil war, a Union Captain, James R. Percy. The Captain was a brave and gallant engineer of the 53rd Ohio Regiment. Capt. Percy was killed by a Confederate sniper at the Battle of Atlanta in August 1864. Rufus March was discharged after Shiloh with a disability but re enlisted later and fought at the Battle of Monacacy River at Frederick, Maryland. He returned to Ohio after the War had two children and was killed by a falling log in 1872. Rufus is buried in Bourneville, OH

1911 or so, Percy Cochran March and his wife Margaret moved to El Paso, TX where Percy worked at a large wholesale hardware company. (Notes from researcher Fred Preston, which he indicates were supplied by John Percy March.

1900 Federal census shows the family enumerated with two children in Marion, Smythe Co., VA. Percy is a bookkeeper, born in Ohio.
Children:

753.   i   **Josephine S. MARCH**, b. 1 Jul 1891 in VA.

754.   ii   **John Preston MARCH**, b. 1 Mar 1899 in VA.

755.   iii   **Jane Cochran MARCH**, b. ABT 1901.

756.   iv   **Arthur MARCH**, b. ABT 1903.

440. **Eleanor Fairman SHEFFEY**, (139.John[5], 29.Eleanor[4], 5.John[3], 2.Robert[2], 1.John[1]) b. 11 Jul 1866 in Marion, Smythe Co., VA, d. 9 Nov 1952. She married **Benjamin Franklin BUCHANAN**, married 2 Mar 1887, b. ABT 1866 in Smythe Co. VA. Marriage and children mentioned in Notable Southern Fam., Z. Armstrong 1922.
    Children:

+ 757.   i   **John Preston BUCHANAN** b. 30 Jan 1888.

  758.   ii   **Patrick Campbell BUCHANAN**, b. 24 Feb 1889 in VA?, d. 10 Nov 1890. Died young.

  759.   iii   **Josephine Spiller BUCHANAN**, b. 22 Aug 1891 in VA?.

  760.   iv   **Virginia B. BUCHANAN**, b. 11 Oct 1894 in VA?. Had 2 daughters. She married **Guy Blair 'Gen.' DENIT**, married 11 Dec 1917, b. ABT 1894.

  761.   v   **Frank BUCHANAN**, b. 29 Nov 1896 in VA?, d. 17 Dec 1896. Died young.

  762.   vi   **Eleanor Fairman 'Nellie' BUCHANAN**, b. 6 Feb 1901 in VA?. She married **Harry Watson STARCHER**, b. ABT 1901.

+ 763.   vii   **David H. BUCHANAN** b. 8 May 1907.

441. **Susan 'Susie' Montgomery SHEFFEY**, (139.John[5], 29.Eleanor[4], 5.John[3], 2.Robert[2], 1.John[1]) b. 12 Aug 1867 in Marion, Smythe Co., VA. She married **E. Marcellus COPENHAVER**, b. ABT 1867 in VA?.
    Children:

  764.   i   **Preston COPENHAVER**, b. ABT 1890 in VA?.

  765.   ii   **Elizabeth Marcellus COPENHAVER**, b. ABT 1892 in VA?.

443. **James White SHEFFEY**, (139.John[5], 29.Eleanor[4], 5.John[3], 2.Robert[2], 1.John[1]) b. 13 Sep 1871 in Marion, Smythe Co., VA, d. 11 Nov 1932. 1930 Federal census shows the family enumerated in Marion, Smyth Co. VA living on West Main St.;

Sheffey, James W., head, owns home, value $5,000, no radio, 57, b. VA to VA parents, lawyer.
-- Lucy C., wife-h, 50, b. VA to parents b. in TN.
-- Caroline, daughter, 21, single, b. VA, teacher, public school.
-- Josephine, daughter, 18, single, b. VA.
-- Elenor, daughter, 16, single, b. VA.
-- Harold, son, 14, single, b. VA.
-- Mary P., daughter, 8, b. VA. He married **Lucy Lee CARLOCK**, married 3 Oct 1900, b. 29 Mar 1880 in VA, d. 30 Mar 1956.
Children:

766.   i   **Lucy Lee SHEFFEY**, b. 5 May 1903 in VA, d. 10 Jul 1947.

767.   ii   **James White SHEFFEY Jr.**, b. 14 Oct 1904 in VA, d. 24 May 1922.

768.   iii   **Carolyn Carlock SHEFFEY**, b. 7 Apr 1909 in VA.

769.   iv   **Josephine Spiller White SHEFFEY**, b. 6 Jul 1911 in VA. 1930 she appears enumerated with her parents in the Federal Census in Marion, Smyth Co., VA, single, age 18.

Had 3 sons. She married **R. C. HORNSBY**, married AFT 1930, b. ABT 1911.

770.   v   **Eleanor Fairman SHEFFEY**, b. 3 Oct 1913 in VA.

771.   vi   **Harold Carlock 'Capt.' SHEFFEY**, b. 16 Nov 1915 in VA, d. 16 Jul 1944. He was killed in WWII.

772.   vii   **John Preston SHEFFEY**, b. 7 Nov 1918 in VA, d. 29 Feb 1920. Died young.

773.   viii   **Mary Preston SHEFFEY**, b. 11 Jun 1921 in VA.

445.   **John Preston SHEFFEY Jr.**, (139.John[5], 29.Eleanor[4], 5.John[3], 2.Robert[2], 1.John[1]) b. 1 Nov 1876 in Marion, Smythe Co., VA. 1930 Federal census shows the family enumerated in Marion, Smyth Co., VA, living at 306, Strother Street;
    Sheffey, John P., head, owns house, value of house $6,000, has radio, age 53, married at 35, b. VA, farmer of own farm.

-- Virginia, wife, age 49, married at 23, b. VA to parents born in VA.
-- Margaret, daughter, age 16, b. VA.
-- Virginia, daughter, age 14, b. VA.
-- John P. Jr., son, age 11, b. VA
Rainey, Lucy, servant, age 52, single, b. VA. He married **Virginia HARRINGTON**, b. 1881 in VA.
> *Children:*

    774. i   **Margaret L. SHEFFEY**, b. 1914 in VA.

    775. ii   **Virginia SHEFFEY**, b. 1916 in VA.

    776. iii   **John Preston SHEFFEY III. III.**, b. 1919 in VA.

446. **James Sheffey PENDLETON**, (141.Elizabeth[5], 29.Eleanor[4], 5.John[3], 2.Robert[2], 1.John[1]) b. 1 Nov 1874 in VA?. He married **Margaret FUDGE**, b. ABT 1874 in VA?.
> *Children:*

    777. i   **Albert G. PENDLETON**, b. ABT 1900 in VA?.

    778. ii   **Granville F. PENDLETON**, b. ABT 1902 in VA?.

448. **Eleanor Lynn RHEA**, (142.Ellen[5], 29.Eleanor[4], 5.John[3], 2.Robert[2], 1.John[1]) b. 7 Aug 1871 in Marion, Smythe Co., VA, d. 2 Sep 1927. Eleanor married twice. Had 2 sons by her first husband. Married second, 4 years after the death of William, who died in 1899. (Notable Southern Families., Z. Armstrong 1922)

1900 Federal census she is enumerated with her two young sons, a widow, with her parents in Marion, Smyth Co., VA. She married (1) **William H. or S. ADAMS**, married 26 Dec 1895, b. ABT 1871 in Bristol, Sullivan Co., TN, d. 5 Jul 1899 in Bristol, Sullivan Co., TN, buried in Marion, Smythe Co., VA. She married (2) **Sturm W. CARSON**, married 19 Nov 1903 in Americus GA, b. 1 Mar 1867 in TN. He lived in Rogersville, TN. Married twice - two distant cousins.

Lived in Atlanta GA with Eleanor.
> *Children by William H. or S. ADAMS:*

    779. i   **Charles Linwood ADAMS**, b. 14 Dec 1896 in Sullivan Co., TN.

780.   ii   **Brainard Rhea ADAMS**, b. 26 Jul 1898 in Sullivan Co., TN, d. 20 Sep 1953.

449. **Margaret Preston RHEA**, (142.Ellen[5], 29.Eleanor[4], 5.John[3], 2.Robert[2], 1.John[1]) b. 22 Jan 1876 in VA?, d. 23 Aug 1945. She married **Henry Boyd STALEY**, married 23 Jun 1898 in Marion, Smythe Co., VA, b. 9 Jul 1871 in Marion, Smythe Co., VA, d. 27 Dec 1948.

Children:

781.   i   **Ellen Sheffey STALEY**, b. 25 May 1899 in Marion, Smythe Co., VA.

+ 782.   ii   **Pauline Hill STALEY** b. 6 Jul 1900.

783.   iii   **Henry Boyd STALEY Jr.**, b. 5 Jan 1903 in Marion, Smythe Co., VA, d. 1939.

453. **Don Preston PETERS**, (143.Mary[5], 29.Eleanor[4], 5.John[3], 2.Robert[2], 1.John[1]) b. 1 Dec 1877 in VA. He was a physician in Lynchburg, VA.

1930 Federal census shows he and his family at 1215 Church Street, Lynchburg, Campbell Co. VA:
  Peters, Don P. head, owns home, value $30,000, has radio, age 55, married at 35, b. VA, physician, surgery.
  -- Rhett, M, wife-H, 40 married at 20, b. MD.
  -- Mary S., daughter, 17, b. MD.
  -- Don P. Jr., son, 14, b. MD.
  -- John P. son, 10, b. VA.
  -- Rhett P., daughter, 7 b. VA.
  McDaniel, Theresa, servant, 16, single, b. VA.
  Smith, Marshall, servant, 30, divorced, b. VA.

He and the family had lived first in Maryland the home state of Rhett and came to Virginia where John was born, before 1920. He married **Rhetta MENCKE**, b. 1 Apr 1888 in Baltimore, Baltimore Co., MD. 1900 a Retta A Mencke does appear with her parents John and Kate in Baltimore, she was born in April 1888, and was 12 at the time.

Another source showed her maiden name as 'Hangh.'
Children:

228

784. i   **Mary Sheffey PETERS**, b. 1913 in MD.

785. ii   **Don Preston PETERS Jr.**, b. 1916 in MD.

786. iii **John P. PETERS**, b. 1920 in VA.

787. iv   **Rhett P. PETERS**, b. 1923 in VA.

454. **Eleanor Fairman PRESTON**, (145.Martha[5], 29.Eleanor[4], 5.John[3], 2.Robert[2], 1.John[1]) b. 11 Aug 1873 in Marion, Smythe Co., VA, d. 9 Jun 1952 in San Francisco, CA. 1880 Federal census shows her enumerated with her parents in Abingdon, Washington Co., VA at age 4.

Her cousin, John Fairman Preston, a Presbyterian minister, performed her marriage ceremony.

California death index notes her dates of birth and death. She married **James Thomas WATKINS**, b. 1872 in Maryland. 1900 Federal census shows only two white James Watkins born in Maryland. One has middle initial 'B' and the other 'T'. 'James T' is enumerated in Baltimore, age 25, secretary/treasurer, with his parents Frank (a dealer of sash and ---) and Augusta Watkins. It is not clear this is a record of the future husband of Eleanor. An obituary of a daughter in law indicates the son of Elearnor Preston Watkins was James Thomas Watkins IV.

1910 April 30 Federal census shows the family enumerated in San Francisco, San Francisco Co., CA living a 3 Beach Terrace, off 25th Ave.
    Watkins, James T. head, 38, married 6 years, b. MD to parents from MD, physician, General Practice.
    " Eleanor P., wife, 34, married 6 years, 4 children, 3 living, b. VA to VA parents, not employed.
    " James T., Jr., son 3, single, b. CA.
    " Robert P., son, 1 4/12, single, b. CA (December 1908 birth).
    " William O., son, 0/12 single, b. CA. (This record would indicate April birth, but CA birth records indicate May 22, which would have been after the date of the census.)
    McManus, Katherine, servant, 23, single, b. Ireland to Irish parents, servant, private house.
    McHugh, Maggie, servant 22, single., b. Ireland to Irish parents, servant, private house.

Schott, Carola, servant, 18, single, b. Switz. German to Switz. German parents, servant, private house.

1920 Federal census shows the family enumerated in San Francisco, San Francisco Co., CA living at 3 25th Avenue.

Watkins, James T., head, owns home, 47, b. MD to parents from CA and MD, Surgeon.

" Eleanor., wife, 43, b. VA to parents from VA, not employed.

" James T. Jr., son,12, single, b. CA.

" Robert, son, 11, single, b. CA.

" William, son, 9, b. CA.

" Sherman, son, 6, single, b. CA.

Habe, George, servant 31, immigrated 1908, b. Japan to parents from Japan, house man, private family.

" Sanna, servant, 23, male, 23, immigrated 1919, b. Japan, to Japanese parents, cook.

Moss, Josephine, servant, 16, immigrated 1913, b. Ireland to parents from Ireland, nurse, private family.

1930 Federal census shows the family enumerated in Stanford Precinct #2, of Palo Alto Township, Santa Clara Co., CA living at 610 Cahillo Street.

Watkins, James T., head, rents $200/ month, 58, married first at 31, b. MD to parents from MD, Surgeon, Orthopedic.

" Eleanor P., 53, wife, married at 26, b. VA, not employed.

" James T., son, 22, single, b. CA.

" Robert P., son, 21, single, b. CA.

" William, son, 19, b. CA.

" H. M. Sherman, son 16, single, b. CA.

Caragay, Pedro, servant, 50, married first at 30, widower, b. Philippines to parents from Philippines, cook, private family.

Whitaker, Albert M., brother-in-law, 21, single, b. CA to parents from PA and CA.

He was a physician in Oakland, CA.

Children:

+ 788.   i   **James Thomas WATKINS IV Jr.** b. 1908.

   789.   ii   **Robert Preston WATKINS**, b. 1 Feb 1909 in CA. Some researchers show his middle name as Sheffy, but others show Preston, and the census records show middle initial P in 1910, 1920 and 1930.

790.   iii   **William O. WATKINS**, b. 22 May 1910 in San Francisco, CA, d. 15 Feb 1967 in CA.

791.   iv   **Arllian O. WATKINS**, b. 22 May 1910 in San Francisco, CA. 1910 California birth records indicate Arllian and William were twins born on the same day in May.

792.   v   **Harry Mitchellsher Sherman WATKINS**, b. 16 Jul 1913 in San Francisco, CA, d. 26 Jun 1993 in Santa Clara, CA.

455. **Robert Sheffey PRESTON II.**, (145.Martha^5, 29.Eleanor^4, 5.John^3, 2.Robert^2, 1.John^1) b. 30 Jul 1885 in Marion, Smythe Co., VA, d. 28 Oct 1953 in Richmond, Henrico Co., VA. 1900 Federal census shows Robert enumerated in Worsham, Prince Edward Co., VA at Hampton-Sidney College.
Preston, Robert S., partner, July 1885, 14, single, b . VA to VA parents, at school.
His mother had passed away, and his father was now superintendent and living at the State Hospital in Marion VA. He married **Alice Burwell REED**, married 3 Oct 1916, b. 19 Jul 1895 in VA?, d. 25 Aug 1979.
Children:

+ 793.   i   **Robert Sheffey PRESTON, Jr. III.** b. 15 Aug 1917.

+ 794.   ii   **William Reed PRESTON** b. 3 Jun 1920.

+ 795.   iii **Alice Burwell PRESTON** b. 24 Feb 1927.

459. **Anne PRESTON**, (156.Robert^5, 33.Francis^4, 5.John^3, 2.Robert^2, 1.John^1) b. 1 Mar 1887 in VA. 1920 Federal census shows the family enumerated in Charleston, South Carolina living at 277 Calhoun Street. Anne's brother Robert W. Preston is living with the family.
Wilson, Geo. H. head, 40, b. SC, Medical Doctor, general practice..
-- Anne, wife 38, b. VA.
-- Margaret b. daughter, 9 b. SC.
-- Hugh H. son, 7, b. SC.
-- Wm (?) F. son 1 2/12 b. SC.
Preston, Robt. W., Brother-in-law, age unk, single, b. VA, Medical Doctor, general practice.
(also in the same household as follows)

Braun, Sue, aunt, 75, single, b. SC.

Plawder, Henry, lodger, 24, single, b. SC, Medical Doctor, Western Med. Col.

Fain, Marion, lodger, 18, single b. SC, student, medical college.

Hughes, James B. lodger, 28, single, b. SC, Medical Student, Medical College.

Owens, Frank, C. lodger, 21, single, b. SC, Medical Student, Medical College.

Crawford, Frank, C., lodger 21, single b. SC, student, medical college. She married **George 'Dr.' H. WILSON**, b. 1880 in SC.

Children:

796.　i　**Margaret B. WILSON**, b. 1911 in SC.

797.　ii　**Hugh H. WILSON**, b. 1913 in SC.

798.　iii　**William F. WILSON**, b. 1 Oct 1918 in SC.

462.　**Hayward CRAIGHEAD**, (163.Preston[5], 34.Jane[4], 5.John[3], 2.Robert[2], 1.John[1]) b. 1892 in Marengo Co., AL. 1920 Federal census shows him enumerated with his parents in Uniontown, AL. He is a merchant.

1930 Federal census shows Hayward now married and enumerated in Faunsdale, Marengo Co., AL:

Craighead, Haywood, head, rents home, has radio, age 37, married first at 32, b. AL, farmer.

-- Maud, wife, age 30, married first at 27, b. AL.

-- Haywood, son age 10/12, b. AL. He married **Maud wife of Hayward CRAIGHEAD**.

Children:

799.　i　**Haywood CRAIGHEAD**, b. 1 Jun 1929 in Marengo Co., AL.

468.　**Walter White PRESTON**, (166.John[5], 35.James[4], 5.John[3], 2.Robert[2], 1.John[1]) b. 18 Apr 1880 in Seguin, Guadalupe Co., TX, d. 23 Aug 1938. 1930 Federal census shows the young family enumerated in Lockhart, Caldwell Co., TX:

Preston Walter W., head, owns home, value $6,000, no radio, 49, married 22 years, . TX, Auditor, Caldwell Co.

-- Mary Amy (sic) wife H, 49, married 22 years, b. TX.

-- Lewis F., son, 13, b. TX

-- Frances, daughter 13, b. TX. He married **Annie Marie BONHAN**, b. 23 Aug 1879 in TX, d. 3 Nov 1941. 1930 Federal census notes her father was born in Virginia and mother in Maryland.

Children:

800.   i   **Walter Bonham PRESTON**, b. 13 Apr 1904 in TX. 1930 Federal census shows him in Precinct 3, Wharton Co., TX a roomer with 20 other men at a mine:
> Preston Walter B., roomer, 21, single, b. TX, mechanical engineer, at Sulphur Mine.

801.   ii   **John Courtney PRESTON**, b. 1912 in TX.

802.   iii   **Frances PRESTON**, b. 2 Sep 1916 in TX.

803.   iv   **Lewis Fredrick PRESTON**, b. 2 Sep 1916 in TX. Twin of Frances. Lived in Oak Ridge TN.

469. **John Lewis PRESTON**, (166.John[5], 35.James[4], 5.John[3], 2.Robert[2], 1.John[1]) b. 24 Mar 1883 in Seguin, Guadalupe Co., TX. He practiced dentistry in Austin TX.

His name appears in the early Federal census records with his family as Lewis or Louis.

1920 Federal census John L. is living with his mother in law in Forney, Kaufman Co., TX, a widower at a young age. No children listed.
 McKellar Emma, head owns home free of mortgage, 61, widow, b. TX.
 Preston John L son in law, 36, widower, b. TX, dentist, at own office.

1930 Federal census there is a John L. Preston who is an officer at the Wichita Falls State Hospital, age age 47, widowed, had married at 30, b. TX, with father born VA and mother born in TX who would appear to be Lewis. He married **Leonora MCKELLAR**, b. ABT 1883 in TX?, d. BEF 1920. Died at the birth of her first child.

Children:

804.   i   **John Lewis PRESTON, Jr.**, b. ABT 1920 in TX?. Died shortly after birth.

485. **Preston Henry BAILEY**, (174.Ellen[5], 37.Henry[4], 5.John[3], 2.Robert[2], 1.John[1]) b. 25 May 1891 in VA, d. 11 Oct 1928. He married **Elizabeth Marie LEFTWICH**, married 1917, b. ABT 1891.

       Children:

    805.   i   **Otway Giles BAILEY Jr.**, b. 1924.

    806.   ii   **Ellen Olivia BAILEY**, b. 1926.

486. **Otway Giles BAILEY, Jr.**, (174.Ellen[5], 37.Henry[4], 5.John[3], 2.Robert[2], 1.John[1]) b. 20 Jan 1895, d. 1974. 1930 Federal census shows the family enumerated in the Madison District of Cumberland Co., VA, perhaps on Stony Point Road. [there is also a note of Cumberland CH road on the first page where the family appears]:
  Bailey, O G Jr, head, owns home, value $4,000, has radio, age 35, married first at 28, b. VA, Supt. Schools, county.
  -- Ella, wife, 34, married first at 27, b. VA.
[next page of census]
  -- Bailey O. G. III son, 5 b. VA.
  -- Ellen O. daughter, 3, b. VA.
  -- O. G. Sr., Father, 76, widowed, b. VA. He married **Ella DEFORD**, married 5 Sep 1923, b. 8 Jun 1895, d. 2 May 1979.

       Children:

+ 807.   i   **Otway Giles BAILEY III.** b. 5 Sep 1924.

+ 808.   ii   **Ellen Olivia BAILEY** b. 10 Oct 1926.

+ 809.   iii   **Jeanne Deford BAILEY** b. 18 Jul 1930.

489. **Henry PRESTON III**, (176.Henry[5], 37.Henry[4], 5.John[3], 2.Robert[2], 1.John[1]) b. 27 Jun 1895. Married, had a child and grandchild. He married **Leta Perry WILSON**, married 18 Jun 1930, b. ABT 1895.
       Children:

    810.   i   **Don PRESTON**, b. ABT 1920.

495. **Robert Earhart RHEA**, (183.Joseph[5], 40.Sarah[4], 6.Jane[3], 2.Robert[2], 1.John[1]) b. 12 Jul 1870 in Sullivan Co., TN, d. 1942. Born on his grandfathers farm.

1910 family with 3 children and Mother Eliza A. living in the household. He married **Margaret Rebecca RHEA**, married 1905 in Sullivan Co., TN, b. 1873 in Sullivan Co., TN, d. 13 Jul 1942 in Bristol, Sullivan Co., TN, buried in East Hill Cem., Bristol, Wash. Co., VA. 1910 census shows she had 4 children, 3 living.

1942 obituary - Well known Bristol resident who died unexpectedly at 5:30am
Monday at her home 641 Alabama St after being in declining health for approximately one year. Spent her entire life in Bristol, being a member of one of the first families of the section. Surviving are her husband; 2 daughters Lindsey Rhea of Bristol and Helen Rhea of Washington, DC; one brother Will Rhea of Bristol.

Children:

811.   i   **Margaret Lindsay RHEA**, b. 21 Dec 1906 in Sullivan Co., TN, d. 24 Aug 1974 in Bristol, Sullivan Co., TN, buried in East Hill Cem., Bristol, Wash. Co., VA. Twin of Helen Bruce Rhea. 1910 census shows she was a twin of Mary E.?

   1974 obituary - Former City Educator Dies. Margaret Rhea of 821 Alabama St. Bristol, TN died 1:30 pm Sunday at Bristol Memorial. Hospital following a brief illness. Educated at VA Intermount College and King College and Western Reserve in Cleveland. Prior to her retirement in 1972 Miss Rhea taught 39 years in the Bristol TN school system and at the time of her retirement was chairman of the Math department at TN high school.

812.   ii   **Mary Eleanor RHEA**, b. 1907 in Sullivan Co., TN?, d. 2 1919 in Bristol, Sullivan Co., TN, buried in East Hill Cem., Bristol, Wash. Co., VA. 1919 obituary - Miss Mary Eleanor Rhea the 12 year old daughter of Mr. and Mrs. R Rhea died at her home on Alabama St. early yesterday morning. She was taken with typhoid which later developed into double case of typhoid-pneumonia. Miss Rhea is survived by her parents, her twin sister Lindsay and a younger sister Helen.

813.   iii   **Helen Bruce RHEA**, b. 1 Aug 1908 in Sullivan Co., TN. Twin of Margaret Rhea. Lived in Bristol, TN.

1942 she was living in Washington, DC.

499. **Margaret Davis RHEA**, (183.Joseph[5], 40.Sarah[4], 6.Jane[3], 2.Robert[2], 1.John[1]) b. 1 Oct 1876 in Sullivan Co., TN. It appears from the settlement of her fathers estate that she married Mr. Bullard by 1911.

1920 Federal census shows the family enumerated in Bluefield, Mercer Co., WV, living at 216 Fairfax St.:
Bullard, Chester, head, rents, 44, b. VA to parents from VA and CT, Machinist, Steam Railroad.
-- Margaret R., wife, 43, b. TN to parents from TN and VA.
-- Margaret, daughter, 17, single, b. Texas, parents from VA and TN.
(next page of census)
-- Joseph R., son, 15, b. Texas, parents from VA and TN

1930 Federal census she is enumerated in the household headed by her brother Alex Rhea, living at 314 Taylor St., Bristol, TN, age 52, a widow.

She also appears in her brother Alexander Rhea's obituary as Mrs. Chester Bullard. She married **Chester BULLARD**, married 3 Jan 1900, b. 1876 in Radford, Pulaski Co., VA, d. BEF 1930.
Children:

814. i **Willie Margaret BULLARD**, b. 1903 in TX. She married **Cameron MCCUE**, b. ABT 1900.

815. ii **Joe Rhea BULLARD**, b. 1905 in TX.

501. **Elizabeth 'Bettie' Dysart RHEA**, (184.Frances[5], 40.Sarah[4], 6.Jane[3], 2.Robert[2], 1.John[1]) b. 1856 in Blountville, Sullivan Co., TN. She married **Alexander ANDERSON**, b. 1856 in Rodgersville TN, (son of Audley ANDERSON).
Children:

+ 816. i **Audley Rhea ANDERSON** b. 28 Mar 1881.

503. **Robert Preston RHEA**, (184.Frances[5], 40.Sarah[4], 6.Jane[3], 2.Robert[2], 1.John[1]) b. 6 Mar 1859 in Blountville, Sullivan Co., TN, d. 3 1930 in Whichita Falls, TX. Moved to Forney TX. Married Bell in TX. He had gone there, started in business and identified himself

with all her public interests of church and state. Was made an elder in the church. ('Genealogy of the Rhea Family by W.L.Rhea, 1895)

1930 obituary - Robert Preston Rhea Funeral Rites Held at Forney Texas -
The following item from Forney Texas newspaper will be of interest to many people in this section.
Funeral services for Robert Preston Rhea were held at the First Methodist Church at Forney Sunday Feb. 2, 1930. Mr. Rhea's sudden death was the result of a collision of his automobile with a freight train at Wichita Falls, TX on Friday January 31st. This tragic event was a distinct shock and grief to the entire citizenship of Forney where Mr. Rhea had lived for many years.

He came to Texas October 12, 1877 from Blountville, TN in which place he was born March 8, 1859. He first settled in Valley View community where he farmed and taught school for several years. After his marriage to Miss Nannie Belle Gillespie he moved to Forney and entered the mercantile business. He followed this line of work for 33 years during which time he built up and maintained a general merchandise store that was a credit to the community. He married **Nannie Belle GILLISPIE**, b. 22 Jan 1851 in Texas, d. 17 Apr 1932 in Texas.
Children:

+ 817. i **Joseph Earhart RHEA** b. 3 Aug 1882.

+ 818. ii **Frank Bland RHEA** b. 9 May 1884.

   819. iii **Lillian Buris RHEA**, b. 24 Aug 1889 in Forney, Kaufman Co., TX.

   820. iv **Robert Preston RHEA Jr.**, b. 21 Jun 1894 in Forney, Kaufman Co., TX.

504. **James Theodoric RHEA**, (184.Frances[5], 40.Sarah[4], 6.Jane[3], 2.Robert[2], 1.John[1]) b. 11 Jun 1860 in Blountville, Sullivan Co., TN, d. 15 Nov 1920 in Forney, Kaufman Co., TX. 1880 Sullivan Co. TN census shows him living in TN alone at the age of 20. Later, he was a bookkeeper for his brother Robert in Forney TX. Robert had the management of two stores and did the buying for both.

1900 Federal census shows the family in Forney, Kaufman Co., TX. James is a bookkeeper at a dry goods store. Caroline has had 2

children, both living: Clarence W. 9 and William E., 5. His sister
Sally and brother in law are enumerated as the household next door.

1909 July 9, reported in the Bristol Herald Courier
- Mrs. Bettie Rhea Anderson of this city is in receipt of a letter from
Forney Texas telling of a thrilling automobile accident in which
James T Rhea formerly of this county was seriously injured.

Mr. Rhea and a partner were returning from a trip to a nearby point
when the large automobile in which they were riding ran over a
bridge and all were hurled into a deep ravine below. Mr. Rhea
suffered two broken ribs and was internally injured ... It is thought
all will recover.

1910 Federal census shows the family enumerated in Forney,
Kaufman Co., TX living at Houston St.
  Rhea, James T., head, 49, married 20 years, b. TN to TN parents,
Cashier, Nat. Bank.
(next page of census)
  Rhea, Caroline L., wife, 43, married 20 years, 3 children, 3 living,
b. Texas to parents from TN.
  -- Clarence W., son, 19, b. Texas.
  -- William E., son, 15, single, b. Texas.
  -- James T., son, 7, b. Texas.

1920 Federal census shows the family enumerated in Forney,
Kaufman Co., TX again. The family of Frank B. Rhea 35 is
enumerated three households away:
  Rhea, James T., head, owns free of mortgage, 59, b. TN, farmer.
  -- Caroline L., wife, 53, b. TX.
  -- Edwin, son, 24, b. TX, bookkeeper, Bank.
  -- James T., son, 17, b. TX.

His family is mentioned in 'Notable Southern Families' by Z.
Armstrong, 1922. He married **Caroline Lee 'Carrie' RIGGS**,
married 6 Nov 1889 in Terrell, TX, b. 23 Apr 1866 in Dallas, Dallas
Co., TX, d. 8 Mar 1956 in Dallas, Dallas Co., TX.
                Children:

+ 821.   i   **Clarence Ward RHEA** b. 27 Sep 1890.

  822.   ii   **William Edwin RHEA**, b. 25 Jul 1894 in Forney,
              Kaufman Co., TX, d. 13 Oct 1977 in Dallas, Dallas
              Co., TX, buried 15 Oct 1977 in Ferris Memorial Park

North, Dallas, TX. 1920 Federal census shows him enumerated with his parents at their home in Forney, TX. He is 24, single, a bookkeeper at a bank. The enumerated recorded his name as Edwin.

1977 Dallas Morning News - A veteran of WWI and a member of barracks #3051. Survivors Otsie and James Rhea. Lived at 4300 Deere St, Dallas, TX. Died at Baylor Hospital. He married **Ottsie MCCARSON**, b. ABT 1894, d. 4 Apr 1998.

+ 823.   iii   **James Theodoric RHEA, Jr.** b. 20 Jun 1902.

505. **Sarah 'Sally' Gilleland RHEA**, (184.Frances[5], 40.Sarah[4], 6.Jane[3], 2.Robert[2], 1.John[1]) b. 1 Mar 1862 in Sullivan Co., TN, d. in Forney, Kaufman Co., TX. Lived with Frank in Forney, TX.

1900 Federal census shows her family living in the household next to her brother James T. Rhea in Forney, Kaufman Co,. TX.
  Adams, Frank M., head, July 1868, 43, married 13 years, b. Texas to parents from TN and MS, no employment reported.
  -- Sallie G., wife, Mar 1862, 38, married 13 years, 3 children, 3 living, . TN to TN parents.
  -- Frank M. Jr., son, May 1888, 12, b. TX.
  -- Leta Rhea, daughter, Jan 1894, 6, b. TX.
  -- Yancey Dailey, son, Mar 1899, 14/12, b. TX.

1930 Federal census shows Sallie, now a widow, living with her son Yancey and his wife Louise in Forney, TX. The list of neighbors indicates they are still living in the same home as in 1900. She married **Frank Milton ADAMS**, married 1888 in TX?, b. 1 Jul 1858 in TX, d. BEF 1930 in Forney, Kaufman Co., TX.
        Children:

    824.   i   **Frank Milton ADAMS, Jr. Jr.**, b. 26 May 1888 in Forney, Kaufman Co., TX. His marriage is mentioned in Notable Southern Fam., Z. Armstrong 1922. He married **Jessie Lee FRENCH**, b. ABT 1888 in TX?.

    825.   ii   **Leta Rhea ADAMS**, b. 1894 in Forney, Kaufman Co., TX.

826.   iii   **Yancey Dailey ADAMS**, b. 1 Mar 1899 in Forney, Kaufman Co., TX. 1930 Federal census shows the young couple enumerated in Forney, Kaufman Co., TX, probably in the old Adams home.
Adams, Yancey D., head, owns home, value $2,000, had radio, age 31, married first at 29, b. TX, Shipping clerk, wholesale drugs.
-- Louise G., wife, 23, married first at 21, b. TX to parents from NC and TX, clerk, drug store.
-- Sallie G., Mother, 68, widow, b. TN, Operator, Telephone. He married **Louise G. wife of Yancey ADAMS**, b. 1907 in TX.

827.   iv   **Nathan ADAMS**, b. ABT 1902. Child listed in this family by James Pillow, 1998.

508.   **Charles Balfer EARHART II.**, (185.Margaret[5], 40.Sarah[4], 6.Jane[3], 2.Robert[2], 1.John[1]) b. 23 Nov 1864 in Bristol, Sullivan Co., TN, d. 1 Nov 1932 in Bristol, Sullivan Co., TN, buried in Blountville Cemetery, Sullivan Co., TN. Infant Charles hidden by his Mammie when Union came through valley. The Federals burned his future wife's family house and store in Blountville TN.

1910 Federal census the family is enumerated in the 4th Civil District, Sullivan Co., TN;
 Earhart, Charles B. head, 44, married 26 years, b. TN to TN parents, farmer, general farm.
 -- Etta E., wife, 43, married 26 years, 8 children, 5 living, b. TN to TN parents.
 -- Powell, son, 24, single, b. TN.
 -- Margaret, daughter, 16, single, b. TN
(next page of the census)
 -- Violet, 11, . TN.
 -- Ralph, P., 5, b. TN.
(This is about the time a photograph was taken of Ralph in a sailor suit and Violet with the class of the Sullivan Co., TN 'Red School House'.)

1930 Sullivan Co. TN census 4th Civil Dist. shows he and Etta at home with Powell Earhart living next door.

His family is mentioned in Notable Southern Families., Zella Armstrong, 1922. He married **Etta Emma POWELL**, married 6 Mar 1884 in Blountville, Sullivan Co., TN, b. 1 Aug 1866 in

Blountville, Sullivan Co., TN, d. 1935 in Blountville, Sullivan Co., TN, buried in Blountville Cemetery, Sullivan Co., TN. Her family had a dry good business operated on Main Street in Blountville. The War came down the valley and store burned. The cabin they lived in was across from Courthouse behind their store. The family hid silver in the yard; silver ladle from this stash was handed down to James O. Bouton and then to his daughter Janet.

Etta's mother thought her too young to marry Charles. Emma was 17 and Charles was but 19 years old. She finally gave consent to for them to wed in their home. To show she didn't fully approve, her mother the left room during the ceremony and they could hear her grinding coffee in the kitchen. The marriage would last 48 years.

1935 obituary - Mrs. Etta Earhart 68, Succumbs Here.
Funeral services for Mrs. Etta Powell Earhart 68, who died at the home of her son Pierce Earhart, Spruce St. at 4:20 am yesterday following a week's illness of pneumonia, will be conducted from the Blountville Presbyterian Church. Mrs. Earhart was the widow of Charles B. Earhart, prominent Sullivan Co. farmer.

Born in Blountville in 1867 she spent her entire life in Sullivan Co. She was a lifelong member of the Blountville Presbyterian Church. Mrs. Earhart's home is at Thomas' Bridge TN where she resided since the death of her husband on Nov. 1, 1932. She was widely known and beloved throughout Sullivan Co. and leaves a host of friends and relatives in this city. Her son Pierce is connected with the Moore-Earhart Company of Bristol, VA. Surviving are 5 children, Powell and Pierce, both of Bristol; Ralph of Thomas' Bridge; Mrs. Margaret E. Doane of Holston Institute, TN and Mrs. James O. Bouton of Washington, DC. Two sisters, Mrs. Ellen Shockley and Miss Gertrude Powell, two nieces and 8 grandchildren survive.

Numerous family photographs of Etta still exist. They show her in many settings, from working on the family farm, playfully sitting in washtub, riding a horse and other scenes which show her to be a hardworking woman full of life.
Children:

+ 828.   i   **John Powell EARHART** b. 1 Jul 1885.

+ 829.   ii   **Samuel Pearce EARHART** b. 5 Dec 1887.

+ 830.   iii   **Margaretta R. EARHART** b. 1 Apr 1893.

   831.   iv   **Charles B. EARHART**, b. 1 May 1896 in Blountville, Sullivan Co., TN, d. BEF 1920. Died of diphtheria. He died from the same disease as his younger brother Robert in 1912.

+ 832.   v   **Violet Etta EARHART** b. 29 Oct 1898.

   833.   vi   **Robert Rhea EARHART**, b. 1 May 1900 in Blountville, Sullivan Co., TN, d. 1912 in Sullivan Co., TN. Died at age of 12 years from diphtheria.

   834.   vii   **Nellie Roller EARHART**, b. 1901 in Sullivan Co., TN, d. 7 Nov 1904 in Blountville, Sullivan Co., TN, buried in Blountville Cemetery, Sullivan Co., TN. 1904 obituary - Nellie, the bright little three year old daughter of Mr. and Mrs. Charles B. Earhart died at the family home 3 miles east of here this morning. The little girl had been ill for more than a week. Her death was due to tonsillitis and stomach trouble.

   835.   viii   **Ralph Preston EARHART**, b. 1905 in Bristol, Sullivan Co., TN, d. ABT 1950. 1920 Federal census shows he is the only child living with parents at home.

Appears in the 1940 Bristol TN City Directory - salesman Moore-Earhart Co.

Died about the age of 40. Had no children. He married **Lillian HOUSTON**, b. ABT 1905 in Bluff City, Sullivan Co., TN, d. AFT 1982 in West Palm Beach, Palm Beach Co., FL. Appears in the 1940 Bristol TN City directory - Saleslady Long's – res. 1101 Virginia Av.

Married after the death of Ralph to Mr. Crusser.

Moved to Florida and there she passed away in a nursing home.

509.   **Sarah Ella EARHART**, (185.Margaret[5], 40.Sarah[4], 6.Jane[3], 2.Robert[2], 1.John[1]) b. 1866 in Sullivan Co., TN. 1910 Sarah,

William and family were enumerated near her brother Joseph's family. They lived on a 245 acre farm inherited from her father John T. Earhart near Bristol Raceway, where Rogers Gardens stands today. She married **William Edgar 'Ed' CARTER**, married 16 Sep 1896, b. 19 Jun 1856 in Sullivan Co., TN, d. 1932. 1920 Federal census shows the family enumerated near the Earhart homestead, as neighbors of Henry, Joseph and Powell Earhart, in Sullivan Co., TN:

Carter, Joe E., head, owns home with mortgage, 22, single, b. TN, farmer, general farm.
-- Edward, father, 63, b. TN.
-- Ella, mother, 53, b. TN
-- Hubert, brother, 20, single, b. TN
-- Carrie, sister, 17, single, b. TN.

1930 Federal census shows couple enumerated together with their youngest daughter, in the 4th Civil District of Sullivan Co. TN. The road is marked in the margin as 'Dirt Road'.

Carter, Edd (sic), head, rents, 74, married at 40, b. TN, farmer.
-- Sarah E., wife-h, 63, married at 30, b. TN.
-- Carrie H., daughter, 27, single, b. TN, no employment.
Children:

836.   i   **Alfred M. CARTER**, b. 12 Jan 1851 in TN. Died in infancy.

837.   ii   **Mary Brown CARTER**, b. 16 Apr 1860, d. 26 Apr 1900.

838.   iii   **Anna Evalina CARTER**, b. 8 Sep 1865. Died in infancy.

839.   iv   **Margaret CARTER**, b. 3 1870. Died in infancy.

840.   v   **William Hubert CARTER**, b. 27 Sep 1889 in Sullivan Co., TN, d. 31 Mar 1965. Served in WWI.

He came to Smythe Co. VA about 1920.

Worked as a meat cutter in Saltville for Matheston Alkaline and Steve Clear, and as a coal miner in Bartley and Gary WV. After leaving their farm on Smythe Chapel Rd. in Meadowview, he built a home on Lee Highway in Abingdon, VA where they lived until their deaths.

841.   vi   **Joseph Evans CARTER**, b. 1898 in Sullivan Co., TN.

842.   vii **Cara 'Carrie' H. Preston CARTER**, b. 1903 in Sullivan Co., TN.

510. **Joseph Preston EARHART**, (185.Margaret[5], 40.Sarah[4], 6.Jane[3], 2.Robert[2], 1.John[1]) b. 1 Dec 1869 in Bristol, Sullivan Co., TN, d. 14 Nov 1933 in Sullivan Co., TN, buried in Blountville Cemetery, Sullivan Co., TN. 1896 he inherited 260.5 acres from his parents, including the old homestead, the 'Elms' farm on Sperry road Blountville, Sullivan Co, TN.

1900 census Joseph is living at home with mother and brother John.

1901 mother Margaret still living with the family at age 75.

1920 Federal census shows the family enumerated in District 4, Sullivan Co., TN on the homestead, adjacent to families of Powel Earhart, Henry Earhart, and Joseph and Bessie Rhea.
  Earhart, Joseph P., head, 50, farmer, b. TN
  -- Sadie, wife 41, b. TN.
  -- Lillian, daughter, 16, single, b. TN.
  -- Phillip, son, 9, b. TN.

1933 Obituary - Joseph Preston Earhart, 64, one of the most beloved and highly respected citizens of Sullivan County, died at 8 o'clock Monday morning after a lingering illness. A son of John T. and Peggy Rhea Earhart, he was a descendant of a long line of distinguished ancestry, in a direct line from the Rev. Joseph Rhea, first Presbyterian minister in Tennessee. He was united in marriage on June 5, 1901 to Miss Sadie Boy who survives him. To this union were morn four children, two of whom survive: Mrs. James Patton of Bristol and Philip B. Earhart who resided with his parents at the lovely old family home "Beech Hill". Two sons died several years ago. Two sister and one brother, Mrs. Ella Carter and John Henry Earhart of Thomas' Bridge and Mrs. Margaret Fain of Norris, Montana, and two grandchildren Sarah Louise and Sidney Patton of Bristol also survive. He married **Sarah Ann 'Sadie' BOY**, married 10 Jun 1901 in Sullivan Co., TN, b. 1871 in Sullivan Co., TN, d. 9 Oct 1967 in Bristol, Sullivan Co., TN. She and Joseph appear in a Boy family photo on page 52 of 'Sullivan Co. Pictorial History, 1999.

1967 Obituary - Sarah Earhart 89, Bristol Dies - of Rt. 1 Bristol, TN and widow of Joseph Preston Earhart, died at 1pm Monday at her home after a long illness. Mrs. Earhart was a native and lifelong resident of Sullivan Co. She was the daughter of Philip and Mary Akard Boy, pioneer residents of the county. Survivors are a daughter Mrs. J. B. Patton; a daughter in law.

Children:

843.   i   **Mary Lillian EARHART**, b. 1904 in Sullivan Co., TN. Her marriage is mentioned in her mother's 1967 obituary. She married **J. B. PATTON**, b. ABT 1904.

844.   ii   **John Sidney EARHART**, b. 9 Mar 1906 in Sullivan Co., TN, d. 8 Aug 1909 in Sullivan Co., TN, buried in Blountville Cemetery, Sullivan Co., TN.

+ 845.   iii   **Philip Boy EARHART** b. 30 Nov 1910.

511. **Margaret Jane 'Maggie' EARHART**, (185.Margaret[5], 40.Sarah[4], 6.Jane[3], 2.Robert[2], 1.John[1]) b. 1872 in Sullivan Co., TN, d. 24 Apr 1944 in Broadwater Co., MT. 1920 Federal census shows the widow Fain in Hot Springs, Madison Co., MT.

Fain, Margaret J., head, owns free of mortgage, 48, widow, b. TN, farmer.

-- John W., son 20, single, b. VA, farm worker, at home.

-- Carrie R., daughter, 16, single, b. MT.

1930 Federal census shows the widow Fain in School District 8, Powder River Co., Montana, living in a household with her unmarried daughter:

Reed, Thomas C., head, owns home, 54, married at 44, b. ND. a farmer.

-- Amy, wife-h, 49, married at 39, b. Iowa to parents from Iowa (?)

Fain, Margaret L (?)., mother, 58, widow, married at 27, b. TN.

-- Ruth, daughter, 24, single, b. MT, to parents from TN.

(Margaret's designation as mother in this household is odd. She may simply be boarding with an unrelated couple.)

1944 Montana Office of Vital Statistics recorded her death at age 72, index #Br 681. She married **Thomas J. FAIN**, married 25 Apr 1899 in Sullivan Co., TN, b. 1872 in Sullivan Co., TN, d. 29 May 1909 in Norris, MO. Moved to Montana due to his weak lungs.

1909 the Montana Office of Vital Statistics recorded his death at age 37, index number 23-0095.

Children:

846.   i   **John William FAIN**, b. 1900 in VA, d. 21 Jul 1980 in Madison, MT.

847.   ii   **Carrie Ruth FAIN**, b. 1904 in MT.

848.   iii   **Thomas J. FAIN II.**, b. ABT 1902.

849.   iv   **Florence FAIN**, b. 1906 in MT, d. 14 Apr 1908.

850.   v   **Margaret Preston FAIN**, b. 1907 in MT, d. 2 Sep 1908.

513.   **Lewis Preston SUMMERS**, (190.Nannie[5], 43.John[4], 6.Jane[3], 2.Robert[2], 1.John[1]) b. 2 Nov 1868 in Abingdon, Washington Co., VA, d. 10 Dec 1943 in Abingdon, Washington Co. VA. 1890-1894 he was the Abingdon VA Post Master.

1895 he began his legal practice.

1920 Federal census shows the family enumerated in Abingdon, Washington Co., VA living at 409 East Valley Street:
Summers, Lewis, P., head, 52, b. VA, lawyer, general practice.
-- Katherine, wife 42, b. VA.
-- Gay W., daughter, 18, single, b. VA.
-- Douglas, daughter (?), 17, single, b. VA.
-- Lewis, son, 15, b. VA.
-- Katherine, daughter, 14, b. VA.
-- John, son, 13, b. VA.
-- Andrew, son, 7, b. VA.
-- Olivia, daughter, 5, b. VA.

1922 he was appointed US District Attorney by President Haring.

He was a member of the Virginia Bar Association and the Presbyterian Church. He was also the chairman of the Walnut Grove Cemetery Association in Washington Co., VA. His Preston ancestors donated the land for the cemetery and many are laid to rest there. Lewis was the author of 'Summers History of Southwest Virginia'.

1930 Federal census shows the family enumerated in Abingdon, Washington Co., VA living at on East Valley Street:
Summers, Lewis P., head, owns home, value $5000, 61, married at age 29, b. VA, Lawyer, General Practice.
-- Katherine B., wife H, 52, married at 19, b. VA.
-- Andrew R., son 17, b. VA.
-- Olivia W., daughter, 15, b. VA. He married **Katherine Annie BARBEE**, b. 1878 in VA.

> *Children:*

851.   i   **Gay White SUMMERS**, b. 1902 in Washington Co., VA.

852.   ii   **Jane Douglas SUMMERS**, b. 1903 in Washington Co., VA.

853.   iii   **Lewis Preston SUMMERS, Jr.**, b. 1905 in Washington Co., VA.

854.   iv   **Katherine Barbee SUMMERS**, b. 1906 in Washington Co., VA.

+ 855.   v   **John Grant SUMMERS** b. 1907.

856.   vi   **Andrew Rowan SUMMERS**, b. 1913 in Washington Co., VA. A Folk Music musician.

857.   vii   **Olivia Wirt SUMMERS**, b. 1915 in Washington Co., VA.

514. **John Fairman SUMMERS**, (190.Nannie[5], 43.John[4], 6.Jane[3], 2.Robert[2], 1.John[1]) b. ABT 1870 in Abingdon, Washington Co., VA. He married **Mary ELDER**, b. ABT 1870 in Sullivan Co., TN?.

> *Children:*

858.   i   **Von Moltke SUMMERS**, b. ABT 1900 in Sullivan Co., TN?.

859.   ii   **Mary Elder SUMMERS**, b. ABT 1902.

516. **Robert James SUMMERS**, (190.Nannie[5], 43.John[4], 6.Jane[3], 2.Robert[2], 1.John[1]) b. 1 Oct 1874 in Abingdon, Washington Co., VA. 1920 Federal census shows robert and his young family living in Abingdon, Washington Co., VA on East Valley Street:

Summers, Robert J., 46, b. VA to parents from WVA and VA, Lawyer, Commonwealth Attorney.

-- Della E., wife, 23, b. VA.

-- James G., son, 7, . VA.

-- Sunshine A., son, 5, b. VA.

-- Lewis P., son, 3, b. VA. He married **Della E. wife of Robert SUMMERS**, b. 1897 in VA.

Children:

860. i   **James G. SUMMERS**, b. 1913 in Abingdon, Washington Co., VA.

861. ii   **Sunshine A. SUMMERS**, b. 1915 in Abingdon, Washington Co., VA.

862. iii **Lewis P. SUMMERS**, b. 1917 in Abingdon, Washington Co., VA.

520. **Fannie Rhea SUMMERS**, (190.Nannie[5], 43.John[4], 6.Jane[3], 2.Robert[2], 1.John[1]) (See marriage to number 396.)

522. **John Carlisle SUMMERS**, (190.Nannie[5], 43.John[4], 6.Jane[3], 2.Robert[2], 1.John[1]) b. 1 Mar 1887 in Abingdon, Washington Co., VA. Named for his distinguished cousin. He married **Billie MCCLUNG**.

Children:

863. i   **Richard M. SUMMERS**, b. 1923 in Welch, WVA, d. 22 Nov 2002 in Abingdon, Washington Co., VA. 2002 obituary Bristol Herald Courier Sunday, November 24, 2002 - Richard M. Summers ABINGDON -- Richard M. Summers, 79, died Friday, Nov. 22, 2002, at Johnston Memorial Hospital in Abingdon. He was preceded in death by his mother and father, John Carlisle and Billie McClung Summers; his brother, John Summers; his second wife, Betty Orr Summers; and his grandson, Brandt Buffington.

He is survived by his daughter, Jean Buffington Gable and her husband, Tony Gable of Lawrenceville, Ga.; two granddaughters, Kacey Buffington of Lawrenceville and Keri Balsamo of

Basking Ridge , N.J.; and his sister, Eugenia
Summers Phillips of Abingdon.

Mr. Summers was born in Welch, W.Va. He grew up
spending the summers in Abingdon until his family
moved permanently to Abingdon in 1945. In 1942 he
graduated from Riverside Military Academy,
Gainesville, Ga., and in 1943 he entered the U.S.
Army where he was assigned to Company B, 171st
Combat Engineer Battalion, 84th Infantry Division.
He served in England and Europe and participated in
the Northern France, Rhineland and Central Europe
Campaigns. He was award the American Theater
Ribbon, European African Middle Eastern Theater
Ribbon and the World War II Victory Ribbon.

Following his discharge from the Army in 1946, he
attended National Business College, Roanoke. After
graduation, he moved to Abingdon in 1949. In
Abingdon he worked as an accountant for several
businesses and for a time was deputy clerk in the
Circuit Court Clerk's Office of Washington County.

Funeral services will be conducted at 11 a.m.
Monday, Nov. 25, at Sinking Spring Presbyterian
Church with the Rev. Robert Tolar Jr. officiating.
Burial will follow in Knollkreg Memorial Park with
military honors by the Highland Fellowship Honor
Guard. Pallbearers will be Tony Gable, John S.
Phillips, Dr. Thomas Phillips Jr., Stephen Smith,
Preston Smith and Hank Grant.

The family will receive friends from 6-8 p.m. on
Sunday evening at Campbell Funeral Home. Instead
of flowers, memorial contributions can be sent to
Sinking Spring Presbyterian Church Building Fund,
136 E. Main St., Abingdon, VA 24210.   Those
wishing to express sympathy online may do so at
www.campbell-funeralhome.com. Campbell Funeral
Home of Abingdon is in charge of arrangements.

864.   ii   **John SUMMERS**, b. ABT 1920.

865.   iii   **Eugenia SUMMERS**, b. ABT 1925. Eugenia
Summers Phillips was Regent, Black's Fort Chapter
DAR, Abingdon, VA.

524.   **Jane Rhea BAILEY**, (192.Sarah[5], 43.John[4], 6.Jane[3], 2.Robert[2],
1.John[1]) b. 15 Dec 1872 in Bristol, Washington Co., VA, d. 9 Sep
1948 in Old Derry Inn, Blountville TN, buried in East Hill Cem.,
Bristol, Wash. Co., VA. She was educated at the Andrew Jackson
Institute in Abington VA. She was a Presbyterian. She married
Joseph Cloyd BYARS, married 30 Sep 1896 in Bristol, Washington
Co., VA, b. 9 Dec 1868 in Southern View Plantation, Washington
Co. VA, d. 17 May 1954 in Old Derry Inn, Blountville TN, buried in
East Hill Cem., Bristol, Wash. Co., VA. Born on his fathers farm in
VA 'Southern View'. Educated at Pantops Academy and University
of VA.

1891 located to Bristol.

1896 he was admitted to the bar.

1900 he was elected City Attorney for Bristol and was elected to the
State Senate from the 1st Senatorial District in the year 1901.

1920 Federal census shows the family enumerated in Richmond,
Henrico Co., VA living at 6 Franklin Street East:
 Byars, Joseph C. head, rents, age 51, b. VA lawyer, general
practice.
  -- Jane B. wife, 57, b. VA.
  -- Joseph C. Jr., son, 21, single, b. VA
  -- Virginia D., daughter, 18, single, b. VA.
  -- Bailey, P. son, 14, single, b. VA.
 Tart, Walter, servant, black, 16, single, b. NC, butler, private
family.
                    Children:

866.   i   **Richard B. BYARS**, b. in VA?. Died in infancy.

867.   ii   **Joseph Cloyd BYARS Jr.**, b. 1898 in Bristol,
Washington Co., VA, d. 2 Jun 1933 in Brooklyn,
Borough of Kings, NY. He married **Dorsey COLE**,
b. ABT 1898.

+ 868.   iii   **Virginia Douglas BYARS** b. 21 May 1901.

869.   iv   **Bailey Preston BYARS**, b. 2 Mar 1906 in Bristol, Washington Co., VA. He married **Ruth Elizabeth ASHTON**, b. 10 Apr 1909, d. 11 Feb 1977.

525. **Julia Flourney BAILEY**, (192.Sarah[5], 43.John[4], 6.Jane[3], 2.Robert[2], 1.John[1]) b. 20 Feb 1874 in Sullivan Co., TN, d. 13 May 1960. 1920 Federal census shows the family enumerated in Emporia, Greenville Co., VA living on Church Street. Julia's parents are living with them.

Tillar, William T., Head, owns, 45, b. VA, retain merchant.
-- Julia B., wife, 45, b. TN.
-- Flourney B., son, 23, b. VA, clerk, hardware.
-- Mabel, daughter in law, 22, b. VA.
-- William T. Jr., son, 18, single, b. VA.
-- Julia, daughter, 13, b. VA
-- Don P., son, 10, b. VA

1930 Federal census shows the family enumerated in Emporia, Greenville Co., VA living on Church Street:

Tillar, William T., head, owns home, value $10,000, has radio, 55, married at 9, b. Virginia to parents from Virginia and North Carolina, merchant, hardware.
-- Julia B., wife-h, 56, married at 20, b. Tennessee, to parents from Virginia.
-- Donilson P. ab, (?), son, 20, single, b. VA
-- Beirruss (or Barruss), Sallie, T, sister, 57, widow, first married at 25, b. VA.

Watts, Ray E, roomer, 28, single, b. MS, clergyman, Presbyterian Church. She married **William Thomas TILLAR**, married 25 Apr 1894, b. 20 Jun 1874 in VA?, d. 9 Jul 1934.

Children:

870.   i   **Sarah Eleanor TILLAR**, b. 21 Feb 1895 in VA. She married **William LAND**, married 4 Apr 1917, b. ABT 1895 in VA?TN?.

+ 871.   ii   **Flournoy Benjamin TILLAR** b. 7 Oct 1896.

872.   iii   **William Preston TILLAR**, b. 1 Jun 1898 in VA, d. 1 Jul 1898.

873.   iv   **William Thomas TILLAR, Jr.**, b. 2 May 1901 in VA. 1930 Federal census shows the family

enumerated in Emporia, Greenville, VA living on
Church Street:
  Tillar William T Jr, head, owns home, value
$10,000, has radio, age 28, married at 27, b. VA,
merchant, hardware.
  -- Margaret M., wife-h, age 29, married at 27, b.
Maryland to parents from Virginia and Maryland.
  -- Schoenewolf (Jean written above), daughter, 7, b.
Maryland to parents b. in Maryland.
[Although she is shown as having the surname Tillar
by the enumerator's notation, Jean must be Margaret's
daughter from a previous marriage, since this couple
had been married only about a year.] He married
Margaret Haines MARSTON, married 29 Aug
1928, b. ABT 1901.

+ 874.   v   **Julia Bailey TILLAR** b. 15 Feb 1906.

   875.   vi   **Donaldson Preston TILLAR**, b. 28 Dec 1909 in
            VA. He married **Elizabeth BELLINGSLY**, married
            28 Dec 1934, b. ABT 1909.

526. **Martha Preston BAILEY**, (192.Sarah[5], 43.John[4], 6.Jane[3],
2.Robert[2], 1.John[1]) b. 25 Jun 1876 in Sullivan Co., TN?, d. 4 May
1930. She married **John W. PRICE**, married 2 Jun 1897, b. 11 Apr
1869, d. 30 May 1947. 1920 Federal census shows the couple
enumerated in Washington D.C.
  Price John W., head, renting, age 50 b. VA, lawyer, general
practice.
  -- Martha B. wife, 43, b. VA.
            Children:

   876.   i   **John W. PRICE Jr.**, b. 23 Apr 1900. He married
            Marcelle Pauline Jeanne LANDOLT, married 23
            Apr 1929 in Lousanne, Switzerland, b. ABT 1900.

529. **Seaton Tinsley PRESTON**, (193.James[5], 43.John[4], 6.Jane[3],
2.Robert[2], 1.John[1]) b. 29 Mar 1892 in Bristol, Sullivan Co., TN, d.
20 Mar 1977 in Volusia Co., FL. 1910 Federal census shows Seaton
and his father enumerated in the household of his uncle and aunt,
Thomas and Jeannie Newman. Seaton is 18, b. TN. Three teachers
are also boarding in this household at 412 Spencer Street, Abingdon
VA.

1917 June 5 Seaton registered for the draft. He was living at 224 South Washington, Alexandria, VA. Birth March 29, 1892, in Bristol, TN. He was then employed as an Asst. Engineer, at Alexandria Stat. VA. He was single, medium height, slender, with blue eyes, 'R. Brown' hair.

The family lived in Kentucky about 1921 where their two oldest boys were born. The youngest was born after they had moved to West Virginia.

1930 Federal census shows the family in Charleston, Kanawha Co., WV living at 1312, Virginia Street (Benjamin Preston age 51 lives at 1300 on the same street).
  Preston, Seaton PT., head, rents $100/month, has a radio, age 38, first married at 25, . VA, engineer, electrical.
  -- Kathryn B., wife-h, 31, first married at 21 (?), b. PA to parents from PA.
  -- Seaton T., son, 8, b. KY.
  -- James B., son, 7, b. KY.
  -- Fredrick L, son 2/12 (April census), b. West Virginia.

Lived in Florida. Had 3 sons.

Social security death index indicated his dates of birth and death, and indicated his last residence was Orange City, Volusia Co., FL. He married **Sara Kathryn BARBER**, married 20 Jul 1920, b. 20 May 1898 in PA, d. 28 Nov 1976 in Volusia Co., VA.
        Children:

+ 877.   i   **Seaton Tinsley PRESTON, Jr. Jr.** b. 29 Aug 1921.

+ 878.   ii   **James Brainard PRESTON** b. 30 Mar 1923.

+ 879.   iii **Frederick 'Fred' Leigh PRESTON** b. 27 Jan 1930.

530. **John Fairman PRESTON**, (194.Samuel[5], 43.John[4], 6.Jane[3], 2.Robert[2], 1.John[1]) b. 1 Apr 1875 in Fernandina Beach, Nassau Co., FL, d. 6 Jun 1975 in Decatur, GA. (Fairman Cumming November 23, 2005 phone conversation Foley from Decatur GA with Ed Foley) He was born in Florida because that was his father's first pastorate. But it was loaded with mosquitoes we guess his wife could not take it during the summers. Samuel Rhea Preston stayed in Fernandina only one year and was fortunate enough to get a pastorate at Athens TN. My grandfather was only 2 years old and stayed there about 4

years. Samuel Rhea got back to Athens when his mother (Jane Rhea Preston) was still living in Abingdon and got to visit with her as a married man with a young child and she would have been able to see her first grandchild. Samuel Rhea Preston was the youngest son of John Fairman Preston I. Samuel Rhea Preston was a very sentimental fellow. They had been ruined up there on the farm. It was hard to run a farm at that time. Whether any of the African Americans stayed on after the war we do not know. From his diary, it appears there were 7 or 8 slaves. Until I saw the diary I had not thought about that.

My grandfather John Fairman Preston went to Princeton. One of his teachers was Woodrow Wilson, who was also born in Virginia of Northern Parents. My father as born in Virginia in the same town as Woodrow Wilson. Wilson started school in the south and decided to go north to school to Princeton and later became a professor at Princeton. My grandfather was born right after the civil war. He stated school in the south. Graduated from Furman (the school founded in 1826 in Greenville SC). His father had founded a college, Chicora College (the college opened in 1893 in Greenville SC as a special ministry of the First Presbyterian Church of that City. The campus was located on the Reedy River in downtown Greenville within view of Furman University. In 1915 the Presbyterian Synod voted to move Chicora to Columbia SC. In 1930 it closed its doors, a victim of the depression. Several members of the faculty jointed the faculty of Queens College in Charlotte and until the 1940's that institution was known as Queens-Chicora College.) which later joined with Queens College. While John was a student at Furman, he was his father's secretary at Chicora College. His father wanted him to stay on there and run the college. He was extraordinarily talented and had already learned shorthand. He did the business correspondence for the college. But after 2 or 3 years he finished at Furman and left to go north to Princeton Theological Seminary and also Princeton University. Studied at both place and got a masters degree at Princeton University. One of his professors was Woodrow Wilson; one was Bliss Perry, who about that time became the editor of the Atlantic monthly. Another teacher was a prolific author Henry Van Dyke who was the author of the hymn Joy to the World.

There is a picture of my grandfather at the YMCA. Somewhere along the way he learned shorthand and actually clerked in the court. John Fairman Preston wrote hundreds and hundreds of pages of shorthand in his life. He put himself through Princeton by taking down notes of the lectures and typing them up and selling them to his classmates. I have one of the shorthand books for the courses and his typing. He tried to teach me the shorthand. Here is another connection with Woodrow Wilson. Here is another man from the South and most of the students were not from the south, from the same part of the country where Wilson was born, a young man who arrives for seminary who is a little bit older than the other students, taking down the lectures in shorthand, in fact the same type of shorthand that Wilson himself used. Wilson was dyslexic and had a great deal of difficulty to read. He began reading shorthand when he was 10 or 12 years old that helped him to read. He then became proud of his shorthand.

Bernard Baruch hired a young man who was a wiz at shorthand, a new kind of shorthand. He came over at a time when Wilson was president, with a message to the house for Wilson from Baruch. He left the message and a word came back to the door for him to come in the President wants to meet you. Wilson said the Baruch had told him that he was very good at shorthand and would like to seem an example of his work. I enjoy shorthand. Billy Rose was in his early 20's. Wilson says I will read to you and you read it back to me from your shorthand notes. He does it and he challenges Wilson. Wilson takes up the challenge and says don't go so fast, I am not as good as you and I use an old fashioned type of shorthand.

Therefore Wilson might have noticed 20 years before taking down notes in shorthand, whose mother know Wilson as a boy. Just speculation.

John received a Master of Philosophy degree from Princeton.

My grandmother (Annie Wiley) came back at age 22 from a trip overseas with her mother to France, Scotland and England. The day after she got back she met my grandfather who was traveling around trying to raise money for world missions for the newly formed Southern Presbyterian Church. So the summer after they were married in September

He went out (to Korea as a Presbyterian missionary) when he was 28. He was a mature and accomplished young man when he went out there. He took this young woman who was 4 years younger, and took her mother too, when she couldn't go back with them, she mailed them a book just a few weeks after my mother and her mother left, 'The Folklore of Korea. She must have really missed them. They were back there the winder of 1908, February. and they came back the next year and she was still living, although in poor health. They were all living in this house, which must have been quite crowded, which g-ma was born in and my mother was born in, and while they were there, one of the Wiley cousins was born there. When my grandmother died, they all left. The house was turned back to the Wiley side. That Wiley couple was already building a house next door, which our Wiley cousin still lives in.

He writes and extraordinary letter on his way out. He writes these travel letters about Japan and Hawaii. As soon as he gets to Korea, where he is going to spend 1/3 of his life, he goes to church that very afternoon and it is just as though he knows he belongs there. He does not feel he is in a strange place at all. They were not the first missionaries, there had already been missionaries for 10 years, but he was considered one of the pioneers. He took up at a place where there were no missionaries before and they welcomed him. They arrived in early Nov. in 1903. Their letters are written within a day or two to his parents and her parents. Daniel had married the youngest daughter of a widow, Mrs. Wiley, who already had lost two sons. One son had been living in London, but returned and settled across the block. She turned her house over to one of her sons in Salisbury and one was living across the block. Mrs. Wiley made arrangements to come to live in Korea. She arrived in Korea and lived with the Prestons for 3 years. That first baby died and was buried in Korea. Four more children were born in Korea and 2 were born back in Salisbury in the same house that Annie Wiley Preston was born in.

Mrs. Wiley, Miriam Murdock Wiley, came out and lived with them in Korea. Annie Wiley and John Fairman Preston had 7 children and the first one lived only 6 weeks. They had lost their first child and that time must have been very difficult for them. She (Mrs. Wiley) lived in Korea for 3 years until her health failed. They had to bring her home on an emergency trip. My grandfather (John Fairman Preston) had become well settled in Korea by then. My grandmother stayed 8 or 10 months in North Carolina and my mother was born on that trip back to this country.

The youngest daughter was the pride of her mother, and the comfort of her mother in her old age. Miriam went to live with them from 1904 to 1907 and then had to come back because of her heath. But her daughter managed to come back to see her for the last year of her life and become a Salisbury citizen for one last year of her life.

They went back out again with a doctor who became a very close friend. Mr. Wilson wanted to go to Mexico to work as a missionary, but was willing to go to Korea. He lasted until retirement. He founded leper colonies and brought modern medicine to Korea. He accompanied my grandmother; my mother and my mother's older sister back to Korea. My mother was just 8 or 10 weeks old January 1908 when they went back to Korea. (Dr. R. M. Wilson's center began in 1909 when Dr. Forsythe, a Presbyterian missionary saw a woman lying in a ditch, picked her up, and took her to his own home to Kwangju. She was the first of many patients with Hansen's disease to be treated by the Kwangju Hospital. By 1925 Dr. Wilson had so many patients living near the hospital that the government, then Japanese, demanded he move them to an isolated peninsula of SoonChun, which it provided. www.Pcusa.org)

My Grandfather John Fairman Preston, wrote and introduction for admittance to Princeton, for the fellow who would become the first president of the Republic of Korea (1948-1961), Syngman Rhee. He came as a young man to the US and stayed many years. He stayed in the country through the Second World War. He was forced out after he became dictatorial. It has only become a true democracy in the last few years.

Missionary people knew that they were very isolated. My father was a bachelor out there for 14 years. Extremely isolated, dependant on their parents to keep them up on things. In one of my mother's letters from 1918, she had gone out 15 years before; she says I don't get any news. She was cut off because her own Salisbury relatives no longer kept her up on the news. A man who became a professional genealogist, the husband of her niece, really began to communicate with her when she retire back to this country and moved to Decatur GA. They bought a house in Decatur in 1942, but moved to the house in 1946. My grandfather lived in Decatur, but they were gone each summer 6 weeks a year. Lived in Decatur for 31 years and my grandmother more than that.

My grandfather (John) and grandmother (Annie) were missionaries for 37 years and 33 of those years in Korea. My grandfather lived to be 100 years old and lived 33 years, or 1/3 of his life in Korea.

He lived to be 100; 1946 to 1975 in Decatur, they had already lived in Decatur on furloughs twice therefore adds two more years which makes 31 years of his life in Decatur, and about 18 years in Virginia.

He spent 3 years in Princeton and 2 years in SC and 4 years in Mississippi and other than that Korea or Virginia or Georgia. My grandmother outlived him by 8 years so you can add that and she also went to Agnes Scott Institute for 2 years so you can add 10 years to 31 to get that she lived in GA for 41 years. She died in 1983 and she was nearly 105. Her eldest daughter (Miriam Wiley Cumming St. Clair) died this year at the age of 99. She was born in Seoul in 1905. My grandmother did not even use a hearing aide, but her mother was extremely deaf and so those years in Korea were quite difficult in that respect. Mrs. Wiley was a very faithful Christian and a very lonely woman. She had turned her house over to her middle son, but got along better with her youngest daughter. She did not coddle her daughter, but they enjoyed each others company and she went out to help her daughter and for her own comfort and managed to stay there from 1904 to 1907. She was then an elderly woman. She was born in 1838 so when she went to Korea in 1904 she was getting on 70 years old.

My grandmother (Annie Wiley Preston) had 21 grandchildren. He married **Annie Shannon WILEY**, married 2 Sep 1903 in Salisbury, Rowan Co., NC, b. 1879 in Salisbury, NC, d. 1983 in Decatur, GA. She attended Agnes Scott College in Decatur, GA.

1918 she wrote to two Salisbury friends that she doesn't get any news. Her own relatives had not kept up with her news but a number of family letters does show cousins and friends did write with news occasionally during the family's years isolated in Korea..
Children:

880. i **Samuel Rhea PRESTON**, b. 1904 in Korea, d. 1904 in Seoul, Korea. The family's first child, he died at just 6 weeks. He is buried in the Foreign cememtery in Seoul Korea.

+ 881. ii **Miriam Wiley PRESTON** b. 26 Sep 1905.

+ 882. iii **Annie Shannon PRESTON** b. 21 Oct 1907.

+ 883. iv **John Fairman PRESTON, Jr.** b. 21 Aug 1909.

+ 884. v **Florence Sutphen PRESTON** b. 16 Sep 1911.

885. vi **William Wiley PRESTON**, b. 26 Apr 1915 in Seochang, Korea, d. 2 Mar 2000 in Oxford, MS.

(Fairman Cumming November 23, 2005 phone conversation Foley from Decatur GA with Ed Foley) William Wiley Preston the next one up, was born in 1915 in Soonchun Korea. He worked for the Red Cross for a long time. He was a WWII veteran in Patton's army. He was in the spear that went the farthest in the shortest time. His letter said we have crossed three rivers in three weeks. He was in Czechoslovakia when he wrote that - he couldn't say that at the time, but they had crossed France, all of Germany and was in Czechoslovakia at the end of March 1945. He died in 2000 at age 84. He moved a lot, they had to, but spent the last 25 years of his life in Miss, they had inherited her family's house. Aunt Sarah is still living in this house. She keeps up with her sister and her few relatives. She was willing to be adopted into the Prestons and was involved in everything the Prestons did.

William had received his BS in Biology at Davidson College, Davidson, NC. He was a teacher. He married **Sarah Tankersley TOLSON**, b. 25 Dec 1918 in College Hill, Oxford, MS. She received her BC at the Mississippi University for Women. She was and teacher and librarian.

2005 she was living in Oxford, MS.

+ 886.   vii   **Rhea Sutphen 'Dr.' PRESTON** b. 15 Mar 1921.

531.   **Samuel Rhea PRESTON, Jr.**, (194.Samuel[5], 43.John[4], 6.Jane[3], 2.Robert[2], 1.John[1]) b. 22 Mar 1877 in SC, d. 1938, buried in Marietta National Cemetery, Marietta, GA. 1898 Presbyterian Ministerial Directory notes: Samuel Rhea Preston, SC, Born Abingdon VA, ordained Nov. 6, 1874 in Greenville, SC.

1910 Federal census shows the family enumerated in Columbia, Richland Co., SC at 1423 Pendleton St., in the home of his father in law:
   Cooper, William, head, 52, married 30 years, b. SC to SC parents, Planter, general farm.
   -- Esther A., wife, 49, married 30 years, 11 children, 9 living, b. SC to SC parents.
   -- Paul A., son, 20, single, b. SC to SC parents, collector, at bank.

-- Grace, daughter, 15, single, b. SC to SC parents.

-- Josephine, daughter, 11, b. SC to SC parents.

Alderman, George A, son in law, 32, married 5 years, b. SC to SC parents, commercial --, shoes.

-- Esther, E., daughter, 27, married 5 years, 0 children.

Preston, Samuel R., son in law, 33, married 1 year, b. VA to VA parents, commercial --, typewriters.

-- Mecca E., daughter, 23, married 1 year, 1 child, 1 living, b. SC to SC parents.

-- Elizabeth, granddaughter, b. 7/12. (April 28, 1910 census).

1930 Federal census shows the family enumerated in Columbia, Richland Co., SC at 1527 Senate(?) St.

Preston S., Rhea, head, rents $100/month, has radio, 53, married first at 32, b. VA, Agents, Real Estate.

-- Mecca, wife h, 42, married at 21, b. SC, enumerator, census.

-- E. Rhea, daughter, 17, b. SC.

-- Mary, daughter, 17, b. SC.

-- Samuel, son 15, b. Alabama.

-- Jane, daughter, 12, . SC.

Hughes, William, boarder, 41, married at 27, b. SC, agent, express co. He married **Mecca COOPER**, b. ABT 1877 in SC.

Children:

887.　i　**Elizabeth Rhea PRESTON**, b. 1 Aug 1909 in Columbia, Richland Co., SC. She married **John HENRY**, b. ABT 1900.

888.　ii　**Annie Shannon PRESTON**, b. ABT 1902.

889.　iii　**Mary PRESTON**, b. ABT 1904.

890.　iv　**Samuel Rhea PRESTON III**, b. 4 Feb 1914 in Columbia, Richland Co., SC, d. 1987 in Winterhaven, FL.

891.　v　**Jane PRESTON**, b. ABT 1906.

534.　**James Brainard PRESTON**, (194.Samuel⁵, 43.John⁴, 6.Jane³, 2.Robert², 1.John¹) b. 27 May 1882 in VA, d. 1926, buried in Birmingham, AL. He married **Margaret STEWART**, b. ABT 1882.

Children:

892.   i   **James PRESTON**, b. ABT 1910.

893.   ii   **Margaret PRESTON**, b. ABT 1912, d. 2001 in Birmingham, AL. She married **Walter FLETCHER**, b. ABT 1912.

536. **Ida Sutphen PRESTON**, (194.Samuel^5, 43.John^4, 6.Jane^3, 2.Robert^2, 1.John^1) b. 16 Sep 1889 in VA, d. 9 Jan 1971 in Decatur, GA. 1930 Federal census shows the family enumerated in Greenville SC living at 16 Daniel (?) Street on April 5.
Warden, Arthur H. head, rents, $40/month, has radio, 41, married at 27, b. VA to VA parents, engineer, electrical.
-- Ida S. P., wife, 40, married at 26, b. VA to parents from VA and SC.
-- Elizabeth R., daughter, 13, single, b. VA to parents from VA.
Preston, Ida S., mother in law, 76, widowed, married at 20, b. SC to parents from PA and NJ. She married **Arthur Hills WARDEN**, b. 21 Jul 1888 in VA. Florida death index shows an Arthur H. Warden died in May 1956 in Duval Co., FL.
Children:

894.   i   **Elizabeth WARDEN**, b. 1 Aug 1916. She married **Mott MARSHALL**, b. ABT 1916.

538. **Carol Montgomery NEWMAN**, (195.Jennie^5, 43.John^4, 6.Jane^3, 2.Robert^2, 1.John^1) b. 1879 in Wytheville, VA, d. 1941. She attended King College in Bristol then entered the University of Virginia where he earned his MA degree. While teaching at U. of VA he also received a PhD in English, Latin and German.

He then went to Virginia Polytechnic Institute, Blacksburg, VA where he was an English Professor and later a department head until his death in 1941.

1956 May, a $1.8 Million library was dedicated to Carol Newman. He married **Carolyn 'Carrie' Amelia FAIN**, married 1902 in Bristol, VA, b. ABT 1879.
Children:

+ 895.   i   **Thomas Fain NEWMAN** b. 1902.

896.   ii   **Virginia NEWMAN**, b. 1907. She married **Walter 'Professor' WAKEFIELD**, b. ABT 1907. He was a professor at State Teachers College in Potsdam, NY.

+ 897.   iii   **Carol Montomery NEWMAN, Jr.** b. 1910.

+ 898.   iv   **James Preston NEWMAN** b. 1913.

541. **William Alexander STUART**, (207.Katherine[5], 45.James[4], 8.John[3], 3.Walter[2], 1.John[1]) b. 24 Oct 1889 in Washington Co., VA, d. 10 Aug 1976. He married **Ellen BRODY**, b. ABT 1889 in Louisville, Jefferson Co. KY. Her name has also been written as Bodley by researcher Fred Preston. He notes she was from Louisville KY.
Children:

    899.   i   **William Alexander STUART Jr.**, b. ABT 1920 in VA?. Lived in 'Rosedale'.

    900.   ii   **George Roger Clark STUART**, b. ABT 1922 in VA?. Lived in Abington, VA.

542. **Katherine Greenway STUART**, (207.Katherine[5], 45.James[4], 8.John[3], 3.Walter[2], 1.John[1]) b. 1890 in Washington Co., VA. She married **James Dabney COLLIER**, b. ABT 1891 in Memphis, Shelby Co., TN.
Children:

    901.   i   **James Dabney COLLIER Jr. Jr.**, b. ABT 1920.

    902.   ii   **John Stuart COLLIER**, b. ABT 1922.

543. **Henry Carter STUART**, (207.Katherine[5], 45.James[4], 8.John[3], 3.Walter[2], 1.John[1]) b. 1892 in Washington Co., VA. He married **wife of Henry Stuart**, b. ABT 1893.
Children:

    903.   i   **Henry Carter STUART Jr.**, b. ABT 1925 in VA?.

550. **Anne Montgomery GRAY**, (212.Elizabeth[5], 47.John[4], 8.John[3], 3.Walter[2], 1.John[1]) b. 22 Mar 1898. She married **Edwin Eugene JUDKINS**, married 26 Oct 1927, b. ABT 1898.
Children:

+ 904.   i   **Elizabeth Gray JUDKINS** b. 10 Oct 1928.

+ 905.   ii   **Anne Peyton JUDKINS** b. 8 May 1931.

551. **Robert Asher GRAY V.**, (212.Elizabeth[5], 47.John[4], 8.John[3], 3.Walter[2], 1.John[1]) b. 1 Sep 1900, d. 16 Jul 1948. He married **Irene L. HARRISON**, married 1922, b. ABT 1900.
Children:

+ 906.　i　**Robert GRAY VI. VI.** b. 29 Sep 1922.

+ 907.　ii　**Elizabeth Harrison GRAY** b. 3 Jul 1931.

+ 908.　iii　**Laura Melinda GRAY** b. 17 Apr 1939.

+ 909.　iv　**Mary Preston GRAY** b. 17 Apr 1939.

554. **John Montgomery PRESTON**, (213.Cochran[5], 47.John[4], 8.John[3], 3.Walter[2], 1.John[1]) b. 4 Jul 1906 in VA. He married **Lula White. ELLIS**, b. ABT 1906.
Children:

+ 910.　i　**John Montgomery PRESTON V.** b. 1938.

+ 911.　ii　**Charles Dean PRESTON** b. 1938.

+ 912.　iii　**Leslie Daffin PRESTON** b. 24 Nov 1939.

562. **Frank Blair PRESTON**, (241.Thomas[5], 61.Amelia[4], 11.Robert[3], 3.Walter[2], 1.John[1]) b. 1903 in Washington Co., VA. He married **Helene IVERSON**, b. ABT 1902 in IL.
Children:

913.　i　**Sinclair PRESTON**, b. ABT 1930 in VA?. He married **Barbara SIMPSON**, b. ABT 1930.

914.　ii　**Sandra PRESTON**, b. ABT 1932 in VA?.

915.　iii　**Frank Blair PRESTON Jr.**, b. ABT 1934 in VA?.

563. **Sarah Pierce PRESTON**, (241.Thomas[5], 61.Amelia[4], 11.Robert[3], 3.Walter[2], 1.John[1]) b. ABT 1906 in Washington Co., VA. Married and lived in North Carolina. She married **Henry FAIRLEY**, b. ABT 1904. Lived in Salisbury, NC.
Children:

916.　i　**Blair Preston FAIRLEY**, b. ABT 1935.

917. ii   **Henry Nathan FAIRLEY**, b. ABT 1937 in VA?.

568. **Mary CUMMINGS**, (254.Robert[5], 73.Anne[4], 13.Fairman[3], 3.Walter[2], 1.John[1]) b. 9 Jun 1894. She married **Edward Terrell BRODNOX**, b. 17 Jul 1891, d. 12 Apr 1961.
Children:

+ 918. i   **Elizabeth Covette BRODNOX** b. 8 Jul 1917.

919. ii   **Edward Terrell BRODNOX Jr.**, b. 31 Mar 1919, d. 1943.

920. iii **Mary Cummings BRODNOX**, b. 20 May 1920. She married **William Thmoas BARHAM**, married 1 Jul 1940, b. 17 Nov 1906.

921. iv   **Millicent Carter BRODNOX**, b. 12 Jul 1927. She married **Virgil LeRoy MCKOIN**, married 29 Apr 1958, b. 1921.

604. **Walter Preston RHEA**, (304.Oscar[5], 95.Walter[4], 20.Joseph[3], 4.Jannette[2], 1.John[1]) b. 13 Mar 1915 in Salem, Fulton Co., AR. When his father died (he was 10) he went to live with an aunt on his mother's side. His brother Orion left Salem for CA. Walter spent winters with his stepmother who ran a boarding house for school teachers during the school term. At age 15, his brother took him to CA where he lived with an aunt and uncle (mother's side). Never went back to Arkansas.

At age 80, he was a member of the SAR. He married (1) **Audrey Marie OVERTON**, married 20 May 1938 in Venice, Los Angeles CA, b. 16 Feb 1919 in New York City, NY, d. 31 Jul 1947 in North Hollywood, Los Angeles CA. He married (2) **Catherine Marcella 'Marsha' GRAAL**, married 8 Dec 1951 in Las Vegas NV, b. 7 Jan 1925 in Stoke ENGLAND, d. 24 Jul 1994 in Orange, Orange Co. CA.
Children by Audrey Marie OVERTON:

922. i   **Richard Rand RHEA**, b. 28 Mar 1942 in Santa Monica CA, d. 1962. Had no children.

923. ii **Lorelyn Lee RHEA**, b. 24 Jul 1944 in Santa Monica CA. Unmarried in 1996.
Children by Catherine Marcella 'Marsha' GRAAL:

924.   iii   **Deborah Catherine RHEA**, b. 29 Mar 1954 in Los Angeles, CA. Unmarried in 1996.

605.   **Sara Lee RHEA**, (304.Oscar^5, 95.Walter^4, 20.Joseph^3, 4.Jannette^2, 1.John^1) b. 24 Jul 1923 in Salem Fulton Co., AR. Born in Salem but later moved with her mother to Batesville, Ark when she was 8 years old and grew up there.

After the war, she and Edwin moved to Little Rock, Ark. She married **Edwin KROUSE**, married 5 May 1943, b. ABT 1923. Married Sara while he was in the Air Force.
Children:

925.   i   **Edwin Eric KROUSE**, b. 5 Nov 1946.

926.   ii   **Kristen Rhea KROUSE**, b. 16 Dec 1950 in Little Rock, Pulaski Co., AR.

927.   iii   **Kerrin Lou KROUSE**, b. 27 Sep 1954 in Little Rock, Pulaski Co., AR.

610.   **Hugh Gans RHEA**, (306.Holmes^5, 95.Walter^4, 20.Joseph^3, 4.Jannette^2, 1.John^1) b. ABT 1907 in TN?. He married **Wife of Hugh RHEA**, b. ABT 1907.
Children:

928.   i   **Hugh Gary RHEA**, b. ABT 1930.

619.   **Gladys RHEA**, (321.Joseph^5, 98.John^4, 21.Robert^3, 4.Jannette^2, 1.John^1) b. ABT 1902. She married **Hampton J. HYDER**, b. ABT 1900.
Children:

929.   i   **Jane Rhea HYDER**, b. ABT 1930. She married **Neville T. CLAYTON**, b. ABT 1930.

930.   ii   **Marjorie Nelle HYDER**, b. ABT 1932. Served as the commissioner of Department of Mental Health and Mental Retardation for State of TN. Resigned after 19 months in Sept. 1996. She married **R. E. CARDWELL**, b. ABT 1932.

623. **Eva Preston RHEA**, (322.John[5], 98.John[4], 21.Robert[3], 4.Jannette[2], 1.John[1]) b. 25 Feb 1910 in Sullivan Co., TN, d. 15 Jul 2000 in Bristol, Sullivan Co., TN, buried in Glenwood Cem. Bristol TN. Taught school in Sullivan Co, TN and Bristol City school systems for 30 years.

2000 obituary -
Eva Preston Rhea Buckles, 90, of Bristol Tennessee died Saturday, July 15, 2000, in Wellmont Hospice House.

A lifelong resident of Sullivan County, she was a daughter of the late Ada Carmack Rhea and Dr. John Preston Rhea. She was the widow of Claude Buckles. She was a member of First Presbyterian Church. She was a graduate of Fairmount School, Bristol Tennessee High School, Virginia Intermont College and East Tennessee State University. She taught for six years in the Sullivan County School System before serving for 27 years as the librarian at Fairmount School.

Mrs. Buckles was a member of Sullivan County Historical Society, Business and Professional Women's Club, Volunteer Chapter of DAR, Matthew Fontain Maury Chapter of UDC and Sullivan County and Bristol Tennessee Retired Teachers associations.

Surviving are a daughter, Jane B. Hersch of Maxon, N.C.; and a grandson, William Preston Hersch of Wilmington, N.C. Funeral services will be conducted Monday at 2 p.m. at the grave side in Glenwood Cemetery. Dr. Gordon A. Turnbull will officiate. The family will receive friends from 12:30 to 1:30 p.m. Monday in Oakley-Cook Funeral Home. In lieu of flowers, memorial contributions may be sent to Wellmont Hospice House, 280 Steele's Road, Bristol, TN. She married **Claude J. BUCKLES**, married 30 May 1938, b. 10 Jul 1904 in Sullivan Co., TN, d. 17 Jul 1968 in Sullivan Co., TN.
   Children:

+ 931.   i   **Jane Preston BUCKLES** b. 11 Feb 1944.

625. **Lysle Edward RHEA**, (324.Josiah[5], 98.John[4], 21.Robert[3], 4.Jannette[2], 1.John[1]) b. 1 May 1906 in Bristol, Sullivan Co., TN, d. 21 Jun 1971 in Panama City, Bay Co., FL, buried in Greenwood Cem., Panama City, FL. From and E-mail message:
Subj: Ancestry
Date:99-01-23 16:34:51 EST

From:sallinger@@panacom.com (Richard Sallinger)
To:EFoley1@@aol.com (Ed Foley)
Dear Ed,

How wonderful!! I am totally ecstatic, having received all of this
information [from you] on the Rhea family.

We bought our personal computer late 1997 and my husband wanted
to start researching his family and bought some family tree CD's.
That sparked my interest to research the Rhea family. Then I ran
across this website and thought there might be a possibility of
someone out there who might have some information. And ... there
you were!

Daddy spelled his name "Lysle," but I don't know if he decided to
change it from "Lyle," or what. He had changed his birth year to
1905 to enable him to get into the military service and we didn't
discover that he actually was born in 1906 until he died June 21,
1971. I think he had actually forgotten in which
year he was born because he told us that he had changed his age by
two years, so we thought perhaps he was born in 1907. He was
wanting to retire, became ill with cancer and worked until three
weeks of his death. Ironically, when Mother and I found out that he
was born in 1906, we realized that he could have retired a month and
a half before he died.

He told me many wonderful stories about his immediate family but
never gave me names of uncles, aunts or cousins but said his
descendants were from Scotland and Ireland. He told me how his
grandfather (John Preston Rhea) used to take barter in exchange for
medical services ... that he would take eggs, a pig, or whatever the
family had if they had no money to pay. He said his mother, Nancy,
taught school in a one-room school house on Lookout Mountain,
wrote poetry (which my father did also), and had a collection of
poems bound, but they burned when their house caught fire. They
moved to Panama City, Florida when my dad was about 16 years
old. Nancy taught chemistry and science at the high school, which
later became the high school at which I graduated. The principal at
my junior high school told me that he went to school with my daddy
and that my grandmother was one of his teachers. I have seen a
picture of her which was published in the yearbook. She became ill
and my father had to quit school in his eleventh year in order to
work and care for her. He never said what type of work his father,
Josiah, did. Daddy told me that he (Lysle) had a scholarship to

become a doctor but he didn't want to be a doctor. He was a very intelligent, honest man (except for lying about his age, I guess) and worked hard all his life. He worked most of his life driving city transit buses, cabs, and a school bus. During the Depression he and Mother "gigged" frogs and he trapped alligators in South Florida. He worked during the summers on a commercial fishing boat. Before his death, he worked about 16 years as a security guard at an oil-tank facility in Lynn Haven, Florida. He had a grand sense of humor and was a very kind, gentle man who taught me to "buck dance," as he called it, and taught me how to cook.

My mother, Ora Geraldine Cullen Rhea (I typed it wrong in the e-mail notice) (she legally changed the spelling of Geraldine to Jeraldine), was born Dec. 5, 1912 in Apalachicola, FL and died Nov. 19, 1993 in Panama City, FL. Her father was Brainard Fuller CULLEN, born Sept. 29, 1877 in Apalachicola, FL and died March 16, 1951 in Pensacola, FL. He married Ora Bertha HOUSEMAN on Oct. 24, 1911. She was born March 16, 1892 in Freeport, FL and died Feb. 9, 1931 in St. Andrews, FL.

We remodeled our home, with some rooms being shifted around, and I cannot find his obituary or the picture of his mother. If I don't come across them, next week I will go to the public library and obtain the obituary from the public files. His father, Josiah, is buried in the Greenwood Cemetery in Panama City, FL in an unmarked grave, next to my mother's parents. I don't know where my grandmother, Nancy, was buried, but it was probably in Apalachicola, FL, near her daughter, Gwendolyn Rhea Kervin. I will research that out in the near future When I get all this information together, I will send it to you.

You have indeed been a blessing. Thank you.
Evanda. He married **Jeraldine Ora 'Teady' CULLEN**, married 21 Jul 1930 in Apalachicola, Franklin Co., FL, b. 5 Dec 1912 in Apalachicola, Franklin Co., FL, d. 19 Nov 1993 in Panama City, Bay Co., FL, buried in Lynn Haven Cem. Ora Geraldine Cullen legally changed her name to Jeraldine.

1932 move to Panama City, FL. She was a homemaker and attended the Family Worship Center and Central Assembly of God.
Children:

+ 932.   i   **Evanda Lee RHEA** b. 18 Sep 1942.

626. **Gwendolyn Preston RHEA**, (324.Josiah^5, 98.John^4, 21.Robert^3, 4.Jannette^2, 1.John^1) b. 17 May 1907 in Bristol, Sullivan Co., TN, d. 23 Aug 1947 in Apalachicola, Franklin Co., FL, buried in Magnolia Cem., Apalachicola, FL. Became a teacher like her mother. Taught in Auburn FL. She played the piano. She married **Jessie Joseph KIRVIN**, married 16 Feb 1927 in Apalachicola, Franklin Co., FL, b. 16 May 1906 in Apalachicola, Franklin Co., FL, d. 16 Dec 1982 in Apalachicola, Franklin Co., FL, buried in Magnolia Cem., Apalachicola, FL. Lived in Apalachicola, FL. Married twice. He was in the seafood business.
> *Children:*

+ 933.   i   **Walter Joseph 'Joe' KIRVIN** b. 10 Nov 1929.

+ 934.   ii   **Jesse Franklin KIRVIN, Sr.** b. 26 Nov 1932.

+ 935.   iii   **Virginia KERVIN** b. ABT 1934.

+ 936.   iv   **Susie Virginia KIRVIN** b. ABT 1940.

633. **Charles Meigs DULANEY, Jr.**, (329.Nancy^5, 102.Robert^4, 21.Robert^3, 4.Jannette^2, 1.John^1) b. 1902 in Sullivan Co., TN, d. 12 Apr 1958 in Bristol, Sullivan Co., TN. 1958 obituary - Dr. Charles M. Dulaney, 56, owner of the Dulaney Drug Store in Blountville, died at 4:30 am Saturday at Bristol Memorial Hospital. A Native of Mountain City, TN, he was the son of the late Dr. Charles M. and Martitia Rhea Dulaney. He was a graduate of the U. School of Pharmacy at Memphis and was associated with Bunting Drug Store for 28 years. Dr. Dulaney was instrumental in forming the medical center pharmacy. He was a member of NARD, Blountville Kiwanis Club and Fist Presbyterian Church of Bristol. Survivors include his wife, Mrs. Evelyn Dungan Dulaney, one daughter Mrs. Nancy Freeman, Winnecmac IN, two stepsons W. Vance Rucker, Greensboro, NC, Richard Rucker, Wilmington, DE. He married (1) **Pauline STONE**, b. 4 Jun 1899 in Abingdon, Washington Co. VA, d. 15 Mar 1946 in Bristol, Sullivan Co., TN, buried in Blountville Cemetery, Sullivan Co., TN. 1946 obituary - Funeral services for Mrs. Charles M. Dulaney: [She] died Friday night at her home at 110 Johnson St., will be conducted at 4 o'clock. The former Miss Pauline Stone daughter of the late Riley and Fannie Rush Stone. Mrs. Dulaney was born in Abingdon VA June 4, 1899. She had lived the greater part of her life in Bristol and was well known there. Surviving are her husband, a well known

druggist of Bunting's drug store, one daughter Nancy, two sisters. He married (2) **Evelyn DUNGAN**, b. ABT 1902.

Children by Pauline STONE:

937.   i   **Nancy DULANEY**, b. ABT 1937 in Sullivan Co., TN. 1958 lived in Winnemac, IN. She married **Mr. FREEMAN**.

938.   ii   **Charles Meigs DULANEY III**, b. 1939 in Sullivan Co., TN, d. 11 Apr 1939 in Sullivan Co., TN, buried in Blountville, Sullivan Co., TN. 1939 obituary - the infant son of Mr. and Mrs. Charles M. Dulaney, died at 5:30 o'clock yesterday afternoon in a local hospital. Surviving are the parents, one sister Nancy and the paternal grandmother Mrs. C. M. Dulaney of Blountville, TN.

634.   **Robert Nathaniel DULANEY**, (329.Nancy⁵, 102.Robert⁴, 21.Robert³, 4.Jannette², 1.John¹) b. 21 Nov 1903 in Blountville, Sullivan Co., TN, d. 17 May 1947 in Chattanooga, Hamilton Co., TN, buried in Blountville Cemetery, Sullivan Co., TN. 1947 obituary - former resident of Blountville, TN, died Friday at his home in Chattanooga.
Robert Dulaney, son of the late Dr. and Mrs. Meigs Dulaney, a native of Blountville, is survived by 3 children: Mary Ann, Charles, and Robert Dulaney. He was a member of the Virginia High School faculty prior to work at Kingsport and Chattangooga. For periods he was temporarily out of the city on government construction projects. He was the architect selected for the State Tuberculosis Surgical Hospital in Chattanooga. He married **Elizabeth MINTON**, b. ABT 1897. She is named in an obituary of her husband as Mrs. Elizabeth Minton Dulaney.

Children:

939.   i   **Mary Ann DULANEY**, b. 21 Sep 1929. 2005 was living Scottsdale, AZ. She married **Mr. POSTERO**, b. ABT 1929.

940.   ii   **Charles Wright DULANEY**, b. 8 Sep 1931 in TN?. 1996 lived in Kingsport TN.

Forwarded Message:
Subj: Rhea Genealogy

Date: 7/23/2005 11:13:36 A.M. Central Daylight
Time
From: Dulaneyxx@@cs.com
To: EFoley1
CC: Dulaneyxx@@cs.com, execdir@@kbgc.org
Dear Ted;

We have been in possession of your very thorough
book on The Descendants of the Rev. Joseph Rhea
for some time. You have really done fine work and I
have been remiss in not sending you some
corrections in my line, as you request in your
forward.

My line is (1) Joesph Rhea, (2) Matthew Rhea IV, (3)
Robert Preston Rhea, (4) Robert Campbell Rhea,
MD, (5) Nancy Martitia Rhea Dulaney (not
MATILDA) who married my grandfather, Dr.
Charles Meigs Dulaney, of Blountville. Martitia was
born in 1870 in Johnson County, TN (not Sullivan)
and died in 1942. Charles Meigs Dulaney was born in
1868, and died in 1934 and (6) Robert Nathaniel
Dulaney (not NATHAN) as shown on p.130. My
father was born Nov. 21, 1903 (not about 1897) and
died 5/17/47.

I can probably come up with the birth and death dates
of my father's siblings if that would be of interest. My
parents had three children - Mary Ann Dulaney
Postero, of Scottsdale, AZ,, born 9/21/1929 and twin
sons, Robert Rhea Dulaney, and Charles Wright
Dulaney (me), born 9/8/31. Robert died in 1965.

I have been in contact with Chuck Owens, who gave
me your e-mail address. We are thrilled that Chuck
and Sherry have done such a wonderful job of
restoring the Dulaney/Anderson house in Blountville.
Their house was built by my great-great-great
grandfather, Dr. Elkanah Roberts Dulaney, so we are
delighted to see it restored so beautifully.

Chuck tells me that you are starting a "Rhea Trust" in
Blountville. We are very interested in the history of

the Rheas and the Dulaneys, so we hope to meet you in Blountville one of these days.

Most cordially,

Charles W. Dulaney (Charlie)
2009 Westwind Drive
Kingsport, TN 37660-3444
(423) 247-1652. He married **Marion S. wife of Charles DULANEY**, b. ABT 1920.

941.　iii　**Robert DULANEY**, b. 8 Sep 1931, d. 1965.

635.　**William Davis DULANEY**, (329.Nancy[5], 102.Robert[4], 21.Robert[3], 4.Jannette[2], 1.John[1]) b. 1907 in Sullivan Co., TN, d. 24 Mar 1994 in Bristol, Sullivan Co., TN, buried in Blountville Cemetery, Sullivan Co., TN. 1994 obituary - Wm. D. Dulaney Sr. 87, of 326 Highway 75 died Thursday in Bristol Regional Medical Center. He was native of Mountain City, TN but had lived in Sullivan Co. for most of his life. Survivors include his wife Mrs. Dorothy Brown Dulaney; 2 daughters Mrs. Margaret Matlock Lakeland, FL, and Mrs. Carold Boonsue, Blountville TN; one son William Dulaney Jr. Blountville. He married **Dorothy BROWN**, b. 1907 in Sullivan Co., TN, d. 7 Oct 1995 in Bristol, Sullivan Co., TN. 1995 obituary - Dorothy Brown Dulaney 88 326 Hwy. 75, Blountville died Saturday Oct. 7, 1995 at Bristol Regional Medical center. She was a lifelong resident of Sullivan Co. A member of the Blountville Presbyterian Church. She was widow of W D Dulaney. Surviving are two daughters Mrs. Carol Dulaney Honsue (?) and Mrs. Margaret (Peggy) Matlock, FL; one son W. D. Dulaney Jr., Blountville.
Children:

+ 942.　i　**William D. DULANEY, Jr.** b. ABT 1920.

943.　ii　**Carol DULANEY**, b. ABT 1922 in TN?. 1994 was living in Blountville. She married **Mr. BOONSUE**, b. ABT 1820.

944.　iii　**Margaret DULANEY**, b. ABT 1928 in Sullivan Co., TN. 1994 she was living in Lakeland FL. She married **Mr. MATLOCK**, b. ABT 1928.

640. **Alice Laura FICKLE**, (337.Oscar[5], 105.Robert[4], 22.Margaret[3], 4.Jannette[2], 1.John[1]) b. 1 Dec 1878 in Sullivan Co., TN. She married **John KEYS**, b. 7 Nov 1871, d. 1 Oct 1968.
Children:

    945.   i   **Perry KEYS**, b. 4 Apr 1904.

654. **Beulah Grace FICKLE**, (340.Samuel[5], 105.Robert[4], 22.Margaret[3], 4.Jannette[2], 1.John[1]) b. 18 May 1896 in TN, d. 3 Feb 1990, buried in New Bethel Cem, Piney Flats TN. Had 3 children. First died as an infant, Max died at 5, but the youngest lived to adulthood. After the death of her husband, she lived with her son in Piney Flats, TN. She married **Allison SPURGEON**, married 28 Nov 1918, b. ABT 1896 in TN, d. 23 Nov 1944. Died tragically in a fire.
Children:

    946.   i   **Max Allen SPURGEON**, b. ABT 1920 in TN?. Died at age 5.

+ 947.   ii   **Lyle Blake SPURGEN** b. 5 Mar 1927.

658. **Haskew Devault 'Hass' FICKLE**, (340.Samuel[5], 105.Robert[4], 22.Margaret[3], 4.Jannette[2], 1.John[1]) b. 1 Feb 1903 in Sullivan Co., TN, d. 20 Jul 1960 in Sullivan Co., TN?, buried in Muddy Creek Cem., Sullivan Co. TN. Divorced Margaret and married Evelyn. He is buried with his second wife. He had been hit on the head with a tree in a field he was clearing. After the accident, he was never the same. 18 months before he died the court took all 6 of the children away from him and Evelyn. The accident it thought to be partly the reason. (reported by Kim Smalley, 1997). He married (1) **Margaret Katherine JONES**, married 9 Aug 1928, b. 24 Sep 1912. She was sister of Lovick Fickle's first wife. He married (2) **Evelyn Louise TAYLOR**, married 29 Sep 1945, b. 14 Jun 1927, d. 19 Nov 1960 in Sullivan Co., TN?, buried in Muddy Creek Cem., Sullivan Co. TN.
Children by Evelyn Louise TAYLOR:

+ 948.   i   **James Haskew 'Jerry' FICKLE** b. 5 Dec 1946.

+ 949.   ii   **Dorothy Eileen FICKLE** b. 29 Aug 1948.

    950.   iii   **Samuel Bruce FICKLE**, b. 14 Feb 1950 in TN?.

+ 951.   iv   **Judy Ann FICKLE** b. 11 May 1953.

952. v **Roy Bell FICKLE**, b. 20 Jul 1954 in TN?. He married **Helen Marie ABSHER**, b. ABT 1954.

+ 953. vi **Lynda Sue 'Susie' FICKLE** b. 5 Aug 1955.

675. **Lucy Mary 'Lula Mae' RHEA**, (349.Matthew⁵, 107.Elizabeth⁴, 23.Matthew³, 4.Jannette², 1.John¹) b. 9 Aug 1876 in Somerville, Fayette Co., TN, d. 6 Mar 1912 in Memphis, Shelby Co., TN. She and her infant died after childbirth. She died at the home of her brother Thomas at 942 S. Willett St. in Memphis. She married **George M. SHAW**, married 7 Dec 1912 in Somerville, Fayette Co., TN, b. 1863 in Robinsonville MS, d. 26 Apr 1941, buried in Elmwood Cemetery, Shelby Co., TN.
Children:

954. i **Lucy Adelaide SHAW**, b. 27 Nov 1911 in Robinsonville MS, d. 3 Dec 1911 in Robinsonville MS, buried 4 Dec 1911 in Elmwood Cemetery, Shelby Co., TN. Died as an infant.

676. **Edward Francis RHEA**, (349.Matthew⁵, 107.Elizabeth⁴, 23.Matthew³, 4.Jannette², 1.John¹) b. 30 Jan 1878 in Somerville, Fayette Co., TN, d. 10 Jun 1957 in Memphis, Shelby Co., TN. He was a station agent; telegrapher with the railroad. He was sent to Mississippi where he met and married his wife.

1925 moved back to Sommerville. His daughter Frances had typhoid when visiting relatives in Memphis. Edward's brother convinced him to move back to TN after her 3 month hospital stay and go into his retail coal business. All the children were born in Lexington MS. He also founded the MS Valley Audit Co. which he operated till his death. Also owned a farm just SW of Lexington named 'Banner Farm'. He married **Mary Adele HERBERT**, married 27 Mar 1909 in Lexington, Holmes Co. MS, b. 30 Oct 1885 in Acona, Holmes Co. MS, d. 20 Dec 1969 in Memphis, Shelby Co., TN. Moved from Acona to Lexington MS at about the age of 12. She attended Mississippi State College for Women, Columbus MS. She received a certificate in stenography. She served as President of the Power Literary Society and was a member of the Calloway Orr Literary Society. She was employed as a secretary for Noel, Booth, and Pepper, attorneys; Tackett and Smith, attorneys; Barrett Grocery Co.; Sutton-Lewis Cotton Co. After her marriage she worked for Elmore and Ruff, attorneys 1914-16. Bookkeeper for Rhea Coal Co. 1938-57.

Children:

+ 955. i **Frances Adele RHEA** b. 27 Oct 1916.

+ 956. ii **Thomas Edward RHEA** b. 6 Jan 1920.

+ 957. iii **Stephen Herbert RHEA** b. 18 Aug 1922.

679. **James Wilson RHEA**, (350.James[5], 107.Elizabeth[4], 23.Matthew[3], 4.Jannette[2], 1.John[1]) b. 20 Jan 1883 in Fayette Co., TN, d. 12 Nov 1965 in Somerville, Fayette Co., TN, buried in Somerville City Cemetery, Somerville TN. They lived for a short while in the Glade Springs neighborhood then bought land from R.T. Cross and built a home. They lived there until 1919 when he bought the old Stainbeck home north of Somerville where he lived until his death. He was a farmer and a member of the Shiloh Methodist Church. He married **Mary Lou CROSS**, married 20 Jan 1904, b. 15 May 1884 in TN?, d. 16 Jul 1947.

    Children:

    958. i **Frances Elizabeth RHEA**, b. 7 Sep 1905 in Fayette Co., TN, d. 26 Aug 1908.

    959. ii **Marion Overton RHEA**, b. 23 Jul 1909 in Fayette Co., TN, d. 18 Oct 1977 in Somerville, Fayette Co., TN. Lived in Memphis most of her adult life. Moved back to Sommerville in 1953 and lived at the old home place until her death. She married (1) **Fred P. HALLUM**, b. ABT 1909. She married (2) **C. M. WILKINSON**, b. ABT 1909. She married (3) **Harry GASSAWAY**, b. ABT 1909.

    960. iii **Sarah Bell RHEA**, b. 2 Jun 1911 in Fayette Co., TN. She married **Charles Tyrone MCNAMEE**, married 8 Jun 1941 in Sommerville, Fayette Co., TN, b. 17 Jan 1910 in Lagrange TN, d. 7 Sep 1978.

+ 961. iv **James Samuel RHEA** b. 7 Jun 1913.

+ 962. v **Betty Cross RHEA** b. 15 Aug 1915.

    963. vi **William Cross RHEA**, b. ABT 1918 in TN?.

+ 964. vii **Mary Louise RHEA** b. 18 Jan 1925.

The Preston Family of Walnut Grove, Virginia

680. **John Edmondson RHEA**, (350.James[5], 107.Elizabeth[4],
23.Matthew[3], 4.Jannette[2], 1.John[1]) b. 1885 in Fayette Co., TN, d. 18
Apr 1925 in Somerville, Fayette Co., TN, buried in Somerville City
Cemetery, Somerville TN. Lived in Sommerville; had farming
interests a few miles north of Sommerville. He married **Fannie
Kemp WATKINS**, married 26 Nov 1902, b. 7 Feb 1883 in Salmon
Mill, Fayette Co. TN, d. 2 Mar 1966 in Memphis, Shelby Co., TN,
buried in Somerville City Cemetery, Somerville TN.
    Children:

965. i **Addie Frances RHEA**, b. 4 May 1908 in Fayette
Co., TN. Spent most of her life in Sommerville. She
and her mother moved to Memphis shortly after the
death of John Edmonson. Frances worked there for
International Harvester for 45 years. Fannie moved
back to Sommerville and built a house on some of the
old Watkins land NW of Sommerville on Highway
59 next to her brother Tom.

+ 966. ii **Thomas Watkins RHEA** b. 14 Feb 1910.

681. **Sarah Bell RHEA**, (350.James[5], 107.Elizabeth[4], 23.Matthew[3],
4.Jannette[2], 1.John[1]) b. 9 Aug 1889 in Fayette Co., TN, d. 20 Jun
1976 in Fayette Co., TN, buried in Somerville City Cemetery,
Somerville TN. Lived in Fayette Co. until she was married.

1943 she returned to Somerville where she became active in the
church. She married **Sidney Albert BAYNES**, married 16 Mar
1915, b. 1885 in Brownsville, Haywood Co., TN, d. 1976. Held a
degree in law firm the Cumberland Law School.

1930 Federal census shows the family enumerated in Brownsville,
Haywood Co., TN at 611 Lafayette Street where they owned a home
in which they also rented to two other families. His age is not
consistent with the 1885 date from other researchers - should be age
45.
    Baynes, Sid, head, owns, value $4000, has radio, age 75, married
25 years, b. TN to parents from NC, no employment shown.
    -- Sarah, wife H, 40, married at 25, b. TN.
    -- Mary V., daughter, 8, single, b. TN.
    Children:

967.   i   **Mary Virginia BAYNES**, b. 12 Mar 1922 in Brownsville, Haywood Co., TN.

682.   **William Abraham RHEA**, (350.James[5], 107.Elizabeth[4], 23.Matthew[3], 4.Jannette[2], 1.John[1]) b. 27 Jul 1891 in Fayette Co., TN, d. 14 Oct 1958 in Somerville, Fayette Co., TN, buried in Somerville City Cemetery, Somerville TN. Served in the US Army during WWI and was stationed in Europe. Both of his sons were stationed in Europe with the Army Air Corps in WWII. He was a pharmacist and later served as postmaster in Somerville for 23 years. He was a member of the First Presbyterian Church in Somerville and was an Elder when he died.

1930 Federal census shows him enumerated in Somerville, Fayette Co., TN near to his relatives; widow of Alfred Long Rhea and her family, and the family of Herman and Jeannie Rhea (his first cousin) Butts.
  Rhea, William A., rents, $20/month, no radio, 38, married at 26, b. TN, Clerk, at Drug Store.
  -- Jessie, wife, 33, married at 21, b. TN.
  -- William A., son, 8, b. TN.
  -- Reuben, son, 3, b. TN.
  McCaskel, Cardin, boarder, rents, $5/month, 22, single, b. TN, Teacher, Public School. He married **Jessie Evelyn SCOTT**, married 29 Dec 1917 in west of Sommerville TN, b. 1896, d. 1 Jun 1971 in Somerville, Fayette Co., TN, buried in Somerville City Cemetery, Somerville TN.

Children:

+ 968.   i   **William Abraham RHEA Jr.** b. 8 Apr 1921.

+ 969.   ii   **Reuben Scott RHEA** b. 2 Jun 1926.

690.   **Louise RHEA**, (364.Richard[5], 111.Abram[4], 23.Matthew[3], 4.Jannette[2], 1.John[1]) b. 1907 in TN?, d. 1973 in TN?, buried in Whiteville, Hardeman Co. TN. She married **Joseph Thompson ALFORD**, b. 1906, d. 1982 in TN?, buried in Whiteville, Hardeman Co. TN.

Children:

+ 970.   i   **Joseph ALFORD Jr.** b. ABT 1930.

698. **Walter Preston RHEA III**, (373.Walter[5], 116.Walter[4], 23.Matthew[3], 4.Jannette[2], 1.John[1]) b. 20 Jan 1909 in Covington TN, d. 1978. He married **Bertie BUTLER**, b. 1907.
Children:

    971.   i   **Walter Preston RHEA IV.**, b. 2 Jan 1937, d. 15 Apr 1990. Died of Leukemia.

    972.   ii   **Anne Stewart RHEA**, b. ABT 1940. She married **Thomas Richard 'Dick' BRUCE**, b. ABT 1940.

    973.   iii **William Brock RHEA**, b. 27 Sep 1940 in TN?.

699. **Henry Sale 'Hal' RHEA**, (373.Walter[5], 116.Walter[4], 23.Matthew[3], 4.Jannette[2], 1.John[1]) b. 1912 in TN?, d. 27 Jan 1985 in Memphis, Shelby Co., TN. He married **Sara HARRELL**, b. ABT 1913.
Children:

+ 974.   i   **Carol Louise RHEA** b. 1944.

+ 975.   ii   **Henry Sale RHEA, Jr.** b. 1948.

+ 976.   iii **Maizie RHEA** b. 3 Jul 1953.

700. **Eleanor Marion RAGLAND**, (377.Eleanor[5], 117.Ellen[4], 23.Matthew[3], 4.Jannette[2], 1.John[1]) b. 8 Jun 1907 in TN?. She married **Norfleet TURNER**, b. ABT 1907.
Children:

+ 977.   i   **Elinor TURNER** b. ABT 1930.

702. **Fairfax Cary RAGLAND**, (377.Eleanor[5], 117.Ellen[4], 23.Matthew[3], 4.Jannette[2], 1.John[1]) b. 15 May 1914 in TN?. She married **Richard HARWOOD**, b. ABT 1914.
Children:

    978.   i   **Fairfax Cary HARWOOD**, b. ABT 1940. She married **Geroge Edward BAILEY**, b. ABT 1940.

705. **Mary Frances RHEA**, (380.Alfred[5], 118.Mary[4], 23.Matthew[3], 4.Jannette[2], 1.John[1]) b. 1914 in TN?, d. 1992. She married **James Hughes DANCY**, b. 1910, d. 1968.
Children:

+ 979.   i   **Mary Kay DANCY** b. 1948.

706.   **Ellen Preston RHEA**, (380.Alfred[5], 118.Mary[4], 23.Matthew[3], 4.Jannette[2], 1.John[1]) b. 31 Dec 1918 in Somerville, Fayette Co., TN. She married **Jasper Leland BARKER**, married 6 Apr 1942 in Somerville, Fayette Co., TN, b. 15 Jan 1903.
>   *Children:*

>   980.   i   **Mary Josephine BARKER**, b. 5 Feb 1954 in Memphis, Shelby Co., TN.

Seventh Generation

708.   **Margaret 'Maggie' M. SHEFFEY**, (391.Robert[6], 124.Elizabeth[5], 25.Robert[4], 5.John[3], 2.Robert[2], 1.John[1]) b. 1 Feb 1880 in Washington Co., VA. 1937 she had in her home an unusual looking safe which was the medicine chest of Dr. Robert Fairman Preston who spent his whole life at Walnut Grove. She also had a beer mug which belonged to the wife of Robert Preston, said to be 300 years old. She also had an old trunk, a walnut washstand, dresser, wardrobe, and mirror which may have come from Ireland, also a large Indian axe which was found on the Walnut grove. (WPA researcher interview of Mrs. Minnick by Victoria Gilliam).

Margaret's great aunt Mary inherited from her father left her some old silver consisting of a coffee pot, tea pot, water pot, cream pitcher, sugar dish, etc. Mary gave these to Mrs. Minnick with the request they be left in the family. Two children of Robert F. Preston were married and Mrs. Minnick gave four of these to nephew Albert and four to nephew Harold Sheffey as wedding presents.

Mrs Minnick had the old family Bible giving data on the Preston family. (1937 WPA VA report by Victoria Gilliam). She married **Robert C. 'R. D.' MINNICK**, married 1902, b. 1874 in VA. 1880 Virginia census shows Robert enumerated with his parents in the Goodson District of Washington Co., VA.

1902 the census indicates the couple was married. They struck west and were in Missouri for the births of three children from 1903 to 1907. The young family was in Kansas by 1910 where they appear in that state census.

1910 Kansas Census shows Robert and Margaret in Leroy Township, Coffey Co., KS enumerated in April of that year.

Minnick, Robert C., head, 36 married 8 years, b. VA, parents b. VA, farmer, general farm.
-- Maggie M., wife, 31, married 8 years, had 3 children, 3 living, b. VA, parents b. VA.
-- Jennie, daughter, 7 b. MO, parents b. VA.
-- Ewdard (sic - Edward?), son, 5 b. MO, parents b. VA.
--Kathryn, daughter, 3, b. MO, parents b. VA.

1920 Virginia census shows the family in Goodson District of Washington Co, VA, enumerated next to Margaret's parents. Their oldest child would be 17 at this point, but there are no children enumerated with them now back in Virginia.
Minnick, Robert C., head, 46, b. VA, parents b. VA, Farmer, general farm.
- Margaret, wife, 39, b. VA, parents b. VA.

Children:

981.　i　**Jennie MINNICK**, b. 1903 in MO.

982.　ii　**Edward MINNICK**, b. 1905 in MO.

983.　iii　**Kathryn MINNICK**, b. 1907 in MO.

710.　**Robert P. SHEFFEY Jr.**, (391.Robert[6], 124.Elizabeth[5], 25.Robert[4], 5.John[3], 2.Robert[2], 1.John[1]) b. 1886 in Washington Co., VA, d. 1935. 1880 his family is enumerated in the Virginia census as the household next to his grandfather Robert Preston and his father Ezra Sheffey in Goodson District of Washington Co., VA.
Sheffey, Robert 25, farmer b. VA
Mary 25, wife b. VA
Maggie M. 3/12 (February) daughter b. VA

1910 May, only Robert and his aunt are enumerated in the Virginia census in the household in Goodson District, Washington Co, VA
Sheffey, Robert P. head of house, 21, single
Carmack, Sallie, aunt, 40.

The next household is that of James Carmack age 31 and his wife with 3 children.

1920 January, Robert and family are enumerated in the Goodson District of Washington Co., VA, the household next to his sister Margaret and her husband Robert Minnick.
Sheffey, Robert, head 31, b. VA, farmer of general farm.

-- Olivia, wife, age 24, b. VA
-- Albert, son, age 7, b. VA.
-- Harold, son, age 4 9/12, b. VA
Carmack, Sallie, aunt, age 63, b. VA

1935 lived in the original Preston home 'Walnut Grove'. Owned it after the death of his father from 1935-37. He married **Olivia B. wife of Robert SHEFFEY**, b. 1890 in VA. 1949 Olivia Sheffey was given the family house at Walnut Grove. By this time, most of the farmland had been sold either by her father or by her great aunt Mary Preston Winston.

1960 the nieces of E. Summers Sheffey, Susan Schmette and Sarah Steenis inherited Walnut Grove.
                Children:

984.   i   **Albert SHEFFEY**, b. 1913 in Washington Co., VA.

985.   ii   **Harold SHEFFEY**, b. 1 Sep 1915 in Washington Co., VA.

986.   iii **Elmo Summers SHEFFEY**, b. ABT 1920. 1955 graduated from University of Virginia Law School.

Washington County News, Thursday, September 5,1985, article by Joy Tucker, related the Preston history of Walnut Grove as told by its last owner E. Summers Sheffey. Although Mr. Sheffey had firsthand knowledge of the place he grew up, later research would put more facts around a number of the legends and myths about the family and its plantation at Walnut Grove. Keeping an eye to the facts later discovered, its is still wonderful to read the interview and article which read as follows:

I was born and reared right her in this house as were all my ancestors" said E. Summers Sheffey, standing outside the Pr4eston-Sheffery homes place near Bristol, VA.
Sheffey can trace his family back to two John Prestons, unrelated, who came to this country from England in the late 1700's. One of them settled in Augusta County. The other had apparently done a great service for the King and was granted a large tract of land in Virginia stretching from the North Fork of the Holston River to the South Fork.

This Preston arrived in the New World in 1770 and built his home in 1772, on a hill near a spring at Walnut Grove. The white, two-story structure, which has been in the Preston family for nine generations, is believed to be the oldest frame house in Washington County.

A grandson of John Preston of Walnut Grove married the daughter of John Preston of Augusta County, joining the two families. Two generations later there were no male Prestons to carry on the family name and in 1855 Elizabeth Virginia Preston married Dr. Ezra Sheffey.

"The family would have social functions from time to time and legend has it that one of their guests was Robert E. Lee", related E. Summers Sheffey. "What I call the living room was their ballroom, where they danced". The numerous pegs that line the walls of the foyer, and were used to hang cots, indicated that the Preston and Sheffeys did a great deal of entertaining.

In addition to being the site of many social events, the property was also the scheme of a battle during the War Between the States, according to family history. A cannonball went through the roof of one of the outbuildings during the fight that was raging along two nearby ridges.

"That battle has been attributed to the same regiment that had a skirmish at Saltville", Sheffey said. "The story is probably true because I have dug lead out of the old log building that apparently was shot into it during the war."

Accomplished members of the Sheffey branch include a colonel in the Confederate army during the War Between the States, a congressman during the post Civil War period, as well as a number of judges.

E. Summers Sheffey has continued the tradition. A graduate of law school at University of Virginia, he was a first lieutenant in the U.S. Marine Corps for three and a half years and was elected as commonwealth attorney twice in the early 1960's. He now lives in Dade City, Fla., where he practices law. Not forgetting his roots, Sheffey said, "I'm a farmer at heart." He uses the family home in Washington County as a summer home and this year has begun renovation work on the old building.

With the help of Wright Brothers Construction of Wallace, which also leases the property for farming, Sheffey repainted the outside of the house, including the roof, as well as repaired the shutters and replaced rotten weather boards.

"I want to make sure it lasts for another hundred years," said Sheffey. "It's a lot of work but I want to be remembered for being faithful to the old home place." He added, "I'm doing this for me."

This winter he will begin work on the inside of the house, stripping the paint off the floor and the wainscoting and deciding what to do about the old wallpaper that covers the uneven plaster of the walls.

"There's a theory that one room downstairs was log and then the rest of the house was built around that, but I haven't gone tearing into it to find out," Sheffey explained. "Fortunately, this home has never suffered any catastrophe, such as fire, or had to be rebuilt."

The house originally consisted of four rooms, two downstairs. Hand carved laths were covered with plaster that was roughly smoothed over. "Later, when wallpaper came along, it was put over the unsightly plaster," said Sheffey.

Pegs and blacksmith nails were used to put the house together. The blacksmith also made the large hinges and locks on all the doors. Huge, hand-hewn beams provide the foundation for the structure.

"One of the most unique aspects of the house is the majestic chimneys," Sheffey pointed out. Each of the stone chimneys is actually two chimneys into one, providing a flue for the four fireplaces, one in each room.

"To me as a layman, I can't comprehend how, 200 years ago with clay for mortar and limited tools, they built something that today is perfect from the point of stability," said Sheffey.

A door off the upstairs hallway stands as a reminder that at one time there was an outside porch on the second floor. The door now leads to the roof of a downstairs porch, which was also added on.

Later, the house was expanded to include the modern conveniences of a kitchen and indoor bathroom. For many years the family carried water up from the spring in front of the house. A cistern and pump were built outside the back door around 1915 and in the late 1930's, someone came up with the idea of building a reservoir on the hill behind the house.

This water source, relying on gravity, was used by Sheffey's mother until she died seven years ago. Sheffey has since remodeled the bathroom and found the reservoir to be insufficient.

Growing near the front of the house is an old, gnarled Catalpa or Indian bean tree that has been on the property almost as long as the Preston family. "It used to be massive but it's on its way out," Sheffey said. "John Preston brought it over here or else he ordered it from the Old Country.

That's the only reason I leave it here. It was much prized as an ornamental tree back then."

Behind the house, there were two log cabins that were used for slave quarters and kitchen. One has been taken down, and the other is supported by two trees. "I can remember meat being hung in here during hog killing season when I was a boy," Sheffey said. Other fond memories of his childhood include catching muskrats and mink in Beaver Creek that runs in front of the house.

"To make my allowance, I caught muskrats by the creek. I'd try to set traps so they would drown by the time I went to get them, but the second or third most exciting thing in the world is to go down, early in the morning, and hear them splashing. Then you knew you'd caught one."

"I'd skin them and hang them in here (the log cabin) to cure. Then I'd send them to Sears and Roebuck. They paid $3.50 for each pelt back then. I'd catch maybe two mink a month as opposed to 20 muskrats a month," he reminisced.

"The mink were harder to trap. They were more elusive and very vicious. You had to be very careful with both mink and muskrats so you didn't damage the pelt."

Although Sheffey's two daughters, Susan and Sarah did not grow up on the old home place, Sheffey hopes that they will feel a strong attachment, as he does, to their heritage. He would like to see the house and the 80 odd acres of property stay in the family for another two hundred years.

711.   **Walter A. SHEFFEY**, (392.Henry[6], 124.Elizabeth[5], 25.Robert[4], 5.John[3], 2.Robert[2], 1.John[1]) b. 1885 in VA. 1910 Federal census shows he and his wife of 8 months living in the household of his parents in Sullivan Co., TN.

　　1920 Walter and his young family appear enumerated in the Federal census of TN in Warren Co., TN, living on Shelbyville Rd.:
Sheffey, Walter, head, owns his home with no mortgage, age 35, farmer.
-- Nettie, wife age 38,
-- Emerson (?), son, 7, b. TN
-- Preston, son age 4 3/4, b. TN.

　　1930 Federal census shows the family in the Third District of Washington Co., TN.

Sheffey, Walter A. [Valter in the index], rents, age 44, married at
age 24, b. VA, general farmer.
-- Nettie R., wife, 48, married at 28, b. TN
-- Emmerson [again difficult to read], son, 17, . TN
-- Preston H., son, 14, b. TN
Bolton, Lars (?) A., boarder, 65, widowed, b. TN to TN parents. He
married **Nettie R. wife of Walter SHEFFEY**, married 1909, b.
ABT 1885 in TN.

Children:

987.　i　**Emerson SHEFFEY**, b. 1913 in TN.

988.　ii　**Preston H. SHEFFEY**, b. 1 Oct 1905 in TN.

716. **Frances CUMMINGS**, (396.James[6], 125.Elizabeth[5], 26.Margaret[4],
5.John[3], 2.Robert[2], 1.John[1]) b. 1908 in Washington Co., VA. She
married **Eldridge H. MOORE**, b. 26 Mar 1903 in Hawkins Co.,
TN, d. JAN 1970. Social Security death index shows an Eldridge
Moore born in 1903 who died in Jan 1970 with his last residence as
Abingdon, VA. Researcher assumes this is the Record of Eldridge
H.

Children:

989.　i　**Eldridge H. MOORE, Jr.**, b. 1 May 1929 in
　　　　Washington Co., VA.

721. **Annie Preston WHITE**, (404.James[6], 128.John[5], 26.Margaret[4],
5.John[3], 2.Robert[2], 1.John[1]) b. 1 Feb 1880 in Austin, Travis Co., TX.
She married **George Gilbert 'Dr.' CRAWFORD**, b. 1 Mar 1876 in
VA. 1900 Federal census shows George enumerated in
Charlottesville, Albemarle, VA, as a student, born March 1876, in
VA, boarding with other students at 119 Westland Ave.

After 1900 and before 1910 George and Anne married and were
living in Delaware when the had their first two children Anne and
Ellen. They are living in Virginia by 1910.

1920 Federal census shows the family enumerated in Strasburg,
Shenandoah Co., VA living on Main St. (They were living on Main
St. in 1910 as well. At that time, mother Emma B., b. 54 widow b.
VA was also living with the family).
Crawford, George G., head, owns home, 43, b. VA to parents from
VA, Physician, General Practice.
-- Anne P., wife, 48, b. Texas to parents from Texas and Virginia.

-- Ellen C., daughter, 15, b. Delaware to parents from VA and TX.
-- Anne P., daughter, 12, b. Delaware to parents from VA and TX.
-- James J., son, 9, b. VA to parents from VA and TX.
-- Jean N., daughter, 6, b. VA to parents from VA and TX.

1930 Federal census shows the family still enumerated in Strasburg, VA, living at 121 West King St. Two children are still at home: Crawford, George G., head, owns home, value $9,000, has radio, married at 27, 54, b. VA, Medical Doctor, General Practice.
-- Anne P., Wife-H, 50, married at 23, b. TX to parents from TX and VA.
-- Jean C., daughter 17, single, b. VA, Bank Clerk, Bank.
-- David L., son, 7, b. VA.

Children:

990.   i   **Ellen Clark CRAWFORD**, b. 1905 in Delaware.

991.   ii   **Annie Preston CRAWFORD**, b. 1908 in Delaware.

992.   iii   **Jean Maxwell CRAWFORD**, b. 1913 in Shenandoah Co., VA.

993.   iv   **James Jamison CRAWFORD**, b. ABT 1914 in VA?.

994.   v   **David L. CRAWFORD**, b. 1923 in Shenandoah Co., VA.

722. **Colin Clarke WHITE**, (404.James[6], 128.John[5], 26.Margaret[4], 5.John[3], 2.Robert[2], 1.John[1]) b. 1884 in TX. 1910 Federal census shows Colin C. White, age 25, lodging in Manhattan, NY, married but not wife enumerated here, born in Texas to parents from Virginia, working as a Salesman, Feed Bank(?)

1920 Federal census shows only one Colin White, age 35, b. Texas to parents from Virginia, living in Washington D.C., a music teacher, married to Margaret, age 36, b. PA to parents from PA and NY. No children enumerated with them.

The couple was in Washington at least until 1922 since their daughter as born.

1930 Federal census shows a Colin C. White in Beaverdam District, Hanover Co., VA.

White, Colin C., 49, first married at 24, b. TX to parents from VA, a Miller. (There are a number of farmers and mill laborers shows in this district.)

-- Margaret, wife H., 49, first married at 36, b. PA to parents from NY (sic).

-- Sally, daughter, 8, b. District of Columbia. He married (1) **Ethel HALLORAN**, b. ABT 1884 in VA?. He married (2) **Margaret wife of Colin WHITE**, b. 1884 in PA.

Children by Ethel HALLORAN:

995.   i   **Phyllis Halloran WHITE**, b. ABT 1910 in VA?.
Children by Margaret wife of Colin WHITE:

996.   ii   **Sarah WHITE**, b. 1922 in Washington, DC.

728. **Lucille YOUMANS**, (415.Margaret⁶, 131.Ellen⁵, 26.Margaret⁴, 5.John³, 2.Robert², 1.John¹) b. 20 Dec 1891 in VA?. She married **William Walter HAINES**, b. ABT 1894 in VA?.
Children:

+ 997.   i   **Margaret Preston HAMES** b. ABT 1920.

+ 998.   ii   **Boyd Lemuel HAMES** b. ABT 1922.

739. **Malcolm McDonald CAMPBELL**, (420.Frank⁶, 131.Ellen⁵, 26.Margaret⁴, 5.John³, 2.Robert², 1.John¹) b. 4 Oct 1904 in Bonham, Fannin Co., TX, d. 25 Jan 1996 in Dallas, Dallas Co., TX. 1922 graduate of Bonham High School. Attended Texas A&M. He was with the Soil Conservation Service. Instrumental in building Lakes Fannin, Crockett and Coffee Mill. He was a veteran of WWII. In later life, he worked in oil and gas until his retirement. He was an active member of the Town North Bible Church. He married (1) **Mildred NEVILL**, married 10 Feb 1927 in Bonham, Fannin Co., TX, b. 2 Jul 1904 in Bonham, Fannin Co., TX, d. 12 Jan 1956 in Bonham, Fannin Co., TX. He married (2) **Harriet CARRIERE**, married 1958, b. 1911, d. 1997.
Children by Mildred NEVILL:

+ 999.   i   **Martha Ellen CAMPBELL** b. 27 Jul 1930.

+ 1000.   ii   **Carolyn CAMPBELL** b. 4 Sep 1932.

741. **Edward Malcolm CAMPBELL**, (422.Preston⁶, 131.Ellen⁵, 26.Margaret⁴, 5.John³, 2.Robert², 1.John¹) b. 20 Jun 1917 in

Abingdon, Washington Co. VA. He married **Ellen Chandler WORTHY**, married 4 Nov 1950, b. ABT 1917.
Children:

    1001. i   **Eleanor Worthy CAMPBELL**, b. 21 Sep 1951, d. 1 Jul 1966 in TN.

+ 1002. ii   **Preston White CAMPBELL** b. 15 Jul 1953.

+ 1003. iii   **Ray Worthy CAMPBELL** b. 16 Jun 1955.

    1004. iv   **Malcolm McDonald CAMPBELL**, b. ABT 1957. He married **Charlene SCHULTZ**, married 18 Aug 1990, b. ABT 1957.

    1005. v   **Volney Howard CAMPBELL**, b. ABT 1960.

    1006. vi   **Louise Howard CAMPBELL**, b. 23 Jun 1969.

757. **John Preston BUCHANAN**, (440.Eleanor[6], 139.John[5], 29.Eleanor[4], 5.John[3], 2.Robert[2], 1.John[1]) b. 30 Jan 1888 in VA?, d. 15 Sep 1937. He married **Annabelle M. MORRIS**, married 14 Aug 1912, b. ABT 1890 in VA?.
Children:

    1007. i   **Eleanor Fairman BUCHANAN**, b. ABT 1913 in VA?.

    1008. ii   **John Preston BUCHANAN Jr.**, b. ABT 1915 in VA?.

763. **David H. BUCHANAN**, (440.Eleanor[6], 139.John[5], 29.Eleanor[4], 5.John[3], 2.Robert[2], 1.John[1]) b. 8 May 1907 in VA?. Had one child. He married **Katherine PRITCHELL**, married 24 Aug 1929, b. ABT 1907.
Children:

    1009. i   **Cynthia Dee BUCHANAN**, b. 17 Jan 1937.

782. **Pauline Hill STALEY**, (449.Margaret[6], 142.Ellen[5], 29.Eleanor[4], 5.John[3], 2.Robert[2], 1.John[1]) b. 6 Jul 1900 in Marion, Smythe Co., VA. She married **Preston COLLINS**, married 2 Jan 1926, b. 25 Dec 1896, d. 20 Sep 1952.
Children:

288

1010. i   **Preston COLLINS Jr.**, b. 17 Dec 1928.

788. **James Thomas WATKINS IV Jr.**, (454.Eleanor[6], 145.Martha[5], 29.Eleanor[4], 5.John[3], 2.Robert[2], 1.John[1]) b. 1908 in CA, d. 1982. His wife's obituary in 2004 notes she married James Thomas Watkins IV. He married **Elise Valerie GETTIER**, b. 17 Jun 1914 in Baltimore, Baltimore Co., MD, d. 22 Jan 2004. 2004 Obituary - Baltimore Sun -
ELISE VALERIE GETTIER was born in Baltimore, Maryland, June 17, 1914. After her prep school days at Roland Park Country School she attended Smith College from which she graduated in 1936 Magna Cum Laude and Phi Beta Kappa. She spent her Junior year at the Sorbonne in Paris. Elsie continued her studies at the Graduate Institute of International Studies in Geneva, Switzerland. There she met her husband James T. Watkins, IV. They were married in 1938. After Jim's discharge from the U.S. Navy in 1946 the Watkins' returned to Palo Alto, and Jim joined the Stanford faculty as assistant professor of Political Science. Their home in Professorville, where they shared their lives with so many friends and students, is the same in which Elise died peacefully, with loved ones at her side, January 11, 2004. For many years Elise was an active volunteer at Allied Arts. But in 1954 the career that she loved, and which enriched a multitude of lives, began. Through 1970 she regularly escorted groups of Stanford students for summers in Europe. She served as travel counselor for Sequoia Travel Center housed in Tresidder Union until 1985, and organized and led tours for the Committee for Art at Stanford for more than two decades. Characterized as a "walking encyclopedia", she loved to teach as well as travel, and her legacy will live long in those who sought her counsel. Following her tenure at Sequoia she founded Watkins Ward Travel. She retired at the age of 85 to her Emerson Street home in Professorville, that was a home away from home for generations of Stanford students. An avid gardener and gourmet cook she delighted in entertaining her friends of all ages. The establishment of the James T. Watkins, IV and Elise V. Watkins Professorship in the School of Humanities and Sciences and the first appointment to this distinguished Chair was celebrated in October at Stanford. Elise is survived by many beloved friends, godchildren and namesakes. Jim predeceased Elise in 1982. Other survivors include nieces and nephews, Eleanor Watkins Lanye of Dallas, TX, Dr. Robert Preston Watkins, Jr. of Port Angeles, WA, Jennifer Watkins Bales of San Jose, CA, Harry S. Watkins, Jr. of San Diego, CA, Virginia Watkins Green of Olympia, WA, Richard R. Jones, Fred Jones and Beth

Jones Elkins, all of Baltimore, MD. In lieu of flowers, donations to the Professorship Fund are appreciated. Please direct correspondence to Stephen Player, Office of Development, Stanford, CA 94305. Email splayer@@stanford.edu or tel: 650-725-5509 or a gift may be made to the Elizabeth Gamble Garden Center, 1431 Waverly Street, Palo Alto, CA 94301. A Memorial Service will be held on March 3 at 4:00 PM at the Faculty Club on the Stanford University Campus. Arrangements by Bay Area Cremation and Funeral Services, 650-365-3909.

Published in the Baltimore Sun on 1/21/2004.ones.

793. **Robert Sheffey PRESTON, Jr. III.**, (455.Robert[6], 145.Martha[5], 29.Eleanor[4], 5.John[3], 2.Robert[2], 1.John[1]) b. 15 Aug 1917 in Richmond, Henrico Co., VA, d. 28 Oct 1991. 1941 Feb 3 Robert S. Preston Jr., b. 1917, Henrico Co., VA, enlisted in Infantry, in the National Guard in Richmond, VA. His record indicated he had 4 years of college, was single without dependants, 71 inches in height, weighed 157 pounds.

Social Security records indicate Robert S. Preston, b. Aug. 15, 1917, who received his number in VA, died Oct. 28, 1991, and last resided at Manakin Sabot, Goochland, VA. He married **Louisa DARRAGN**, married 14 Aug 1943, b. 23 Jan 1919.

Children:

1012. i   **Mary Louisa PRESTON**, b. 1 Nov 1944.

1013. ii   **Alice Valeria PRESTON**, b. 22 May 1947.

1014. iii   **Carolyn Reed PRESTON**, b. 27 May 1950.

1015. iv   **Robert Sheffey PRESTON IV.**, b. 9 Nov 1953.

1016. v   **Fredrick D. PRESTON**, b. 28 Sep 1963.

794. **William Reed PRESTON**, (455.Robert[6], 145.Martha[5], 29.Eleanor[4], 5.John[3], 2.Robert[2], 1.John[1]) b. 3 Jun 1920, d. 18 Jul 1971. He married **Suzanne Cosley PULLIAM**, married 1 1947, b. 8 Dec 1922.

Children:

+ 1017. i   **William Reed PRESTON Jr.** b. 2 Dec 1948.

+ 1018. ii   **Martha Colsey PRESTON** b. 17 Mar 1951.

1019. iii **Thomas Burwell PRESTON**, b. 19 Mar 1954.

1020. iv **Suzanne Crenshaw PRESTON**, b. 26 Jan 1962.

795. **Alice Burwell PRESTON**, (455.Robert[6], 145.Martha[5], 29.Eleanor[4], 5.John[3], 2.Robert[2], 1.John[1]) b. 24 Feb 1927. She married **Parke Farr SMITH**, married 10 Apr 1948, b. 24 Jan 1920.
Children:

1021. i **Christie Reed SMITH**, b. 1 Nov 1950. She married **M. B. VANDOREN III.**, married 27 Jan 1979, b. 16 Jun 1949.

1022. ii **Preston Sheffey SMITH**, b. 5 Jan 1953. He married **Cynthia Gay VELOM**, married 27 Sep 1980, b. 15 Sep 1956.

1023. iii **James Alexander SMITH**, b. 5 Jan 1953. He married **Janet Lynn RHODES**, married 26 Nov 1977, b. 15 Feb 1956.

1024. iv **Parke Burwell SMITH**, b. 15 Jul 1959.

807. **Otway Giles BAILEY III.**, (486.Otway[6], 174.Ellen[5], 37.Henry[4], 5.John[3], 2.Robert[2], 1.John[1]) b. 5 Sep 1924. He married **Elsie WATSON**, married 18 May 1945, b. 5 Feb 1923.
Children:

1025. i **Anna Lynn BAILEY**, b. 25 Dec 1950.

1026. ii **Barbara Leigh BAILEY**, b. 25 Feb 1955.

808. **Ellen Olivia BAILEY**, (486.Otway[6], 174.Ellen[5], 37.Henry[4], 5.John[3], 2.Robert[2], 1.John[1]) b. 10 Oct 1926. She married **Curtis V. GIANNINI**, married 28 Aug 1948, b. ABT 1926.
Children:

1027. i **Steven P. GIANNINI**, b. 20 Jun 1949.

1028. ii **David Curtis GIANNINI**, b. 22 Nov 1950.

1029. iii **Giles Anderson GIANNINI**, b. 4 Feb 1956.

809.　**Jeanne Deford BAILEY**, (486.Otway[6], 174.Ellen[5], 37.Henry[4], 5.John[3], 2.Robert[2], 1.John[1]) b. 18 Jul 1930.　She married **Robert Pierce WHITMAN**, married 20 Dec 1952, b. ABT 1930.
　　　　　Children:

　　　1030.　i　**Robert Pierce WHITMAN Jr.**, b. 15 Dec 1953.

　　　1031.　ii　**Jeanne Preston WHITMAN**, b. 12 Jan 1957.

　　　1032.　iii　**Sarah Sutton WHITMAN**, b. 4 Nov 1959.

816.　**Audley Rhea ANDERSON**, (501.Elizabeth[6], 184.Frances[5], 40.Sarah[4], 6.Jane[3], 2.Robert[2], 1.John[1]) b. 28 Mar 1881 in Sullivan Co., TN?.　He married **Bertha Eleanor SHORT**, b. ABT 1881.
　　　　　Children:

　　　1033.　i　**Audley Rhea ANDERSON Jr.**, b. ABT 1910.

817.　**Joseph Earhart RHEA**, (503.Robert[6], 184.Frances[5], 40.Sarah[4], 6.Jane[3], 2.Robert[2], 1.John[1]) b. 3 Aug 1882 in Forney TX, d. 12 Jan 1978 in Maywood, CC, Il.　Notable Southern Families., Z. Armstrong 1922 notes Joseph married Jeanette McNabb. He married (1) **Jeanette MCNABB**, b. ABT 1882 in TX?.　He married (2) **Mabelle Benjama LARSEN**, married 4 Jun 1921 in Pittsburgh, Allegheny Co., PA, b. 8 May 1894 in Chicago, Cook Co., IL, d. 6 Jul 1977 in Chicago, Cook Co., IL.　Daughter of Benjamin Larsen and Susanna Marie Hagensen both born Norway.
　　　　　Children by Mabelle Benjama LARSEN:

　　　1034.　i　**Mabelle Lenox RHEA**, b. 17 Jul 1922 in Chicago, Cook Co., IL.　She married **Wallace John EWALD**, married 27 Apr 1946 in Chicago, Cook Co., IL, b. ABT 1920.

818.　**Frank Bland RHEA**, (503.Robert[6], 184.Frances[5], 40.Sarah[4], 6.Jane[3], 2.Robert[2], 1.John[1]) b. 9 May 1884 in Forney, Kaufman Co., TX.　He married **Nell HILL**, b. ABT 1884 in TX?.
　　　　　Children:

　　　1035.　i　**Sara Carolyn RHEA**, b. ABT 1910 in TX?.

　+　1036.　ii　**Robert Milton RHEA** b. 1918.

821. **Clarence Ward RHEA**, (504.James[6], 184.Frances[5], 40.Sarah[4], 6.Jane[3], 2.Robert[2], 1.John[1]) b. 27 Sep 1890 in Forney, Kaufman Co., TX. He married **Dorothy FITZGERALD**, married 14 Feb 1918 in St. Louis, MO, b. 1 Oct 1892.
        Children:

    1037. i   **Dorothy Jane RHEA**, b. 12 Jul 1922 in St. Louis, MO.

    1038. ii   **Clarence Ward RHEA Jr.**, b. 11 Nov 1923 in St. Louis, MO.

823. **James Theodoric RHEA, Jr.**, (504.James[6], 184.Frances[5], 40.Sarah[4], 6.Jane[3], 2.Robert[2], 1.John[1]) b. 20 Jun 1902 in Forney, Kaufman Co., TX. Borne and raised in Forney, Texas. At the age of ten, he had his first job - delivering Cardui (?) Almanac for 50 cents per copy. He was paid by his Uncle Frank Adams who ran the pharmacy
in Forney(A historical Marker ins on the Store now).

1920, James Rhea attended Austin College in Sherman, Texas, majoring in Business or Accounting (it was the first year for the Military school to be Co-Ed.) When his father died he dropped out to support his mother. The family took him in to their hotel business as a bookkeeper.

1925 Forney was world famous for it's Forney Black Land Cotton - there was a "bumper crop" that
year. James while working at the cotton Gin, went with his boss that year to Tulsa, Oklahoma, to sell the cotton. This is the time when James decided to be a bookkeeper instead of breaking his back hauling cotton, drinking black coffee, and eating bologna sandwiches. James Rhea met the Love of his Life in Forney, Texas. Dr. Fowler, I believe his cousin asked him to meet a nice young nurse named Delma Houser who was working at the Forney Sanitarian (The Superintendent was a Dr. BoBo.) He
took this young lady out and his single life was over. He later met a Mr. D.P. Houser at Josephine, Texas. While there after several attempts to get Mr. Houser out of the house and alone, he asked for her hand. D.P. knew what was coming down the pike and played it very coy. James said he wished to marry her in Dallas at the First Presbyterian Church to which D.P. replied "There's enough Methodist Minister in Josephine to marry Delma." He gave his blessing- James was the only son-in-law to ask him for his

daughter's hand. On June 28, 1928, Dr. William M. Anderson, Minister at First Presbyterian Church of Dallas, united James and Delma, with witnesses Gladys and Charlie Drake(He was a teller who had worked for James's father). They drove to Waco, Texas, for their honeymoon. When they arrived at the hotel the room was ready, but something was very wrong. They were given a room with two single beds - THIS would not do. James told them that he was on his honeymoon and the single beds were out of the question. They got the Honeymoon Suite on the top floor with a fantastic front view. During a 1996 visit with Uncle James, I asked about his brother, James Rhea had no comment, only acknowledged that he had a brother. Mrs. Rhea had said or told him that Edwin was " worthless and whereabouts unknown. " James still living in 1998. (From e-mail of James Pillow, Houston TX 1998.) He married **Mary Delma HOUSER**, married 28 Jun 1926 in Dallas, Dallas Co., TX, b. ABT 1902. Went to nursing school in east TX. After graduation she worked at a Sanitarium in Forney TX where she met James Rhea. She became a registered nurse and liked surgery. She was a very quick crotchetier because she was left handed and therefore skipped a step. She was always trim and walked or biked with James every morning and evening.

Children:

1039. i   **Gladys Ann RHEA**, b. 14 Apr 1927 in Forney, Kaufman Co., TX, d. 11 Jun 1927 in Dallas, Dallas Co., TX. Died of Cataral fever.

828. **John Powell EARHART**, (508.Charles[6], 185.Margaret[5], 40.Sarah[4], 6.Jane[3], 2.Robert[2], 1.John[1]) b. 1 Jul 1885 in Bristol, Sullivan Co., TN, d. 30 Mar 1946 in Sullivan Co., TN, buried in Shelby Hills Cem., Bristol, TN. Appears in the 1940 Bristol City Directory - Carrier USPO - home Rd 1 Bluff City TN.

1930 and 1930 Federal census shows the family enumerated in Sullivan Co. 4th Civil District #82; shows Powell a farmer, Kate and two sons.

1930 census shows Gypsie Millard is a boarder. She is a public school teacher, possibly at the little Red School house on the property. She was 21.

1932 obituary - J. Powell Earhart of the Thomas Bridge community of Sullivan Co., TN, died suddenly as the result of a hear attach at his home at 9:30 am yesterday.

Mr. Earhart was born July 15, 1855 and son of Charles B. and Etta Powell Earhart, descendants of prominent pioneer families, was well known throughout this section. He was a lifelong resident of Sullivan Co. and an employee of Bristol TN Post Office for 26 years. He retired from post office work about a year ago due to ill health.

He is survived by his widow, Mrs. Kate Sanders Earhart, one son Lt. Lawrence P. Earhart, two brothers S. Pearce and Ralph P. Earhart, both of Bristol, 2 sisters Mrs. Margarita Doane, Holston Institute, and Mrs. Violet Bouton, Washington DC, and one granddaughter Julia Katherine Earhart. One son, Charles S. Earhart preceded him in death June 3, 1945. He married **Kathleen 'Kate' Viola SANDERS**, b. 1888 in TN, d. 14 May 1959 in Bluff City, Sullivan Co., TN, buried in Shelby Hills Cem., Bristol, TN. Obituary - Mrs. Powell Earhart Dies after Trash Fire Tragedy.
A 72-year old woman who was burned Wednesday when flames enveloped her clothing died early yesterday, at Bristol Memorial Hospital. The Victim was Mrs. Powell Earhart of Rt. 1, Bluff City. Mrs. Earhart lived on the Thomas Bridge home of a son Lawrence Earhart at the intersection of Sperry Access Rd. and the highway which runs from Bluff City to Blountville.

Members of the family said they were unable to provide information on the tragedy. They said Mrs. Earhart apparently was burning trash at the time and that her clothing caught fire. They said they believed that it was some time before she was found since the trash had all burned out. Mrs. Earhart was rushed to the hospital here. She died at 5 a.m. yesterday.

Mrs. Earhart is survived by son Lawrence Earhart, three sisters Mrs. Glen Doane and Mrs. W. H. Cox, both of Blountville and Mrs. F. H. Price, Coral Gables FL; two brothers Dr. M. A. Sanders, Johnson City, and R. A. Sanders Bristol VA and a granddaughter Judy Olson, Abingdon, VA.
Children:

+ 1040. i **Charles Sanders EARHART** b. 1914.

+ 1041. ii **Lawrence Powell EARHART** b. 29 Aug 1918.

829. **Samuel Pearce EARHART**, (508.Charles[6], 185.Margaret[5], 40.Sarah[4], 6.Jane[3], 2.Robert[2], 1.John[1]) b. 5 Dec 1887 in Blountville, Sullivan Co., TN, d. 3 Aug 1977 in Sullivan Co., TN. Traveled a

good bit on RR. Met Mr. Moore who had leather goods business; soon partner. When Moore died Pierce ran the Co.. Brother Ralph also worked there at Moore-Earhart Co. on State St. in Bristol (1900-1976). Made harnesses on second and third floor; retail on first floor. Sold shoe fittings and athletic goods for 69 years. Named after uncle Sam Pearce (husband of Betsy Roller).

1920 lived 22 Ashe St. Bristol, TN.

1940 appears in the 1940 Bristol City Directory : Moore-Earhart Co. h 104 Spruce.

Died after short illness. He married **Eveleen Bryley MAUK**, married 16 Jun 1914 in Bristol, Sullivan Co., TN, b. 1894 in Morristown TN, d. 1965 in Bristol, Sullivan Co., TN. Moved to Bristol with her parents when she was nine.

Had Earhart family history by genealogist to get into DAR - through the Rhea side.
Children:

+ 1042. i **Margaret Kathleen EARHART** b. 24 Nov 1915.

+ 1043. ii **Etta Elizabeth EARHART** b. 1 Mar 1917.

830. **Margaretta R. EARHART**, (508.Charles[6], 185.Margaret[5], 40.Sarah[4], 6.Jane[3], 2.Robert[2], 1.John[1]) b. 1 Apr 1893 in Blountville, Sullivan Co., TN. She married **Archie T. DOANE**, b. 1893 in Sullivan Co., TN. 1930 the family is enumerated in the 18th Civil District of Sullivan Co. TN. Archie's brother Eugene is enumerated as the next household in the census.
   Doane, Argie T. (sic), head owns home, 37 married at 26, . TN, farmer.
   -- Margaret, wife-h, 37, married at 25, b. TN
(on the next page of the census)
   -- Doane, Balfour, son, 12, b. TN.
   -- Violet H., daughter, 4 11/12, b. TN (April 19 census date)
   -- Alice, mother, 63, widow, b. TN.
Children:

+ 1044. i **Balfour DOANE** b. 1917.

 1045. ii **Violet Helen DOANE**, b. 1 May 1925, d. BEF 1990. She married **Mr. ARCHER**, b. ABT 1930.

832. **Violet Etta EARHART**, (508.Charles[6], 185.Margaret[5], 40.Sarah[4], 6.Jane[3], 2.Robert[2], 1.John[1]) b. 29 Oct 1898 in Blountville, Sullivan Co., TN, d. 23 Jul 1949 in Sibley Hosp, Washington D.C., buried in Ft. Lincoln Cem. Prince George's Co MD. 1916 James' King College yearbook, 'Mephisto', was engraved with the name Violet Earhart. She was not a student, and it must have been a give from James, who was the yearbook editor. She would have been 17, and he 21 a the time.

1919 marriage license shows James was 24 and she 20 when they wed.

She and her family are enumerated in 'Notable Southern Families', by Zella Armstrong, 1922. She died of leukemia.

Obituary - Mrs. James Bouton - S. Pearce Earhart of this city has been notified of the death yesterday of his sister Mrs. Violet Earhart Bouton in Sibley Hospital, Washington, D.C. Mrs. Bouton was the daughter of the late Mr. and Mrs. Charles B. Earhart of Sullivan Co. and was born Oct. 29, 1898. In 1919 she married James O. Bouton and moved to Washington where her husband was employed in the Post Office Department. She joined the Presbyterian Church at Blountville at an early age and was a member of Sherwood Presbyterian Church at the time of her death. Besides S. Pearce Earhart, Mrs. Bouton is survived by her husband and two sons, James Bouton and Charles Bouton. She married **James O'dell BOUTON**, married 22 Apr 1919 in Sullivan Co., TN, b. 1 May 1893 in Emmitt, Sullivan Co. TN, d. 8 Jun 1978 in Dennisville, Cape May CO, NJ, buried 10 Jun 1978 in Cold Spring Presbyterian Cape May NJ. James grew up on farm in Emmet TN. It is said that his homestead is now under South Holston Lake as result of Tennessee Valley Authority dam project.

1909 he appears as a young baseball player in a 1909 photo published in Families and History of Sullivan Co. as a member of the Beidleman's school baseball team along with 9 other boys from the Hickory Tree area of the county.

When his father passed away, his family wanted him to run the farm. He attended college instead. 1908 attended King College. Left after two years, and in 1910 taught school at the one room Rhea School house. He boarded with the Earhart family in their home across the farm from the schoolhouse. This is when he met Violet Earhart, his future bride.

1911 he returned to King college and graduated in 1915. He was editor of the College Yearbook, 'Mephisto'. The graduating class of seniors numbered 12 that year. His class picture is accompanied by the notations: James O'Dell Bouton, B.S., Emmett, Tenn. Phiothesmian Literary Society, Winner Improvement Medal '10-11; Declaimer's Medal '10-'11,; Debater's Medal '12-'13, Oratorical Medal '12-'13; President Philothesmian Literary Society '12-'13; Anniversary Debater '12-'13, '14-'14; Editor "Mephisto'".

"Jim is noted for his much speaking. He entered King College with his mouth open and has not closed it since. But that he has spoken well may be gathered from the above list - for he has won every medal his society has offered. "J. O." would be a lawyer; after a course at Columbia, he is sure to rise rapidly in this profession, until some day he will plead cases before the united States Supreme Court - if not indeed sit on that bench."

1915 he was the winner, third honor Tennessee State Intercollegiate Oratorical Contest held as Maryville College, Maryville, Tenn, April 25, 1915 according to note in Violet Earhart's copy of the 1915 Mephisto.

After graduation he took a job with the Post office in Washington DC making $900. When his salary reached $1200 he went back to Bristol and married Violet Earhart. They bought a house on Monroe St. in Washington DC for $6500. Family speculation is that James promised to return each year with Violet for a visit with the TN family in exchange for his taking her so far from home. There are a quite a number of family photos showing he and Violet at the Earhart home in Blountville both before they were married and after the birth of their first son James Jr.

1920 Federal census index and in the enumeration has the family name misspelled as 'Boulten'. The name is written over seemingly to correct the spelling to Boulten. The couple appear enumerated in Washington D.C. at 2706 24th St. NE; the second family living in the residence, James renting from the owner:
  Boulten (sic), James O., head, rents, 25, b. TN, Clerk (General), U.S. Government.
  -- Violet, wife, 21, b. TN, no employment.

1930 Federal census index has the family name misspelled as 'Bonton.. They appear enumerated in Washington D.C. at 2857 Monroe Street N.E.:

  Bouton, James O., head, owns home, value $8,000, has radio, 35, married at 24, b. TN, Clerk, Federal Government.

  -- Violet E., Wife H, 31, married at 20, b. TN

  -- James O. Jr, son, 8, b. District of Columbia.

After his retirement he was very active for many years. He worked in his garden in Dennisville and traveled. He drove a bright yellow Chevy Camaro. Ed Foley remembers 'Pops' coming for a visit in 1975. 'Pops' had been expected to come visiting from New Jersey that day. When a yellow sports car with New Jersey license plates zoomed by while he was driving on the Beltway around Washington DC , he knew just who it was - 'Pops'.

'The Press' Cape May Edition, Saturday June 10, 1978- Obituary - James Bouton, 85 Was Postal Executive. Dennisville - James O Bouton, 85, of 52 Tuckahowe Road died Thursday in Burdette Tomlin Memorial hospital, Cape May Court House.

He was an attorney and executive of the U.S. Post Office Department in Washington D.C. for 47 years and was a will known speaker for the department at conventions and meetings throughout the country.

Born in Sullivan County Tenn., he attended King College and was a graduate of Southeast Law School in Washington D.C.

Mr. Bouton's grandfather was a colonel (James Odell) in the confederate army during the Civil War.

A resident of this community for 10 years, Mr. Bouton was a member of the Cape May Court House Historical Society ; a former president of the Cape May Kiwanis; a mason in Zollicoffer Lodge 444 F&AM of Tennessee; and chairman of the Dennis Township Board of Adjustments. He also served on the Cape May County Park Commission and was an elder in the Cold Spring Presbyterian Church.

Surviving are his wife, Charlotte Eldredge Bouton, two sons, James O. Jr. of Myrtle Beach SC and Charles E. of Chicago; and four grandchildren.

Services will be at 2 pm Sunday in the Cold Springs Presbyterian Church. Burial will be in the church cemetery. A viewing will take place one hour before the services. Expressions of sympathy in Mr. Bouton's memory may be in the form of donations to the Cold Spring Presbyterian Church. Arrangements are by the John C. Sudak Funeral Home, Cape May.

Children:

+ 1046. i   **James O'Delle BOUTON Jr.** b. 20 Apr 1921.

+ 1047. ii   **Charles Earhart BOUTON** b. 16 Jun 1930.

845. **Philip Boy EARHART**, (510.Joseph[6], 185.Margaret[5], 40.Sarah[4], 6.Jane[3], 2.Robert[2], 1.John[1]) b. 30 Nov 1910 in Blountville, Sullivan Co., TN, d. 13 Mar 1967 in Nashville, Davidson Co., TN, buried in Blountville Cemetery, Sullivan Co., TN. 1967 obituary - prominent Sullivan Co. farmer and political leader died of a heart attack in Nashville Monday morning. Mr. Earhart was stricken as he was leaving Southern Airways early morning flight to the state capital. Emergency aid was rendered at the airport, and he was rushed to Nashville General hospital where he was pronounced dead on arrival.

He had flown to Nashville for a scheduled meeting yesterday, of the State Soil Conservation committee of which he was a member. Mr. Earhart was president of the Sullivan Co. Farm Bureau and had been active for many years in Democratic Party affairs of the county and the state.

He was a close friend of Governor. Buford Elllington's and served on Ellington's campaign committee in Sullivan Co. last year. A native of Sullivan Co., Mr. Earhart lived on the Bluff City highway, just outside Bristol. He was a graduate of Maryville College and a member and elder of Blountville Presbyterian Church; a member of the State Farm Bureau's board of directors; a director of Milk Sales and the Appalachian Dairy Council; president of the Sullivan Co. Artificial Breeders Association and a director of East TN ABA. Survivors include his wife Mrs. Katy Brown Earhart, 2 sons Charles Philip Earhart and Robert Joseph Earhart both of Bristol; his mother Mrs. Joseph P. Earhart of Bristol; a sister, Mrs. J. P. Patton of Bristol, a nephew Sidney Patton, a niece Mrs. David Morris of Decherd TN.

Left 125 acres of the family farm to his family on his death in 1967. Farming of tobacco and silage for the Holstein cattle continue to this day. He married **Kathryn BROWN**, married 12 Apr 1947 in McMinnville, Warren Co., TN, b. 20 Aug 1922 in Viola, Warren Co., TN, d. 25 Apr 1980 in Bristol, Sullivan Co., TN, buried in Blountville Cemetery, Sullivan Co., TN. 1980 obituary - Mrs. Kathryn Earhart died Friday afternoon in Bristol Memorial Hospital of an apparent heart attack. She was the widow of Philip Earhart, a scion of the early settlers of Sullivan Co. They made their home at 'The Elms' farm on Volunteer Parkway.

Mrs. Earhart was a prominent leader in educational, civic, religious and social circles in Sullivan Co. She came to Bristol from McMinnville TN as assistant Home Demonstration Agent for Sullivan Co. in charge of the Girl's 4-H Clubs. She was a former teacher in Bluff City TN. At the time of her death, Mrs. Earhart was chairman of District V and vice president of the TN State Farm Bureau of Women. She was a volunteer adult leader in Sullivan Co. for 4-H Clubs. She was a member of the Sullivan Co. Farm Bureau and served as advisor of the Young Farmers and Homemakers of Sullivan Co. She had also served on the agriculture committee of the County Court and the Family Home Loan Administration. She was treasurer of the Sullivan Co. Retired Teacher's Association, president of the Bluff City Music Club, vice regent of the Volunteer Chapter of the DAR, membership chairman of the Sullivan Co. Historical Society and was representative for Sullivan Co. on the TN State Commission for "The Year of the Child".

Mrs. Earhart was scheduled to leave on May 7 for Hamburg, Germany, serving as a delegate for the TN State Farm Bureau Women to the 1980 meeting of the Associated Country Women of the World. She attended a similar conference in Nairobi, Kenya in 1977. She was an active member of the Democratic Party of Sullivan Co. and was a member of the Blountville Presbyterian Church. 2 sons, Charles P. and Robert Earhart both of Bluff City, TN, and one brother survive Mrs. Earhart, Lawrence Brown, Los Angeles, CA.

Children:

+ 1048. i **Robert Joseph EARHART** b. 2 Jul 1955.

+ 1049. ii **Charles Phillip EARHART** b. 2 Jul 1955.

855. **John Grant SUMMERS**, (513.Lewis[6], 190.Nannie[5], 43.John[4], 6.Jane[3], 2.Robert[2], 1.John[1]) b. 1907 in Washington Co., VA. He married **Leila JACKSON**, b. 27 Sep 1908 in Smyth Co., VA, d. 20 Jan 1998 in Palm Harbor, FL. 1998 her obituary appears in the New River Notes, of Upper New River Valley, NC and VA - age 89, died Tuesday Jan. 20, 1998 at the home of her daughter and son in law, Suzanne and Donald Farren, in Palm Harbor, FL.
Children:

> 1050. i **Suzanne SUMMERS**, b. ABT 1930. She married **Donald FARREN**.

868. **Virginia Douglas BYARS**, (524.Jane[6], 192.Sarah[5], 43.John[4], 6.Jane[3], 2.Robert[2], 1.John[1]) b. 21 May 1901 in Bristol, Washington Co., VA, d. 5 Oct 1999 in Bristol, Washington Co., VA, buried in Glenwood Cem. Bristol TN. She was educated at Sullins College, Bristol, VA.

1926 Kenneth, her first husband, passed away. She returned to Bristol, VA sometime after his death.

1930 Federal census shows Virginia a widow, living with her young son with her parents in Alcova Heights, Arlington Co., VA at Alvoca Avenue:
  Byars, J. Cloyd, head, owns home value $25,000, has radio, 61, married at 28, b. VA, attorney, private office.
  -- Jane B., Wife-H, 57, married at 23, b. VA.
  -- Bailey P., son, 24, single, b. VA, salesman, real estate.
  Coontz, Virginia, daughter, 27, widow, married at 22, b. VA, typist, U.S. Government.
  -- Robert Joseph, grandson, 4, single, b. VA

There were so many lovely parties at Virginia's home, especially her "Loving Hearts" dinners and her "Burning of the Greens" party every Christmas. One of the loveliest of these was on her birthday party May 1976 when she gave a beautiful buffet dinner and dance in the garden of her home, Old Derry Inn, in Blountville, TN. Educated at Sullins College, Bristol VA.

1940 Judge Caldwell and Virginia bought the Old Deery Inn and restored it to its former grandeur. There were so many lovely parties at Virginia's home, especially her "loving Hearts" dinners and her "Burning of the Greens" party every Christmas. One of the loveliest of these was on her birthday May 1976 when she gave a beautiful buffet dinner and dance in the garden of her home, Old Derry Inn, in Blountville.

Her obituary appeared in the Bristol News, Oct. 6, 1999. Virginia Byars Caldwell, 98, died in NHC Healthcare of Bristol VA. She lived in Norfolk and Arlington Co. VA, CA, Hawaii and again in Arlington County before returning to Bristol in 1931. She was the widow of US Navy LT. Kenneth Coontz and Judge Joseph Caldwell.

She was a member of Blountville Presbyterian Church, the National Society for Historic Preservation, the Washington Co. Historical Society and Fort Chiswell Chapter of the Daughters of the American Revolution.

She and Judge Caldwell began the restoration of the Old Derry Inn in Blountville in 1940 and she lived there until 1990 when she entered NHC Healthcare.

Surviving are a son Capt. Robert Joseph Coontz, US Navy retired of Alexandria VA, a brother Bailey Preston Byars of Falls Church VA, three stepsons, three grandchildren, a great grandchild, 14 step grandchildren, 22 step great grandchildren and several step great great grandchildren.

Mrs. Caldwell was also preceded in death by a stepson, Joseph Anderson Caldwell, Jr. Her interests were antiques, spinning and weaving cloth on antique wheels and looms, quilt making, chair caning, basket weaving in the manner of the Cherokee Indians, making apple butter in the pioneer style and preservation of old crafts. She married (1) **Kenneth Lee COONTZ**, married 8 May 1924 in Washington D.C., b. 5 May 1897 in San Francisco CA, d. 12 Sep 1926 in Washington D.C., buried in Arlington National Cemetery. Educated at the US Naval Academy in Annapolis MD, class of 1917. He was a LT. in the US Navy.

His only son was just 9 months old when Kenneth died. She married (2) **Joseph Anderson CALDWELL**, married 1932, b. 1884 in Bristol, Sullivan Co., TN. Joseph was a widower with four children when he married Virginia Byars Coontz a widow with one son. They were 3rd cousins.

Children by Kenneth Lee COONTZ:

+ 1051. i   **Robert Joseph COONTZ** b. 7 Jan 1926.

871. **Flournoy Benjamin TILLAR**, (525.Julia⁶, 192.Sarah⁵, 43.John⁴, 6.Jane³, 2.Robert², 1.John¹) b. 7 Oct 1896 in VA. 1930 Federal census shows the family enumerated in Emporia, Greeneville Co., VA living on Main Street, near Annie and Peter Tillar.

Tillar Flourney B. head, rents, pays $15/month, has a radio, age 34, married at 23, b. VA, merchant, hardware.

-- Mabel C., wife-h, 32, married at 21, b. VA.

-- Thomas C. son, 6, b. VA.

-- Francis (sic) L., daughter, 11/12, b. VA. He married **Mabel F. CATO**, married 15 Apr 1919, b. 1898 in VA.

Children:

1052. i   **Thomas C. TILLAR**, b. 1924 in VA.

1053. ii   **Frances L. TILLAR**, b. 1 May 1929 in VA.

874. **Julia Bailey TILLAR**, (525.Julia⁶, 192.Sarah⁵, 43.John⁴, 6.Jane³, 2.Robert², 1.John¹) b. 15 Feb 1906 in VA. She married **John Campbell ANDERSON III.**, married 12 Nov 1925, b. 1904 in Sullivan Co., TN, b. 1904 in TN. John and Julia were distant cousins, with Rev. Joseph Rhea, their common immigrant ancestor.

1930 Federal census shows the family enumerated in Louisville, Jefferson Co., KY living at 2120 Douglas Blvd.:

Anderson, John C., head, rents home for $75/month, has radio, age 26, married at 21, b. TN to parents from TN and NC, purchasing agent, tobacco corporation.

-- Julia T., wife-h, 24, married at 19, b. VA to parents from VA and TN.

-- Julia T, daughter, 2 (although written over), b. VA to parents from TN and VA.

Anderson, Thomas F., Brother, 23, single, b. TN to parents from TN and NC, credit manager, Tin Foil Co.

Children:

1054. i   **Julia T. ANDERSON**, b. 1928 in VA.

877. **Seaton Tinsley PRESTON, Jr. Jr.**, (529.Seaton⁶, 193.James⁵, 43.John⁴, 6.Jane³, 2.Robert², 1.John¹) b. 29 Aug 1921 in KY, d. 24 Sep 1994 in Winnetka, Cook Co., IL. 1951 Texas birth records shows Thomas Gaines Preston born in Travis Co. to Seaton and Aline Marie.

Social security death index confirms his date of birth and notes his death in 1994 in Cook Co., IL. He married **Aline Marie DEBBEAUT**, married 26 Jul 1945 in Antwerp, Belgium, b. ABT 1921 in Belgium?.

Children:

+ 1055. i   **Seaton Tinsley PRESTON III III.** b. 19 Jun 1946.

+ 1056. ii   **Christiane Marie PRESTON** b. 4 Sep 1947.

+ 1057. iii **JohnThomas PRESTON** b. 18 Mar 1949.

  1058. iv   **Thomas Gaines PRESTON**, b. 8 Sep 1951 in Travis Co., TX.

  1059. v   **Philip Keneth PRESTON**, b. 9 Aug 1956.

878. **James Brainard PRESTON**, (529.Seaton[6], 193.James[5], 43.John[4], 6.Jane[3], 2.Robert[2], 1.John[1]) b. 30 Mar 1923 in KY. He married **Cynthia Joan Houghton GLASSEN**, married 14 Apr 1951, b. ABT 1923.

  Children:

+ 1060. i   **Cynthia Houghton PRESTON** b. 5 Mar 1952.

+ 1061. ii   **James Brainard PRESTON, Jr. Jr.** b. 8 Aug 1954.

  1062. iii **Martha Leigh PRESTON**, b. 19 Mar 1960. She married **David Michael POWELL**, married 21 Aug 1982, b. ABT 1960.

879. **Frederick 'Fred' Leigh PRESTON**, (529.Seaton[6], 193.James[5], 43.John[4], 6.Jane[3], 2.Robert[2], 1.John[1]) b. 27 Jan 1930 in Charleston, Kanawha Co., WV. 1997 he began to maintain a Preston family home page. E-mail address - fpreston@ @iAmerica.net

1951 he graduated from Virginia Tech as a metallurgical engineer. He did consulting for gray, ductile and malleable iron foundries, also created web pages for individual and organizations.

Fred is from Charleston WV and his wife from Fair Haven NH. He had lived in Blacksburg, VA, Ft. Monmouth, NJ, Fredonia, NY, Natrona Heights, PA, Orange City, FL, St. Joe/ Benton Harbor, MI, Bisbee, AZ, Davis CA (not necessarily in that order) Lufkin, TX.

He has children in Fontana CA, St. Joe MI, Irving, TX, and Nacogdoches, TX. He has 9 grand daughter, and one great grand daughter and a two grand sons.

He retired, be entered real estates with Gann Medford Real Estate in Lufkin, TX. His hobbies include model railroading, video collecting, stamps, gardening, genealogy, wine making and computer programming. Also tennis and gold. He married **Betty Louise AUMACK**, married 15 Jan 1955, b. ABT 1930. 1996 she earned a Bachelor's in Social Work from SFA and worked part time.

Children:

+ 1063. i   **Frederick Leigh PRESTON, Jr. Jr.** b. 10 Oct 1955.

+ 1064. ii   **Linda Louise PRESTON** b. 23 Oct 1956.

+ 1065. iii   **Robert James PRESTON** b. 14 Aug 1961.

+ 1066. iv   **Rebecca Ann PRESTON** b. 11 Jun 1964.

881.   **Miriam Wiley PRESTON**, (530.John[6], 194.Samuel[5], 43.John[4], 6.Jane[3], 2.Robert[2], 1.John[1]) b. 26 Sep 1905 in Seoul, Korea, d. 22 Mar 2005 in Fairfax, MO. (Fairman Cumming November 23, 2005 phone conversation Foley from Decatur GA with Ed Foley) Miriam Wiley Preston was born in Seoul in September 1905. The family did not live in Seoul, but they went up to Seoul to have the baby because they thought the medical care would be better. They were living on the southwest coast of the country at the time. Annie had lost her first child and had concerns about the second just one year later. The first-born was buried in the Seoul Foreign cemetery after dying at 6 weeks.

Miriam received her BA at Agnes Scott College and her MA at Yale University, preparing her for her occupation as a college teacher.

Aunt Miriam married at the same time as the Bockhorsts (sister Florence) in a double wedding in Montreat, NC. Miriam helped her husband finish his PHD at Ohio State that summer and the following year. She was 4 or 6 years older, but did not find a man until after she got her masters degree at Yale. Although during the depression she managed to find several teaching jobs.

She died in Tarkio in 1964. She had just moved there when her son Fairman Preston St. Clair was killed in a car accident. There was a Tarkio College that has since closed about 10 years ago.

She would go out to visit her eldest daughter in Oregon who went to Stanford for her masters, cousin Mimi. (Cousin) Miriam was glad to get out of the Middle West and went to California and stayed at Stanford for many years. Married a fellow who was a computer wiz. They founded a computer company and she quit teaching and moved to Oregon.

(Aunt) Miriam would go out to visit and come back to Montreat every summer. She came to Montreat without a miss since 1938. Her husband was Kenneth St. Clair a history teacher. They had 4 children. Fairman died at 19. Charles St. Clair lives in Asheville NC in very nice house with a porch. He is the youngest. His wife is a teacher. Kenneth Jr. lives in Indiana. He works for Social Security Administration and has a stepdaughter, a daughter and a son (of his present wife, his high school sweetheart). He was married 3 times.

(Aunt) Miriam lived to be 99 and got to know her grandchildren very well even though they came along late in life.

2005 Indianapolis Star - Obituary - Miriam Wiley St. Clair
1905 - 2005 Age 99, of Tarkio, MO died Tuesday, March 22, 2005 at Community Hospital, Fairfax, MO. She was very active in the Presbyterian Church her entire life. Funeral services will be held 11 a.m. Saturday, March 26 at Tarkio Presbyterian Church, Tarkio, MO, with calling there 10 a.m. until time of service and 4 to 6 p.m. Friday, March 25 in Davis Funeral Home, Tarkio, MO. Interment will be held in Decatur Cemetery, Decatur, GA. Memorial contributions may be made to Tarkio Presbyterian Church, Tarkio, MO. She was preceded in death by her parents, John Fairman & Annie Shannon (Wiley) Preston; husband, Dr. Kenneth E. St. Clair; son, Fairman Preston St. Clair; two brothers, Rhea Preston, William Preston; one sister, Shannon Cumming. She is survived by her two sons, Kenneth E. St. Clair, Jr. & his wife, Mary Lea, Lanesville, IN, Charles St. Clair & his wife, Sue, Asheville, NC; one daughter, Miriam Wiley St. Clair & her husband Charles Guzis, Eugene, OR; three grandchildren, Heather Lea St. Clair, Michael Aaron St. Clair, Eric Kenneth St. Clair; one step-granddaughter, Leslie Chastain. She married **Kenneth Edison ST. CLAIR**, married 3 Sep 1938 in Montreat, Buncombe Co., NC, b. 3 Jul 1908 in Appleton, WI, d. 16

Nov 1996 in Montreat, Buncombe Co., NC. He was a professor of history at Tariko College, Tariko,,MO. After retirement, he took part in senior citizens running events. A member of the Rotary Club, he had perfect attendance for 15 years. His funeral service took place in the same chapel where he married 58 years earlier. He is buried in the Preston family plot in Decatur, GA. (!BIR,MAR,DEA,BUR: J & S Weihing, NE; Van Patten Family Records).

Children:

1067. i   **Miriam Wiley ST. CLAIR**, b. 30 May 1941 in Pikesville, KY. She received her BA from Agnes Scott College in Decatur, GA preparing her for her occupation as a teacher.

2005 she is mentioned in her mother's obituary as living in Eugene, OR. She married (1) **James E. GERARD**, married 1 Sep 1964, b. ABT 1941. She married (2) **Charles GUZIS**, married 1 Jul 1990, b. ABT 1941. He was educated at Purdue University.

Chuck Guzis is one of the principal founders of NTI. He provides advice based on his extensive experience with software companies and as a utility software developer. He also has developed several of NTI's computer forensics software tools. Mr. Guzis is also the President of Sydex, Inc. which is located in Eugene, Oregon. Sydex has specialized in the development of custom low level software applications and computer hardware devices.

Mr. Guzis has specialized expertise writing low level software utilities which directly access floppy diskettes, tape drives and hard disk drives. He is considered by many to be one of the few experts in the world regarding these specialized technical areas. He has been under contract to large corporations, such as IBM, to develop specialized software and computer hardware for specialized corporate needs. Mr. Guzis is also the author of several computer forensics software utility programs which have become the standards used in the field of computer forensics by military, government and law enforcement agencies throughout the United States,

Canada and other foreign countries, e.g., SafeBack, AnaDisk, and CopyQM. These programs were acquired by NTI in March 2000 from Sydex, Inc. and Mr. Guzis continues to provide software upgrade support for these unique forensic and security review products. He is also an expert concerning computer networks and in the development of forensic utilities for operating systems such as Unix, DOS, Windows 95, Windows 98, Windows NT and Windows 2000.

Mr. Guzis previously has worked in leadership roles for Control Data Corporation, Durango Systems, Inc., Stellar Software Systems and Peritus International, Inc. He also has participated as a technical editor for some of the major computer technology authors in the writing of books and publications which are popular with computer users worldwide. Mr. Guzis has a Bachelor of Science degree from Purdue University in Computer Science. He is also mentioned in the book, Computer Forensics, Computer Crime Scene Investigations by John R. Vacca concerning his pioneering work in the development of SafeBack. (http://www.forensics-intl.com/guzis.html).

+ 1068. ii **Kenneth Edison ST. CLAIR, Jr.** b. 30 Mar 1943.

1069. iii **Fairman Preston ST. CLAIR**, b. 10 Mar 1945 in Lexington, KY, d. 19 Oct 1964 in Tarkio, MO.

+ 1070. iv **Charles Ainsworth ST. CLAIR** b. 1 Apr 1948.

882. **Annie Shannon PRESTON**, (530.John[6], 194.Samuel[5], 43.John[4], 6.Jane[3], 2.Robert[2], 1.John[1]) b. 21 Oct 1907 in Salisbury, Rowan Co., NC, d. 8 Dec 2003 in Decatur, GA. (Fairman Cumming November 23, 2005 phone conversation Foley from Decatur GA with Ed Foley) My father and grandfather tried to tell me some of the family history; my grandfather especially tried. The last time I asked him to tell me the stories, he couldn't tell me any because he was getting a little fussy. He had a very good memory until he was 95, but when he was 70 or 75 I lived with him and that is when he tried to teach me his shorthand. He was living in the house and had a whole lot of history. He at that time was trying to trace some of his family history. His old letters were in the house, and the house burned, and

he was able to save a few of the old letters. It is extraordinary that he was able to keep up with the family since he was a missionary his whole life.

One of the cousins he kept up with was Caldwell and they ran an inn in TN. My grandparents kept up the their cousins the Caldwell's in Blountville. Interestingly they visited them shortly after they got back from Korea when they retired. It is remarkable that they could keep up with their former lives but they wrote letters. These people who were able and willing to write letters all their lives really left us a legacy. (This cousin was Virginia Douglas Byars Caldwell who owned the Derry Inn in Blountville TN - EFF). We have a number of cousins of some kind on the TN side of the border, and his family was on the Virginia side of the border. She was a cousin of my grandfather and one of the three or four of his cousins he kept up with, even while he was overseas.

Some of these cousins he kept up with for 50 or 60 years. That was remarkable. He did not go up to VA that much after he retired. In one of his letters just after he came back from Korea just before the Second World War start, when he was 70 years old. Summer of 1941 he wrote about a trip they took to Kentucky for just one day. They went to Pikeville KY and back to Asheville, Black Mountain. He was driving, and hadn't driven in this country that much. They managed to stop for lunch, visit his Caldwell relatives and get back to Black Mountain all in one day.

Two of the Preston cousins took a trip around the world and stopped in Hawaii and China but stopped to visit their cousin in Soonchong Korea. They continued on to Oberammergau and home after being away for a year. The trip ended in 1934. The book is called the Hitching Post.

The family kept up closely with the Watkins in California. My grandfather (John Fairman Preston) performed the wedding ceremony for Eleanor Fairman Preston and James Thomas Watkins after he was married, before he went to Korea. Eleanor was a doctor and she married a doctor. When they moved to San Francisco. His grandparents and parents would stay with them on their way back and forth across the continent from Korea.

Three brothers came from Scotland, we don't know who their parents were, about 1810. One was William; he may have already had a son. He had a son Daniel James Cumming who married a woman who may have been a cousin. Daniel James had an extremely long life in Baltimore. He delivered milk, and worked in a grocery and then became a teacher. He was a teacher all the way through the Civil War and lived a long and stable life in Baltimore and made enough to make a stable living as a teacher instead of delivering milk. One of his children was William Cumming, my grandfather who also did some of these odd jobs but eventually became a Presbyterian minister. He supplied a church in Longwood VA first, up in the mountains beyond Iron Gate. It was logging and mining country in the 1890's. He was in Blacksburg VA one year. Stanton Virginia was his third pastorate. Then he went up to Baltimore and came back to Stanton for a few years, then back to Baltimore and then for a long time to Kentucky. Would have stayed in KY, but lost that job and went back to Baltimore

My father Daniel James Cumming became a minister and had a master's degree from Columbia Teachers College. I am not sure why he came south (Daniel Cumming) except that it was cheaper to go to school in the south and he didn't have much money. He only went to seminary for only one year, but I think he was an effective minister.
In Korea he was in charge of various high school for most of his career. The high schools were closed when the Japanese wanted the students to bow down to the emperor. So my father was sort of out of a job the last 3 years there. He was born 1892 in Stanton VA. His father William Cumming was a native of Baltimore. He married a Stokes, a native Virginian. Leila Stokes (written as Louise, born in Virginia, in the 1900 Federal census for Maryland).

The place where I was place where I was born and where my brother and sister and two of my uncles were born in Soonchun Korea, the Presbyterian hospital, failed, but there is still a large catholic hospital there. When my own family needed medical help they would sometimes go over to the Catholic Hospital there. The leprosy center is still there. One of our neighbors was an Emery trained orthopedist who was the last head of the Wilson Leprosy Center. There is a nice little hospital there with 300 acres. This area near the town of Yasu at the very southern tip of Korea is where my brothers and sisters grew up. It is warm enough that they rarely had snow.

(Fairman Cumming November 23, 2005 phone conversation Foley from Decatur GA with Ed Foley)

311

Annie Shannon Preston, My mother was born in Salisbury NC in Oct 21 1907. She was a little girl when Daniel Cumming went to Korea. They married in 1934 in Decatur GA at home where they rented a house for furlough. She later was a lonely woman who lived 1/3 of her life after her husband died. They were married for 36 years, that's a good marriage.

My mother had 17 grandchildren.

When my mother finished college and went back again to Korea my father became reacquainted with her, the Georgia Peach. She and her older sister both made Phi Beta Kappa, as did their daughters and their granddaughters.

My mother died just 2 years ago. She kept her emotions under control, but I can see that some of these memories overwhelmed her. She was willing to let all of these things lie around. They went to school at home in Korea. They were in the Calvert system and read a whole lot. I just came across a list of the books they would have had at home in Korea. They had a live-in teacher in Korea who stayed with them to make sure they were ready to come to school back in this country.

My sister is living in Black Mountain. Her husband is in Korea. He is still acting like a missionary. He is in South Korea and will be going to North Korea soon. He speaks Korean very well. The northern language has diverged some though. He has gotten a drill rig to carry to North Korea to drill wells at hospitals so they can get water from underground. This is a project he invented. He was there helping them to set up a dental van and a TB van. He is trying to help make contact should the two countries begin to open up.

2003 Black Mountain News, Black Mountain, NC - obituary - Annie Shannon Preston Cumming
Decatur, Ga.

Annie Shannon Preston Cumming, of Decatur, Ga., who was born in Salisbury, on October 21, 1907, died Monday, December 8, 2003.

Her parents, John Fairman Preston and Annie Shannon Wiley Preston, raised her in Soonchun, Chulla Namdo, Korea, where they were missionaries for the Presbyterian Church, US, from 1903 to 1940. She and her husband, Daniel James Cumming (deceased in

1971) also served in Korea from 1934-40 and 1963-66; and at the First Presbyterian Church of Monroe, Ga., from 1966-68.

She is survived by three siblings, Miriam Wiley Preston St.Clair, of Tarkio, Mo., John Fairman Preston, Jr., of Pebble Beach, Calif., and Florence Preston Bockhorst, of Kirkwood, Mo. Her surviving children are William Cumming, of Nashville, Tenn., Fairman P. Cumming, of Decatur, Ga., Sarah Stokes C. Mitchell, of St. Louis, Mo., Shannon C. McCormick, of Decatur, Robert Bruce Cumming, of Christiana, Del., and Margaret C. Union, of Black Mountain (NC). She was also the beloved grandmother of 17 grandchildren.

A memorial service was held at Decatur Presbyterian Church on Monday, December 15. Gifts in lieu of flowers may be sent to Agnes Scott College, or to Decatur Presbyterian Church. She married **Daniel James 'Kim' CUMMING**, married 19 May 1934 in Decatur, GA, b. 1 Aug 1893 in Staunton, VA, d. 8 Jan 1971 in Decatur, GA. Researcher Roland Bockhorst shows his date of birth as Dec. 17, 1886 in Staunton, VA.

He received a BS in Chemistry from Kentucky Wesleyan and a BD from Louisville, Seminary in Kentucky. He became a Presbyterian Minister serving and raising his family in Korea.

1942 they moved back to the US to Decatur.
Children:

+ 1071. i **William CUMMING** b. 14 Feb 1935.

    1072. ii **Fairman Preston CUMMING**, b. 4 Mar 1937 in SoonChun, Korea. Received his BS in biology from Davidson College, Davidson, NC.

        1999 he donated a copy of the 1827 letter from James Preston in Co. Derry to Robert Preston to the Washington Co., VA Historical Society. The document notes it is from Fairman Preston Cummings for his mother Shannon Preston Cummings, 520 Ponce De Leon Place, Decatur, GA 30030.

        He was living with his mother in her last years at the family home.

+ 1073. iii **Anne Shannon CUMMING** b. 15 Jan 1939.

+ 1074. iv **Sarah Stokes CUMMINGS** b. 22 Feb 1942.

  1075. v **Robert Bruce 'Rev.' CUMMING**, b. 14 Apr 1946 in Homestead, FL. Received his BA in music from Florida Prebyterian College and his Master of Divinity from the San Francisco Seminary.

  2003 lived in Christiana, Delaware where he was associated with the Presbyterian Church there on Old Baltimore Pike.

+ 1076. vi **Margaret Wiley CUMMING** b. 5 Mar 1953.

883. **John Fairman PRESTON, Jr.**, (530.John[6], 194.Samuel[5], 43.John[4], 6.Jane[3], 2.Robert[2], 1.John[1]) b. 21 Aug 1909 in Kwangju, Korea. (Fairman Cumming November 23, 2005 phone conversation Foley from Decatur GA with Ed Foley)
The next is John Fairman Preston Jr. who is still living. He was born in Kwangju in 1909 August 22. He has lived in Pebble beach since 1977 and lived next to Stanford at one time.

Uncle Johnny had a number of reasons to go back and forth. When he finished college he took a trip around the world. Uncle William got TB and had to be brought back and Uncle Johnny went to meet him. Our Watkins cousins lived in California. There were four Watkins sons; one became and orthopedist, one became a professor of Economics at Stamford University. This is a line that the family stayed close to. Uncle Johnny often visited with them. Their house for years was on a bluff over the Golden Gate.

He married a woman who had spent nearly 2 years in Korea. She was a duke university graduate. She had grown up and lived her life in Washington, except for the time she would spend with her family at a place they had in Martha Vineyard in the summer. She was Imogene Bird. Not any connection to the Birds who were political. It was her mothers and grandmothers side, which had the money. Her father had founded a Presbyterian church especially for visiting tourists called Church of the Pilgrims. The Presbyterian ministers' wife left the money to build that church, and the mother of that person was said to have donated the money to restore Salem North Carolina.

My aunt (Imogene Bird Cumming) spent money traveling and did not have much money to pass on to their son and daughter. They took a nice cruise around the world every year or two.

He had spent 3 years as a doctor in Korea and came back in Oct 1940. He was a very well trained and experienced doctor but needed a job when he returned from Korea. Within a few months of their returning he was called up to Virginia as a plant doctor at the Hercules Powder Plant in Radford VA. He lived just up the road from Abingdon (the location of Walnut Grove, the ancestral Preston home in Virginia). His wife was living in a hot little valley in Virginia for a number of years and welcomed a change to live in California. They moved to California to live nicely. Has lived in California since 1957, half of his life. He made enough money to buy a retirement home in Pebble Beach, but it took everything he had. He turned blind within a few months of retiring. He had cataracts.

He had a son who was an air force pilot, piloted Phantoms, who was shot down in Vietnam, but survived that one. He was later killed in a Phantom crash in the Chesapeake Bay at age 40 while flying on a mission for the Reserves. His memorial is in Arlington Cemetery, his mother being from Washington DC. His son who was John Fairman Preston IV was killed in a hang gliding accident shortly after he was married in California. He got the wrong wind. He died in a hang glider, John Preston III died in a Phantom, and John Preston II is still alive in his 90's. John Fairman Preston I lived to be 100 and the first of that name is ruminating up at Walnut Grove bone yard.

1990 I visited the Walnut grove cemetery when they were building a shopping center there. My father has some letters where they sent some money to keep up the cemetery. He married **Imogene BIRD**, b. ABT 1913.

Children:

+ 1077. i **John Fariman PRESTON III** b. 1942.

   1078. ii **Andrew Bird PRESTON**, b. 1945 in Chattanooga, TN. Attended the University of California at Santa Barbara.

   1079. iii **Sally ANne PRESTON**, b. ABT 1946.

884.   **Florence Sutphen PRESTON**, (530.John[6], 194.Samuel[5], 43.John[4], 6.Jane[3], 2.Robert[2], 1.John[1]) b. 16 Sep 1911 in Salisbury, Rowan Co., NC. (Fairman Cumming November 23, 2005 phone conversation Foley from Decatur GA with Ed Foley)
Aunt Florence (Florence Sutphen Preston Bockhorst) is still living. She was born in Salisbury Sept 1911, in a house that is still standing, during that year that was my grandmothers last year as a Salisbury belle. When she got married in 1938, her husband, who was a professor of architecture at Washington University in St. Louis, built the house that she is still living in. Her son wants her to come to Florida this year, but she is still living in the house she moved into in 1938 after she got married to Roland Bockhorst.

In 1934 the Cumming family was going back over to Korea. After staying in the US a year, mother Annie Preston got married in Decatur and her sister Florence had finished at Agnes Scott College (Atlanta's Presbyterian Women's College since 1889). They were on board ship after seeing the Watkins family and were going out under the golden gate bridge. Florence, called Sacha ('Say-gee' a Korean nickname) was returning to live for 2 years and teach the younger children. Each of the other 2 daughters also did this. She also received her MS at the University of Tennessee.

Meanwhile, Roland Bockhorst was in dire straights when he started school, but he eventually put himself through Washington University (St. Louis). He did so well that Mr. Bockhorst had won an architectural prize right in the middle of the depression. He had been putting himself though college working in filling stations and now he was being sent around the world to study architecture expenses paid. He was standing on the deck when they went through the Golden Gate. Aunt Florence, who was extremely cute and pretty, climbed up waving a sheet at the Watkins not far away. Roland noticed this cute girl and managed to introduce himself. He was very good looking and becoming an accomplished architect. He was ready 4 years later to marry her and to move into the house that Florence has lived in for 70 years. That is how they met.

Their son Fairman Bockhorst has done work on the family on the computer. Fairman Bockhorst's only son is Jonathan Fairman Bockhorst who is now a sophomore at the University of Florida.

2003 obituary of her sister Annie Shannon Preston Cumming of Decatur GA indicated Florence Preston Bockhorst lived in Kirkwood, MO. She married **Roland Walter BOCKHORTST**, married 3 Sep 1938 in Montreat, Buncombe Co., NC, b. 16 Jan 1905 in St. Louis, MO,[1] d. 31 May 1995 in Kirkwood, MO. 1920 Federal census shows Roland as a young man living with his widowed mother and 4 siblings in St. Louis MO, age 15.

He was a Professor of Architecture at Washington University, St. Louis, MO.

1995 June 3, St. Louis Post-Dispatch
Roland Walter Bockhorst, professor emeritus at the Washington University School of Architecture, died Wednesday (May 31, 1995) of infirmities at his home in Kirkwood. He was 90.
Mr. Bockhorst taught courses in descriptive geometry, architectural graphics and materials of construction and specifications for 36 years at Washington University. He retired from the university in 1972.

He was past secretary, treasurer and vice president of the St. Louis chapter of the American Institute of Architects (AIA). In 1991, Mr. Bockhorst received the AIA St. Louis.
Children:

+ 1080. i **Roland Preston BOCKHORTST** b. 14 Jul 1940.

+ 1081. ii **Rhea Wiley BOCKHORTST** b. 29 Sep 1942.

+ 1082. iii **Mary Ann BOCKHORTST** b. 12 Jun 1944.

+ 1083. iv **Fairman Kennedy BOCKHORTST** b. 21 Dec 1950.

886. **Rhea Sutphen 'Dr.' PRESTON**, (530.John[6], 194.Samuel[5], 43.John[4], 6.Jane[3], 2.Robert[2], 1.John[1]) b. 15 Mar 1921 in Soon Chun, Korea, d. 5 Jan 1995. Educated at Davidson College and Duke University Medical School.

(Fairman Cumming November 23, 2005 phone conversation Foley from Decatur GA with Ed Foley)
The youngest uncle was born in 1923 and was unexpected. Rhea Sutphen Preston born the same house in Korea I was born in. This is the house my grandfather had built when they moved from Soonchun from Kwangju. Kwangju sometimes makes the national

[1] *Social Security Death Index.*

news about Korea. Yasu has a huge steel mill just 20 miles south of
Soonchun. Uncle Ray was an air force surgeon. It was an
extraordinary amount of stress. He had the genetics to live to be 85
but died at 71. (Researcher Fairman Bockhorst indicated Rhea's
birth date was March 15, 1921 and his death occurred in 1992).

Emory University School of medicine 1998 Spring newsletter notes
in Deaths of Residency Training and Fellowship Alumni: Rhea
Sutphen Preston (surgery) of Prattveill, Ala, on Jan 5, 1995. He
married **Katherine GAINES**, b. ABT 1923.
Children:

   1084. i   **Katherine Gaines PRESTON**, b. 1949. She
married **Samuel FOREMAN**, b. ABT 1949.

   1085. ii   **Annie Shannon PRESTON**, b. 1952.

   1086. iii **Rhea Stphen PRESTON, Jr.**, b. ABT 1954.

+ 1087. iv **Patsy PRESTON** b. ABT 1956.

895. **Thomas Fain NEWMAN**, (538.Carol[6], 195.Jennie[5], 43.John[4],
6.Jane[3], 2.Robert[2], 1.John[1]) b. 1902. He married **Marjorie COLE**,
married 1926.
Children:

   1088. i   **Carolyn NEWMAN**, b. ABT 1930.

   1089. ii   **Thomas NEWMAN**, b. ABT 1932. He was a
geologist who lived in Ft. Worth, TX.

897. **Carol Montomery NEWMAN, Jr.**, (538.Carol[6], 195.Jennie[5],
43.John[4], 6.Jane[3], 2.Robert[2], 1.John[1]) b. 1910 in VA. He taught
several periods at Virginia Polytechnic Institute

1949-1969 he pursued a career in Journalism that included working
as an editor of the New Yorker for 20 years. He married **Jean
MILLS**, married 1942, b. ABT 1910.
Children:

   1090. i   **Nancy NEWMAN**, b. ABT 1940.

   1091. ii   **Steven NEWMAN**, b. ABT 1942.

898. **James Preston NEWMAN**, (538.Carol[6], 195.Jennie[5], 43.John[4], 6.Jane[3], 2.Robert[2], 1.John[1]) b. 1913, d. 1982. 'Preston' was an instructor, Assistant Professor and Associate Professor from 1939 to 1978 at Virginia Polytechnic Institute. The Newmans lived on 'Faculty Row' on campus. He married **Katherine LONG**, b. ABT 1913 in Blacksburg, VA.
Children:

   1092. i   **Florence NEWMAN**, b. ABT 1940.

   1093. ii   **James Preston NEWMAN, Jr.**, b. ABT 1942.

904. **Elizabeth Gray JUDKINS**, (550.Anne[6], 212.Elizabeth[5], 47.John[4], 8.John[3], 3.Walter[2], 1.John[1]) b. 10 Oct 1928. She married **George FURGE**, married 23 Apr 1952, b. ABT 1928.
Children:

   1094. i   **Mary Anne Elizabeth FURGE**, b. 15 Oct 1952.

   1095. ii   **Teresa Georgia FURGE**, b. 18 Apr 1954.

   1096. iii   **George FURGE Jr.**, b. 3 Dec 1956.

   1097. iv   **Edwin Judkins FURGE**, b. 1 1958.

905. **Anne Peyton JUDKINS**, (550.Anne[6], 212.Elizabeth[5], 47.John[4], 8.John[3], 3.Walter[2], 1.John[1]) b. 8 May 1931. She married **Richard 'Dr.' Eugene HAGER**, married 1 Aug 1955, b. ABT 1931 in Huntington, Cabell Co. WV.
Children:

   1098. i   **David Peyton HAGER**, b. 8 Jul 1958.

   1099. ii   **Peter Chrispin HAGER**, b. 24 Jul 1959.

   1100. iii   **Anne Ferrell HAGER**, b. 16 Sep 1961.

   1101. iv   **Elizabeth Henry HAGER**, b. 27 Feb 1963.

   1102. v   **Thomas Preston HAGER**, b. 13 May 1965 in Huntington, Cabell Co. WV.

   1103. vi   **John Wallace HAGER**, b. 13 May 1965. Twin of Thomas.

906. **Robert GRAY VI. VI.**, (551.Robert[6], 212.Elizabeth[5], 47.John[4], 8.John[3], 3.Walter[2], 1.John[1]) b. 29 Sep 1922. He married **Evelyn LOGGANS**, married 16 Sep 1943, b. ABT 1922.
Children:

    1104. i   **Gloria GRAY**, b. 14 Apr 1947.

    1105. ii   **Barbara GRAY**, b. 6 May 1948.

    1106. iii   **John Robert GRAY**, b. 17 Jan 1950.

907. **Elizabeth Harrison GRAY**, (551.Robert[6], 212.Elizabeth[5], 47.John[4], 8.John[3], 3.Walter[2], 1.John[1]) b. 3 Jul 1931. She married **Alfred Lester HACKLEROAD**, married 2 Aug 1951, b. ABT 1931.
Children:

    1107. i   **Alfred L. HACKLEROAD**, b. 3 Oct 1952.

    1108. ii   **Richard Asher HACKLEROAD**, b. 2 Jul 1954.

    1109. iii   **Amelia Nell HACKLEROAD**, b. 28 Dec 1957.

    1110. iv   **Jennifer Irene HACKLEROAD**, b. 14 Mar 1965.

908. **Laura Melinda GRAY**, (551.Robert[6], 212.Elizabeth[5], 47.John[4], 8.John[3], 3.Walter[2], 1.John[1]) b. 17 Apr 1939. She married **Frank Winston FLEU**, married 26 Feb 1961, b. ABT 1939.
Children:

    1111. i   **Frank Winston FLEU Jr.**, b. 5 Apr 1962.

    1112. ii   **Robert Asher FLEU**, b. 19 May 1963.

    1113. iii   **Helen Kate FLEU**, b. 19 Dec 1967.

909. **Mary Preston GRAY**, (551.Robert[6], 212.Elizabeth[5], 47.John[4], 8.John[3], 3.Walter[2], 1.John[1]) b. 17 Apr 1939. Twin of Laura. She married **Bruce Jeffries BLACK**, b. ABT 1939.
Children:

    1114. i   **Bruce Jeffries BLACK Jr.**, b. 26 Jan 1965.

    1115. ii   **Mary Katherine BLACK**, b. 27 Jun 1967.

910. **John Montgomery PRESTON V.**, (554.John[6], 213.Cochran[5], 47.John[4], 8.John[3], 3.Walter[2], 1.John[1]) b. 1938 in VA?. He married **Elizabeth Dean SESSIONS**, married 15 Jul 1961 in E, b. 5 Dec 1939 in Eufaula, AL.
Children:

+ 1116. i **Louise Virginia PRESTON** b. 19 Jul 1962.

1117. ii **Elizabeth 'Betsy' Dean PRESTON**, b. 22 Mar 1970.

1118. iii **John Montgomery PRESTON**, b. 15 Dec 1970 in Chattanooga, TN.

911. **Charles Dean PRESTON**, (554.John[6], 213.Cochran[5], 47.John[4], 8.John[3], 3.Walter[2], 1.John[1]) b. 1938. Twin of John. He married **Patricia OWENS**, b. 8 Mar 1939 in Kings Mountain, NC.
Children:

1119. i **Charles Dean PRESTON**, b. 14 Oct 1966.

+ 1120. ii **Elinor Catharine PRESTON** b. 19 Dec 1968.

912. **Leslie Daffin PRESTON**, (554.John[6], 213.Cochran[5], 47.John[4], 8.John[3], 3.Walter[2], 1.John[1]) b. 24 Nov 1939. He married **Esther Carla KIRKPATRICK**, married 26 Aug 1962, b. ABT 1939 in Newport, TN.
Children:

1121. i **Miriam Graham PRESTON**, b. 2 May 1968. She married **Kevin DAVIE**, b. ABT 1968.

918. **Elizabeth Covette BRODNOX**, (568.Mary[6], 254.Robert[5], 73.Anne[4], 13.Fairman[3], 3.Walter[2], 1.John[1]) b. 8 Jul 1917. She married **John Fredrick CARPENTER**, married 17 Aug 1935, b. 13 Sep 1909, d. 10 Mar 1961.
Children:

1122. i **Elizabeth B. CARPENTER**, b. 6 Aug 1935 in VA?. She married **Bobby Gerald SMITH**, married 26 Dec 1956, b. 24 Dec 1933.

931. **Jane Preston BUCKLES**, (623.Eva[6], 322.John[5], 98.John[4], 21.Robert[3], 4.Jannette[2], 1.John[1]) b. 11 Feb 1944 in Sullivan Co., TN.

Holds degrees from University. of Tennessee Knoxville, George Peabody College of Vanderbilt University. and West Ga. College. She, like her mother is a librarian. ('Family History of Sullivan Co.', 1992)

2000 she was living in Maxon, NC. She married **Robert C. HERSCH**, married 13 Mar 1971, b. 17 Mar 1941 in NC, d. 18 Oct 1989 in NC.

Children:

1123. i **William Preston HERSCH**, b. 14 Jul 1976 in Maxton NC. 2000 he was living in Wilmington, NC.

932. **Evanda Lee RHEA**, (625.Lysle[6], 324.Josiah[5], 98.John[4], 21.Robert[3], 4.Jannette[2], 1.John[1]) b. 18 Sep 1942 in Greenville, FL, d. 10 Sep 2004 in Bay Co., FL, buried in Lynn Haven Cem., Bay Co., FL. Worked in programming for radio stations; then as a registered nurse (1999). She married **Richard Lee SALLINGER**, married 20 Apr 1962 in Panama City, Bay Co., FL, b. 25 Oct 1939 in Niangua, MO. 1999 worked as a supervisor for a gas company. Retired from USAF.

Children:

1124. i **Wesley Edward SALLINGER**, b. 15 Apr 1963 in FL?. Unmarried in 1999, working as an insurance and financial advisor.

+ 1125. ii **Kenneth Wade SALLINGER** b. 17 Apr 1964.

+ 1126. iii **Patrick Rhea SALLINGER** b. 19 Feb 1974.

933. **Walter Joseph 'Joe' KIRVIN**, (626.Gwendolyn[6], 324.Josiah[5], 98.John[4], 21.Robert[3], 4.Jannette[2], 1.John[1]) b. 10 Nov 1929 in Apalachicola, Franklin Co., FL, d. 21 Apr 1999 in Apalachicola, Franklin Co., FL, buried in Magnolia Cem., Apalachicola, FL. He was a lifelong resident of Apalachicola. He was a house painter and worked in the seafood industry. He was a Baptist. He married **Barbara Abb WORDEN**, b. ABT 1930 in Rainbow Springs, WV.

Children:

1127. i **Cindy Ann KIRVIN**, b. 16 Oct 1949 in Apalachicola, Franklin Co., FL. Attended Chapman HS, Chipola Jr. College and North FL Jr. College in Madison Co., FL. She married (1) **Robert VOLZ**, b. ABT 1949. She married (2) **James Donald**

YEAGER, married 6 Oct 1984 in Tallahassee, Leon Co., FL, b. 3 May 1939 in Indianapolis, Marion Co., IN.

1128. ii **Madelyn KIRVIN**, b. ABT 1955. 1998 lived in Tallahassee FL; 1999 at Wayside Farm Rd., Havana FL 32333, ph. (850)539-3714. She had children. She married **Joe PULLEN**, b. ABT 1955.

1129. iii **Steven Joseph KIRVIN**, b. ABT 1964. Lived in Tallahassee in 1999 at 1438 Tami Trail, ph (850)877-5730.

1130. iv **Walter Joseph KIRVIN Jr.**, b. ABT 1966. Died when he drown in a flooded storm culvert attempting to save a friend.

934. **Jesse Franklin KIRVIN, Sr.**, (626.Gwendolyn[6], 324.Josiah[5], 98.John[4], 21.Robert[3], 4.Jannette[2], 1.John[1]) b. 26 Nov 1932 in Auburn, Bay Co., FL, d. 17 Aug 2002 in Lacombe, LA, buried in Magnolia Cem., Apalachicola, FL. His name has been spelt variously with 'e' and 'ie'.

1999 lived in Lacombe, LA at 60418 W. Spruce Ln. He had attended Chapman HS in Apalachicola, FL. Was in the National Guard, BIOC, Ft. Benning GA. Retired as seafood dealer and station manager. He married **Margaret Shirley STEPP**, married 29 Jul 1951 in Clarksville, Calhoun Co., FL, b. 17 May 1933 in Carlsbad, Eddy Co., NM. Attended Chapman HS in Apalachicola FL and Southern Louisiana University at Hammond, LA.
Children:

1131. i **Jesse Franklin KIRVIN Jr.**, b. 5 Nov 1952 in Apalachicola, Franklin Co., FL.

1132. ii **Jason Allen KIRVIN**, b. 24 Jul 1954 in Apalachicola, Franklin Co., FL, d. 1974, buried in Magnolia Cem., Apalachicola, FL. Died in an automobile accident.

1133. iii **Jonathan Preston KIRVIN**, b. 22 Aug 1959 in Apalachicola, Franklin Co., FL. 1999 lived at 318 Avery Dr. Slidell LA 70461 ph (504)646-3435.

1134. iv **Jennifer Velora KIRVIN**, b. 12 Feb 1962 in Apalachicola, Franklin Co., FL. She married **Mr. LOTT**, b. ABT 1962.

935. **Virginia KERVIN**, (626.Gwendolyn[6], 324.Josiah[5], 98.John[4], 21.Robert[3], 4.Jannette[2], 1.John[1]) b. ABT 1934. Married several times. 1999 lives in Biloxi, Miss. She married (1) **Danny HARTLEY**, b. ABT 1934. She married (2) **Mr. SNEED**, b. ABT 1932.

Children by Danny HARTLEY:

1135. i **Patricia HARTLEY**, b. ABT 1960.

936. **Susie Virginia KIRVIN**, (626.Gwendolyn[6], 324.Josiah[5], 98.John[4], 21.Robert[3], 4.Jannette[2], 1.John[1]) b. ABT 1940. 1999 lived at 2113 O'Donnel Blvd, Gulfport, MS 39507 (228)896-1071. She married **Sylvan S. SNEED**, b. ABT 1940.

Children:

1136. i **Patricia SNEED**, b. ABT 1970.

1137. ii **Gwendolyn SNEED**, b. ABT 1972.

1138. iii **Melinda SNEED**, b. ABT 1974.

942. **William D. DULANEY, Jr.**, (635.William[6], 329.Nancy[5], 102.Robert[4], 21.Robert[3], 4.Jannette[2], 1.John[1]) b. ABT 1920 in TN?. He married **Wife of William DULANEY**, b. ABT 1920.

Children:

1139. i **David DULANEY**, b. ABT 1960 in Blountville, Sullivan Co., TN.

1140. ii **Suzanne DULANEY**, b. 1961 in Blountville, Sullivan Co., TN, d. 15 Apr 1966 in Blountville, Sullivan Co., TN, buried in Blountville Cemetery, Sullivan Co., TN. Obituary - A 5 year old Blountville girl died yesterday of injuries received when she fell from a swing at her home. Bristol Memorial Hospital reported Suzanne Dulaney, daughter of Mr. and Mrs. W. D. Dulaney Jr. died about noon of internal injuries.

1141. iii **Charlotte DULANEY**, b. ABT 1962.

947. **Lyle Blake SPURGEN**, (654.Beulah⁶, 340.Samuel⁵, 105.Robert⁴, 22.Margaret³, 4.Jannette², 1.John¹) b. 5 Mar 1927 in TN, d. 24 Nov 1991. He married **Patty REPASS**, b. ABT 1935.
Children:

+ 1142. i   **Debrah Lynn 'Debbie' SPURGEON** b. ABT 1960.

   1143. ii   **Howard SPURGEON**, b. ABT 1962.

948. **James Haskew 'Jerry' FICKLE**, (658.Haskew⁶, 340.Samuel⁵, 105.Robert⁴, 22.Margaret³, 4.Jannette², 1.John¹) b. 5 Dec 1946 in TN?. He married **Deanne Carol wife of James FICKLE**, married 25 Oct 1970, b. 5 Dec 1946.
Children:

+ 1144. i   **Lisa FICKLE** b. 22 Jul 1966.

+ 1145. ii   **David FICKLE** b. 30 Dec 1967.

   1146. iii   **Michael FICKLE**, b. 21 Oct 1971.

949. **Dorothy Eileen FICKLE**, (658.Haskew⁶, 340.Samuel⁵, 105.Robert⁴, 22.Margaret³, 4.Jannette², 1.John¹) b. 29 Aug 1948 in TN?. She married **Ronald Ray ENSOR**, b. ABT 1948.
Children:

+ 1147. i   **Kristi Leigh ENSOR** b. 21 May 1970.

   1148. ii   **Cynthia Ann ENSOR**, b. 1 May 1971.

+ 1149. iii   **Kimberly Renee ENSOR** b. 26 Apr 1973.

   1150. iv   **Rhoda Lea ENSOR**, b. 11 Mar 1975.

951. **Judy Ann FICKLE**, (658.Haskew⁶, 340.Samuel⁵, 105.Robert⁴, 22.Margaret³, 4.Jannette², 1.John¹) b. 11 May 1953. She married **Roger Hurley PHILLIPS**, married 27 Jul 1973, b. 3 Sep 1974.
Children:

   1151. i   **Amanda Susanne PHILLIPS**, b. 3 Sep 1974. She married **Ronald HOLTSCLAW**, married 24 Jul 1995, b. ABT 1974.

1152. ii   **Roger Matthew PHILLIPS**, b. 22 Apr 1977. He
married **Michelle Lea BOYD**, married 29 Jul 1996,
b. ABT 1977.

953. **Lynda Sue 'Susie' FICKLE**, (658.Haskew[6], 340.Samuel[5],
105.Robert[4], 22.Margaret[3], 4.Jannette[2], 1.John[1]) b. 5 Aug 1955 in
TN?. She married **Virgil Ray GARLAND**, married 3 Jun 1978, b.
12 Jul 1985.

Children:

1153. i   **Ashely Renee GARLAND**, b. 12 Jul 1985.

1154. ii   **Benjamin Hunter GARLAND**, b. 10 Apr 1988.

1155. iii   **Joshua James GARLAND**, b. 27 Oct 1992.

955. **Frances Adele RHEA**, (676.Edward[6], 349.Matthew[5],
107.Elizabeth[4], 23.Matthew[3], 4.Jannette[2], 1.John[1]) b. 27 Oct 1916 in
Lexington, Holmes Co. MS. 1924 moved with the family to
Memphis TN to receive medical care for Typhoid fever.

1935 graduated from Central HS in June 1935. Attended Memphis
State University on scholarship 1935-37 and Miller-Hawkins
Secretarial School 1937-38. Selected as a member of the National
Honor Society.

1938-49 moved to Philippine Islands while her husband was in the
Army. Lived in Memphis since 1949. Secretary at a chemical
company. She married (1) **Richard Hanslow HARRISON**, married
9 Feb 1938 in Memphis, Shelby Co., TN, b. 1 Apr 1911 in Meridian,
MS, d. 29 Nov 1989 in Arlington, Fairfax Co., VA. After his
father's death, moved with his mother to Atlanta, GA, her native
state. Attended schools in Atlanta and Georgia Tech. Received civil
service commission with US Engineering Corps in Memphis TN in
1937. Transferred to Poplar Bluff MO to work on Wappapello Dam
project as soils engineer. Held reserve officer commission in US
Army and was called to active duty May 1941.

Served New Caledonia, Germany and Canada. Later employed by
the Federal Aviation Agency in Leesburg VA. Married Twice. She
married (2) **James Albert MURPHY**, married 8 Oct 1949 in
Hernando, Desoto Co. MS, b. 10 Aug 1910 in Newark, Essex Co.
NJ. 1928 graduated from Belleville HS. In business with his

brothers in Newark, NJ until 1939 when he went to England and served until 1945 with the Royal Air Force.

1947-49 US Security Division and Army Ordinance in Philippine Islands.

1950 until he retired worked as a precision inspector for Hunter Division of Robbins and Myers.

2000 obituary - JAMES ALBERT MURPHY, 89, of Memphis, retired quality-control supervisor for Hunter Fan Co., died of heart failure Sunday at Kirby Pines Nursing Home. Forest Hill Funeral Home East has charge. He was a Catholic and a World War II Royal Air Force veteran. Mr. Murphy, the husband of Frances Rhea Murphy for 50 years, also leaves a stepdaughter, Lynne Harrison Gardner of Charlottesville, Va.; two stepsons, Richard Harrison Jr. of Columbia, Md., and Gene Lee Harrison of Leesburg, Va., three step grandchildren and two step great-grandchildren. The family requests that any memorials be sent to a charity of the donor's choice.
Reprinted from Commercial Appeal, on-line 4-18-2000.
Children by Richard Hanslow HARRISON:

+ 1156. i **Lynn HARRISON** b. 16 Sep 1941.

+ 1157. ii **Richard Hanslow HARRISON. Jr.** b. 23 Jun 1944.

   1158. iii **Gene Lee HARRISON**, b. 25 Feb 1946 in Brownwood, Brown Co., TX. Married twice but has no children. Flys search and rescue. His father had been living in Leesburg and he came to the area and lives there (1995). Graduated with a degree in electrical engineering from Virginia Tech. Worked at Mitre Corp. He married (1) **Ellen SIMON**, married in Strasburg, Shenandoah Co., VA, b. ABT 1946 in TN?. He married (2) **Suzanne Marie OLSEN**, married 20 Jun 1970 in Springfield, Fairfax Co., VA, b. ABT 1946 in TN?.

956. **Thomas Edward RHEA**, (676.Edward[6], 349.Matthew[5], 107.Elizabeth[4], 23.Matthew[3], 4.Jannette[2], 1.John[1]) b. 6 Jan 1920 in Lexington, Holmes Co. MS, d. 2 Jan 1999 in Paris, Lamar Co. TX, buried 6 Jan 1999 in Denison Cemetery, Idabel, OK. 1937 graduated from Central HS.

1941 received a BS from Mississippi College. Received medical training at University of TN in Memphis. After his time in the service a friend asked if he would like to come to Oklahoma and work as the company doctor for Dirks Paper company. Took the job in Oklahoma and also had his own

Lived in Idabell OK (1995).

private practice there for 50 years. Died of a heart attack at St. Joseph Hospital. He married (1) **Helena Annette CARD**, married 5 Feb 1944 in Memphis, Shelby Co., TN, b. 11 Aug 1918 in Palo Alto, Santa Clara Co. CA, d. 31 May 1990 in Idabel, McCurtain Co. OK, buried in Denison Cemetery, Idabel, OK. Was a pharmacists mate 2nd class in the Navy in WWII. One of the original WAVES. Died of carcinoid cancer. He married (2) **Josephine TOWNSEND**, married 25 Nov 1991 in Idabel, McCurtain Co. OK, b. 18 Feb 1943 in Farris OK.

Children by Helena Annette CARD:

+ 1159. i **Thomas Edward RHEA, Jr.** b. 2 1945.

+ 1160. ii **Allene Adele RHEA** b. 23 Sep 1946.

1161. iii **Catherine RHEA**, b. 28 Jan 1949 in DeQueen, Sevier Co. AR, d. 28 Jan 1949 in DeQueen, Sevier Co. AR, buried in Denison Cemetery, Idabel, OK.

+ 1162. iv **George Matthew RHEA** b. 6 Oct 1950.

+ 1163. v **Sarah Elizabeth RHEA** b. 27 Dec 1951.

+ 1164. vi **Richard Card RHEA** b. 20 Feb 1956.

+ 1165. vii **Herbert Card RHEA** b. 20 Feb 1956.

+ 1166. viii **Robert Eugene RHEA** b. 6 Nov 1958.

957. **Stephen Herbert RHEA**, (676.Edward[6], 349.Matthew[5], 107.Elizabeth[4], 23.Matthew[3], 4.Jannette[2], 1.John[1]) b. 18 Aug 1922 in Lexington, Holmes Co. MS. On May 13, 1995 Rhodes College, Memphis TN conferred an honorary Doctor of Humanities degree on S. Herbert Rhea. The college cites the following. "Herbert Rhea, doctor of humanities is a long time supporter and member of the

board of trustees. President of Rhea Financial Corp. and a graduate of the University of Tennessee, he became a licensed CPA in 1950. Since then he has been a managing partner of the Rhea and Ivy CPA firm and founder and president of SSM Corp. He is a past president of the Tennessee Society of CPA's. The recipient of Rhodes' Distinguished Service Medal in 1980 for outstanding service to the college, he serves on the boards of several companies and is chairman of Memphis' Dixon Gallery and Gardens. He is a board member of the Thomas W. Briggs Foundation, which provided construction of the student center in the mid 1960's, renovation of the facility in the 1980's and recently a major challenge gift for the construction of the Campus Life Center. Rhea also provided the Linda Williams Rhea Scholarship in honor of his wife. The Rhea Lounge in Briggs Student Center is named in the couple's honor."

General partner of the Private Investment Consortium, and President of Rhea Financial Corp. Founder of Rhea and Ivy CPA's in 1954. 1973 he started SSM Corp., a financial consulting business. He stepped down in 1983. He was an elder of the Second Presbyterian Church. He married **Sarah Linda WILLIAMS**, married 7 Sep 1945 in Memphis, Shelby Co., TN, b. 4 Oct 1923 in Brownsville, Haywood Co., TN. 1938 moved to Memphis with her family.

1941 she graduated Central HS.

1941-42 attended Memphis State University. Worked in business office of Southern Bell Telephone and Telegraph Co. 1942-45.
Children:

+ 1167. i   **Stephen Herbert RHEA, Jr.** b. 3 Jul 1949.

   1168. ii   **Suzanne McCleish RHEA**, b. 16 Oct 1951 in Memphis, Shelby Co., TN. 1995 working as PA for 3 kidney specialists in Macon.

       Received her training at Emory University and Duke University's Physician Assistant Program. She married **Paul BURGAR**, married 30 Mar 1984 in Memphis, Shelby Co., TN, b. 21 Oct 1948 in Buffalo, NY. 1995 teaching at the Georgia School of Business.

   1169. iii   **Linda Lavenia RHEA**, b. 8 Jun 1956 in Memphis, Shelby Co., TN, d. 8 Jun 1956 in Memphis, Shelby

Co., TN, buried in Forest Hill Cemetery, Memphis, TN.

1170. iv **Marilyn Baird RHEA**, b. 31 Aug 1959 in Memphis, Shelby Co., TN. She married **Van Lee CHEESEMAN**, married 27 Sep 1997 in Memphis, Shelby Co., TN, b. 17 Oct 1957.

961. **James Samuel RHEA**, (679.James[6], 350.James[5], 107.Elizabeth[4], 23.Matthew[3], 4.Jannette[2], 1.John[1]) b. 7 Jun 1913 in Fayette Co., TN, d. 24 Jul 1973. He was a farmer and owner of JS Rhea Gin. Married at the historic Darcyville Methodist Church, the oldest in West TN. He married **Annie Marie CRAWFORD**, married 14 Jun 1939 in Dancyville, TN, b. ABT 1913.
Children:

1171. i **Ann Crawford RHEA**, b. 30 Oct 1940 in TN. Graduated from the University of Mississippi with a BS in Art Education and from the Memphis Academy of Arts with a BS in Fine arts. She was an interior designer and lived in Scottsdale AZ in 1986.

+ 1172. ii **James Samuel RHEA, Jr.** b. 6 Sep 1943.

+ 1173. iii **David Charles RHEA** b. 18 May 1951.

962. **Betty Cross RHEA**, (679.James[6], 350.James[5], 107.Elizabeth[4], 23.Matthew[3], 4.Jannette[2], 1.John[1]) b. 15 Aug 1915 in Fayette Co., TN. She married **Claude Powell SNOWDEN Jr.**, married 28 Nov 1940 in Somerville, Fayette Co., TN, b. 24 Aug 1917.
Children:

+ 1174. i **James Wilson SNOWDEN** b. 27 Jun 1941.

1175. ii **Mary Lou SNOWDEN**, b. 29 Oct 1950.

964. **Mary Louise RHEA**, (679.James[6], 350.James[5], 107.Elizabeth[4], 23.Matthew[3], 4.Jannette[2], 1.John[1]) b. 18 Jan 1925 in Fayette Co., TN. 1947 she graduated from Fayette Co. HS and Southwestern (now Rhodes) College. After graduation she moved to Memphis and was employed at Prudential Insurance Co. for 5 years. Later she worked at Chapman Chemical Co. until her marriage. Since then she lived in Park Forest IL. She was active in the Federated Women's Clubs and Daughters of the American Revolution. She

married **Arthur Frank SPENGLER Jr.**, married 17 Nov 1956, b.
17 Nov 1956. Was a metallurgist with International Harvester Co
for 20 years and later with Miller & Co. Retired and acted as
consultant to several companies.
Children:

+ 1176. i   **Sarah Ann SPENGLER** b. 2 Sep 1957.

  1177. ii   **Mary Margaret SPENGLER**, b. 22 Aug 1960.
             Graduated from Grinnell College, Grinnell IA. She
             earned a Library Science degree from the U. of Iowa
             where she worked as a a librarian in 1986.

966. **Thomas Watkins RHEA**, (680.John^6, 350.James^5, 107.Elizabeth^4,
23.Matthew^3, 4.Jannette^2, 1.John^1) b. 14 Feb 1910 in Fayette Co.,
TN, d. ABT 1982. Spent his whole life in Fayette Co. Engaged in
farming some of Watkins land he inherited and built a home 7 miles
NW of Somerville there. He married **Lillie Boyd HIGHTOWER**,
married 15 Nov 1933, b. 10 Dec 1909 in Greenwood MS.
Children:

+ 1178. i   **Thomas Watkins RHEA, Jr.** b. 28 Nov 1934.

968. **William Abraham RHEA Jr.**, (682.William^6, 350.James^5,
107.Elizabeth^4, 23.Matthew^3, 4.Jannette^2, 1.John^1) b. 8 Apr 1921.
He married **Martha Deborah DAVIS**, b. 3 Apr 1924 in Murray,
KY.
Children:

+ 1179. i   **Martha Deborah RHEA** b. 29 Dec 1952.

+ 1180. ii   **William Humphrey RHEA** b. 27 Nov 1954.

969. **Reuben Scott RHEA**, (682.William^6, 350.James^5, 107.Elizabeth^4,
23.Matthew^3, 4.Jannette^2, 1.John^1) b. 2 Jun 1926. He married (1)
Whitney Wheeler BURNETTE, b. ABT 1926, d. 9 Dec 1984. He
married (2) **Nancy PARSONS**, b. ABT 1926.
Children by Whitney Wheeler BURNETTE:

+ 1181. i   **Reuben Scott RHEA Jr.** b. 8 Aug 1950.

+ 1182. ii   **Boyd Burnette RHEA** b. 16 Feb 1953.

970. **Joseph ALFORD Jr.**, (690.Louise[6], 364.Richard[5], 111.Abram[4], 23.Matthew[3], 4.Jannette[2], 1.John[1]) b. ABT 1930. He married **Thelon ROBERTS**, b. ABT 1930.
Children:

    1183. i   **Joseph ALFORD III.**, b. ABT 1960.

    1184. ii   **James Rhea ALFORD**, b. ABT 1962.

974. **Carol Louise RHEA**, (699.Henry[6], 373.Walter[5], 116.Walter[4], 23.Matthew[3], 4.Jannette[2], 1.John[1]) b. 1944. She married **William Roy FORD**, married 1 Jun 1965 in Florence AL, b. ABT 1944.
Children:

    1185. i   **Christopher Lane FORD**, b. 7 Apr 1966.

    1186. ii   **Clinton Ray FORD**, b. 1970. He married **Angela WARD**, b. ABT 1970.

975. **Henry Sale RHEA, Jr.**, (699.Henry[6], 373.Walter[5], 116.Walter[4], 23.Matthew[3], 4.Jannette[2], 1.John[1]) b. 1948. 1997 a physician in Memphis. He married **Sally HARRISON**, b. ABT 1948.
Children:

    1187. i   **Blake Sale RHEA**, b. 1976.

    1188. ii   **Kelly Alden RHEA**, b. 1978.

    1189. iii   **Wade Harrison RHEA**, b. 1980.

976. **Maizie RHEA**, (699.Henry[6], 373.Walter[5], 116.Walter[4], 23.Matthew[3], 4.Jannette[2], 1.John[1]) b. 3 Jul 1953 in Memphis, Shelby Co., TN. She married **John KELLER**, married 1 Nov 1979 in Memphis, Shelby Co., TN, b. ABT 1942.
Children:

    1190. i   **Rhea Lauren KELLER**, b. 23 Nov 1980.

977. **Elinor TURNER**, (700.Eleanor[6], 377.Eleanor[5], 117.Ellen[4], 23.Matthew[3], 4.Jannette[2], 1.John[1]) b. ABT 1930. She married **Edward GIOBBI**, b. ABT 1930.
Children:

    1191. i   **Gena GIOBBI**, b. ABT 1960.

The Preston Family of Walnut Grove, Virginia

1192. ii   **Lisa GIOBBI**, b. ABT 1962.

1193. iii **Chambliss GIOBBI**, b. ABT 1964.

979. **Mary Kay DANCY**, (705.Mary⁶, 380.Alfred⁵, 118.Mary⁴, 23.Matthew³, 4.Jannette², 1.John¹) b. 1948. She married **Kenneth Radford SMITH**, b. 1944.
      Children:

1194. i   **Kenneth Rhea SMITH**, b. 1968.

Eighth Generation

997. **Margaret Preston HAMES**, (728.Lucille⁷, 415.Margaret⁶, 131.Ellen⁵, 26.Margaret⁴, 5.John³, 2.Robert², 1.John¹) b. ABT 1920. She married **Henry I. MADDEN**, b. ABT 1920.
      Children:

+ 1195. i **Margaret Preston MADDEN** b. ABT 1950.

1196. ii   **Timothy Hames MADDEN**, b. ABT 1952.

1197. iii **David Laurens MADDEN**, b. ABT 1954.

998. **Boyd Lemuel HAMES**, (728.Lucille⁷, 415.Margaret⁶, 131.Ellen⁵, 26.Margaret⁴, 5.John³, 2.Robert², 1.John¹) b. ABT 1922. He married **Marie Ann AYERS**, b. ABT 1922.
      Children:

1198. i   **William Walter HAMES**, b. ABT 1945.

1199. ii   **Joseph Robert HAMES**, b. ABT 1947.

1200. iii **Elizabeth Ann HAMES**, b. ABT 1949.

1201. iv   **Charles Boyd HAMES**, b. ABT 1951.

999. **Martha Ellen CAMPBELL**, (739.Malcolm⁷, 420.Frank⁶, 131.Ellen⁵, 26.Margaret⁴, 5.John³, 2.Robert², 1.John¹) b. 27 Jul 1930 in Bonham, Fannin Co., TX. She married **Robert Harold KENNARD**, married 9 May 1953 in Bonham, Fannin Co., TX, b. 15 Aug 1923 in Williamston, Wood Co., WV.
      Children:

+ 1202. i **Robert Malcolm KENNARD** b. 2 Apr 1955.

1203. ii **Julie Ellen KENNARD**, b. 31 Oct 1956.

1000. **Carolyn CAMPBELL**, (739.Malcolm[7], 420.Frank[6], 131.Ellen[5], 26.Margaret[4], 5.John[3], 2.Robert[2], 1.John[1]) b. 4 Sep 1932 in Bonham, Fannin Co., TX. She married **Joe Cravens DENTON Jr.**, married 13 Jun 1951 in Bonham, Fannin Co., TX, b. 16 May 1931 in Bonham, Fannin Co., TX.
Children:

1204. i **Catherine DENTON**, b. 21 Apr 1954 in Bonham, Fannin Co., TX.

+ 1205. ii **Jane DENTON** b. 30 Oct 1955.

+ 1206. iii **Jo Carolyn DENTON** b. 22 Mar 1957.

1002. **Preston White CAMPBELL**, (741.Edward[7], 422.Preston[6], 131.Ellen[5], 26.Margaret[4], 5.John[3], 2.Robert[2], 1.John[1]) b. 15 Jul 1953 in TN?. 1995 was a pediatric pulmonologist at Vanderbilt University in Nashville TN.

Elder in Christ Presbyterian Church. He married **Elaine MITCHELL**, married 1 Sep 1984, b. ABT 1951.
Children:

1207. i **Eleanor Mary CAMPBELL**, b. 18 Jun 1987.

1208. ii **David Aubrey CAMPBELL**, b. 22 Apr 1988.

1209. iii **Allison Grace CAMPBELL**, b. 8 Jun 1990.

1003. **Ray Worthy CAMPBELL**, (741.Edward[7], 422.Preston[6], 131.Ellen[5], 26.Margaret[4], 5.John[3], 2.Robert[2], 1.John[1]) b. 16 Jun 1955. He married **Elaine CLAAR**, married 8 Oct 1983, b. ABT 1955.
Children:

1210. i **Katherine CAMPBELL**, b. ABT 1984.

1211. ii **Caroline Bonner CAMPBELL**, b. ABT 1985.

1212. iii   **Ellen Claar CAMPBELL**, b. 16 Aug 1986.

1017. **William Reed PRESTON Jr.**, (794.William[7], 455.Robert[6], 145.Martha[5], 29.Eleanor[4], 5.John[3], 2.Robert[2], 1.John[1]) b. 2 Dec 1948. He married **Irene Walker FRALEY**, married 5 Jan 1975, b. 26 Apr 1951.
> *Children:*

    1213. i   **Christopher Reed PRESTON**, b. 27 Sep 1980.

1018. **Martha Colsey PRESTON**, (794.William[7], 455.Robert[6], 145.Martha[5], 29.Eleanor[4], 5.John[3], 2.Robert[2], 1.John[1]) b. 17 Mar 1951. She married **Peter Walsh FARNSWORTH**, married 27 Sep 1975, b. 28 Jan 1949.
> *Children:*

    1214. i   **Suzanne Pulliam FARNSWORTH**, b. 5 Feb 1978.

1036. **Robert Milton RHEA**, (818.Frank[7], 503.Robert[6], 184.Frances[5], 40.Sarah[4], 6.Jane[3], 2.Robert[2], 1.John[1]) b. 1918 in Forney TX. He married **Wife of Robert RHEA**, b. ABT 1918.
> *Children:*

+ 1215. i   **Mark Leinart RHEA** b. ABT 1950.

1040. **Charles Sanders EARHART**, (828.John[7], 508.Charles[6], 185.Margaret[5], 40.Sarah[4], 6.Jane[3], 2.Robert[2], 1.John[1]) b. 1914 in Sullivan Co., TN, d. 3 Jun 1945 in Johnson City, Washington Co., TN, buried in Shelby Hills Cem., Bristol, TN. 1945 obituary - 32, died Sunday at Mountain Home in Johnson City, TN.
Mr. Earhart who had served in the US Army for the past 2 and one-half years, received a medical discharge April 24, and since that time had been a patient at Mountain Home. Surviving besides he parents are his wife Mrs. Elizabeth Kernan Earhart, one daughter Julia Katherine Earhart and a brother Lt. Lawrence Earhart, now serving in the Philippine Islands. He married **Elizabeth KERNAN**, b. ABT 1914.
> *Children:*

    1216. i   **Julia Katherine EARHART**, b. ABT 1940 in Sullivan Co., TN.

1041. **Lawrence Powell EARHART**, (828.John[7], 508.Charles[6], 185.Margaret[5], 40.Sarah[4], 6.Jane[3], 2.Robert[2], 1.John[1]) b. 29 Aug

1918 in Bristol, Sullivan Co., TN, d. 19 Apr 1974 in Sullivan Co.,
TN. 1974 obituary - L. P. Earhart Apparent Heart Attack Victim
Bluff City, TN.
Lawrence P. Earhart, Rt. 5 Bluff City, died in Bristol Memorial
Hospital after an apparent heart attack. Mr. Earhart was a builder-
developer. He was a member of Blountville United Methodist
Church, a graduate of King College and a member of Bristol Elks
Lodge 232, VFW Post 6975, Hackler Wood Post 145 of the
American Legion and Volture 883 of the 40 and 8.
Surviving are his wife Mrs. Linda Earhart and two sons, Powell
Earhart and Mark Earhart, all of the home. SS#411-20-0387. He
married (1) **Lynda DENTON**, b. 7 Mar 1936 in Bristol, Sullivan
Co., TN. He married (2) **Isabel JESSEE**, b. 1924 in Cleveland
TN, d. 10 Apr 1961 in Bluff City, Sullivan Co., TN, buried in
Shelby Hills Cem., Bristol, TN. 1961 obituary - Mrs. Earhart of
Bluff City Succumbs at 37.
Mrs. Isabel Jessee Earhart, 37, of Rt. 1 Bluff City, died at her home
at 9:30 a.m. yesterday after a long illness. Mrs. Earhart was born at
Cleveland VA, the daughter of the late Thomas J. and Dorma
Carroll Jessee. She was a member of Blountville Methodist Church
and for the past 15 years was secretary to Dr. N. J. Chew.
Surviving are her husband, Lawrence P. Earhart, 3 sisters Mrs.
Reed H. Thomas Jr. of Bluff City, Mrs. Ellen Ray of Morristown,
and Mrs. Della Musick of Kimbal, WVA, eight brothers H. C. 'Red'
Jessee of Morristown, TC Jessee of Elizabethton, John H. Jessee of
Princetown WVA, Harmoon C. Jessee of Bluff City, WE Jessee
Merchantsville, NJ, ID Jesse of Ieager WVA, Charles M. Jessee,
Philadelphia, and S-Sgt Samuel C. Jessee of Atlanta.
Children by Lynda DENTON:

1217. i **Lawrence Powell EARHART, Jr.**, b. 26 Apr 1963
in Sullivan Co., TN. Lives in the Old Earhart home.

1218. ii **Mark James EARHART**, b. 10 Nov 1964 in
Sullivan Co., TN, d. 4 Oct 1983 in Johnson City,
Washington Co., TN, buried in Shelby Hills Cem.,
Bristol, TN. Killed by drunk driver. Was a freshman
in college.

1983 obituary - Johnson City, TN - An 18 year old
Bluff City TN man was killed and another man
injured when an alleged drunken driver struck their
car from behind here Tuesday, causing it to flip over

twice and throw both occupants from the car, Johnson City police said.

James Mark Earhart, of Rt. 7, Bluff City, TN, was pronounced dead on arrival at Johnson City Medical Center. He was a passenger in a compact car driven by Shannon M. Wilson of 3312 High Dr., Kingsport, TN. Jackie Wolfe, age and address unavailable, was being held in the Johnson City jail on charges of second degree murder and driving under the influence as a results of the 1:45pm accident at the intersection of West Market and Collins Streets police said. Police said Wolfe will be arraigned on the charges in city court today.

Wilson was being treated Tuesday for multiple injuries at the Johnson City Medical Center. The investigation was continuing and no other information was available from Police.

Earhart was a 1983 graduate of Sullivan Central High School where he was a member of the VICA club. He was a freshman at East TN State University. Survivors include his mother Mrs. Lawrence P. (Lydia Denton) Earhart of Bluff City, one brother Powell Earhart, US Army stationed in Greece, and his maternal grandmother Mrs. James N. Denton, Bristol.

1042. **Margaret Kathleen EARHART**, (829.Samuel[7], 508.Charles[6], 185.Margaret[5], 40.Sarah[4], 6.Jane[3], 2.Robert[2], 1.John[1]) b. 24 Nov 1915 in Blountville, Sullivan Co., TN. 1940 Bristol City Directory - Kathleen M. Earhart - Home lighting advisor East Tenn Light and Poser Co. Residence was: 104 Spruce (This was the home of her father Pearce.) Later in life she suffered greatly from crippling arthritis. She married **Theodore Dale 'Col' PERRY**, married 1 Jun 1939, b. ABT 1920. Retired as Colonel from US army after 30 years service. Veteran of WWII and Korea.
Children:

+ 1219. i **James Samuel PERRY** b. ABT 1940.

1220. ii **Margaret 'Meg' Earhart PERRY**, b. ABT 1948 in Anchorage, Anchorage Co. AK, d. 1955 in

Arlington, Fairfax Co., VA. Died at age 8 of cancer. Her parents were living at 3554 N. Nottingham St, Arlington VA when she died. She had attended Nottingham elementary school. She had been ill over 6 months and was visited by President Eisenhower when he was at Walter Reed Hospital for his annual physical in May of that year. She had begun her schooling at Camp Sendai, Japan. Died from leukemia.

1043.   **Etta Elizabeth EARHART**, (829.Samuel[7], 508.Charles[6], 185.Margaret[5], 40.Sarah[4], 6.Jane[3], 2.Robert[2], 1.John[1]) b. 1 Mar 1917 in Bristol, Sullivan Co., TN. 1935 as a senior at Bristol TN HS she fell in love with a football hero from King College, 'Race Horse' Caldwell. He came to King College from Crosspore NC in 1933. He worked at Moore-Earhart Store for 38 years.

1932 at a Rhea family reunion, she modeled Elizabeth McIlwain's wedding dress (now in a Rocky Mount NC Museum). A picture from that day is in 'Families and History of Sullivan County', 1992. She married **Ford Monroe CALDWELL**, married 12 Apr 1936 in Elizabethton, Carter Co., TN, b. 1914 in Giles Co VA. Eloped just before Etta finished High School. Her father had the marriage annulled. He agreed to the marriage if she graduated. The eventually married. Ford started a management training program for a dime store but Etta could not bear to move and he went to work for the local Moore-Earhart store instead; working there 38 years..
    Children:

+   1221.   i   **Harriet Ann CALDWELL** b. 29 Jul 1937.

+   1222.   ii   **Joyce Eveleen CALDWELL** b. 5 Sep 1940.

+   1223.   iii   **Ford 'Buddy' CALDWELL, Jr.** b. 31 Mar 1947.

1044.   **Balfour DOANE**, (830.Margaretta[7], 508.Charles[6], 185.Margaret[5], 40.Sarah[4], 6.Jane[3], 2.Robert[2], 1.John[1]) b. 1917 in Sullivan Co., TN, d. 9 Dec 1990 in Kingsport, Sullivan Co., TN, buried in Oak Hill Cemetery, Kingsport TN. 1990 obituary - Balfour Doan 73, 409 Manderley Rd. Kingsport died at 9pm at his home. A native and lifelong resident of Sullivan Co. he retired from Mead Corp. and was past president of the Lions Club of Kingsport. He was preceded in death by his parents AT and Margaretta Doan, one sister,

Violette Helen Archer. Surviving are his wife Jean Doane, one daughter Mrs. Jim (Kathy) Cahow, Abingdon VA, one son Tim Doane, Kingsport. He married **Jean wife of Balfour DOANE**, b. ABT 1917.

> *Children:*

    1224. i   **Kathy DOANE**, b. ABT 1950. She married **James CAHOW**, b. ABT 1950.

    1225. ii   **Tim DOANE**, b. ABT 1952.

1046. **James O'Delle BOUTON Jr.**, (832.Violet[7], 508.Charles[6], 185.Margaret[5], 40.Sarah[4], 6.Jane[3], 2.Robert[2], 1.John[1]) b. 20 Apr 1921 in Washington D.C., d. 7 Mar 1995 in North Myrtle Beach, Horry Co. SC, buried in Ft. Lincoln Cem. Prince George's Co MD. Jim was born and spent his early childhood in the Langley section of Washington DC just off Mills Avenue. When he was four the family left their upstairs rented portion of this house and moved to their own home on Monroe Street in Northwest Washington. It was here the James and later his brother Charlie would spend the rest of their childhood.

Each summer the family would travel back to the Holston Valley area of East Tennessee to visit with Jim's mother's family. Many family photographs show Jim as a young boy in East Tennessee during these visits including one where at the age of 2 he is feeding the chickens with grandma Emma Powell Earhart.

Graduated from McKinley High School in Washington DC January 31, 1941.

Attended American University in Washington DC February 1941 to June 1942. Completing a year before he was drafted in the Army.

1942 June 23 US Army Enlistment records she he entered Army at Fort Meyer, Virginia. It notes he was single without dependants, had 2 years of college. His height was 73 inches, and weight 212 pounds. He enlisted for the duration of the war or other emergency, plus six months subject to the discretion of the President. He was a private and was discharged from AAA School Company, Davis NC as a Corporal December 12, 1942. He immediately entered service on December 23, 1942 for Officers Training School. Commissioned as a 2nd Lt. in the Anti-Aircraft Artillery OCS 1942. Instructor AAA School at Camp David NC April 1943 through May 1944.

Platoon Officer in AAA and Infantry May 1944 through June 1945. Commanded approximately 200. Special Service Officer June 1945 through 1946. During his service, made 5 trips on ship to European ports aboard troop transport. He was finally discharged from active service as a Captain on August 1, 1946 at the Fort Meade Separation Center in Maryland.

August 1946 to 20 November 1950 worked as Postal Clerk at the main US Post Office in Washington D.C.

From February 1947 through June 1950 attended Benjamin Franklin University in Washington DC at night. Completed the required courses including Commercial Law, Accounting and Economics to earn a BS in 1950 while working at the post office during the day.

Met his wife Erin on blind date arranged by friends. Married June 30, 1949 in a simple ceremony in a local church due to the illness of his mother who died the following month. In July 1951, using veterans benefits, bought their first home at 2108 Woodberry St. Hyattsville, MD.

November 21, 1950 to August 19, 1951 worked in Washington DC, US Army Department, Ordinance Requirements Branch as a Supply Requirements Clerk. Over the next 32 years he worked in positions of increasing responsibility for the Department of the Army. April 15, 1978 after 32 years of Civil Service he retired from his position at the HQ US Army Material Development and Readiness Command, Alexandria VA.

In 1978 moved to North Myrtle Beach SC to a home they designed on the second fairway of Robbers Roost Golf Course. Where they enjoyed many years of travel, golf, friends and relaxation earned from these years of work. He enjoyed working in his year, saw and played cards with friends and visited often with his grandchildren.

February 1994 he suffered a heart attack and a year later on March 7, 1995 after awaking that morning, he collapsed stricken by a heart attack and was pronounced dead later that day. He now rests with his mother, wife and youngest daughter at Fort Lincoln Cemetery, Bladensburg, Maryland not far from his boyhood house on Monroe Street.

Services were held at the Trinity Methodist Church in North Myrtle Beach. He now rests with his mother, wife and youngest daughter at Fort Lincoln Cemetery, Bladensburg, Maryland not far from his boyhood house on Monroe Street. He married **Erin CONNOR**, married 30 Jun 1949 in Washington D.C., b. 11 Jul 1923 in Greenwood SC, d. 24 Jul 1998 in Myrtle Beach, Horry Co., SC, buried in Ft. Lincoln Cem. Prince George's Co., MD.

Erin was born the tenth child of a tenth child (her mother), also named Erin. She said she was born prematurely and claimed the family took her home in a shoe box. Erin was raised in Greenwood SC where father had moved them when he left the farm to work for the Railroad.

1923 her birth certificate indicated her father operated a filling station. In January 1940 Erin's mother died. Her father had passed away 5 years earlier. She moved to live with her sister Helen's family, the Douglas' in Charlotte, NC. Erin spent her senior year of high school and graduated from Central High School on Elizabeth Av. in Charlotte NC on June 11, 1941, the same day her sister gave birth to Erin's niece Jane Douglas. Helen Douglas of course did not make it to the graduation but her husband Neil Douglas came.

1941 after her graduation, she worked for a brief time as a typist, Aug. 1941 to Oct. 1941 in Charlotte for the Boys Scouts of America. Erin's sister Marian had been working in Wash. DC. In 1942 Marian applied to National Geographic in Washington for Erin and got her a job there. In October 1941 Erin began work as a typist at the Geographic offices on Ekert St. but was soon offered a position on 16th and M St. NW which was near where she was living with Marian. This job was a temporary position but was later extended indefinitely. The letter informing her of this also indicated that the check for her first three days of work was also enclosed - $8.00. While working at Geographic, she took and passed the civil service exam and got a job with the Navy Department.

1942 January she began working for the Navy on 18th and Constitution Avenue NW in Washington as a Clerk Typist within weeks of Pearl Harbor attack. She and Marian would walk from their apartment to work since the buses would be full by the time they arrived at their stop. Erin worked in an office that reviewed contracts for companies who were doing business with the Navy.

Her sister Marian and Peck Brengle married and in June 1942 Erin moved to a boarding house for women on Massachusetts Avenue near the embassies. She lived there during the war, when the girls would all chip in their ration coupons to pay for the groceries their landlady would buy to prepare their meals. Here she met lifelong friends the sisters Joanne and Denise.

1953 March 23, she applied for and was granted 6 months unpaid maternity leave. In September of that same year she resigned to stay home with newborn Janet. March 1966 Erin was reinstated to government service as an accounts maintenance clerk at NASA, Goddard Space flight Center in Greenbelt, Maryland. Retired from the NASA April 1978 when she moved with Jimmy to North Myrtle Beach.

She died after an illness of a few months due to complications from emphysema. In her last few weeks, was cared for at the Manor Care facility in Myrtle Beach, surrounded by daughter, son in law and her visiting grandchildren.

Children:

+ 1226. i **Janet Erin BOUTON** b. 3 Jun 1953.

　　 1227. ii **Sandra Louise BOUTON**, b. 16 Aug 1955 in Washington D.C., d. 20 Oct 1958 in Prince George's Co MD, buried in Ft. Lincoln Cem. Prince George's Co MD. Died of liver disease as a young child.

1047. **Charles Earhart BOUTON**, (832.Violet[7], 508.Charles[6], 185.Margaret[5], 40.Sarah[4], 6.Jane[3], 2.Robert[2], 1.John[1]) b. 16 Jun 1930 in Washington D.C. Went to McKinley High School with Carol. Charlie went to U of Maryland and Carol to American. In ROTC, he joined Air force and was stationed in NM where Mark was born. Returning to Wash DC after service they lived on N.H. Av and he worked at Naval Ordinance Lab. Attended George Washington U at night for Law Degree. Went to work for Swift Foods Co and after obtaining degree was transferred to Chicago IL where he worked till his retirement to FL. He married **June Carol WHITCRAFT**, married 14 Jun 1952 in Washington D.C., b. 5 Aug 1930. Graduated from American University in 1952. Member of Kappa Delta and Cap and Gown, mentioned in Who's Who in American Colleges. Her marriage was held at Brookland Baptist Church, Rev. Ward Hurlburt officiating. Reception was at DAR chapter house on Massachusetts Av. in Washington DC.

Children:

+ 1228. i **Mark Earhart BOUTON** b. 10 Sep 1953.

+ 1229. ii **Leslie Ann BOUTON** b. 5 Mar 1956.

+ 1230. iii **Clare Lynn BOUTON** b. 9 Oct 1961.

1048. **Robert Joseph EARHART**, (845.Philip[7], 510.Joseph[6], 185.Margaret[5], 40.Sarah[4], 6.Jane[3], 2.Robert[2], 1.John[1]) b. 2 Jul 1955 in Bristol, Sullivan Co., TN. Twin. Lives on the old Rhea home place on Rt. 11 E across from the Bristol Speedway. He married **Shelia EATON**, married 7 Jun 1975 in Kingsport, Sullivan Co., TN, b. 4 Mar 1955 in Kingsport, Sullivan Co., TN. Daughter of Herbert Allan Eaton and Janette.

Mother from Sneedville and father from TN as well.
Children:

1231. i **Philip Wheeler ERHART**, b. 24 Jan 1981 in Bristol, Sullivan Co., TN.

1232. ii **Robert Allen EARHART**, b. 4 Aug 1985 in Bristol, Sullivan Co., TN.

1049. **Charles Phillip EARHART**, (845.Philip[7], 510.Joseph[6], 185.Margaret[5], 40.Sarah[4], 6.Jane[3], 2.Robert[2], 1.John[1]) b. 2 Jul 1955 in Bristol, Sullivan Co., TN. Twin. He married **Stephanie STATEN**, married 9 Jun 1979 in Johnson City, Washington Co., TN, b. 14 Jun 1956 in Johnson City, Washington Co., TN. Daughter of William and Betty Staten.
Children:

1233. i **Jennifer Ashley EARHART**, b. 29 Dec 1984.

1234. ii **Allison Brooke EARHART**, b. 2 Apr 1986 in Johnson City, Washington Co., TN.

1235. iii **Aaron Mark EARHART**, b. 1 Jun 1988 in Johnson City, Washington Co., TN.

1051. **Robert Joseph COONTZ**, (868.Virginia[7], 524.Jane[6], 192.Sarah[5], 43.John[4], 6.Jane[3], 2.Robert[2], 1.John[1]) b. 7 Jan 1926 in Alexandria VA. Educated at the US Naval Academy, class of 1949. He was a

Captain in the US Navy. He inherited the Derry Inn in Blountville TN. Sold the historic structure to the Sullivan Co., Historical Society. He married **Patricia Irene PATRICK**, married 12 Feb 1955 in Columbia, Marion Co., MS, b. ABT 1926.

Children:

1236. i   **Robert Joseph COONTZ, Jr.**, b. 25 Jul 1956 in Annapolis, Anne Arundel Co. MD. BA in mathamatics from Swathmore, MS Hydrogeology Stanford. He and his wife divide their time between Waukesha, WI and Ayr Scotland. No children (1998). He married **Susan Margaret HENRY**, married 16 Oct 1990 in La Jolla CA, b. ABT 1956.

+ 1237. ii   **Kenneth Lee COONTZ** b. 27 Nov 1957.

1238. iii   **Constance Patricia COONTZ**, b. 2 Aug 1960 in San Diego, CA. Earned a BA from Byrn Mawr College.

She and her husband lived in Andover MA. No children (1998). She married **Jonathan Jay MAZELSKY**, married 3 Jun 1989, b. 30 Jul 1960.

1055. **Seaton Tinsley PRESTON III III.** (877.Seaton[7], 529.Seaton[6], 193.James[5], 43.John[4], 6.Jane[3], 2.Robert[2], 1.John[1]) b. 19 Jun 1946. He married **Anita HULEFELD**, married 6 Sep 1975, b. ABT 1946.

Children:

1239. i   **Anne Katherine PRESTON**, b. 29 Apr 1979.

1240. ii   **Robert Tinsley PRESTON**, b. 20 Apr 1982.

1241. iii   **Susanna Debbaut PRESTON**, b. 2 Dec 1983.

1056. **Christiane Marie PRESTON**, (877.Seaton[7], 529.Seaton[6], 193.James[5], 43.John[4], 6.Jane[3], 2.Robert[2], 1.John[1]) b. 4 Sep 1947. She married **William WALKER**, married ABT 1980, b. ABT 1947.

Children:

1242. i   **Colin WALKER**, b. 15 Jul 1981.

1057. John Thomas PRESTON, (877.Seaton[7], 529.Seaton[6], 193.James[5], 43.John[4], 6.Jane[3], 2.Robert[2], 1.John[1]) b. 18 Mar 1949. He married **Sean OTIS**, married 28 Oct 1972, b. ABT 1949.
Children:

    1243. i **Patrick PRESTON**, b. 17 Sep 1977.

    1244. ii **Tommy PRESTON**, b. 23 Apr 1981.

1060. Cynthia Houghton PRESTON, (878.James[7], 529.Seaton[6], 193.James[5], 43.John[4], 6.Jane[3], 2.Robert[2], 1.John[1]) b. 5 Mar 1952. She married **Erwin Jay PINKHAM**, married 2 Feb 1974, b. ABT 1952.
Children:

    1245. i **Matthew Owne PINKHAM**, b. 30 Aug 1975.

    1246. ii **Jessica Heather PINKHAM**, b. 30 Jun 1980.

1061. James Brainard PRESTON, Jr. Jr., (878.James[7], 529.Seaton[6], 193.James[5], 43.John[4], 6.Jane[3], 2.Robert[2], 1.John[1]) b. 8 Aug 1954. He married **Peggy Anne SMOYER**, married 24 Aug 1974, b. ABT 1954.
Children:

    1247. i **Andrew James PRESTON**, b. 19 Dec 1979.

    1248. ii **Scott Roy PRESTON**, b. 23 Feb 1984.

1063. Frederick Leigh PRESTON, Jr. Jr., (879.Frederick[7], 529.Seaton[6], 193.James[5], 43.John[4], 6.Jane[3], 2.Robert[2], 1.John[1]) b. 10 Oct 1955 in Fort Huachuca, AZ. He married **Corrima SMITH**, married 11 Oct 1980, b. 28 Jan 1959, d. 22 Apr 1998.
Children:

    1249. i **Melissa Louise PRESTON**, b. 27 Feb 1982. She married **Nicholas HENNON**, married 24 May 2003, b. ABT 1982.

    1250. ii **Kelly Ann PRESTON**, b. 29 Aug 1986.

1064. Linda Louise PRESTON, (879.Frederick[7], 529.Seaton[6], 193.James[5], 43.John[4], 6.Jane[3], 2.Robert[2], 1.John[1]) b. 23 Oct 1956 in

Dunkirk, NY. She married **Charles Edward SNYDER**, b. 22 Oct 1954.
> *Children:*

    1251. i   **JoAnn Margaret SNYDER**, b. 16 Jun 1980.

    1252. ii   **Cynthia Arlene SNYDER**, b. 9 Jan 1982.

1065. **Robert James PRESTON**, (879.Frederick[7], 529.Seaton[6], 193.James[5], 43.John[4], 6.Jane[3], 2.Robert[2], 1.John[1]) b. 14 Aug 1961 in Dunkirk, NY. He married **Terresa HARTWICK**.
> *Children:*

    1253. i   **Amanda Rhea PRESTON**, b. 17 Mar 1987.

    1254. ii   **Amy Renee PRESTON**, b. 26 Jun 1989.

    1255. iii   **Samantha Rosie PRESTON**, b. 6 Apr 1998.

    1256. iv   **James Robert PRESTON**, b. 6 Oct 1999.

    1257. v   **Christopher Thomas PRESTON**, b. 2 Apr 2003.

1066. **Rebecca Ann PRESTON**, (879.Frederick[7], 529.Seaton[6], 193.James[5], 43.John[4], 6.Jane[3], 2.Robert[2], 1.John[1]) b. 11 Jun 1964 in Dunkirk, NY. She married **Lynn WEAVER**, b. 26 Sep 1967.
> *Children:*

    1258. i   **Nicole Lynn WEAVER**, b. 22 Dec 1992.

1068. **Kenneth Edison ST. CLAIR, Jr.**, (881.Miriam[7], 530.John[6], 194.Samuel[5], 43.John[4], 6.Jane[3], 2.Robert[2], 1.John[1]) b. 30 Mar 1943 in Lexington, KY. He received his BA at the University of Kentucky. Works for social security. Married 3 times.

2005 lived in Lanesville, IN. 2005 son just started at Stamford. He married (1) **Dianne Sue GELBAND**, married 1 Oct 1968 in Council Bluff, IA, b. 13 Aug 1950. He married (2) **Mary Lea SPRAY**, married 4 Aug 1980 in Kansas City, MO, b. 1 Mar 1943 in Medora, IN. She received her education at Indiana Central College and an MA from Indiana University. She is a teacher.
> *Children by Dianne Sue GELBAND:*

1259. i **Heather Lea ST. CLAIR**, b. 28 Mar 1973 in Kansas City, MO.
Children by Mary Lea SPRAY:

1260. ii **Michael ST. CLAIR**, b. 3 Apr 1983 in Mission, KS.

1070. **Charles Ainsworth ST. CLAIR**, (881.Miriam[7], 530.John[6], 194.Samuel[5], 43.John[4], 6.Jane[3], 2.Robert[2], 1.John[1]) b. 1 Apr 1948 in Indianapolis, IN. Earned his BS from UNCA and his MS from MIT. He is a teacher.

2005 lived in Asheville, NC. He married **Susan HEATON**, b. ABT 1948.
Children:

1261. i **Eric ST. CLAIR**, b. 24 Apr 1984 in Boston, MA.

1071. **William CUMMING**, (882.Annie[7], 530.John[6], 194.Samuel[5], 43.John[4], 6.Jane[3], 2.Robert[2], 1.John[1]) b. 14 Feb 1935 in SoonChun, Korea. Earned his BS in biology from Peabody College and his MA from Vanderbilt, both in Nashville, TN.

(Fairman Cumming November 23, 2005 phone conversation Foley from Decatur GA with Ed Foley)
My brother is named William and his second son is named Daniel James Cumming. The family traded the names William and Daniel James for many generations. This Daniel James has a good job in Nashville and commutes from Murfreesboro. He has just become engaged. He has a sister who had a child a year ago.

2005 lived in Nashville, TN. He has taught for over 30 years at Tennessee State University where he is Assistant Professor, Biology, Physics and Chemistry and Coordinator of Elementary Education. He married **Janice ESLICK**, married 26 Nov 1969.
Children:

1262. i **Lisa Anne CUMMING**, b. 24 Dec 1970 in Nashville, Davidson Co., TN.

1263. ii **William Franklin Preston CUMMING**, b. 8 Apr 1976 in Nashville, Davidson Co., TN.

1264. iii **Daniel James CUMMING**, b. 27 Sep 1977 in Nashville, Davidson Co., TN.

1265. iv **Mary Kim CUMMING**, b. 30 Apr 1980 in Nashville, Davidson Co., TN.

1073. **Anne Shannon CUMMING**, (882.Annie[7], 530.John[6], 194.Samuel[5], 43.John[4], 6.Jane[3], 2.Robert[2], 1.John[1]) b. 15 Jan 1939 in SoonChun, Korea. Earned her BA in Biology from Agnes Scott College and her MS in Biology from Washington University in St. Louis.

2005 she was living in Decatur GA. She married **Joseph Bedford 'Dr.' MCCORMICK**, married 1968 in Decatur, GA, b. 17 Oct 1942. Joseph earned his MD from Duke University, and a degree from Harvard. He is a public health virologist.
Children:

1266. i **Christopher Robert MCCORMICK**, b. 25 May 1970 in Boston, MA.

1267. ii **Peter Joseph MCCORMICK**, b. 7 Nov 1973 in Atlanta, GA. Earned his BS from Washington University and his Ph D from Texas A&M.

1268. iii **Anne Shannon MCCORMICK**, b. 27 Oct 1977 in Atlanta, GA. Earned her BA from the University of Portland and her MA from American University.

1074. **Sarah Stokes CUMMINGS**, (882.Annie[7], 530.John[6], 194.Samuel[5], 43.John[4], 6.Jane[3], 2.Robert[2], 1.John[1]) b. 22 Feb 1942 in Nashville, Davidson Co., TN. Earned her BA from Agnes Scott College in Decatur, GA and her MA from Johns Hopkins. She was a mathematics teacher. She married **Francis Marion MITCHELL III**, married 20 Jun 1970 in Decatur, GA, b. 2 May 1940 in Charleston, SC. Earned his BS in Mechanical Engineering from Georgia Tech, and his MS in Mechanical Engineering at MIT.
Children:

1269. i **Francis Marion MITCHELL IV**, b. 23 May 1972 in Chapel Hill, NC. Earned his BA in Anthropology from Davidson College, Davidson NC.

1270. ii **Anne Wiley MITCHELL**, b. 28 Dec 1974 in Chapel Hill, NC. Earned her BA in History and French from Agnes Scott College in Decatur, GA and her JD from

Northwestern University. She married **Peter
Leonard TIGNOR**, married 21 Jun 1997 in Severna
Park, MD, b. 5 Jul 1975. Earned his AA from
Baltimore Culinary Institute.

1271. iii **Caroline Hay MITCHELL**, b. 16 Apr 1978 in New
Orleans, LA. Earned her BA in biology at Agnes
Scott College in Decatur, GA. She married **Thomas
HAMILTON**, b. ABT 1978.

1076. **Margaret Wiley CUMMING**, (882.Annie[7], 530.John[6],
194.Samuel[5], 43.John[4], 6.Jane[3], 2.Robert[2], 1.John[1]) b. 5 Mar 1953
in Nashville, Davidson Co., TN. Earned her BA at North Georgia
College.

2003 her mother's obituary in the Black Mountain News indicated
Margaret C. Union (sic), daughter, was living in Black Mountain,
NC. She married **James Reavis LINTON**, married 29 Dec 1978 in
Decatur, GA, b. 9 Apr 1953 in Princeton, NJ. He is a consultant
and builder.

2005 James was working in Korea on a project to bring a drill rig
into North Korea in order to drill for fresh water to supply the needs
of hospitals in the north. Working with the Christian Friends of
Korea in Black Mountain, he and his family have helped bring
relief to the North Korean people and to provide a bridge until the
relations between North and South are normalized.
Children:

1272. i **Elizabeth Shannon LINTON**, b. 29 Nov 1983 in
Asheville, Buncombe Co., NC.

1273. ii **Hugh Nathaniel LINTON**, b. 25 Nov 1985 in
Asheville, Buncombe Co., NC.

1274. iii **Wililam Evan LINTON**, b. 24 Feb 1988 in Black
Mountain, Buncombe Co., NC.

1275. iv **Michael Duncan LINTON**, b. 10 Apr 1990 in Black
Mountain, Buncombe Co., NC.

1276. v **Anna Evangeline LINTON**, b. 17 Mar 1992 in
Black Mountain, Buncombe Co., NC.

1277. vi **Daniel Allen LINTON**, b. 14 May 1994 in Black Mountain, Buncombe Co., NC.

1278. vii **Peter James LINTON**, b. 7 Oct 1996 in Black Mountain, Buncombe Co., NC.

1077. **John Fariman PRESTON III**, (883.John[7], 530.John[6], 194.Samuel[5], 43.John[4], 6.Jane[3], 2.Robert[2], 1.John[1]) b. 1942 in CA, d. 16 Jul 1983 in MD. 1966 July 18, he was rescued after his plane was shot down in Viet Nam.

1983 he died in the crash of an F4 Phantom into the Chesapeake Bay while on a reserves mission. He married **Judy wife of John Fairman PRESTON**, b. ABT 1942.
        Children:

1279. i **John Fairman PRESTON IV**, b. ABT 1965, d. 1987.

1280. ii **Randolph PRESTON**, b. ABT 1967.

1080. **Roland Preston BOCKHORTST**, (884.Florence[7], 530.John[6], 194.Samuel[5], 43.John[4], 6.Jane[3], 2.Robert[2], 1.John[1]) b. 14 Jul 1940 in St. Louis, MO. Earned hsi BS in Electical Engineering from Washington University, St. Louis, MO. (His father was a professor there). Works as an engineer.

He married **Dianne OHARE**, married 1966, b. 21 Sep 1939.
        Children:

1281. i **Adam BOCKHORTST**, b. 21 Apr 1969. 1999 earned his Bachelor's degree from Webster University. Works as a teacher.

1081. **Rhea Wiley BOCKHORTST**, (884.Florence[7], 530.John[6], 194.Samuel[5], 43.John[4], 6.Jane[3], 2.Robert[2], 1.John[1]) b. 29 Sep 1942 in St. Louis, MO. Earned his BS from Washington University, St. Louis, MO. Worked as an engineer. He married (1) **Leslie BISHOP**, married 14 Jun 1969, b. 14 May 1947 in Long Island, NY. She was a counselor. He married (2) **Anna Marcel DEHERMANAS**, married 21 Jun 1991 in Marietta, GA, b. 24 Apr 1947 in Freemont, OH.
        Children by Leslie BISHOP:

1282. i   **Peter Rhea 'Dr.' BOCKHORTST**, b. 24 May 1971 in Baltimore, MD. Earned his MD at the University of Delaware. Works as a Doctor of osteopathy. He married **Jennifer Rebecca GRIESBACH**, married 28 May 1994 in Jefferson, VA, b. 29 Nov 1971. Earned her BA in International Relations at the University of Delaware, her MA in Education from the University of New Mexico and her JD from Stanford. Works as a lawyer.

1283. ii   **Andrew Bishop BOCKHORTST**, b. ABT 1972. Earned his BA in English from Ohio University and his MA in Anthropology from the University of Arizona.

1082. **Mary Ann BOCKHORTST**, (884.Florence[7], 530.John[6], 194.Samuel[5], 43.John[4], 6.Jane[3], 2.Robert[2], 1.John[1]) b. 12 Jun 1944 in St. Louis, MO. Earned her degree from Washington University. She is a nurse. She married (1) **Charles Jacob KUNKLE III**, married 1964, b. 21 Apr 1945 in St. Louis, MO. She married (2) **James S. KNICKREHM**, married 1992, b. 22 Jan 1940.
Children by Charles Jacob KUNKLE III:

+ 1284. i   **Charles Jacob KUNKLE IV** b. 23 Aug 1967.

+ 1285. ii   **Amanda KUNKLE** b. 30 Sep 1979.

1083. **Fairman Kennedy BOCKHORTST**, (884.Florence[7], 530.John[6], 194.Samuel[5], 43.John[4], 6.Jane[3], 2.Robert[2], 1.John[1]) b. 21 Dec 1950 in St. Louis, MO. Earned his BS in Electrical Engineering and his MS EM.

Listed as a member of the crew of the submarine USS Pollack, SSN603:
Fairman K. "Bock" Bockhorst Rank: ET1 (SS) nuke, Years aboard: 1976-1981

He married **Julie WARD**, married 24 Aug 1975 in Idaho Falls, ID, b. 17 Jul 1957 in Glendale, CA.
Children:

1286. i   **Lindsey Grey BOCKHORTST**, b. 5 Oct 1981 in San Jose, CA. 2003 earned her BS in Hearing

Disorders from Florida State University, Tallahassee, Florida.

1287. ii **Jonathan Fairman BOCKHORTST**, b. 1 Dec 1984 in Phoenixville, PA.

1087. **Patsy PRESTON**, (886.Rhea[7], 530.John[6], 194.Samuel[5], 43.John[4], 6.Jane[3], 2.Robert[2], 1.John[1]) b. ABT 1956. She married **Julian BROADHEAD**, b. ABT 1956.
Children:

1288. i **Rhea BROADHEAD**, b. ABT 1980.

1289. ii **Preston BROADHEAD**, b. ABT 1982.

1290. iii **Brandon BROADHEAD**, b. ABT 1984.

1291. iv **Sacha BROADHEAD**, b. ABT 1986. Bears the Korean nickname of her great aunt Florence 'Sacha' Preston Bockhorst. (It was pronounced 'Say-chee).

1116. **Louise Virginia PRESTON**, (910.John[7], 554.John[6], 213.Cochran[5], 47.John[4], 8.John[3], 3.Walter[2], 1.John[1]) b. 19 Jul 1962 in Chapel Hill, NC. She married **Matt TRICE**, married 30 Dec 1988, b. ABT 1962.
Children:

1292. i **Virginia Carroll TRICE**, b. 10 Sep 1993.

1293. ii **Emily Elizabeth TRICE**, b. 31 Mar 1998.

1120. **Elinor Catharine PRESTON**, (911.Charles[7], 554.John[6], 213.Cochran[5], 47.John[4], 8.John[3], 3.Walter[2], 1.John[1]) b. 19 Dec 1968. She married **Craig BEVIER**, married 8 Aug 1992, b. 4 Jul 1968.
Children:

1294. i **Olivia BEVIER**, b. ABT 1993.

1125. **Kenneth Wade SALLINGER**, (932.Evanda[7], 625.Lysle[6], 324.Josiah[5], 98.John[4], 21.Robert[3], 4.Jannette[2], 1.John[1]) b. 17 Apr 1964 in FL?. 1999 worked as a Special Agent with the Office of Special Investigation, USAF. He married (1) **Karen Kimberly**

ROBERSON, married 15 Jun 1985, b. ABT 1964. He married (2) **Jamie Louise STRENGTH**, married 8 Jun 1996, b. 20 Sep 1961.
Children by Karen Kimberly ROBERSON:

   1295. i   **Tara Marie SALLINGER**, b. 15 May 1987.

   1296. ii   **Michael Ellis SALLINGER**, b. 24 Aug 1989.

1126. **Patrick Rhea SALLINGER**, (932.Evanda[7], 625.Lysle[6], 324.Josiah[5], 98.John[4], 21.Robert[3], 4.Jannette[2], 1.John[1]) b. 19 Feb 1974 in FL?. 1999 owned a carpet installation business. He married (1) **Beverly Rhea HOLMES**, married 20 Aug 1993, b. ABT 1974. Had no children during her 2 years of marriage with Patrick. He married (2) **Heather Robin DENDEKKER**, married 28 Jun 1997, b. 17 Jul 1976.
Children by Heather Robin DENDEKKER:

   1297. i   **Joshua Stephen SALLINGER**, b. 25 Sep 1998.

1142. **Debrah Lynn 'Debbie' SPURGEON**, (947.Lyle[7], 654.Beulah[6], 340.Samuel[5], 105.Robert[4], 22.Margaret[3], 4.Jannette[2], 1.John[1]) b. ABT 1960. She married **Mr. HOLLINGWORTH**, b. ABT 1960.
Children:

   1298. i   **Kaytlin Blake HOLLINGWORTH**, b. ABT 1990.

1144. **Lisa FICKLE**, (948.James[7], 658.Haskew[6], 340.Samuel[5], 105.Robert[4], 22.Margaret[3], 4.Jannette[2], 1.John[1]) b. 22 Jul 1966. She married **Kent BLEVINS**, married 20 Sep 1987, b. ABT 1966.
Children:

   1299. i   **Tiffany BLEVINS**, b. 26 Aug 1989.

   1300. ii   **Tiarra BLEVINS**, b. 27 Aug 1991.

1145. **David FICKLE**, (948.James[7], 658.Haskew[6], 340.Samuel[5], 105.Robert[4], 22.Margaret[3], 4.Jannette[2], 1.John[1]) b. 30 Dec 1967. He married **Michelle WHITED**, b. ABT 1967.
Children:

   1301. i   **Jacob FICKLE**, b. ABT 1990.

The Preston Family of Walnut Grove, Virginia

1147. **Kristi Leigh ENSOR**, (949.Dorothy[7], 658.Haskew[6], 340.Samuel[5],
105.Robert[4], 22.Margaret[3], 4.Jannette[2], 1.John[1]) b. 21 May 1970.
She married **David RUSSELL**, married 9 Feb 1991, b. ABT 1970.
Children:

    1302. i   **Jennifer Renee RUSSELL**, b. 20 Aug 1991.

1149. **Kimberly Renee ENSOR**, (949.Dorothy[7], 658.Haskew[6],
340.Samuel[5], 105.Robert[4], 22.Margaret[3], 4.Jannette[2], 1.John[1]) b. 26
Apr 1973. She married **Consort of Kimberly Ensor**, b. ABT
1973.
Children:

    1303. i   **Shawna Renee ENSOR**, b. 26 Apr 1995.

1156. **Lynn HARRISON**, (955.Frances[7], 676.Edward[6], 349.Matthew[5],
107.Elizabeth[4], 23.Matthew[3], 4.Jannette[2], 1.John[1]) b. 16 Sep 1941
in Tampa Fl. 1990 began working at State Farm as a loss
prevention specialist. Had gone to nursing school in
Charlottesville VA and there met her husband. She married **Donald
Wayne GARDNER**, married 20 Jun 1962 in Charlottesville,
Albemarle Co., VA, b. 20 Apr 1935 in VA?. Graduated from HS in
Charlottesville. Served in the armed forces and worked in real
estate.

1996 worked at Rudy's dry cleaners.
Children:

+ 1304. i   **Stephen Allen GARDNER** b. 7 Oct 1964.

    1305. ii   **David Todd GARDNER**, b. 19 Jun 1967 in
Staunton, Augusta Co., VA. Majored in
anthropology at Mary Washington College in
Fredericksburg VA (1994).

                1996 lived in Fredericksburg VA. He married
Christine Marie STURM, married 27 Jul 1991 in
Charlottesville, Albemarle Co., VA, b. 10 Apr 1966
in St. Louis, Missouri. Received PhD in
anthropology.

1157. **Richard Hanslow HARRISON. Jr.**, (955.Frances[7], 676.Edward[6],
349.Matthew[5], 107.Elizabeth[4], 23.Matthew[3], 4.Jannette[2], 1.John[1]) b.

23 Jun 1944 in Louisiana. Had fellowship at Purdue. Had received engineering degree at Virginia Tech.

Since 1963 worked for Baltimore Aircoil - 1994 systems production manager.

1994 lived in Columbia, MD. He had attended school in Blacksburg as a military corpsman on a cooperative program. He alternated school work with employment at Atlantic Research Corp. near Leesburg, VA, majoring in mechanical engineering. He married **Ellen Doris Katharina STEGLICH**, married 30 Jun 1972, b. 17 Oct 1947 in Mainz, Germany. Met her husband when he was in the service in Germany.

Children:

1306. i **Mark Gotthard HARRISON**, b. 6 Apr 1976 in Columbia, Howard Co., MD. 1996 in his second year at U of Maryland.

1159. **Thomas Edward RHEA, Jr.**, (956.Thomas[7], 676.Edward[6], 349.Matthew[5], 107.Elizabeth[4], 23.Matthew[3], 4.Jannette[2], 1.John[1]) b. 2 1945 in Memphis, Shelby Co., TN. Retired from the US Navy on 30 September 1993 at Norfolk VA. Served for 20 years. Works at Micromax, a computer manufacturing company. Active in Church of the Ascension (Episcopal). Licensed Chalicer of the church. Moved in 1996 because of a fire at previous home. He married (1) **Donna Fern THOMAS**, married 2 May 1966 in Pauls Valley, Garvin Co. OK, b. 12 Jul 1947 in St. Pauls Valley, OK. He married (2) **Karen Patricia EVANS**, married 28 Nov 1981 in Idabel, McCurtain Co. OK, b. 13 Mar 1948 in Chicago, Cook Co., IL.

Children by Donna Fern THOMAS:

1307. i **Thomas Edward RHEA III.**, b. 29 Jan 1972 in Charleston, Charleston Co., SC.

1308. ii **Lynnette Frances RHEA**, b. 28 Jan 1977 in Charleston, Charleston Co., SC. Graduated from Stillwater Oklahoma High School May 25, 1995.

1160. **Allene Adele RHEA**, (956.Thomas[7], 676.Edward[6], 349.Matthew[5], 107.Elizabeth[4], 23.Matthew[3], 4.Jannette[2], 1.John[1]) b. 23 Sep 1946 in Riverside, Riverside Co. CA. Attended Southeastern State College i Durant. Worked as a receptionist for her father for many years. She married **Johnie Dale GRIMES**, married 1 Jun 1967 in

Idabel, McCurtain Co. OK, b. 17 Oct 1947 in Idabel, McCurtain Co. OK. Worked for Choctaw Electric Rural Cooperative for many years. An avid genealogist.
Children:

1309. i   **Rebecca Jane GRIMES**, b. in Idabel, McCurtain Co. OK.

+ 1310. ii   **Rachel Lenette GRIMES** b. 28 Oct 1969.

1311. iii   **Katherine Allene GRIMES**, b. 19 Jul 1972 in Idabel, McCurtain Co. OK. Graduated from East Central State U. Nursing School in spring of 1995. She married **Jamie SAMPSON**, married 24 Jun 1995 in Ada, Pontotoc Co. OK, b. 12 Nov 1970 in Ada, Pontotoc Co. OK. Attended Ada public school, graduated from Ada HS 1989.

1312. iv   **Victoria Rhea GRIMES**, b. 12 Oct 1983 in Idabel, McCurtain Co. OK.

1162. **George Matthew RHEA**, (956.Thomas[7], 676.Edward[6], 349.Matthew[5], 107.Elizabeth[4], 23.Matthew[3], 4.Jannette[2], 1.John[1]) b. 6 Oct 1950 in DeQueen, Sevier Co. AR, d. 3 Apr 1997 in Idabel, McCurtain Co. OK, buried in Denison Cemetery, Idabel, OK. 1997 obituary in McCurtain Daily Gazette, Idabelle OK:
"Rhea joined the staff in 1972, a year after Superintendent Glass came there. Glass said he was a respected leader of youth who wore many hats and has been a key person at the school for 25 years. Other than Glass, Rhea was the senior member of the staff at Tom School.

Rhea headed the Chapter I program there, instructing students at all grade levels in language and English. He was a curriculum coordinator and official in the county curriculum contests.

A 4-H leader, he was a member of Forest Heritage Center's board of directors. Also active in community theater productions. He was treasurer of the St. Luke's Episcopal Church in Idabel.

Survivors include his wife Gail Rhea and children April and Stephen Rhea. He is also survived by his father Thomas E. Rhea, and stepmother Jo Rhea of Idabell, sisters and brothers-in-law Arlene R. Grimes and Johnie D. Grimes, Sarah R. White and

Robert J. White of Alexandria TN, a brother Thomas E. Rhea Jr. of
Norfolk VA, brothers and sisters-in-law Richard Rhea and Lanney
C. Rhea, Herbert C. Rhea and Nellie F. Rhea of Jenks, Robert R.
Rhea MD and Lisa m. Rhea of Franklin TN; his mother-in-law
Clara Russell Johnson and husband Louie Johnson of Hochatown
and 22 nieces and nephews."

George married Gail Russell in Idabel on August 14 1971. He had
been a teacher for the Tom Public Schools for the past 25 years.
George died of colon cancer complicated by renal failure. He
married **Gail Anita RUSSELL**, married 14 Aug 1971 in Idabel,
McCurtain Co. OK, b. 24 Nov 1949 in Idabel, McCurtain Co. OK.
Children:

    1313. i   **April Anita RHEA**, b. 12 Oct 1977 in Idabel,
                McCurtain Co. OK. Graduated from Idabel High
                School 19 May 1996 in Idabel OK.

    1314. ii   **Stephen Matthew RHEA**, b. 13 Jun 1983 in Idabel,
                McCurtain Co. OK.

1163. **Sarah Elizabeth RHEA**, (956.Thomas[7], 676.Edward[6],
349.Matthew[5], 107.Elizabeth[4], 23.Matthew[3], 4.Jannette[2], 1.John[1]) b.
27 Dec 1951 in Hugo, Choctaw Co. OK. 1995 worked at Baptist
Dekalb General Hospital. She married **Robert James WHITE**,
married 19 May 1973 in Idabel, McCurtain Co. OK, b. 22 Apr 1951
in Smithville, Dekalb Co. TN. 1994 ran an antique store in
Smithville. An avid collector. He worked on special assignment
for the Tennessee State Museum.
         Children:

    1315. i   **Elizabeth Adele WHITE**, b. 23 Aug 1976 in
                Smithville, Dekalb Co. TN.

    1316. ii   **James Harrison WHITE**, b. 2 Apr 1980 in
                Smithville, Dekalb Co. TN.

    1317. iii **John Rhea WHITE**, b. 8 Sep 1983 in Smithville,
                Dekalb Co. TN.

1164. **Richard Card RHEA**, (956.Thomas[7], 676.Edward[6],
349.Matthew[5], 107.Elizabeth[4], 23.Matthew[3], 4.Jannette[2], 1.John[1]) b.
20 Feb 1956 in Idabel, McCurtain Co. OK. Worked in Oklahoma
City until 1998 then took a position with Abbott Laboratories in the

diagnostic equipment division. Lived in Little Rock, Arkansas. He married **Lanney Louise COOPER**, married 30 Oct 1981 in Oklahoma City, Oklahoma Co., OK, b. 20 Feb 1957 in Hugo, OK.
Children:

1318. i   **Amy Elizabeth RHEA**, b. 30 Jan 1983 in Oklahoma City, Oklahoma Co., OK.

1319. ii   **Bradley Adam RHEA**, b. 26 Sep 1985 in Oklahoma City, Oklahoma Co., OK.

1320. iii   **Amanda LeeAnn RHEA**, b. 14 Jul 1987 in Oklahoma City, Oklahoma Co., OK.

1321. iv   **Melissa Annette RHEA**, b. 9 Jan 1990 in Oklahoma City, Oklahoma Co., OK.

1165. **Herbert Card RHEA**, (956.Thomas^7, 676.Edward^6, 349.Matthew^5, 107.Elizabeth^4, 23.Matthew^3, 4.Jannette^2, 1.John^1) b. 20 Feb 1956 in Idabel, McCurtain Co. OK. Twin. 1994 moved to Jenks OK, a suburb of Tulsa. Was as athletic trainer for Jenks Public Schools. He married **Nellie LaVonne FRY**, married 4 Dec 1976 in Stillwater, Payne Co. OK, b. 9 Oct 1955 in Stillwater, OK.
Children:

1322. i   **Joshua Glen RHEA**, b. 1 Dec 1980 in Enid, OK. Confirmed in the Episcopal Church at Hollins College, Roanoke VA in 1994.

1323. ii   **Ashley Marie RHEA**, b. 8 Mar 1984 in Enid, OK.

1166. **Robert Eugene RHEA**, (956.Thomas^7, 676.Edward^6, 349.Matthew^5, 107.Elizabeth^4, 23.Matthew^3, 4.Jannette^2, 1.John^1) b. 6 Nov 1958 in Idabel, McCurtain Co. OK. 1977 graduated from Idabel Gray High School.

1977-78 was spent in Korbach Germany as an exchange student. Graduated from Oral Roberts U., Tulsa OK 1982 with a B.A.

1986 earned his M.D. Degree. In family practice residency in Jackson TN 1986-89. Practiced in Stoud, OK 1989-92. Practiced Ashland City, TN since 1993. Member of the Episcopal Church and has served on the vestry. He married **Lisa Jane MARTIN**, married 1 Aug 1981 in Tulsa, Tulsa Co., OK, b. 19 Aug 1960 in

San Jose, CA. 1978 graduated from LeMars Community HS
(Iowa). Graduated from Oral Roberts U., Tulsa OK with B.S.
degree in 1982.
Children:

1324. i   **Matthew Robert RHEA**, b. 17 Oct 1987 in Jackson,
Madison Co. TN.

1325. ii   **Alexander Samuel RHEA**, b. 29 Jul 1992 in Tulsa,
Tulsa Co., OK.

1167. **Stephen Herbert RHEA, Jr.**, (957.Stephen⁷, 676.Edward⁶,
349.Matthew⁵, 107.Elizabeth⁴, 23.Matthew³, 4.Jannette², 1.John¹) b.
3 Jul 1949 in St. Louis, Missouri. Worked for Union Planters
Bank. He married **Leigh SCHOPFER**, married 6 Mar 1982 in
Dallas, Dallas Co., TX, b. 20 Mar 1952 in Memphis, Shelby Co.,
TN.
Children:

1326. i   **Emily Keith RHEA**, b. 7 Nov 1983 in Dallas, Dallas
Co., TX.

1327. ii   **Elizabeth Leigh RHEA**, b. 29 May 1986 in Dallas,
Dallas Co., TX.

1172. **James Samuel RHEA, Jr.**, (961.James⁷, 679.James⁶, 350.James⁵,
107.Elizabeth⁴, 23.Matthew³, 4.Jannette², 1.John¹) b. 6 Sep 1943.
Attended Memphis State University

1986 was engaged in farming and operating the family gin. Lived
in the old Rhea family home. He married **Rebecca Lee OZIER**,
married 7 Apr 1966, b. 22 Jun 1944 in Monroe, LA.
Children:

1328. i   **Lee Ann RHEA**, b. 24 Dec 1968.

1329. ii   **Jamie Rebecca RHEA**, b. 17 Nov 1972.

1330. iii   **Samantha Courtney RHEA**, b. 2 Sep 1983.

1173. **David Charles RHEA**, (961.James⁷, 679.James⁶, 350.James⁵,
107.Elizabeth⁴, 23.Matthew³, 4.Jannette², 1.John¹) b. 18 May 1951
in TN. Attended Draughons Business College.

1986 was assistant manager of the Colonial Country Club in Memphis. He married **Mary Patricia RILES**, married 16 Aug 1974, b. ABT 1951.
Children:

    1331. i   **David Charles RHEA Jr.**, b. 16 Aug 1980.

    1332. ii   **Chad Alan RHEA**, b. 4 Feb 1986.

1174. **James Wilson SNOWDEN**, (962.Betty[7], 679.James[6], 350.James[5], 107.Elizabeth[4], 23.Matthew[3], 4.Jannette[2], 1.John[1]) b. 27 Jun 1941. He married **Betty Lou WHITE**, married 15 Feb 1963, b. ABT 1941.
    Children:

    1333. i   **Any Denise SNOWDEN**, b. 9 Dec 1963.

    1334. ii   **James Wilson SNOWDEN Jr.**, b. 25 Dec 1972.

1176. **Sarah Ann SPENGLER**, (964.Mary[7], 679.James[6], 350.James[5], 107.Elizabeth[4], 23.Matthew[3], 4.Jannette[2], 1.John[1]) b. 2 Sep 1957. Graduated from Carleton College, Northfield MN.

1986 they were living in Northfield. She married **Allen Lee JANKE**, b. ABT 1957.
    Children:

    1335. i   **Zachary Arthur JANKE**, b. 29 Sep 1984.

1178. **Thomas Watkins RHEA, Jr.**, (966.Thomas[7], 680.John[6], 350.James[5], 107.Elizabeth[4], 23.Matthew[3], 4.Jannette[2], 1.John[1]) b. 28 Nov 1934 in Fayette Co., TN. Was a draftee and served in US Military from 1957 to 1959. Came back to Somerville and followed in his fathers footsteps. Farmed the Watkins land and built a house on Highway 59 next to his mother and father. He married **Suzanne MARSHALL**, married 13 Jun 1958, b. 17 Jan 1940 in Mason, TN.
    Children:

    1336. i   **Susan Blanche RHEA**, b. 12 Sep 1962 in Fayette Co., TN. She and William lived in Little Rock AR in 1986. She married **William Selby KENNEDY V.**, married 14 May 1983 in Somerville, Fayette Co., TN, b. 13 Jul 1960 in AR.

1337. ii **Martha Boyd RHEA**, b. 17 Sep 1964 in Fayette Co., TN. 1986 lived in Memphis and worked for a travel agency.

1179. **Martha Deborah RHEA**, (968.William^7, 682.William^6, 350.James^5, 107.Elizabeth^4, 23.Matthew^3, 4.Jannette^2, 1.John^1) b. 29 Dec 1952. She married **Gerald Francis SLATTERY Jr.**, b. ABT 1953.
Children:

1338. i **Thomas Eamon SLATTERY**, b. 1986.

1339. ii **Matthew Rhea SLATTERY**, b. 1987.

1340. iii **Anna Elizabeth SLATTERY**, b. 1990.

1180. **William Humphrey RHEA**, (968.William^7, 682.William^6, 350.James^5, 107.Elizabeth^4, 23.Matthew^3, 4.Jannette^2, 1.John^1) b. 27 Nov 1954. He married **Cathy Howell TIDWELL**, b. 1954.
Children:

1341. i **Catherine Elizabeth RHEA**, b. 1983.

1342. ii **William Andrew RHEA**, b. 1986.

1343. iii **Patricia Scott RHEA**, b. 1989.

1181. **Reuben Scott RHEA Jr.**, (969.Reuben^7, 682.William^6, 350.James^5, 107.Elizabeth^4, 23.Matthew^3, 4.Jannette^2, 1.John^1) b. 8 Aug 1950. He married **Margaret Ann TOMLIN**, b. 1952.
Children:

1344. i **Reuben Scott RHEA III.**, b. 1977.

1345. ii **Gordon Matthew RHEA**, b. 1979.

1182. **Boyd Burnette RHEA**, (969.Reuben^7, 682.William^6, 350.James^5, 107.Elizabeth^4, 23.Matthew^3, 4.Jannette^2, 1.John^1) b. 16 Feb 1953. He married **Jane JOURDON**, b. ABT 1953.
Children:

1346. i **Boyd Burnette RHEA Jr.**, b. 1977.

The Preston Family of Walnut Grove, Virginia

1347. ii **Olen Jourdan RHEA**, b. 1979.

1348. iii **Joshua Harris RHEA**, b. 1982.

Ninth Generation

1195. **Margaret Preston MADDEN**, (997.Margaret[8], 728.Lucille[7], 415.Margaret[6], 131.Ellen[5], 26.Margaret[4], 5.John[3], 2.Robert[2], 1.John[1]) b. ABT 1950. She married **Jeffrey Brook ALLEN**, b. ABT 1950.
> *Children:*

1349. i **Margaret Preston ALLEN**, b. ABT 1980.

1350. ii **Jonathan Brooke ALLEN**, b. ABT 1982.

1202. **Robert Malcolm KENNARD**, (999.Martha[8], 739.Malcolm[7], 420.Frank[6], 131.Ellen[5], 26.Margaret[4], 5.John[3], 2.Robert[2], 1.John[1]) b. 2 Apr 1955 in Dallas, Dallas Co., TX. He married **Beth DOHONEY**, married 27 Dec 1981 in Hillsboro, Hill Co., TX, b. 27 Apr 1958 in Hillsboro, Hill Co., TX.
> *Children:*

1351. i **Kate Campbell KENNARD**, b. 16 Oct 1987 in Dallas, Dallas Co., TX.

1352. ii **Elizabeth Ellen KENNARD**, b. 14 Nov 1991 in Dallas, Dallas Co., TX.

1353. iii **Will Reed KENNARD**, b. 23 Jun 1998 in Dallas, Dallas Co., TX.

1205. **Jane DENTON**, (1000.Carolyn[8], 739.Malcolm[7], 420.Frank[6], 131.Ellen[5], 26.Margaret[4], 5.John[3], 2.Robert[2], 1.John[1]) b. 30 Oct 1955 in Bonham, Fannin Co., TX. She married **Rick JONES**, b. ABT 1955.
> *Children:*

1354. i **Abigail JONES**, b. ABT 1975 in TX.

1355. ii **Allison JONES**, b. ABT 1977 in TX.

1206. **Jo Carolyn DENTON**, (1000.Carolyn[8], 739.Malcolm[7], 420.Frank[6], 131.Ellen[5], 26.Margaret[4], 5.John[3], 2.Robert[2], 1.John[1]) b. 22 Mar

1957 in Bonham, Fannin Co., TX. She married **Peter MUSE**, married in Dallas, Dallas Co., TX, b. ABT 1957.
Children:

   1356. i   **Denton MUSE**, b. ABT 1980 in Dallas, Dallas Co., TX.

   1357. ii   **Ben MUSE**, b. ABT 1982 in Dallas, Dallas Co., TX.

1215. **Mark Leinart RHEA**, (1036.Robert[8], 818.Frank[7], 503.Robert[6], 184.Frances[5], 40.Sarah[4], 6.Jane[3], 2.Robert[2], 1.John[1]) b. ABT 1950. Lived in Greenville TX. He married **wife of Mark RHEA**, b. ABT 1950.
Children:

   1358. i   **Daniel RHEA**, b. ABT 1970. 1998 lives in Fort Worth TX.

1219. **James Samuel PERRY**, (1042.Margaret[8], 829.Samuel[7], 508.Charles[6], 185.Margaret[5], 40.Sarah[4], 6.Jane[3], 2.Robert[2], 1.John[1]) b. ABT 1940 in TN. Attended Washington and Lee High School in Arlington VA.

1964 was living at Wake Forest, NC. Later, Chairman of the psychology department of East Tennessee University. He married **wf of James PERRY**, b. ABT 1950.
Children:

   1359. i   **Theodore 'Thad' Leland PERRY**, b. ABT 1967 in Bristol, Sullivan Co., TN. Working on Doctorate of Psychology at Vanderbilt University (1993).

   1360. ii   **Margaret 'Meg' Alice PERRY**, b. ABT 1974. Graduated from Vanderbilt University. She married **Claude W. MILLICAN III.**, b. ABT 1975.

   1361. iii   **Alexa D. PERRY**, b. ABT 1977 in Blountville, Sullivan Co., TN.

1221. **Harriet Ann CALDWELL**, (1043.Etta[8], 829.Samuel[7], 508.Charles[6], 185.Margaret[5], 40.Sarah[4], 6.Jane[3], 2.Robert[2], 1.John[1]) b. 29 Jul 1937 in Bristol, Sullivan Co., TN. She married **Otto Maurice SPANGLER**, b. ABT 1937. Pastor of the campus of the University of Florida at Gainesville.

1964 lived in Burgin KY.
Children:

    1362. i   **Otto 'Chuck' Maurice SPANGLER, Jr.**, b. ABT 1960. 1995 the family was living in Suffolk, England where Mary was stationed with the US Air Force. He married **Mary wife of Otto SPANGLER**, b. ABT 1960. Worked as lawyer for the US Air Force.

+ 1363. ii   **Victor SPANGLER** b. ABT 1962.

+ 1364. iii **Elizabeth SPANGLER** b. ABT 1964.

1222. **Joyce Eveleen CALDWELL**, (1043.Etta^8, 829.Samuel^7, 508.Charles^6, 185.Margaret^5, 40.Sarah^4, 6.Jane^3, 2.Robert^2, 1.John^1) b. 5 Sep 1940 in Bristol, Sullivan Co., TN. She married **William FLANNAGAN**, married 1958, b. ABT 1940. 1964 was living in Jackson AL.

1995 the family was living in Rome GA.
Children:

    1365. i   **William 'Chip' FLANNAGAN Jr.**, b. ABT 1961 in St. Louis, Missouri.

    1366. ii   **Cindy Marie FLANNAGAN**, b. ABT 1965 in St. Louis, Missouri. She married **Michael STEEN**, b. ABT 1965 in Mo?. 1995 the family was living in St. Louis. Mike was working for Boatmans Bank there. They have 2 children.

1223. **Ford 'Buddy' CALDWELL, Jr.**, (1043.Etta^8, 829.Samuel^7, 508.Charles^6, 185.Margaret^5, 40.Sarah^4, 6.Jane^3, 2.Robert^2, 1.John^1) b. 31 Mar 1947 in Bristol, Sullivan Co., TN. 1995 lives in Plano TX. Works for a chemical company. He married (1) **Sheila wife of Ford CALDWELL**, b. ABT 1947. Ford and Sheila were married 21 years (1995). He married (2) **Kim BOONE**, b. 1955 in TX?. She and Ford met at work. Had two children by previous marriage.
Children by Sheila wife of Ford CALDWELL:

    1367. i   **Brett CALDWELL**, b. ABT 1975. 1995 was student at Texas Tech.

1226. **Janet Erin BOUTON**, (1046.James[8], 832.Violet[7], 508.Charles[6], 185.Margaret[5], 40.Sarah[4], 6.Jane[3], 2.Robert[2], 1.John[1]) b. 3 Jun 1953 in Washington D.C. Born at Doctors Hospital in Washington, D.C. Lived her early years in the Washington suburb of Lewisdale. Attended Lewisdale elementary. Moved to Kettering in Largo Md and attended junior and Senior high school at Fredrick Sasscer High School in Upper Marlboro, Maryland. This was an old rural High school at the Prince George's County seat. In Spanish Class is where she met her future husband. They had both Spanish and geometry together.

1971-73 attended Prince George Community College. The college was located just across the highway from her Kettering subdivision. This was just a short drive in her red Ford Pinto each day. In her Junior year she transferred to the University of Maryland in College Park, MD. During her college years, she worked evenings at Woodward and Lothrop, a high-end department store.

1975 Graduated U. of Maryland B.A. in English Literature 1975. Began her banking career at Unibank in Montgomery Co. MD as a teller. Worked at Unibank until it was taken over in a merger. Stayed in the banking area and took a position at Friendship Savings and Loan as head teller in Bethesda and later Assistant Manager. Worked at the Savings and Loan until the birth of her first child. Went on leave for about 6 months and then returned as Assistant Manager at the Friendship branch at White Flint in Montgomery Co. Md.

1979 left the bank when she moved to NY to follow her husband's work and dedicated herself to raising her family. Managed the rental of the Bowie house while they lived in New York and later when they returned to Maryland in 1985. She was often a school volunteer. She was Den mother for David's age group in Columbia pack 601. She was Room Mother at Singapore American school 5th grade in 1999. Shepherded the children through years of schooling keeping close to the teachers and counselors at each school. While living in Singapore she traveled to many of the countries in Asia and Europe. She played tennis with friends and in an occasional competition (winning a trophy in 1996 in Ladies Doubles from the Fontana Heights Tournament).

2001 she and her youngest moved to Japan to join her husband who had gone ahead before the school year began. There she was a member and served on the board of the American Women's club.

After returning to the U.S. in 2003, she became involved as a board members of the Peoria Easter Seals Auxiliary, hostess of a local a Mahjong group, and served as president of the 100 member Entree Neu newcomers group. She's an avid reader. She married **Edward Francis FOLEY III**, married 23 Oct 1976 in U of Maryland Chapel, b. 13 Oct 1954 in Asheville, Buncombe Co., NC. 1954 Born at St. Joseph's Hospital in Asheville (Buncombe) NC. Baptized at St. Lawrence Roman Catholic Basilica in downtown Asheville.

1955 Ed's father took job as Agent in NYC. Family moved when Ed was 6 months old to a one bedroom apartment on Crocheron Av. and then eventually to a 2 bedroom ground floor apartment at 172nd St. and Crocheron Av. Flushing NY. Eventually four children in one room sleeping on two bunk beds.

1972 attended Notre Dame studying of business for two years. Changed major to biology and transferred to U of Maryland where he graduated in 1976 with a B.S. in Biology.

1976 began working in finance for General Electric Credit where he would hold various positions of increasing responsibility for the next 9 years.

1979 first son Michael was born in Silver Spring, MD.

1980 was transferred to the General Electric Credit offices on Long Island NY. Moved with Jan and Mike to a duplex on Handsome Av. a half block from the Great South Bay in Sayville on Long Island. That year enrolled in MBA program at NY Institute of Technology, Commack NY Campus.

1982 bought a house at 67 Bushwick St. in South Huntington NY 1/2 mile from the GE office.

1985 started to work in as manager for Caterpillar Financial Services in Columbia MD. Bought a house at Campfire Lane Columbia MD, 4 miles from office. The children attended local schools and participated in soccer – Ed as assistant coach. Enjoyed time with the boys in scouts, as den leader; Assistant Scoutmaster.

1992 completed MBA at Loyola College of Maryland, in Baltimore. Concentration was International Business.

1995 accepted position of Director and Treasurer of Caterpillar Asia in Singapore. Supervised a staff of over 60 foreign nationals; also director of a number of Caterpillar Affiliates in the Asia Region. Director V-Trac Infrastructure Co. a Cook Island company through which CAT owns 25% of the dealership in Hanoi, Vietnam. Director, Tractor Engineers Ltd. Bombay, India. This company is a joint venture with Indian company Larson and Tubrough. TENGL manufactures tractor undercarriage for machines in India and engine manufacturer Hindustan Powerplus Ltd., Bangalaore.

2001 was elected Vice President of Caterpillar Financial Services with responsibility for Asia Pacific. That summer the family moved to Tokyo, Japan where Ed administered that company's operations in the nine countries they operated in Asia, and started the company on the path to enter China.

2003 the family returned to the U.S. to Peoria, where he assumed marketing responsibilities for Caterpillar for the Eastern U.S. and Canada.

2004 was awarded a Doctorate of Business Administration from the University of Sarasota in Florida.

2005 Executive Vice President of Caterpillar Financial Services with responsibility for all operations in North America including board responsibility for the company's finance subsidiary, FCC, in Jacksonville, FL.

Source Citation:
Who's Who in the East. 24th edition, 1993-1994. New Providence, NJ: Marquis Who's Who, 1992.
Who's Who of Emerging Leaders in America. Third edition, 1991-1992. Wilmette, IL: Marquis Who's Who, 1991.
Who's Who of Emerging Leaders in America. Fourth edition, 1993-1994. New Providence, NJ: Marquis Who's Who, 1992.
Who's Who in Finance and Industry. 26th edition, 1989-1990. Wilmette, IL: Marquis Who's Who, 1989.
Who's Who in Finance and Industry(R) (Marquis(TM)). 30th edition, 1998-1999. New Providence, NJ: Marquis Who's Who, 1997.
Children:

1368. i **Michael James FOLEY**, b. 26 Oct 1979 in Holy
Cross Hosp, Silver Spring Montgomery Co. MD.
Born in Maryland and spent his first to years in a
four-bedroom cape cod Levitt home. During his
school years Mike participated in Cub Scouts,
earning his Arrow of Light rank and spent a year in
Boy scouts. He played baseball in Middle School
and his first year of high school ran cross country
track.

1996 moved to Singapore. 1998 graduated from
Singapore American School.

2002 graduated from Howard County Community
College, Columbia MD with an A. A. degree while
living in Columbia, MD.

2005 awarded degree from University of Maryland,
Magna Cum Laude, after majoring in history.

1369. ii **David Edward FOLEY**, b. 28 Sep 1982 in
Southside Hosp, Bayshore (Nassau) NY. Born on
Long Island, David spent his first years on the Great
South Bay in Sayville, NY and later in Huntington
when his parents bought a home there near Ted's
office. Before David entered school, he moved with
his family to Columbia, Maryland. He attended
nursery school there and made some long time
friends.

Attended Jeffers Hill Elementary School a short walk
from his home on Campfire Ln. Entered Owen
Brown Middle School where he was active in soccer
and baseball, but moved to Singapore when he was
13. Entered the Singapore American School as a
Freshman at Woodlands in Singapore. During his
stay in Asia he has visited more than 20 countries
with his family. He was part of the school's orchestra
as first chair cellist.

2003 attended Central Illinois College in East Peoria,
IL. 2005 after completing the requirements for his
Associates Degree, he transferred to Temple
University's Tokyo campus. He lived in Kawasaki

Japan at the home of friend Yuriko Yokoyama's grandmother while attending the University.

1370. iii **Ryan Connor FOLEY**, b. 18 Apr 1988 in Howard Co. Hosp. Columbia, (Howard)MD. Born at Howard County Hospital and spend his early years in Columbia.

Attended nursery school and then Jeffers Hill Elementary School just a short walk from his home. Moved in 1996 to Singapore with his family and entered the 3rd grade.

2001 moved with his family to Tokyo. Attended the 8th grade at International Secondary School in Meguro Honcho in Tokyo. He would ride his bicycle each morning to the subway station at Azabu Juban and ride the train to the station not far from the school. The school was small with very personal instruction in a format from the University of North Dakota. 2003 the family move to Peoria IL in the Midwest. Ryan attended and graduated from Illinois Valley Central High School in Chillicothe, IL in 2006.

1228. **Mark Earhart BOUTON**, (1047.Charles[8], 832.Violet[7], 508.Charles[6], 185.Margaret[5], 40.Sarah[4], 6.Jane[3], 2.Robert[2], 1.John[1]) b. 10 Sep 1953 in Albuquerque, Bernillo Co. NM. 1975 received B.A. from Williams College.

1980 received Ph. D in psychology from University. of Washington in Seattle.

From the University of Vermont Web site summary of faculty and curriculum vitae:

Mark E. Bouton Professor of Psychology; Editor (since 1996): Journal of Experimental Psychology: Animal Behavior Processes President-Elect, Eastern Psychological Association, 2003-4 President, Eastern Psychological Association, 2004-5.

Program: Experimental Cluster: Biobehavioral

Curriculum Vitae

Areas of Interest
The goal of my research is to understand the basic mechanisms of learning, memory, and emotion that are represented in classical conditioning, one of the most fundamental examples of associative learning that we know. I have been especially interested in inhibitory processes in learning and memory, and how "contexts," or cues that are present in the background whenever learning and remembering occur, control them. In classical conditioning, the context can be many things, including external cues provided by the setting or environment, the internal state created by drugs, emotions, recent events, and even the passage of time. My students and I study all of these things. I am especially interested in the implications of our findings for theories of conditioning and associative learning, theories of memory, and theories of certain clinical issues, such as relapse after therapy. I am also interested in the brain mechanisms behind our effects. My main interest, though, is learning itself, which I see as the essential process by which humans and animals adapt to the environment during their lives. Since 1998, I have been the Editor of the Journal of Experimental Psychology: Animal Behavior Processes, the American Psychological Association's journal covering animal learning, cognition, and motivation. (see www.apa.org/journals/xan.html)

Representative Publications
Bouton, M. E., & Sunsay, C. (2003). Importance of trials versus accumulating time across trials in partially-reinforced appetitive conditioning. Journal of Experimental Psychology: Animal Behavior Processes, 29, 62-77.

Bouton, M. E. (2002). Context, ambiguity, and unlearning: Sources of relapse after behavioral extinction. Biological Psychiatry, 52, 976-986.

Bouton, M. E., Mineka, S., & Barlow, D. H. (2001). A modern learning theory perspective on the etiology of panic disorder. Psychological Review, 108, 4-32.

Pearce, J. M., & Bouton, M. E. (2001). Theories of associative learning in animals. Annual Review of Psychology, 52, 111-139.

Frohardt, R. J., Guarraci, F. A., & Bouton, M. E. (2000). The effects of neurotoxic hippocampal lesions on two effects of context after fear extinction. Behavioral Neuroscience, 114, 227-240.

Bouton, M. E. (2000). A learning theory perspective on lapse, relapse, and the maintenance of behavior change. Health Psychology, 19(Suppl.), 57-63.

Bouton, M. E., Nelson, J. B., & Rosas, J. M. (1999). Stimulus generalization, context change, and forgetting. Psychological Bulletin, 125, 171-186.

Holland, P. C., & Bouton, M. E. (1999). Hippocampus and context in classical conditioning. Current Opinion in Neurobiology, 9, 195-202.

Rosas, J. M., & Bouton, M. E. (1998). Context change and retention interval can have additive, rather than interactive, effects after taste aversion extinction. Psychonomic Bulletin & Review, 5, 79-83. He married **Suzie LEGAULT**, married in Naperville, IL, b. 1 Apr 1953 in St. Louis, St. Louis Co., MO.

> *Children:*

>> 1371. i **Lindsey LeGault BOUTON**, b. 28 May 1987 in Burlington VT.

>> 1372. ii **Grace Dorothy BOUTON**, b. 28 Dec 1992 in Burlington VT.

1229. **Leslie Ann BOUTON**, (1047.Charles[8], 832.Violet[7], 508.Charles[6], 185.Margaret[5], 40.Sarah[4], 6.Jane[3], 2.Robert[2], 1.John[1]) b. 5 Mar 1956 in Washington D.C. Degree in Russian Language. She married **James C. PETERSON**, married 23 Jul in Naperville, IL, b. 1954 in Rockford, IL. Work as a chemist at Monsanto primarily involving their product 'Roundup' (1993).

Doctorate from Northwestern University.
> *Children:*

>> 1373. i **Brooke Bouton PETERSON**, b. 8 Oct 1989 in Manchester MO.

>> 1374. ii **Christa Whitcraft PETERSON**, b. 1 Sep 1990 in Manchester MO.

1230. **Clare Lynn BOUTON**, (1047.Charles[8], 832.Violet[7], 508.Charles[6], 185.Margaret[5], 40.Sarah[4], 6.Jane[3], 2.Robert[2], 1.John[1]) b. 9 Oct 1961

in Aurora, Kane Co, IL. 1992 lived in Arlington VA. She married **Myles Robert HANSEN**, married 22 Jul 1989 in Chevy Chase United Methodist Church, b. ABT 1961. 1992 lived 3456 South Wakefield Arlington VA 22206.
Children:

    1375. i   **Reuben Henry HANSEN**, b. 1 Sep 1992 in Alexandria VA.

    1376. ii   **Madeleine June HANSEN**, b. 17 Mar 1995 in Washington D.C.

    1377. iii **George Earhart HANSEN**, b. 8 Aug 1996 in Fairfax Va.

1237. **Kenneth Lee COONTZ**, (1051.Robert^8, 868.Virginia^7, 524.Jane^6, 192.Sarah^5, 43.John^4, 6.Jane^3, 2.Robert^2, 1.John^1) b. 27 Nov 1957 in Annapolis, Anne Arundel Co. MD. 1998 lived in Toronto Canada. He married **Sophia PECKMAN**, married 2 Dec 1982 in Toronto, Ontario CANADA.
Children:

    1378. i   **Kendall Lee COONTZ**, b. 4 Sep 1984 in Toronto, Ontario CANADA.

1284. **Charles Jacob KUNKLE IV**, (1082.Mary^8, 884.Florence^7, 530.John^6, 194.Samuel^5, 43.John^4, 6.Jane^3, 2.Robert^2, 1.John^1) b. 23 Aug 1967 in St. Louis, MO. He married **Cheri PITTS**, married 1990, b. 10 Feb 1969.
Children:

    1379. i   **Chelby KUNKLE**, b. 23 Jul 1990.

    1380. ii   **Charles Jacob KUNKLE V**, b. 15 Jan 1995.

    1381. iii **Cayla KUNKLE**, b. 23 Jul 1999.

    1382. iv **Corbin KUNKLE**, b. 29 Mar 2002 in Blue Springs, MO.

1285. **Amanda KUNKLE**, (1082.Mary^8, 884.Florence^7, 530.John^6, 194.Samuel^5, 43.John^4, 6.Jane^3, 2.Robert^2, 1.John^1) b. 30 Sep 1979 in Independence, MO. Works as a secretary. She married **Joel ADAMS**, b. ABT 1979.

Children:

1383. i **Mary Frances ADAMS**, b. 30 Nov 1999 in Atlanta, GA.

1304. **Stephen Allen GARDNER**, (1156.Lynn^8, 955.Frances^7, 676.Edward^6, 349.Matthew^5, 107.Elizabeth^4, 23.Matthew^3, 4.Jannette^2, 1.John^1) b. 7 Oct 1964 in Charlottesville, Albemarle Co., VA. 1995 broadcast editor for USA TODAY in Arlington VA.

1995 lived in Winchester VA. He married **Robin Elizabeth LOGERWELL**, married 6 Jul 1991, b. 30 Dec 1963 in San Diego, CA.

Children:

1384. i **Joshua Thomas Logerwell GARDNER**, b. 19 Feb 1989 in Charlottesville, Albemarle Co., VA.

1385. ii **Kelsey Erin GARDNER**, b. 7 Nov 1991 in Winchester, Frederick Co. VA.

1310. **Rachel Lenette GRIMES**, (1160.Allene^8, 956.Thomas^7, 676.Edward^6, 349.Matthew^5, 107.Elizabeth^4, 23.Matthew^3, 4.Jannette^2, 1.John^1) b. 28 Oct 1969 in Idabel, McCurtain Co. OK. She married **Douglas O'Neal ALLEN**, married 11 Aug 1989 in Idabel, McCurtain Co. OK, b. 3 Nov 1969 in Texarkana, Bowie Co. TX.

Children:

1386. i **Whittney Allene ALLEN**, b. 1991 in Oklahoma City, Oklahoma Co., OK.

1387. ii **Brittney Annette ALLEN**, b. 14 Nov 1991 in Oklahoma City, Oklahoma Co., OK.

Tenth Generation

1363. **Victor SPANGLER**, (1221.Harriet^9, 1043.Etta^8, 829.Samuel^7, 508.Charles^6, 185.Margaret^5, 40.Sarah^4, 6.Jane^3, 2.Robert^2, 1.John^1) b. ABT 1962. 1995 lived on a boat with family in Daytona Fl. He married **Ronica wife of Victor SPANGLER**, b. ABT 1962.

Children:

1388. i   **Elise SPANGLER**, b. ABT 1990.

1364. **Elizabeth SPANGLER**, (1221.Harriet[9], 1043.Etta[8], 829.Samuel[7], 508.Charles[6], 185.Margaret[5], 40.Sarah[4], 6.Jane[3], 2.Robert[2], 1.John[1]) b. ABT 1964. She married **Mr. BERGE**, b. ABT 1964. Works for Secret Service. 1995 stationed in Germany but soon to relocated to Northern Virginia.

          Children:

1389. i   **Christopher BERGE**, b. ABT 1990.

Bibliography

Armstrong, Zella, 1922, *Notable Southern Families*. Lookout Publishing, Chattanooga, TN.

Foley, Edward, 1996, *The Descendants of Rev. Joseph Rhea of Ireland*. Heritage Books, Bowie, MD.

Foley, Edward, 2000, *The Descendants of Matthew 'The Rebel' Rhea of Ireland and Scotland*. Heritage Books, Bowie, MD.

Gray, M., Rolston, H. 1966. The Story of the Walnut Grove Church. Pamphlet dated may 27, 1966, Washington Co. Historical Society Collection.

Rhea Family Papers, Accession Number THS 10, Date of Procession Completion, March 18, 1966, Property of Tennessee Historical Society.

Rhea, William L., 1895, *Genealogy of the Rhea Family*. Unpublished Manuscript, copy held in the Sullivan County (TN) Public Library, Blountville, TN.

Summers, Lewis P., 1903, *History of Southwest Virginia 1746-1786, Washington County 1777-1870*. Overmountain Press, Johnson City, TN.

Summers, Lewis P. 1936. Walnut Grove Cemetery Is Among Section's Most Historical Spots. Bristol Herald Courier, July 4, 1936.

Summers, Lewis P. Walnut Grove, now a business center, once was a Preston Domain. Washington County News, reprinted March 4, 1971.

Tucker, Joy, 1985, Nine Generations. Washington County News, September 5, 1985.

ABSHER
Helen Marie, 274
ADAMS
Brainard Rhea, 228
Charles Linwood, 227
Frank Milton, 239
Frank Milton, Jr. Jr., 239
Joel, 372
Leta Rhea, 239
Louise G. wife of Yancey, 240
Mary Frances, 373
Nathan, 240
William H. or S., 227
Yancey Dailey, 240
AKARD
Bess, 161
ALBRIGHT
Lula Jane, 190
ALDRIDGE
Harriet West, 149
ALFORD
James Rhea, 332
Joseph III., 332
Joseph Jr., 277, 332
Joseph Thompson, 277
ALLEN
Brittney Annette, 373
Douglas O'Neal, 373
Jeffrey Brook, 362
Jonathan Brooke, 362
Margaret Preston, 362
Whittney Allene, 373
ANDERSON
Alexander, 236
Audley, 85, 236
Audley Rhea, 236, 292

Audley Rhea Jr., 292
Calvert B., 94
John Campbell III., 304
Julia T., 304
Mr., 177
ARCHER
Mr., 296
ARNOLD
Cleo, 209
ASHTON
Ruth Elizabeth, 251
AUMACK
Betty Louise, 306
AYERS
Marie Ann, 333
BAILEY
Anna Lynn, 291
Barbara Leigh, 291
David 'Col.' Flournoy, 167
David Ellar, 169
Ellen Olivia, 234, 291
Geroge Edward, 278
Jane Rhea, 169, 250
Jeanne Deford, 234, 292
Julia Flourney, 169, 251
Martha Preston, 169, 252
Nannie Louise Montgomery, 169
Otway Giles, 155
Otway Giles III., 234, 291
Otway Giles, Jr., 156, 234
Preston Henry, 156, 234
Robert Preston, 169
BARBEE
Katherine Annie, 247
BARBER
Sara Kathryn, 253

Caroline Bonner, 334
Carolyn, 287, 334
Daniel Trigg, 139
David Aubrey, 334
Edward Donald, 139
Edward Malcolm, 222, 287
Edward McDonald, 138
Eleanor Mary, 334
Eleanor Worthy, 288
Ellen Claar, 335
Ellen Frances, 221
Frank, 139, 221
Garnett, 96
James White, 139
John Jouett, 221
Joseph Trigg, 96, 140
Josephine Trigg, 139
Katherine, 334
Louise Howard, 288
Malcolm, 139
Malcolm McDonald, 221, 287, 288
Margaret Preston, 139, 219
Martha Ellen, 287, 333
Mary Conley, 96
Mary Ellen, 221
Preston White, 139, 221, 222, 288, 334
Ray Worthy, 288, 334
Robert Robinson Preston, 96, 140
Sussie Trigg, 139, 220
Volney, 222
Volney Howard, 288
William White, 139, 221
CARD
Helena Annette, 328

CARDWELL
R. E., 265
CARLOCK
Lucy Lee, 226
CARMACK
Ada Texanna, 193
Mary, 214
CARPENTER
Elizabeth B., 321
John Fredrick, 321
CARRIERE
Harriet, 287
CARSON
Mary 'Nellie' Helen, 156
Sturm W., 227
CARTER
Alfred M., 243
Anna Evalina, 243
Anne Cary, 79, 216
Cara 'Carrie' H. Preston, 244
Elizabeth Campbell, 137
Joseph Evans, 244
Margaret, 243
Mary Brown, 243
Mary Margaret, 158
Rachel, 76
William Edgar 'Ed', 243
William Hubert, 243
CARY
Eleanor Marion 'Nellie', 126, 212
Hudson, 126
Hudson Fairfax, 126
Marion, 126
Miles Fairfax, 126
Rhea Preston, 126
CATO
Mabel F., 304

Susan Brown 'Susie', 126, 211

Susan Elizabeth, 63, 123, 126, 131

Suzanne McCleish, 329

Theodoric Bland, 161

Thomas Edward, 275, 327

Thomas Edward III., 355

Thomas Edward, Jr., 328, 355

Thomas Tucker, 208

Thomas Watkins, 276, 331

Thomas Watkins, Jr., 331, 360

Virginia, 189

Virginia Sheffey, 146

Wade Harrison, 332

Walter, 124

Walter Preston, 52, 62, 109, 125, 191, 264

Walter Preston III, 212, 278

Walter Preston IV., 278

Walter Preston Jr., 126, 211

Wife of Hugh, 265

wife of Mark, 363

Wife of Robert, 335

William, 63, 124, 125

William Abraham, 209, 277

William Abraham Jr., 277, 331

William Abram, 123, 131

William Andrew, 361

William Brock, 278

William Cross, 275

William Edmondson, 126

William Edwin, 238

William Humphrey, 331,

361

RHODES
Albert Harvey, 211
Gaston Harvey, 210
Janet Lynn, 291
RIDDLE
Mr., 133
RIGGS
Caroline Lee 'Carrie', 238
RILES
Mary Patricia, 360
RILEY
Ann Myers, 108
Pharoh, 108
RIPTOE
Miss, 111
RIVERS
Addie, 113
James, 192
James Gray, 112
James Jr., 113
Nannie Robert, 114, 192
Relms, 192
Robert, 113, 192
ROBBINS
Alfred Gerald, 189
Bernice Preston, 189
Elizabeth, 189
Irma, 189
Lillian, 189
Maude E., 189
Neil R., 189
Pauline Elizabeth, 189
Rufus A., 188
Sarah, 189
ROBERSON
Karen Kimberly, 353
ROBERTS

WHITCRAFT
June Carol, 342
WHITE
Annie Lewis, 137, 153, 218
Annie Preston, 218, 285
Bessie Lelia, 137
Betty Lou, 360
Colin Clarke, 218, 286
Elizabeth Adele, 357
Elizabeth Wilson, 66, 80, 133
Ellen Sheffey, 67, 138
James Harrison, 357
James Lewis, 137, 217
James Lowery, 66
James Lowery Jr., 66
Jane Conn, 66, 135
John Preston, 66, 135, 153
John Rhea, 357
Lewis Nelson, 219
Louis Milton, 137
Margaret Rhea, 66, 134
Margaret wife of Colin, 287
Mary Magdelene, 137, 218
Montgomery Lewis, 137, 219
Pauline Campbell, 138
Phyllis Halloran, 287
Robert James, 357
Sarah, 287
Stuart, 137
Susan Preston, 67, 96, 140
Walter Lewis, 137
William Young Conn, 67, 137
WHITED

Michelle, 353
WHITMAN
Jeanne Preston, 292
Robert Pierce, 292
Robert Pierce Jr., 292
Sarah Sutton, 292
WICKLIFFE
Mary Howard, 68
WILEY
Annie Shannon, 258
WILKINSON
C. M., 275
WILLETS
Mr., 217
WILLIAMS
Sarah Linda, 329
WILLIAMSON
Jean Rhea, 211
Lunnsford Y., 211
WILLS
Corinne Roane, 158
WILSON
Albert, 158
Eleanor 'Ellen', 45
Ellen Meade, 222
George 'Dr.' H., 232
Hugh H., 232
Leta Perry, 234
Margaret B., 232
Shirley, 206
William F., 232
WINSTON
Carrie, 215
Edmund 'Captain', 65
WISEMAN
Hugh C., 210
WOLFORD
Catherine 'Kitty', 105
Charles Ross, 187

Elkanah, 105
Elkanah Walker, 185
Grace, 185
Howard Frank, 186
Ida Lee, 187
Joseph Rhea, 105, 185
Lettie Escott, 186
Louise Jennet, 185
Lula Preston, 187
Margaret Alice, 185
Margaret Jane, 105
Martha E., 107
Rodney Ross, 186
Thomas White, 187
William Henry, 185
William Owen, 107, 186
WOODS
Eward, 178
Thomas 'Rev. T. E. P.', 178
Zellu, 178
WOODSON
Mary, 94
WORDEN
Barbara Abb, 322
WORTHY
Ellen Chandler, 288
WRIGHT
Anne A. wife of Pretson, 184
Charlotte B. 'Charlie', 104
Della D., 103
Jeannette Creigh, 103
Marlene, 184
Preston, 103, 184
Thomas Roane Barnes 'T.R.B.', 101
Thomas Roane Barnes, Jr., 104

William Alfred, 104
William Elliott Clayton, 118
WYLEY
Martha E., 67
YEAGER
James Donald, 323
YOUMANS
Laurens W. 'Col.', 219
Lucille, 220, 287
MacDonald Campbell, 219
Margaret Preston, 220

About the Author

DR. EDWARD F. FOLEY, who married into the Preston clan, is a well-traveled financial executive, having lived in three countries. He is an amateur historian with a keen interest in family history; the author of two other family history books, *The Descendants of Rev. Joseph Rhea of Ireland* and *The Descendants of Matthew "The Rebel" Rhea of Ireland and Scotland*; the owner, restorer and custodian of two structures in the Historic District of Blountville, Tennessee; and a member of historical societies of Virginia, Tennessee and South Carolina.

www.ingramcontent.com/pod-product-compliance
Lightning Source LLC
Chambersburg PA
CBHW050559270326
41926CB00012B/2119